$30.50

Eye-movements and visual perception

R. W. DITCHBURN

Eye-movements and visual perception

CLARENDON PRESS · OXFORD
1973

Oxford University Press, Ely House, London W. 1
GLASGOW   NEW YORK   TORONTO   MELBOURNE   WELLINGTON
CAPE TOWN   IBADAN   NAIROBI   DAR ES SALAAM   LUSAKA   ADDIS ABABA
DELHI   BOMBAY   CALCUTTA   MADRAS   KARACHI   LAHORE   DACCA
KUALA LUMPUR   SINGAPORE   HONG KONG   TOKYO

ISBN 0 19 857371

PRINTED IN NORTHERN IRELAND AT THE UNIVERSITIES PRESS, BELFAST

Preface

THE primary objective of this book is to provide an account of phenomena observed with stabilized retinal images and of the small eye-movements of fixation. It is important to know how these movements are generated, how they are controlled, and the extent to which they are controlled. Certain data on the larger eye-movements of pursuit are included because basic methods of control may be similar for large and small eye-movements, but no attempt is made to treat the general topic of the large eye-movements.

The researches described have been carried out by physiologists and psychologists, physicists, and engineers. It is impossible that any account should please all these people, all the time. For the physical scientists I have provided some background material on those aspects of the anatomy and physiology of vision which are relevant to the interpretation of experiments on eye-movements and on stabilized images. I have to ask the biologists to bear with me if this part of the book appears to them either superfluous or inadequate—or even both at once! I hope it will be understood that in a brief selection made for a special purpose it has not been possible to include the kind of historical treatment which shows what each worker has contributed to the present body of knowledge.

I wish to thank the British Medical Research Council, the Public Health Service of the United States, and the University of Reading for financial provision which made possible my own researches. I am also grateful to numerous collaborators. I particularly thank Dr. Wade Marshall for his interest and encouragement at an early stage of the work.

A considerable section of this book was written while I held a National Science Foundation Fellowship at the University of Rochester, New York. I wish to express my appreciation of this provision. In regard to the production of the book, I am much indebted to the staff of the Clarendon Press, and also to Mr. Drysdale who has read the proofs.

I wish to thank my wife who has given valuable help in the preparation of the manuscript and encouragement at all stages in the writing of this book.

Goring,   R. W. D.
July, 1973

ACKNOWLEDGEMENTS

THE permission of a number of authors (whose names appear below certain figures) to reproduce diagrams, and also that of the following holders of copyright, is gratefully acknowledged:

Academic Press
American Medical Association
American Physiological Society
British Optical Association
Canadian Psychological Society
Institute of Electrical and Electronic Engineers (U.S.A.)
Institute of Perception TNO (Netherlands)
Institute of Physics (U.K.)
Henry Kimpton, Ltd.
Macmillan Journals, Ltd.
Microfilms International Publishing Corporation
C. V. Mosby Co.
Optical Society of America
Plenum Press
Journal of Physiology
Mrs. Stephen Polyak
Rockefeller University Press
Royal Society
Springer-Verlag
Taylor and Francis, Ltd.
University of Toronto Press

Contents

xiv   *Contents*

1

Introduction

1.1. Eye-movements during fixation

Certain small movements of the eyes are present when a well-trained subject fixes his gaze as steadily as he can upon a clearly defined target. The pattern of these movements can, to some extent, be modified by training and by conscious decision, but they cannot be eliminated in this way. Consequently, in normal vision, the retinal image of a stationary target is never completely fixed upon the retina. The question whether these movements of the retinal image significantly affect the process of visual perception is of fundamental interest. Two kinds of experimental evidence are especially relevant in regard to this question: first, a thorough study of the eye-movements and their interpretation in terms of retinal image movements, and, second, experiments on vision when the retinal image has been stabilized. In these experiments the subject views a target whose movements are controlled by his own eye-movements in such a way that its image remains on the same part of the retina even when the eye moves. The detailed study of small eye-movements is also of great interest as an example of physiological control. In this connection it is necessary to consider both the small involuntary movements made while fixating, and also small voluntary movements made while the subject is following a moving target.

In this book we shall not discuss the much larger movements made in reading, scanning an extended field, and other visual tasks.† Their primary function is to bring the retinal image of the point of maximum interest near to the centre of the fovea so that the high visual acuity associated with the central fovea may be used to the greatest advantage. We are concerned with small movements which remain when this condition has been established. It is true that the small movements must operate so that fixation is maintained to a

† Carmichael and Dearborn (1948), Vernon (1928), and Yarbus (1967) describe the large movements. See also Noton and Stark (1971a and b) and Jeannerod (1969).

2

certain degree of precision, but we shall see that they have other functions which are of great importance in relation to visual perception.

1.2. Controlled and uncontrolled movements

When we speak of controlled eye-movements we do not imply that these movements are necessarily under the direct, conscious control of the subject. Many bodily functions are physiologically controlled by elaborate feed-back systems without the subject being aware of the control or able to affect it directly by conscious decision. The pulse rate is an example. However, all control systems are, to a greater or lesser extent, imperfect. There is always a residual 'noise' or 'random error', a fluctuation in the variable which is controlled. This may be regarded as uncontrolled since no observation on the system can predict *in detail* the future course of the fluctuation.

Large eye-movements are in general subject to voluntary control, though they are often made unconsciously. The small movements which remain when a subject fixates are not entirely random because they operate in such a way that fixation is maintained. Therefore they must, in part, be controlled, though they must also contain a random part due to incompleteness or imperfection of the control. One object of the studies which will be described in Chapter 5 and Chapter 14 is to separate the controlled from the random part, and to understand both the control system and its limitations. The subject is normally unconscious of the existence of eye-movements when he is fixating. Nevertheless, these movements are affected by his mental state, and the pattern of eye-movements may be changed, to some extent, by training. In the discussions which follow in later chapters we shall be concerned with physiological control rather than control by conscious decision, though we shall have to take account of the effects of training.

1.3. Problems to be considered

We shall first give an account of the measurement and recording of small eye-movements, leading to a kinematic description of resulting movements of the retinal image during fixation. This stage is a purely empirical study independent of any theory or interpretation. It must be admitted at the outset that the results available are

not as extensive as one would desire. The number of subjects studied
is rather small, and even for those subjects who have been most
intensively studied, the amount of data available is insufficient for
some kinds of statistical analysis. Nevertheless, the material is enough
to allow certain important conclusions to be drawn, and to permit at
least a preliminary discussion of the relevant problems of physiological
control and of the possible effects of small eye-movements on the
process of visual perception.

The most direct way of investigating the effect of retinal image
movements on visual perception is to annul these movements and to
study the resulting changes in visual function. We shall describe
methods for doing this which do not involve the use of drugs, or any
disturbance to the subject, apart from wearing a contact lens. It is
found that in some circumstances total loss of visual function is
produced in this way. It is then possible to make further experiments
in which the natural small movements of the retinal image are replaced by movements under the control of the experimenter, and so
to find out what kinds of movements are important for visual function.

The remainder of this introductory chapter gives an account of
some features of the anatomy† of the eye and of the extra-ocular
muscles in order to provide a background for the later discussion.

1.4. General anatomy of the eye

The shape of the *globe*, which is formed of fairly tough, protective
tissue, is shown in Figs. 1.1 and 1.2. Its dimensions are given in
Table 1.1. The *retina*, which is attached to the posterior part of the
globe, consists of the light-sensitive receptors together with a network of associated nerve fibres. The *sclera*, which is opaque and constitutes about $\frac{5}{8}$ of the globe, is nearly spherical. It has an external
diameter of about 24 mm. The *cornea*, which is transparent, and of
good optical quality, is a meniscus of radii 7·9 mm on the anterior
side and 6·8 mm on the posterior side. The thickness varies from 0·5
mm in the centre to 0·8 mm at the periphery. The cornea is elliptical
(horizontal diameter 11·6 mm and vertical diameter 10·6 mm).

The eyelids are lined with a mucous membrane. The *conjunctiva*
are a continuation of this membrane. They cover the anterior part
of the sclera, and are firmly attached to it in the region where it joins

---

† See Duke-Elder (1961). *System of Opthalmology*. Vol. 2, for a detailed account of the
anatomy of the eye and of the visual pathways.

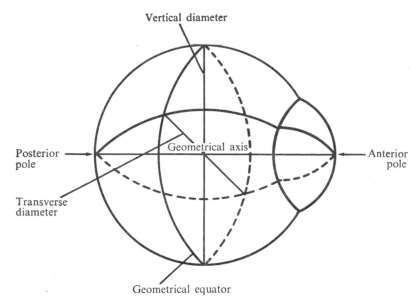

Fɪɢ. 1.1. Diagram of eye to define certain terms. (After Duke-Elder 1938.)

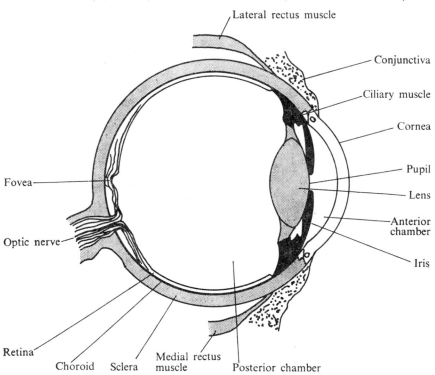

Fɪɢ. 1.2. Section of left eye seen from above. (After Duke-Elder 1938.)

TABLE 1.1
Dimensions of the eyeball

Axial length (anterior surface of cornea to retina)	24·0 mm†
Transverse diameter	23·5 mm
Anterior radius of cornea	7·86 mm‡
Thickness of cornea	0·5 to 0·8 mm
Thickness of sclera	0·3 to 1·0 mm
Width of cornea	10·6 to 11·6 mm
Distance of plane of iris diaphragm§ from anterior surface of cornea	3·6 mm
Instantaneous centre of rotation: 13·8 mm behind the anterior surface of cornea and 1·65 mm to nasal side of visual axis.	

† Range of variation: among a group which did not include very young or very old subjects, from 20·0 mm to 29·5 mm. Standard deviation 1·09 mm.

‡ Range of variation: 7·00 mm to 8·65 mm. Standard deviation 0·26 mm (Stenström 1948).

§ Distances of entrance pupil 3·05 mm and of exit pupil 3·7 mm from anterior surface of cornea.

the cornea. A transition region between cornea and sclera, about 1 mm wide, is known as the *limbus*. At the cornea-scleral junction there is a shallow circular furrow.

The *anterior chamber* and the *posterior chamber* are filled with the *intra-ocular fluid*, whose refractive index (1·3337) is only slightly different from that of water. There is an excess pressure inside the globe. This *intra-ocular pressure* varies between 10 mm and 20 mm (with a median at about 16 mm) in healthy individuals (Davson 1962, Vol. I, p. 158).

The *iris* is an opaque diaphragm whose variable opening, called the *pupil*, is controlled by the *ciliary muscles*. The pupil area is about 3 mm² at high illumination, and it expands to an area of about 45 mm² at low illumination (diameters 2·0 mm and 7·5 mm).† The *choroid*, a pigmented layer between the sclera and the retina, has a nutrient function.

1.5. The retina

The optic nerve enters the globe at a point 3 mm on the nasal side of and about 1 mm below, the posterior pole. It spreads out into the fine network of nerve-fibres which constitute the retina. The light-sensitive ends are called *rods* and *cones*, though the difference must be

† A wider range of diameter (from 1·0 mm to 9·0 mm) is obtained by instilling drugs.

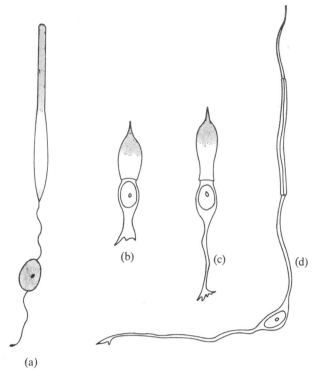

FIG. 1.3. Retinal receptors: (a) rod; (b), (c), and (d) cones. (After Davson 1962.)

regarded as one of function and nervous connection, rather than of anatomical form (Fig. 1.3). Some structures of the retina are shown in Fig. 1.4, and some of the connections are shown diagrammatically in Fig. 7.6. The retina is part of the central nervous system. It contains, (a) the sensitive elements (often called rods and cones), (b) cells that form part of the visual pathway from receptors to cortex (bipolar and ganglion cells), and (c) cells which interconnect branches of the visual path (horizontal and amacrine cells). The interconnections formed by fibres from the bipolar and ganglion cell bodies are very complicated even when seen under an optical microscope. Recently, electron-microscopy (Pedler 1965; Dowling and Boycott 1966) has shown that the number and extent of the horizontal connections are much larger than those revealed by the light microscope. The function of these interconnections is not understood in detail but it is certain that selection and recoding of information take place within the retina itself. The regions (5) to (9) in Fig. 1.4 are known as the cerebral layer of the retina. The rods are about 2 μm in diameter. The smallest

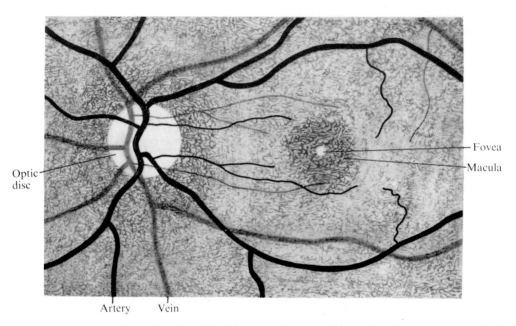

Optic
disc

Fovea

Macula

Artery   Vein

FIG. 1.5. Optic disc and macula. Thick black lines, arteries; grey lines, veins; finer structure, retinal capillaries. (After Davson 1962)

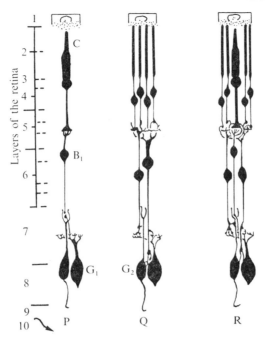

Layers of the retina

F𝗜𝗴. 1.4. Some retinal structures: P, pure cone system with direct connection from cone-receptor C to bipolar B and ganglion G_1; Q, rod-system with several receptors connected to G_2; R mixed rod-cone system with complicated interconnections. (After Polyak 1941.)

cones are about 1 μm in diameter at the tip and 1·5 μm at the base. The largest foveal cones are about three times larger (§ 1.7).

1.6. The optic disc

In the region where the fibres of the optic nerve converge and ultimately leave the globe there are no rods or cones. This region is blind. When the eye is viewed in an ophthalmoscope large retinal blood vessels can be seen in and near this region (Fig. 1.5), though the exact appearance varies considerably even in healthy subjects. From this region the retinal blood vessels spread out into finer and finer branches. These absorb a great deal of light, and we shall have to consider why they are not permanently seen as shadows across the field of view (§ 6.19). They become finer and less dense in a region near the posterior pole.

1.7. Regions of the retina

In a region of 1 mm to 3 mm diameter (corresponding to 4° to 10° of the visual field) there are few blood vessels, and the cerebral layers are spread out so that light can reach the receptors (which are mostly cones) more easily. This central region is called the *macula lutea*, or yellow spot and is covered with a yellow pigment whose function may be to protect against deep blue light. The exact area of the macula cannot be defined precisely. It is not the same as the area of the *rod-free region*, which is smaller. The *central fovea* is smaller still. Precise definition is not possible; most writers use the term for a nearly circular area containing about 7000 cones and within rather less than 2° diameter in the visual field†. Even within this region there is considerable variation of visual acuity and of intercone distance. This led Polyak (1941) to distinguish a *central territory*, or *foveola*, where the cones are most closely packed and the visual acuity is highest. This region is only about 100 μm in diameter (20′ in the visual field) and within it the average intercone distance is about 3·5 μm. Duke-Elder (1961), and Pirenne (1962) have discussed the variation of intercone and inter-rod distances in different regions of the retina.‡ There is no consensus of agreement on the precise definition of these terms. We shall use the following nomenclature. All areas are assumed to be circular and centred on the visual axis: The diameters are assumed to be as follows: macula 5°, fovea 2°, foveola or central territory 0·3° (or 20′). A region from 2° to 10° will be called parafoveal, and all the retina beyond 10° will be regarded as peripheral.

1.8. Refractive system of the eye

Most optical systems such as telescopes and microscopes are constructed with spherical refracting surfaces, and the elements are mounted so that the centres of all the surfaces are on one straight line, which is called the axis. The refracting surfaces of the eye are not quite spherical and the centres of tangent spheres are not exactly collinear. However, these deviations are important chiefly in detailed consideration of the aberrations of the eye, and to a good approximation, the eye may be regarded as a coaxial system which is symmetrical

† Vilter (1949) estimates a smaller average intercone distance ($\sim$2·5 μm), and about 20 000 cones in the central fovea.

‡ Duke-Elder (1961). *System of Opthalmology*, Vol. 2, pp. 264–9.

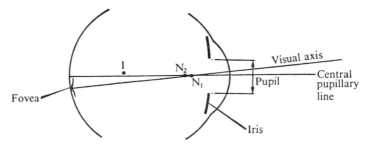

FIG. 1.6. Visual axis (VA), central pupillary line (CPL), and instantaneous centre of rotation (I).

about a line through the middle of the pupil and normal to the cornea (Fig. 1.6). This line is called the *central pupillary line*. It can be operationally located, whereas the geometrical axis and the optic axis cannot be precisely located in a living subject.

The distances of the cardinal points of the refracting system of the eye, both when accommodated and when unaccommodated, have been determined by a number of workers. The values obtained by Gullstrand (1911) are given in Table 1.2. The two principal points are close to each other, and the separation of the nodal points is also small. This led Listing (1853) and Donders (1864) to suggest that the refractive properties might be represented by a *reduced eye* whose principal points coincide with the mean position of the principal points of the eye, and whose nodal points similarly coincide with the mean position of the nodal points of the eye. The principal points of a single refractive surface coincide with each other and with the surface, and both nodal points are situated at the centre of curvature of this surface. It is, therefore, possible to calculate the radius (5·73 mm) and the refractive index (1·336) for a spherical surface whose refractive properties are nearly the same as those of the unaccommodated eye. Table 1.2 gives the relevant measurements for the accommodated and unaccommodated eye, and for the two systems by which they may be replaced. Figure 1.7 shows the position of nodal and principal points (a) for the eye and (b) for the reduced eye. Table 1.2 refers to one eye measured by Gullstrand. There are considerable variations in the length of the eyeball and in the refractive power of the lens. Stenström (1948) has investigated the variation of the more important parameters and summarized the results obtained by earlier workers.

The accommodated eye of Gullstrand has a near-point of 102 mm and differs from the unaccommodated eye much more than does an eye accommodated to the usual near-point at 250 mm. Thus the

TABLE 1.2
Optical system of the eye†

	Unaccommodated Eye		Accommodated Eye	
	Measurement of Gullstrand (mm)	Reduced eye (A) (mm)	Measurement of Gullstrand (mm)	Reduced eye (B) (mm)
Radius of curvature of cornea	8·00		8·00	
First principal point (P_1)	1·358	1·47	1·772	1·93
Second principal point (P_2)	1·60	1·47	2·086	1·93
First nodal point (N_1)	7·08	7·2	6·533	6·69
Second nodal point (N_2)	7·33	7·2	6·847	6·69
First focal point (F_1)	−15·71	−15·58	−12·397	−12·4
Second focal point (F_2)	24·4	24·27	21·06	21·06
Anterior (first) focal length (f_1)	−17·06	−17·05	−14·17	−14·17
Posterior (second) focal length (f_2)	22·79	22·8	18·39	18·39
Power (F) of eye	58·64D	58·63D	70·57D	70·57D
Power of cornea	43·1D	—	43·1D	—
Distance of object in focus on retina (d)			−102·0	−102·0
Second nodal point to retina (g)	17·07	17·07	17·55	17·58

† All distances (except those in the bottom row) are measured from the anterior surface of the cornea.

Reduced eye (A) consists of a single spherical surface of 5·73 mm radius (index 1·336) situated 1·47 mm behind the anterior surface of the cornea (retina 24·27 mm from anterior surface of cornea). *Reduced eye* (B) consists of a single spherical surface of 4·76 mm radius (index 1·290) situated 1·93 mm behind the anterior surface of the cornea (retina 24·27 mm from anterior surface of cornea). The *schematic eye* (Gullstrand) contains both a refracting surface and a lens. By suitably adjusting the radii of curvature and refractive indices, almost exact agreement with the positions of principal points for a real eye is obtained.

normal accommodated eye is about halfway between the accommodated' and 'unaccommodated' eyes measured by Gullstrand.

1.9. Visual axis

The visual axis (Fig. 1.6) is defined as the line from the point of fixation (i.e. the point to which the subject endeavours to fix his gaze) to the corresponding image point in the centre of the fovea. Since the eye is never free from movement, this definition may

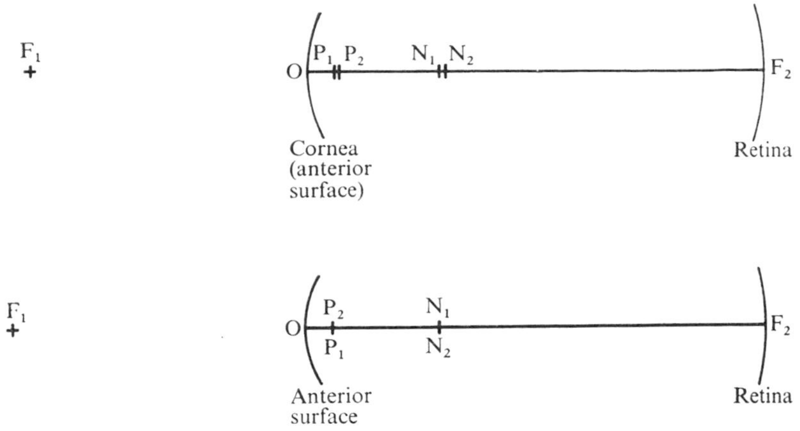

$\underset{+}{F_1}$

$\underset{+}{F_1}$

FIG. 1.7. (a) Cardinal points of the eye; (b) cardinal points of the 'reduced eye'.

be altered to read 'from the point of fixation to the mean position of its image on the retina'. This mean will have to be taken over a sufficient time interval (say, 20 s.). The visual axis necessarily passes through the nodal point of the reduced eye (Fig. 1.7(b)). The angle α between the visual axis and the optic axis is usually about 5°, but there is considerable variation and for some eyes the angle is only about 1°. The fovea is on the temporal side of the point where the optic axis cuts the retina; when the visual axes of the two eyes are parallel the two optic axes thus diverge by about 10°.

Fig. 1.8 shows the relation between the visual axes and the orbits of the eyes. The two orbital axes are inclined at an angle of 45°. When both eyes are looking directly ahead, the angle between each visual axis and the corresponding orbital axis is therefore $22\frac{1}{2}°$. There is a space of 3 mm to 4 mm between the eye and the bony structure of the orbit. This space is filled by the extra-ocular muscles together with some fatty tissue.

1.10. Kinematics of eye-movements

In later chapters we shall need to infer movements of the retinal image from measurements of eye-movements. In some situations it is necessary to take into account both translational and rotational movements of the eye, and in § 1.12 we discuss the analysis of the more general movements of the eyeball, considered as a rigid body.

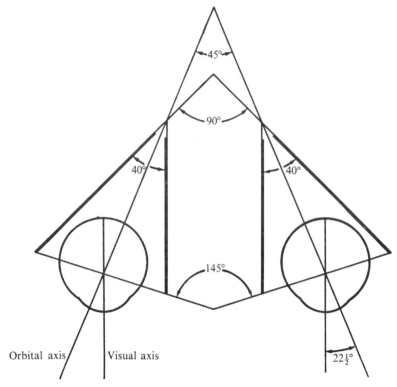

Orbital axis Visual axis $22\frac{1}{2}°$

F IG. 1.8. Relation of orbital axes to visual axes. (After Duke-Elder 1938.)

However, for much of our discussion, we shall need to consider only
the rotational movements, and we therefore start by specifying these.
Suppose that the subject is sitting or standing with the trunk erect,
and that the two eyes are looking straight forward, i.e. the visual
axes are horizontal and parallel. This is called the *primary position*.
Then any rotation of the eye may be resolved into components about
the following three mutually perpendicular directions:

  (a) vertical;
  (b) horizontal and perpendicular to the visual axis in the primary
       position;
  (c) the visual axis.

Movements around the direction (a) are in a horizontal plane and are
denoted by H; those around (b) are in a vertical plane and are denoted by V; and those around (c) are called *torsional* rotations T.
It is usual to regard the H and V axes as fixed relative to the head,
but when the visual axis moves, the axis for torsional rotation moves
with it.

Any direction of regard which is reached by a rotation about *either* direction (a), *or* direction (b), is called a *secondary position*. Any other direction (reached by rotations about both (a) and (b)) is called a *tertiary position*. In some experiments on eye-movements the subject is supine, and in this condition the axes must be regarded as retaining the above-defined relation to the head (i.e. T is now vertical, etc.), and the primary position is one in which the subject is looking in a vertical direction.

So long as we are concerned only with rotations, we specify only *directions* of rotation and not *axes*. However, it is convenient to anticipate later discussions by saying that a point situated 13·8 mm behind the anterior surface of the cornea, and slightly (1·65 mm) on the nasal side of the visual axis, may be regarded as an *instantaneous centre of rotation* for small movements. The eyeball may be assumed to rotate as a rigid body about three axes parallel to directions (a), (b), and (c) and passing through this point (Fig. 1.6). A plane perpendicular to the visual axis and passing through the centre of rotation is called *Listing's plane*.

A horizontal movement which turns the eye in a nasal direction is called *adduction*, and one which turns it in a temporal direction is called *abduction*. A rotation about the visual axis in which the upper part of the eye moves to the nasal side is called *intorsion*, and one in which it moves to the temporal side is called *extorsion*.

1.11. Relation between angles of rotation and movements of the retinal image†

The position in the visual field of a distant object may be specified by stating the angles (in the horizontal and vertical planes) through which the eye must be rotated from the primary position in order to fixate on the chosen point. We usually deal with small angles for which we may put

$$\tan \theta = \sin \theta = \theta, \quad \text{and} \quad \cos \theta = 1, \tag{1.1}$$

where θ is the angle in radians.

It is often convenient to express angles in minutes of arc (*min. arc*) where

$$1' = 1 \text{ min. arc.} = 2 \cdot 9 \times 10^{-4} \text{ radians} \tag{1.2}$$

The symbols which appear in the equations usually represent angles in radians, and a suffix 'm' will be attached to angles measured in

† A more detailed mathematical analysis of eye-rotations and other topics treated in §§ 1.11–1.18 is given by Matin (1964).

min. arc so that
$$2{\cdot}9 \times 10^{-4}\, \theta_{\mathrm{m}} = 0. \tag{1.3}$$

The angle subtended at the eye by a distant object is equal to the angle subtended at the second nodal point by the retinal image. This angle is called the *angular size of the distant object*. The linear dimension x of the retinal image of an object whose angular size θ is given by
$$x = g\theta = 2{\cdot}9 \times 10^{-4}\, \theta_{\mathrm{m}} \tag{1.4}$$

where g is the distance from the nodal point to the retina. Using the value of g given in Table 1.2 we find that the size of the retinal image

TABLE 1.3
Angular dimensions of the eye†

One minute of arc	$= 2{\cdot}89 \times 10^{-4}$ rad
Movement of retinal image corresponding to 1′ of visual angle	$= 5{\cdot}0\ \mu$m
Average distance between centres of neighbouring foveal cones	$3{\cdot}0\ \mu$m or 0·6′
Average distance between centres of neighbouring cones in the foveola	$1{\cdot}75\ \mu$m or 0·35′
Diameter of smallest cones; at tip	$1{\cdot}0\ \mu$m or 0·2′
at base	$1{\cdot}5\ \mu$m or 0·3′
Diameter of fovea	100′ to 120′
Diameter of foveola	20′
Diameter of region with 80 per cent maximum visual acuity	less than 120′
Distance between centres of retinal images of lines which are just resolved in visual perception	$4{\cdot}5\ \mu$m or 0·9′
Standard deviation (from mean of successive readings) of a single vernier acuity setting	$0{\cdot}3\ \mu$m to $0{\cdot}8\ \mu$m or 4″ to 10″
Spatial frequency of sinusoidal grating external to the eye which is just resolved (2·0 mm pupil)	62 cycles deg⁻¹
Spatial frequency which is just resolved in interference fringes on retina	65 cycles deg⁻¹

† Including data from Polyak (1941).

of an object of angular size 1′ is approximately $5{\cdot}0\ \mu$m. When the eye turns through an angle of θ_{m} in a vertical or horizontal plane, the retinal image of a distant object is displaced relative to the retina by a distance $5{\cdot}0\theta_{\mathrm{m}}\ \mu$m. This applies also to a movement in a direction between H and V (i.e. to any small rotation about an axis in Listing's plane). When the eye makes a small torsional rotation ϕ, the retinal image of a point on the visual axis does not move, but the image of a distant point whose direction makes an angle V with the visual axis (Fig. 1.5) moves through a distance $x' = V\phi g$ or, inserting values from Tables 1.2 and 1.3,
$$x' = 1{\cdot}44 \times 10^{-3}\, V_{\mathrm{m}}\phi_{\mathrm{m}}\ \mu\text{m}. \tag{1.5}$$

Table 1.3 gives some details of retinal structure together with the equivalent visual angles.

1.12. Rotation and translation

Suppose that a two-dimensional body (such as a wheel) rotates, with angular velocity ω, about an axis passing through the point A which is located in the body, and that the point A moves with respect to axes $0x$ and $0y$, with velocity V (see Fig. 1.9). It is assumed that, (a) the axis of rotation is normal to the plane of the body, and (b) the axes $0x$ and $0y$ are fixed relative to some system (e.g. the laboratory bench) external to the body. Then a point A' moves, with respect to the axes, with velocity $\mathbf{v'} = \mathbf{v} - \mathbf{r}'\omega$, and it is always possible to find, either within the body or in an imaginary extension of it, a point I for which $\mathbf{v'} = 0$. This point is *momentarily* at rest, and is called the *instantaneous centre of rotation*. The whole motion of the body is *momentarily* a rotation, with angular velocity ω, about an axis through I. This point is not, in general, permanently fixed in relation to either the body or to the frame of reference. For example, the instantaneous centre for a cartwheel is the point of contact with the ground, and this is neither a fixed point in the wheel nor on the ground. The curves along which the centre I moves in the body and in the frame of reference are called *centrodes*, and the whole motion can be regarded as rolling one centrode on another. For the wheel, the

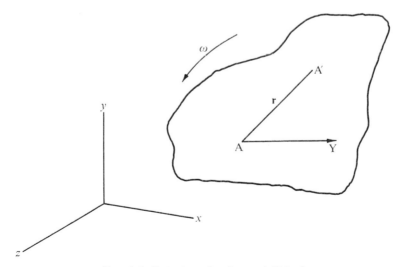

Fig. 1.9. Rotation of a planar rigid body.

rim is one centrode and the other is a line drawn on the ground. In certain situations, for small but finite movements, the movement of the centre of rotation is small enough to be neglected in comparison with the main movements, and the instantaneous centre may be regarded as fixed for small movements.

1.13. General motion of a rigid body

A solid rigid body has six degrees of freedom. These may be specified as components of rotation about three mutually perpendicular axes passing through some point fixed in the body, and three components of velocity of translation (relative to external axes) for this point. Suppose that the components of rotation have been combined by the usual vector methods into one rotation about an axis which we call Oz (Fig. 1.10). Suppose that the translation has been resolved to give one component V_z, and a component in the plane perpendicular to V_z. We choose Ox to be in the direction of this component so that $V_y = 0$. Then an instantaneous centre of rotation O' can be found so that the whole motion, apart from the velocity V_z, is momentarily a rotation about an axis $O'z'$ through O'. Including V_z, the whole motion is a screw motion along and about $O'z'$. Of course it is possible that, in a particular case, V_z may be negligibly small.

When the eyes are rotated, the tone of the eye-muscles as a whole is increased so that the globe is pulled slightly backwards. The rotation is then like that of a screw of very fine pitch. The effect of this small translation on retinal image movements is almost certainly

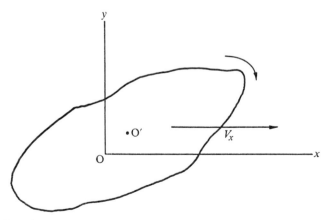

Fɪɢ. 1.10. Rotation of a rigid body (Oz is perpendicular to plane of paper).

negligible, though it may affect the method of measuring eye-movements which is described in § 2.33.

1.14. Instantaneous centre for the eye-rotations

When the eye is in the primary position the instantaneous centre of rotation is about 13·8 mm behind the anterior surface of the cornea, and 1·65 mm to the nasal side of the visual axis (Fig. 1.6). There is some evidence that the centre for V-rotations may be 1·5 mm nearer the cornea than the centre for H-rotations, but this difference may be neglected. G. Park and R. Park (1933) have investigated the movement of the centre of rotation when the eye rotates ±38° from the primary position, and have determined centrodes. The extreme movement is less than 2 mm and the movement in the range ±3° is less than 0·2 mm. Thus, for the movements in which we are mainly interested, the centre may be regarded as fixed.

The exact position of the centre is determined by the precise points of attachment of the extra-ocular muscles and by the elastic properties of the layers of muscle and fatty tissue which are between the globe and the orbit. There is little information about the variation of the position of the instantaneous centre from one person to another, and even in one person it may be affected by fatigue of the eye-muscles or by wearing a contact lens. It is therefore desirable to design experiments on eye-movements and on the stabilized image so that the exact position of the centre need not be known (§ 2.13).

Translations of the eye in its orbit associated with the rotation are taken into account when the centre of rotation is determined. Translations due to volume changes associated with the pulse are not included. There is some evidence that these are less than 0·01 mm.†

1.15. Size of the retinal image of a near object

Suppose that an object of linear dimension l is situated at a distance p from the anterior nodal point of the eye so that the visual angle which it subtends is θ (Fig. 1.11). Let g be the distance of the posterior nodal point from the retina, and x the length of the retinal image. Then, since the angle subtended by the object at the anterior

---

† The change in intra-ocular pressure is of order 1 mm Hg. The corresponding change in volume is less than 1 part in 10^4 (Duke-Elder (1968). *System of Ophthalmology*. Vol. 4, Chap. 4).

3

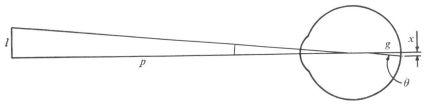

F<small>IG</small>. 1.11.

nodal point equals the angle subtended by the image at the posterior nodal point, we have (when θ is small):

$$\theta = l/p = x/g, \tag{1.6}$$

or

$$x = g\theta = lg/p. \tag{1.7}$$

When $p = 100$ mm and the condition of the eye is that given in column 3 of Table 1.2,

$$x_{100} = 0.165l. \tag{1.8}$$

For an object at 250 mm we assume that the nodal points are about half-way between the positions given in column 1 and the positions given in column 3 of Table 1.2. We then have

$$x_{250} = 0.067l. \tag{1.9}$$

Thus an object of length 1 mm gives an image of 165 μm when it is 100 mm from the nodal point (93 mm from the cornea), and 67 μm when it is at 250 mm from the nodal point (243 mm from the cornea). The corresponding linear magnifications are approximately $\frac{1}{6}$ and $\frac{1}{15}$.

1.16. Effect of eye-movements and head-movements for near object

We now suppose that the eye views a fixed point M. For simplicity we assume that (a) the centre of rotation is fixed, and (b) the two nodal points coincide as in the reduced eye (§ 1.8 and Fig. 1.10). Any small movement of the eye (relative to this point) may be resolved into a rotation of the visual axis about the nodal point together with a displacement of this point (Ditchburn and Ginsborg 1953). In Fig. 1.12 let I_1 represent the initial image on the retina of the point M, and let N represent the initial position of the nodal point. Suppose that N is displaced to N', and the visual axis turned through an angle θ. We assume for the moment that NN' is perpendicular to

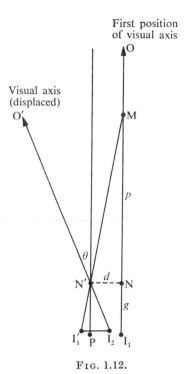

Fɪɢ. 1.12.

MN, and that the angle θ is in the plane MNN$'$. Let I$_1'$ be the new position of the retinal image of M, and let I$_2$ be the new position of the point I$_1$ of the retina, and let N$'$P be parallel to MNI$_1$. Then, the displacement of the retina relative to the image is $x = $ I$_1'$I$_2$ and

$$I_1'I_2 = I_1'P + PI_2, \tag{1.10}$$

and

$$x = g(\theta + d/p), \tag{1.11}$$

where $d = $ NN$'$ is the displacement of the nodal point and the movements are small so that I$_1$, I$_2$, P and I$_1'$ are nearly collinear.

In the above discussion we have neglected possible movements of N: (a) in the direction NM and (b) perpendicular to the plane of rotation (the plane of the paper). Movements in the direction MN which are small compared with p have no effect. The effect of movements perpendicular to the plane of rotation may be calculated from eqn (1.11) by putting $\theta = 0$, giving $y = d'/p$.

In practice two types of movement contribute to θ and to d: (a) rotations of the eye in its orbit and (b) movements of the head. A rotation θ_1 of the eye produces an equal rotation of the visual axis, and a displacement $r\theta_1$ of the nodal point, where r is the distance of the nodal point from the centre of rotation. A head movement may involve both a rotation θ_2 and a displacement d_2 of the nodal point. The total image displacement is then

$$x = g\theta_1(1+r/p)+\theta_2+d_2/p \qquad (1.12)$$

In several experiments $(\theta_1+\theta_2)$ is measured and the other two terms must be regarded as errors; θ_1 is usually large compared with θ_2, and $r = 7$ mm approximately. Thus with $p = 250$ mm the term r/p is about 0·025, but a correction may be made so that no error is introduced. It is fairly easy to reduce d_2 to less than 0·1 mm, and with extreme precautions d_2 may be made somewhat less than 0·01 mm (§ 2.27). For $p = 250$, and $d_2 = 0·1$ mm, $d_2/p = 1/2500$ which is approximately equal to 1·3 min. arc, and for $d_2 = 0·01$ mm, d_2/p is approximately equal to 0·1 min. arc. The fractional error then depends on the size of the angle θ, which is to be detected or measured.

1.17. Accelerated movements

So far the problem has been considered in relation to static situations. Experiments to be described later (§ 4.4) show that retinal image movements due to eye rotations sometimes involve high accelerations. Accelerations of the retinal image at rates of up to 300 cm s^{-2} may occur. Putting $g = 17$ mm and $p = 250$ mm in eqn (1.11) we find that a head acceleration of 4400 cm s^{-2} would be required to produce this rate of acceleration of the retinal image when viewing a target at 250 mm. The force needed to produce this acceleration in a body of 4 kg is so large that, even apart from the constraints applied to fix the head, it is very unlikely that head movements contribute materially to the more rapidly accelerated movements of the retinal image.

1.18. Relation between eye-movements and retinal image movements when using a contact lens or spectacle or optical instrument

Suppose a contact lens is worn to enable a subject to focus an object at a distance d, using an unaccommodated eye. Provided that the contact lens moves with the eye, the situation is very nearly the same as when the eye is accommodated. The only difference is that the contact lens which adds the extra power is in front of the cornea, whereas normal accommodation adds to the power of the system behind the cornea. Thus, with the contact lens, the principal and nodal points are a little further away from the retina than they are with an eye accommodated for viewing at the same distance. The effect is quite small unless a very powerful contact lens is used. For example, a contact lens for viewing an object at 100 mm gives a posterior nodal point at 18·0 mm from the retina instead of 17·6 mm for the accommodated eye (Table 1.2).

When a subject views an object through a lens or optical system which is not attached to the head, the movements of the retinal image caused by rotations of the eye or by translations of the head are the same as they would be if he were using the naked eye to view the image formed by the instrument. If the instrument is adjusted to produce an image at infinity then translation of the head does not affect the position of the retinal image.†

When a subject looks through spectacles attached to the head the situation is rather complicated. In respect of rotations of the eye in its orbit, the effect is the same as if the image formed by the spectacle lens were viewed by the naked eye. In respect of rotation or translation of the head, the effect is the same as if the power of the dioptric system of the eye were increased (by accommodation), except that the nodal point of the combination of lens and eye is further from the retina than with the contact lens.

1.19. The extra-ocular muscles‡

The general arrangement of the extra-ocular muscles is shown in Fig. 1.13, which is a diagrammatic view of the right eye seen from above, and in Fig. 1.14, which is a perspective view. There are three pairs of muscles, the members of one pair being opposed to each other.

(a) *The lateral rectus and the medial rectus.*§ These act so as to give a couple in a horizontal plane producing H-rotations when the eye is in the primary position. Each is attached to the eye by an insertion which is almost symmetrically distributed above and below the horizontal meridian. The insertion into the sclera is about 6 mm behind the periphery of the cornea, and the muscles are wrapped around the globe as indicated in Fig. 1.14. The point of last contact,

† It may, of course, affect the amount of light received by the eye if the exit pupil of the instrument is about the same size as the eye pupil.

‡ Detailed anatomy of the extra-ocular muscles is given by Duke-Elder (1963), *System of ophthalmology*, Vol. 2, and in an article by Alpern which forms Part I of Vol. 2 of *The eye* by Davson (1962).

§ Sometimes called exterior rectus and interior rectus.

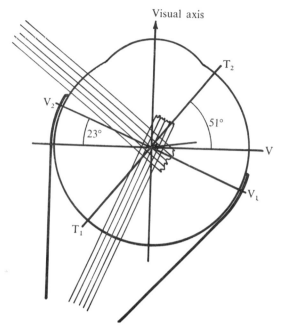

FIG. 1.13. Extra-ocular muscles of right eye seen from above.

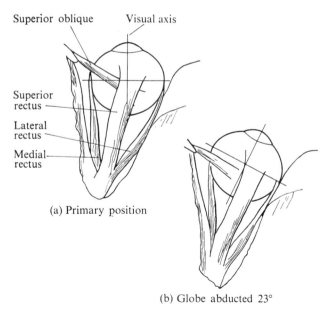

(a) Primary position

(b) Globe abducted 23°

FIG. 1.14. Extra-ocular muscles: perspective view. (From Adler 1965.)

and hence the point of application of the force, alters when the muscle contracts and the eye rotates. Contraction of the lateral rectus produces abduction, and contraction of the medial rectus produces adduction. The lateral rectus is about 50 mm, and the medial about 40 mm, in length. Both of these originate near the apex of the orbit in a zonule called the *annulus of Zinn*.

(b) *The superior rectus and the inferior rectus*. These are attached to the globe symmetrically above and below the cornea. They act approximately along the line of the orbit. When the eye has been adducted to a position about 24° from the primary position they act so as to produce a rotation in a vertical plane (V-rotation), but when the eye is in the primary position their action produces rotation which has H, V, and T components, though the V-component is still the largest. Their insertions are again about 6 mm behind the junction of sclera and cornea, and they also originate in the annulus of Zinn. They are each about 40 mm long.

(c) *The superior oblique and the inferior oblique*. These muscles act in a vertical plane which makes an angle of about 52° with the visual axis when the eye is in the primary position. They thus affect H-, V-, and T-rotations from this position. A pure V-rotation can be produced by the joint action of the superior and inferior recti and the two obliques acting in the correct ratio, which is about 2:1 in favour of the recti (Fig. 1.13). The insertion of the obliques is towards the posterior of the eyeball so that contraction of the superior oblique rotates the eyeball downwards, whereas contraction of the superior rectus (which is inserted forward of the centre of rotation) rotates it upward. Contraction of the inferior oblique rotates the eyeball upward.

The superior oblique originates at the apex of the orbit and passes through a kind of pulley (the *trochlea*) before insertion in the eyeball. The inferior oblique originates more in the side of the orbit. The two obliques do not act in precisely the same plane. The superior oblique is considerably longer than the inferior and is inserted nearer the equator. These asymmetries must complicate any system of control which is to rotate the eye with high precision or to maintain good fixation.

1.20. The action of the different eye-muscles is summarized in Fig. 1.15 which is due to Hering (1879). It shows the path which would be traversed by the point of fixation (on a plane normal to the direction of the visual axis in the primary position) if each muscle were to act alone. The heavy bars at the ends of each line show the projection of an after-image which is initially in the position HH′, and so indicate

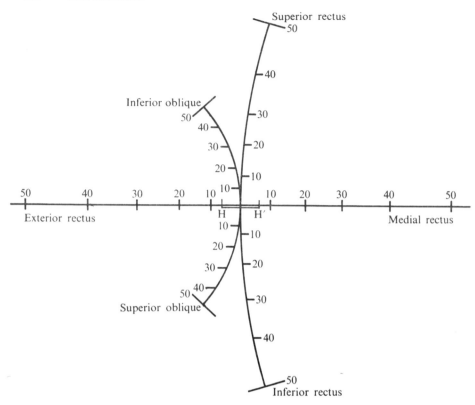

Fɪɢ. 1.15. Effects of actions of individual muscle-pairs of right eye. (After Hering 1879.)

the extent of torsion. It will be seen that the inferior oblique and the inferior rectus produce extorsion, and the superior oblique and superior rectus produce intorsion when they are contracted.

H-rotations or V-rotations (or any other movement about a direction in Listing's plane) can be made voluntarily though perhaps with incomplete control in relation to their exact path (§ 13.24). The question whether the action of the eye-muscles is co-ordinated to reduce torsion can be answered only by experiment (§§ 1.22 and 4.23).

From Fig. 1.15 it may be seen that, while H-rotations can be made by one pair of muscles alone, other movements in Listing's plane require the co-operation of at least two of the three pairs of eye-muscles. A further degree of co-ordination is required when the two eyes move together.

1.21. Torsion

When the eye is in the primary position, the H, V, and T axes are mutually perpendicular, and an H-rotation or a V-rotation to a secondary position does not involve torsion. When, however, the eye is moved from the primary position by an H-rotation, the visual axis, and therefore the T axis,† is no longer normal to the V axis. A V-rotation then includes a component about the T axis. Thus, whenever the eye moves to a tertiary position by successive H- and V-rotations, a certain amount of torsion will occur. *Listing's Law* states that this torsion, which is often called *normal torsion*, is the same for any given tertiary position no matter by what path it has been reached. This torsion can be observed by printing an after-image of a cross on the retina, and then turning the eye to a tertiary position (e.g. by looking upwards and to one side). The cross will then appear tilted relative to the vertical (Fig. 1.15). By viewing the cross against a suitable screen the angle of torsion may be measured and Listing's Law may be verified.

It has been shown by Schubert‡ that the angle of torsion ω is given by

$$\tan \omega = \frac{\tan \alpha (1 - \cos \beta)}{1 + \tan^2 \alpha \cos \beta}, \qquad (1.13)$$

where α is the angle between the axis of rotation and the vertical, and β is the angle of rotation about this axis. It will be noted that this equation correctly gives $\omega = 0$ when $\alpha = 0$ (H-rotation) and when $\alpha = \pi/2$ (V-rotation).

1.22. The superior and inferior recti act about an axis RR′ which makes angle ψ with the V axis. When the eye is in the primary position RR′ makes an angle $\pi/2 - \psi$ with the visual axis. The axis RR′ is in the horizontal plane. When the eye is in the primary position a small rotation θ about RR′ produces a vertical movement of $\theta \cos \psi$ upwards and a torsion of $\theta \sin \psi$. In a similar way the obliques act about an axis 00′ which makes an angle χ with the V axis, and a small rotation ϕ about 00′ has components $\phi \cos \chi$ about the V axis, and $-\phi \sin \chi$ about the visual axis. The combined action of the superior and inferior recti and of the obliques produces

$$\text{(i) V-rotation} = \theta \cos \psi + \phi \cos \chi, \qquad (1.14)$$

---

† See § 1.10.

‡ Duke-Elder. (1938). *Textbook of Opthalmology*. Vol. 1, pp. 598 and 602.

and

(ii) T-rotation $= \theta \sin \psi - \phi \sin \chi.$ (1.15)

If

$$\frac{\theta}{\phi} = \frac{\sin \chi}{\sin \theta} \qquad (1.16)$$

then the torsional component is zero and a simple vertical rotation is produced. The fact that no torsion is observed for vertical movements of the eyes implies that the muscles do normally combine in this way. It is found that ψ is approximately 51° and χ is about 23°, so that zero torsion is obtained when $\theta/\phi = 0.5$. Thus vertical movements are made by the obliques exerting about twice as much effect as the superior and inferior recti.

While this is the normal action of the eye muscles, it is possible for them to combine in such a way as to produce a component of torsion associated with vertical motion or even a pure torsion. The kind of torsion which would be produced in this way is quite different from the normal torsion described in § 1.21 and might be much larger than normal torsion (§ 4.23).

1.23. The eye-muscles

The fibres of the eye muscles are exceptionally thin, the average cross-section being about 150 μm² (with a range of 4:1). The cross-sectional area of the whole muscle is of the order 30 mm² or 2×10^5 times the average area of one fibre. It is possible that some fibres run the whole length of the muscle, but this is not certain. There is an unusually large amount of elastic tissue fibre. This may assist precise control of eye-movements.

1.24. Innervation of eye-muscles

Many muscles have one associated nerve fibre to every 50 to 100 muscle fibres. The eye-muscles have the much greater innervation of one nerve fibre to every 2·5 muscle fibres. It is clear from histological studies that the human eye-muscles contain sensory as well as motor fibres (Cooper and Daniel 1949; Wolter 1955). The function of sensory nerves in the eye muscles of the goat has been investigated by Cooper, Daniel, and Whitteridge[†] (1954). They found that the rate of firing is determined by the rate of contraction of the muscle (i.e. by

† See also Whitteridge (1960).

the angular velocity of the eye). The significance of this in relation to control of eye-movements will be discussed later (§ 15.10).

1.25. Optical quality of the dioptric system

Owing to diffraction, no optical system brings all the light from a point source to a single point in the image. This is shown in Fig. 1.16, where the dashed curves represent the distribution of light in a retinal image for different sizes of pupil and for an ideal lens system. Thus, if the dioptric system of the eye were perfect, the retinal image would become sharper as the diameter of the pupil increased, just

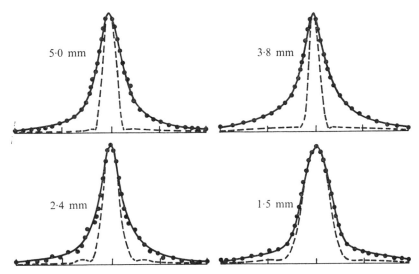

Fig. 1.16. Spread function of retinal image of narrow slit. (a) – – – Calculated for aberration-free lens; (b) —●—●—●— measured values (Campbell and Gubisch 1966) for different pupil diameters.

as the resolving power of a microscope improves when the numerical aperture of the objective is increased.

Defects of lens systems make the image less sharp and may be divided into

(a) regular aberrations which cause the wave front leaving the system to deviate from a sphere (but in a smooth way); these make the central maximum wider and also spread the light in the outer regions; and
(b) small local defects (e.g. bubbles in glass or scratches on the

surfaces) which deviate a small fraction of the light, some of it through fairly large angles, causing 'veiling glare'.

In vision, (a) mainly reduces the sharpness of boundaries and (b) reduces effective contrast. The effect (b) is important when there is a very bright source, such as the sun, within the field of view.

1.26. The spread function

The distribution of light in the image of a point source is difficult to measure because the amount of light available is necessarily small. It is usual, therefore, to measure the *line-spread function* $\sigma(x)$, i.e. the distribution (in a direction perpendicular to the line) of light in the image of a short narrow slit. The point-spread function can be derived from the line-spread function by calculation.

The line-spread function for a camera lens may be measured by exploring the image plane with a photo-multiplier covered by a fine slit. Since it is not possible to explore the retinal image directly, measurements are made on an image formed by light which has *twice* passed through the dioptric system of the eye. The apparatus used by Campbell and Gubisch (1966) is shown in Fig. 1.17. Light leaving the fundal image is reflected from the beam-splitter B to form an image in the plane of the slit S_2. When B is rotated (about an axis normal to the diagram) the image is scanned across the slit. The output from the photo-multiplier is accepted by a computing device which averages the readings for a number of scans, and so reduces the effect of random errors (called 'noise').

The line-spread function in the retinal image can be deduced from the results by a calculation which allows for the fact that the image on S_2 is formed by light which has twice passed through the dioptric

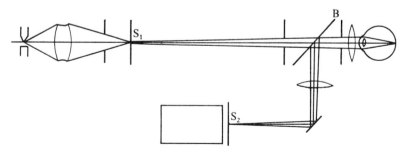

FIG. 1.17. Apparatus for measurement of line-spread function. (From Campbell and Gubisch 1966.)

system of the eye. The results for different pupil diameters are shown in Fig. 1.16. There is a central core and a 'skirt'. There is an optimum pupil size which gives the best image, and these measurements indicate that the optimum is about 2·4 mm.

1.27. Earlier measurements of the line-spread function were made by Flamant (1955), Westheimer and Campbell (1962), and Krauskopf (1962). All of these experiments gave a considerably wider spread than that shown in Fig. 1.16. Since the most recent experiment of Campbell and Gubisch (1966) incorporates significant technical improvements, and since all known systematic errors tend to increase the measured spread, we shall assume that their curves represent the best measurements for subjects who are fairly young and have good vision (any *small* refractive error having been corrected).

The calculation of the line-spread function for the retinal image depends on the assumption that the light received from the fundus is perfectly diffused. Tests made by Campbell and Gubisch showed that the fundus is very much nearer to a perfect diffuser than to a mirror reflector. They also estimated that the line-spread function which they had obtained for white light did not differ significantly from the line-spread function for monochromatic light of wavelength 570 nm.

1.28. Modulation transfer function† (M.T.F.)

An alternative way of specifying the quality of an optical system is based on the use of a series of sinusoidal gratings as test objects. The distribution of light for one of these gratings (Fig. 1.18) is given by

$$L = 1 + C(p)\sin 2\pi px \qquad (1.17)$$

The contrast of a grating is defined to be

$$\frac{I_{\max} - I_{\min}}{I_{\max} + I_{\min}},$$

and since $I_{\max} = 1 + C(p)$ and $I_{\min} = 1 - C(p)$ the contrast is $C(p)$. In measurements on lens systems, x is usually expressed in millimetres and p (called the *spatial frequency*) is the number of lines per millimetre. For the eye it is convenient to measure x in degrees in the visual field and p is expressed in cycles per degree. For any one grating $C(p)$ is a constant. $C(p)$ is always less than 1, since the luminance

† We have allowed for the magnification of the dioptric system of the eye in the definition of angles 'in the visual field'. The loss of light in passage through the optic media (§ 7.16) is not included but is unimportant in this connection.

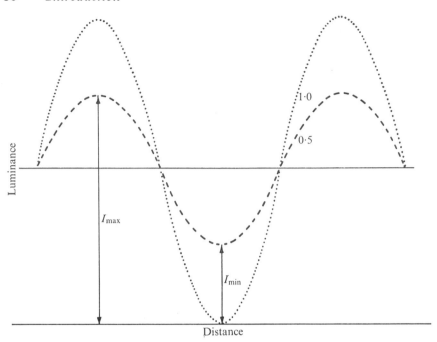

Fɪɢ. 1.18. Sinusoidal grating: distribution of intensity $C = 1 \cdots$; $C = 0\cdot5$ – – –.

cannot be negative. It is found that, provided the aberration is not very large, the distribution of light in the image is sinusoidal but of lower contrast. When the system is working at unit magnification and there is no loss of light, the distribution of light in the image is given by

$$L = 1 + M(p)C(p)\sin 2\pi px, \qquad (1.18)$$

where $M(p)$ is a dimensionless constant called the *modulation transfer factor*. The variation of $M(p)$ with p is called the *modulation transfer function* (M.T.F.) This function is the Fourier transform of the line-spread function $\sigma(x)$. Thus if either $\sigma(x)$ or $M(p)$ is measured, then the other can be calculated. It is usual to assess lens systems by comparing the measured M.T.F. with the M.T.F. calculated for an aberration-free lens of the same aperture.†

† For an introduction to the use of the M.T.F. see Chapter 8 and Chapter 20 of Ditchburn (1963). For a comprehensive account see Fellgett and Linfoot (1955). In a general treatment of lens systems, allowance is made for a possible phase-shift and a complex function, called the optical transfer function (O.T.F.), is used. Since this phase-shift is of no interest in our problem, we have assumed that it is zero in eqn (1.18) and in the following discussion. When the phase-shift is negligible the M.T.F. is equal to the O.T.F.

1.29. The M.T.F. for an ideal lens is 1 for $p = 0$ and falls to zero at some limiting frequency p_L, which is determined by the aperture of the lens. The *normalized frequency* p_N is defined to be equal to p/p_L. When $M(p_N)$ is plotted against p_N a single curve represents any ideal lens. This curve is the line without points in Fig. 1.19 which applies when the illumination is non-coherent.† Any real lens can be compared with an ideal lens of the same aperture by plotting $M(p_N)$ against p_N. The M.T.F. for any real lens approaches unity when $p_N = 0$ but at all other spatial frequencies the value of $M(p)$ is less than that of an ideal lens of the same aperture.

Fig. 1.19 shows values of $M(p_N)$ for the dioptric system of the eye. These are obtained by calculating the Fourier transforms of the function $\sigma(x)$, shown in Fig. 1.17, for pupil diameters 2·0 mm, 2·4 mm, and 3·0 mm. Since the abscissa is p_N, the curve for an ideal lens is the same for all apertures. It may be seen that the departure from an

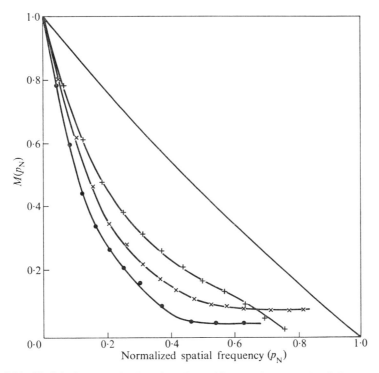

F IG. 1.19. Modulation transfer function: line without points calculated for aberration-free lens: other curves calculated from measurements of line-spread functions (Fig. 1.16) + + + 2·0 mm pupil; × × × 2·4 mm; ● ● ● 3·0 mm.

† In normal vision the illumination is nearly always non-coherent.

ideal lens increases with aperture. The values of p_L are 64 cycles deg^{-1} for 2·0 mm aperture, 77 cycles deg^{-1} for 2·4 mm, and 96 cycles deg^{-1} for 3·0 mm.

The resolution of an ideal lens improves with increasing aperture but the difference, due to aberrations between an ideal lens and a real lens increases as the aperture increases. These two effects oppose one another so that the best retinal image is obtained for an eye-pupil in the range 2·0 to 2·4 mm. For pupils less than 2·0 mm the resolution falls off owing to the increased effect of diffraction, and for pupils greater than 2·4 mm it falls off owing to increased effects of aberrations.

1.30. Threshold contrast

Fringes with the distribution of intensity given by eqn (1.18) may be produced on the screen of a cathode-ray tube. It is then possible to measure the *threshold contrast* $C_T(p)$ for which fringes of frequency p can just be detected. The reciprocal of $C_T(p)$ is called the *response* R of the visual system in respect of the spatial frequency p. Fig. 12.1 (p. 270) shows the results of an experiment in which R is measured for different values of p. (Note that ordinate scale is logarithmic).

Using the apparatus shown in Fig. 1.20, it is possible to form on the retina a set of fringes with a sinusoidal distribution of illumination. The source T_c gives two beams of coherent light which are imaged on the pupil of the eye so as to form two adjacent coherent sources. These, acting alone, would form fringes with $C = 1$, but the contrast of the fringes on the retina can be adjusted to any desired value between 0 and 1 by adding non-coherent light from the source TL.

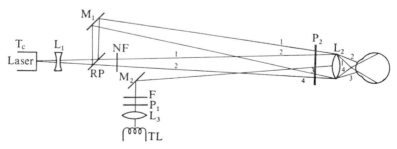

FIG. 1.20. Apparatus for producing interference fringes on the retina. (From Campbell and Green 1965.)

The spatial frequency of the fringes can also be adjusted. This apparatus was used by Campbell and Green (1965) with a helium-neon laser at T_c so that the colour of the light was a fairly deep red ($\lambda = 638$ nm).

If the designed conditions of this experiment are fully realized the fringes are not degraded by aberrations of the dioptric system of the eye, and the true contrast of the retinal image is known. The response R' of the eye in respect of these fringes was measured and was found to be greater than R (Fig. 12.1, p. 270). It is assumed that the threshold contrast *at the retina* is the same whether the fringes are formed externally or internally, so that

$$M(p) = R(p)/R'(p). \tag{1.19}$$

In Fig. 1.21, curve (b) shows the values of $M(p)$ calculated from (1.19) (using the curves of Fig. 12.1); curve (a), which is transferred

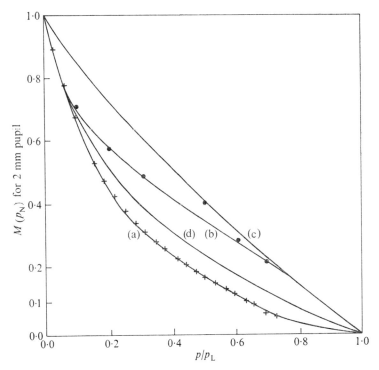

FIG. 1.21. Modulation transfer function (2 mm pupil). Curve (a) from Campbell and Gubisch (1966), curve (b) from Campbell and Green (1965), curve (c) calculated for an ideal lens, and curve (d) geometric mean of (a) and (b).

from Fig. 1.19, shows the results obtained by calculation based on the measurement of $\sigma(x)$ for the same pupil size (2·0 mm), and curve (c) is the theoretical curve for an ideal lens. Curve (b) is consistently above curve (a). This is to be expected since any imperfection in the experimental arrangement of Campbell and Green would make the contrast of the interference fringes lower than it is assumed to be and hence would make the value of $M(p)$ too high. On the other hand any imperfection in the experimental measurement of $\sigma(x)$ would tend to make the observed profile of the image less sharp than the true profile, and this would lead to values of $M(p)$ which are too low. We cannot do better than assume that the best values of $M(p)$ are obtained by taking the geometric mean of the two measured values of $M(p)$. These values are shown in curve (d). The limiting spatial frequency is 65 cycles deg^{-1}.

1.31. Interference fringes on the retina have also been observed by Le Grand (1937), Byram (1944b), Arnulf and Dupuy (1960), and Westheimer (1960). None of these workers had the advantage of a laser source and, in general, the values of R' and of p_{L} are lower than those found by Campbell and Green (e.g. Le Grand found $p_{\mathrm{L}} = 60$ cycles deg^{-1}; Westheimer found $p_{\mathrm{L}} = 50$ cycles deg^{-1}). Byram however reports that at 40 cycles deg^{-1} the fringes appeared perfectly sharp (Fig. 1.22(a)); at 86 cycles deg^{-1} the fringes 'had a wavy appearance (Fig. 1.22(b)) and were subject to a shimmering movement'. At 150 cycles deg^{-1} he still observed structure in the form of

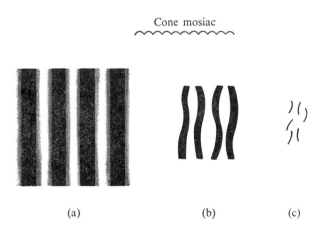

Cone mosiac

(a)   (b)   (c)

FIG. 1.22. Appearance of interference fringes on the retina according to Byram (1944b). (a) Clearly seen (40 cycles deg^{-1}), (b) wavy (86 cycles deg^{-1}), and (c) curved segments (150 cycles deg^{-1}).

a series of wriggling, curved segments (Fig. 1.22(c)). It is possible that the structure seen at and above 85 cycles deg^{-1} was an artefact of the apparatus or that it was due to spurious resolution.† Byram's own explanation that these appearances were due to interaction of the structure of the target and the structure of the receptor mosaic, mediated by the eye-movements, may well be correct.

† Ditchburn (1963), § 8.41.

2

Methods of recording eye-movements (1)

2.1. Historical

Carmichael and Dearborn (1948) include a fairly detailed account of early work on eye-movements, and a review article on eye-movements by Lord and Wright (1950b) gives a summary of these experiments. Most of this early work was concerned with the eye-movements which are made when reading or performing a similar visual task. The movements to be measured in these studies are so large that an error of a degree or more can be accepted, and it is sufficient to be able to resolve events to within about a tenth of a second. In this book we are chiefly concerned with the small eye-movements which remain when a subject is fixating as accurately as he can. This is a situation in which the eye was, at one time, considered to be at rest because the apparatus available was not sufficiently sensitive to record the small movements. We shall see later (§§ 2.3–2.5) that certain features of these small movements may usefully be recorded with a method which has an accuracy of about 2′ and a time-resolution of about 30 ms, but that complete analysis demands about twenty times better sensitivity and ten times better time-resolution.

2.2. Classification of methods

The numerous methods which have been used for recording and measuring eye-movements may be classified in several different ways. We divide them into the following two groups:

    (a) Those methods which do not require an attachment to the eye,
    (b) Those which do require such an attachment.

Group (a) will be described in this chapter and group (b) in Chapter 3. Most of the methods of group (a) have been developed from older methods designed to measure the larger eye-movements. They are less sensitive and less accurate in response to high frequency movements than the methods of group (b). Nevertheless, these methods have two important advantages. They are convenient to apply to large groups of subjects, and it is very unlikely that the eye-movements are affected by the procedure used to measure them.

2.3. The following methods are commonly used for measuring the large eye-movements:

(1) The after-image method.
(2) The corneal reflection method.
(3) The scleral observation method.
(4) The corneo-retinal potential method.

Methods (1) and (4) do not require the subject's head to be fixed. Method (2) has been made the basis of several standard instruments, including the optokinetrograph and a portable instrument called the opthalmograph. Method (2) has also been developed into a commercially produced instrument called the electro-oculargraph (Shackel (1960)). We shall also include in this chapter a description of a fifth method which does not involve any attachment to the eye. This method, due to Cornsweet (1958), involves the direct measurement of movements of a retinal image relative to the retinal blood vessels.

All of the methods described in this chapter, except the corneo-retinal potential method, yield useful information on the small eye-movements of fixation, though none of them has quite enough high-frequency response or sensitivity for accurate reproduction of all features of these movements (§ 2.5).

2.4. Physical characteristics of recording systems

A satisfactory system for recording small eye-movements must possess suitable physical characteristics in respect of, (a) sensitivity, (b) linearity, (c) frequency response, and (d) noise in the appropriate frequency range. To specify these characteristics we need a rough estimate of the size and frequency range of the movements which are to be measured. For this purpose we accept the consensus of present results as showing that the small eye-movements include, (i) slow drifts at the rate of a few minutes of arc per second, (ii) sharp saccadic movements often up to 10' and occasionally up to 60' in 30 ms, and (iii) an irregular tremor of excursus 0·05'–2'. The frequency spectrum of the tremor extends up to 150 Hz though the most important region is 0–30 Hz. The saccadic movements are likely to make more severe demands on the recording system than the other movements.

2.5. Byford (1960) has discussed the frequency response characteristics required for accurate reproduction of the saccadic movements. He assumes that the recording system has a frequency response given by

$$R = \frac{v_0^2}{v^2 + v_0^2},$$

(2.1)

where v_0 is a constant of the system and R is the ratio of the square of the amplitude (of a wave of frequency v) in the record to the corresponding quantity in the input (Fig. 2.1, curve (b)). The response of

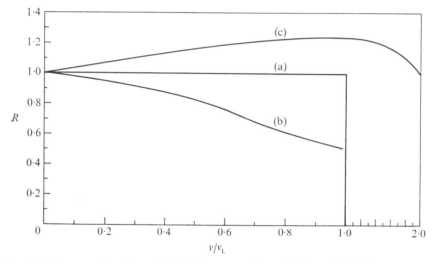

FIG. 2.1. Response functions. (a) Ideal low-pass filter; (b) filter defined by eqn (2.1); (c) filter defined by eqn (2.4).

this system falls off at high frequencies and the value when $v = v_0$ is half the value at $v = 0$. This is the response characteristic of a resistance–capacity coupled amplifier. Millman and Taub (1956) have examined the reproduction of a ramp function (Fig. 2.2) by this system. They define the error E to be the difference between the input and output divided by the input. They then show that

$$E = \frac{1}{2\pi v_0 T} \text{ (approximately),}$$

(2.2)

where T is the rise-time of the ramp (Fig. 2.2). A system whose response is represented by eqn (2.1) and for which $v_0 = 125$ Hz will reproduce a saccadic movement which occurs in $T = 25$ ms to within an error $E = 0.05$ or 5 per cent. This calculation ignores the overshoot of the saccadic movements, but this is less sharp than the steep rise of the main movement, and the conditions for reproduction of the overshoot will be less stringent than those calculated from eqn (2.1). Byford also considers the reproduction of the velocity and the acceleration in the saccadic movement. Since the maximum velocity is reached before the maximum displacement, the conditions for accurate reproduction of velocity are more stringent than those for reproduction of displacement. The conditions for reproduction of acceleration are still more stringent. It thus appears that for a system with frequency response given by eqn (2.1), a system with a value of about

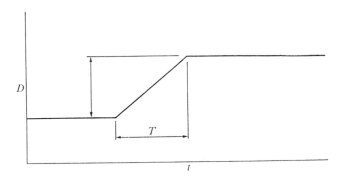

Fɪɢ. 2.2. Ramp function.

200 Hz for ν_0 will be sufficient to give reproduction of the saccades which is good enough for checking any theory of muscular action which may be proposed. This system, provided that it is sufficiently free from noise, will also reproduce the tremor (§ 2.7).

2.6. The above discussion depends on the assumption made concerning the shape of the response curve (Fig. 2.1 curve (b)). We therefore consider two other response curves shown in Fig. 2.1, curve (a) and (c). The one shown in curve (a) is an idealized low-pass system with a sharp cut at some limiting frequency ν_L. If we again assume that the saccade is represented by a ramp function with a rise-time of t_0, it may be represented by the Fourier series

$$f_0(t) = \frac{t_0}{\pi} \left\{ 1 + \sum_{m=1}^{\infty} (-1)^{m+1} \frac{(\sin m\pi t/t_0)}{m} \right\}. \tag{2.3}$$

The fundamental frequency is $2/t_0$, and if $t_0 = 25$ ms this frequency is 20 Hz. Thus a system for which $\nu_L = 160$ Hz would reproduce the first nine terms of the Fourier series and give a good representation.

A sharp-cut system is not obtained in practice. A more realistic system has damped resonance at some frequency ν_r. The response is then given by

$$R = \frac{A}{\gamma^2 + (\nu - \nu_r)^2}.$$

(2.4)

This system gives a good reproduction if (a) the resonance frequency is at least 1·5 times the highest frequency in which we are interested and (b) the damping constant γ has a suitable value (e.g. $\gamma = 2\nu_r$) so that the response curve is nearly flat over the range of frequencies in which we are interested (Fig. 2.1, curve (c)). The eye-movements will be accurately reproduced by a system of this type provided ν_r is at least 220 Hz and γ is of the order $2\nu_r$. This would give a nearly constant response up to 150 Hz.

2.7. Specification for recording system

Two specifications based on the preceding discussion will now be given. Specification (1) describes a system which will accurately reproduce all components of the small eye-movements. Specification (2) is a less stringent specification. It describes a system which will yield useful information in relation to drifts and saccades but will not accurately reproduce the smallest and fastest movements.

Specification (1)

(a) The system should be linear to within 1 per cent over a range from 0′ to 50′.

(b) The frequency response should be flat (to within 3 dB) from 0 to 150 Hz.

(c) The sensitivity should be sufficient to enable a movement of 0·05′ to be detected. If the system produces a visible trace then 1′ should be represented by a deflection of 1 cm and the edge should be sharp enough to read to 0·5 mm. If displacements up to 5′ are to be recorded a dynamic range of 100:1 (20 dB) is required. For displacements up to 50′, to include the largest saccades, the dynamic range over all would be 1000:1 (30 dB), but the system might work with two ranges, each about 50:1, including some overlap.

(d) The noise power in any frequency range should be small compared with the corresponding signal power.

The last item (d) cannot be made precise until we have a more satisfactory Fourier analysis of the movements; low frequency noise (0–3Hz) would affect estimates of magnitude of drift but irregular movements of 0·3′ in this frequency range would produce only a small error. Noise of frequency above 200 Hz could be excluded by band-pass filters. Noise in the range 10–100 Hz of r.m.s. amplitude 0·1′ would interfere with recording of tremor, and especially with a search for dominant frequencies in the tremor.

Specification (2)

(a) The system should be linear to within 5 per cent in the range 0 to 10′.

(b) The frequency response should extend from 0 to 10 Hz without loss of more than 5 dB.

(c) The sensitivity should be sufficient to enable a movement of 1′ to be detected.

(d) The r.m.s. noise amplitude in the range 0–15 Hz should be less than 0·5′.

2.8. After-image methods

Donders (1847), Helmholtz (1866) and many others have used a method in which a well-defined after-image is printed on the retina by asking the subject to fixate a bright source for a short time, or by subjecting him to a flash of light. This flash is made so short that no appreciable movement of the eye can take place during the flash, and so bright that the amount of light received is large enough to print a good image. Barlow (1952 and 1963) has studied the after-image method and estimated its accuracy. He used the apparatus shown in Fig. 2.3. The source A is a carbon arc; the lens L is seen in Maxwellian view and is therefore extremely bright when it is not covered. The plate P is blackened except for a fine line as shown. The shutter S covers the plate P initially, leaving only a small pinhole near the centre which is illuminated in weak red light. The subject fixates on this pinhole and the shutter is then allowed to drop, and two parts of the line are exposed successively. One part is exposed for 20 ms. The other part is exposed 100 ms later, also for 20 ms. If the eye has moved in a vertical direction, the after-image should consist of two misaligned parts. The subject was asked to alter an adjustable vernier until it showed the same gap as the after-image. The mean displacement in 85 tests was 0·07′, and the standard deviation was 0·54′. Two controls were used, (a) a single exposure of a straight line and (b) a line in two parts misaligned by 1·3′. From the results obtained with these, a standard deviation due to errors of judgment was found to be 0·30′. Subtracting the variance due to this cause from the observed variance leads to a standard deviation between two successive positions of the eye of 0·44′. If one regards the two positions as random choices from a 'population' of eye positions then the mean departure from the mean position is 0·31′. This is the mean component in a vertical direction. In 1963 Barlow used this method as a test for accuracy of stabilization of the retinal image (§ A.12).

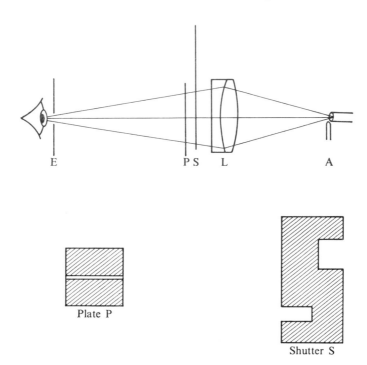

E   P S L   A

Plate P

Shutter S

FIG. 2.3. After-image method. (After Barlow 1952.)

2.9. Bennet-Clark and Ditchburn (1963) also investigated the accuracy of this method. Their target was a single rectangular strip 2′ wide and 1° long. Various steps in this strip were produced by covering half of it with an inclined glass plate. The size of the step in the after-image was estimated by the same method as that used by Barlow. Steps of 2·5′ and 5·0′ were estimated as (2·4′±0·25′) and (4·7′± 0·36′) respectively. These results agree reasonably well with Barlow's estimate of 0·30′ for the standard deviation due to errors of matching. However, when no step at all was introduced, the subjects estimated a spurious step of (0·8′±0·45′), whereas in a similar situation Barlow's subjects estimated (0·0′±0·31′). In some experiments one half of the target was made brighter than the other, but without a step.

The subject then observed a spurious step which diminished with time. With 0·5 log-unit difference of luminance the spurious step was 3·4′ after 20 s, 2·0′ after 60 s, and 1·1′ after 120 s. This suggests that some of the variance observed in Barlow's experiment may have been due to fluctuations in the carbon arc.

2.10. The after-image method has the advantage that there is no attachment to the subject's eye, and his head need not be rigidly fixed. No elaborate apparatus is required. One might hope that in this situation the movements observed would be the normal movements of a comfortable subject. Unfortunately the flash of light which prints the after-image will often produce a violent movement which is followed by smaller movements. These may last until the image has disappeared. Also it is necessary to blink, or to use intermittent illumination to maintain the after-image. In normal vision the subject does not see noticeable after-images. If a well-defined after-image is situated a little away from the centre of the fovea the subject will often try 'to look at it', i.e. to bring it to the centre of the retina by moving his eye. Thus an after-image which is a little off centre may induce eye-movements. Barlow observed the reaction due to the flash, but says that it was subject to a delay of at least 120 ms, and therefore did not affect his tests, which were made after 100 ms or 75 ms.

An after-image method can be used to demonstrate the existence of drifts and saccades to a large audience (Verheijen 1961). The pattern shown in Fig. 2.4 is projected onto a lantern screen in a darkened room and the members of the audience are asked to fixate the spot A for 15 s and then to attempt to fixate the point B. The after-image is seen to be moving relative to the pattern and drifts and saccades are readily observed.† The after-image used in this case is not strong and there is no reaction from a bright flash, so this method, with some modification, might be used to obtain estimates of the number of saccades per minute.

2.11. The counting method

In this method the subject views a uniformly repeated pattern (in the simplest case, a set of equispaced parallel lines). He is asked to count the lines and finds this easy when the visual angle between

---

† The reader may try the experiment in the following way. Place the book on a table so that it is well illuminated by a reading lamp in an otherwise dark room. Cover one eye and fixate as directed in the test. It is advantageous to support the head with the hands to reduce head movements.

adjacent elements of the pattern is about 20′. If the visual angle is reduced, either by using finer patterns or by going farther from one pattern, a stage is reached where the pattern assumes a shimmering appearance and the individual elements can no longer be counted. For most subjects the visual angle between adjacent elements is then

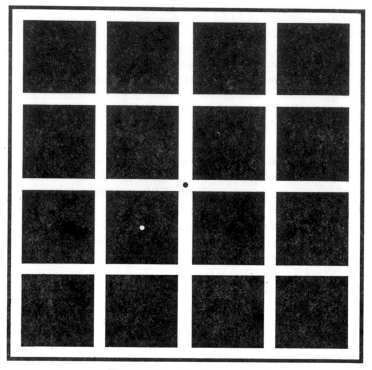

FIG. 2.4. Verhijen's experiment.

in the range 5′–10′. An estimate of the extent to which the eye moves during fixation is thus obtained with a minimum of apparatus and with no constraints on the subject. However, the target is an unusual one and one cannot be sure that the eye-movements occurring when attempting to fixate a single well-defined fixation mark are similar.

2.12. The corneal reflection method

A beam of radiation is reflected from the anterior surface of the cornea. The rotation of the eye about an instantaneous centre which does not coincide with the centre of curvature of the corneal surface

(Fig. 2.5) causes a deflection of the beam. This deviation may (a) be observed visually or (b) be recorded on moving photographic paper or (c) be made to alter the light falling on a photocell and the resulting current recorded on moving photographic paper.

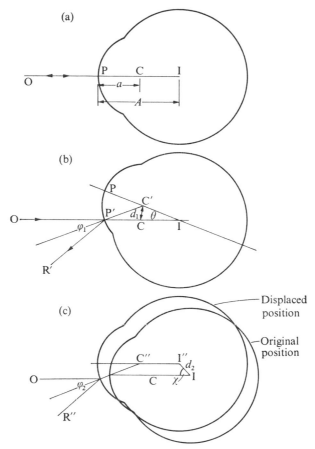

FIG. 2.5. (a) Original position of eye; (b) rotation through angle θ (c) displacement through distance d_2 (original position superposed).

A schematic diagram is shown in Fig. 2.5. Suppose that a narrow parallel beam of light is incident normally upon the cornea as shown in Fig. 2.5(a). C is the centre of curvature of the anterior surface of the cornea, and I is the instantaneous centre of rotation of the eye.†
Fig. 2.5(b) shows the effect of a small rotation about an axis through I (normal to the plane of the paper). This rotation may be regarded as

† For the present discussion the small displacement of I from the visual axis is ignored. This does not introduce any significant error.

the resultant of, (i) a displacement of C to C', and (ii) a rotation θ about C. The rotation about C does not change the angle of reflection since it merely substitutes one part of the spherical surface for another. Let $d_1 = CC'$, $A = IP$, and $a = CP$. Then, for a small rotation,

$$d_1 = (A-a)\theta. \tag{2.5}$$

The change in the angle of reflection ϕ_1 is $2d_1/a$.

Now suppose that the head is translated through a distance d_2 in a direction making an angle χ with CP, then the change in the angle of reflection (ϕ_2) is $\dfrac{2d_2 \sin \chi}{a}$.

When rotation and displacement both occur the total change in the angle of reflection is

$$\phi = \phi_1 + \phi_2 = \frac{2}{a}((A-a)\theta + d_2 \sin \chi). \tag{2.6}$$

Putting $A = 13{\cdot}8$ mm and $a = 7{\cdot}9$ mm (see Table 1.1) we obtain

$$\phi_m = 1{\cdot}5(\theta_m + 600d_2 \sin \chi), \tag{2.7}$$

where ϕ_m and θ_m are expressed in minutes of arc, and d_2 in mm.

Eqn (2.7) indicates that a translation of the head of 10 μm produces about the same deflection as 5' rotation of the eye, provided the translation is along a direction normal to the optic axis. A component of translation along the optic axis has no effect. A torsional rotation does not change the corneal reflection.

When the radiation is incident in a direction making an angle ψ with the radius of the corneal surface at the point of incidence, the geometry is more complicated. It may be shown that approximately

$$\phi' = \frac{2}{a}\{\theta(A-a)\cos \psi + d_2 \sin \chi \cos \psi + d_2 \cos \chi \sin \psi\}. \tag{2.8}$$

When $\psi = 30°$ we have

$$\phi' = 1{\cdot}3(\theta_m + 600d_2 \sin \chi + 300d_2 \cos \chi). \tag{2.9}$$

Thus the effect of a rotation or of a translation perpendicular to the optic axis are little changed, but a translation along the optic axis of 10 μm is now equivalent to 3' of rotation.

2.13. Eqn (2.6) shows that the ratio between the angle of rotation of the eye and the deflection of the beam depends on the distance $(A-a)$ of I from C. This is fairly small and a change during rotation may constitute a fairly large percentage change. For this reason, and also because ψ enters into eqn (2.8), ϕ will not be proportional to θ for angles in excess of 10°. Moreover the ratio of ϕ to θ is known by calculation only to the extent that $(A-a)$ is known (Fig. 2.5). How-ever, the ratio between ϕ and θ can be found by direct calibration when the subject transfers fixation between two well-defined marks whose angular separation is known.

This method has been used a good deal for observation of fairly large angular movements. In this work errors due to head movements are not important if the head is well fixed, but it must be remembered that 0·1 mm of head movement will produce an error of about 1°. Most of the work done with this method has been carried out either with visual observation or with direct photographic recording. At least two commercial instruments for the observation of eye-movements use the corneal reflection technique which is very suitable for projects such as the observation of eye-movements when reading and the study of pathological nystagmus. For accounts of this work see Lord and Wright (1948), Carmichael and Dearborn (1948), and Vernon (1928 and 1930).

2.14. Photo-electric recording of the corneal reflection has been de-veloped by Lord and Wright (1948). A detailed account of their method is given by Lord (1948). A beam of ultraviolet light (wave-length about 365 nm) is directed on to the cornea in such a direction that the radiation which enters the eye falls on the blind spot. The reflected radiation is divided by a beam-splitter into two parts which fall on photo-multipliers P_H and P_V respectively. Straight edges are placed in the paths of the beams in such a way that a rotation of the eye in the H-direction affects the light falling on P_H, and a rotation in the V-direction affects the light falling on P_V. The output from the photomultipliers is used to control a double-beam cathode-ray tube and the display is photographed at suitable intervals. The electrical circuits transmit frequencies up to 1 kHz and have substantially constant responses for frequencies up to 100 Hz. The sensitivity of the method, after allowing for imperfect correction for translational movements† is probably about 1′ to 3′. In another version of the apparatus the beams pass through variable density wedges before falling on the photo-multipliers. This enables larger movements to be measured but with some reduction in over-all sensitivity.

2.15. Head movements

In order to reduce head movements the subject was supine. Part of the weight of the head was supported by a sling, and a dental bite

† See § 2.15 below.

was used to fix the head. In order to estimate the effect of head movements, a reflecting surface of radius equal to that of the corneal surface was mounted on an aluminium strip and attached to the teeth of the subject's upper jaw by a dental regulation band. The movements recorded were periodic at the frequency of the pulse. The movements were estimated to be less than 0·1 μm and about ten times less than the corresponding movements obtained when the subject is vertical.

Ditchburn and Ginsborg (1953) and Fender (1956) found that small *rotations* of the head are possible when the teeth are fixed by a dental bite. This implies that the translation of the head at eye-level may be much larger than the movement recorded by a band attached to the teeth. Findlay (1969a) used a photo-electric method to detect small movements of a mark which could be attached to the head at different points. He obtained the smallest movements when the dental bite was used. At eye-level the movements were (under the best conditions) as follows.

(a) Regular movement at about 1·3 Hz (presumably due to the pulse) of ± 3 μm to ± 4 μm together with some movement at about 8 Hz, probably due to mechanical resonance of the head against its constraints.

(b) Average movement in 1 s: 4 μm.

(c) Maximum movement in 1 s: 11 μm.

(d) Maximum movement in 60 s: 20–40 μm.

These measurements of head movements do not take account of translation of the eye in its orbit due to volume changes associated with the pulse. Duke-Elder (*Ophthalmology*. Vol. I, p. 590) estimates this movement as 'a few hundredths of a millimetre'. However, the records of Lord and Wright suggest that this movement may, under favourable conditions, be less than 10 μm.

It thus appears that the movements of the head lead to changes in the corneal reflection angle equivalent to a rotation of 3′ to 5′ in 1 s, and much larger rotations over periods of 60 s.

2.16. Portable corneal reflection apparatus

Johansson and Backlund (1960a, b) describe a corneal reflection method in which the whole apparatus is mounted on the subject's head. The apparatus weighs about 1·5 lb and can be worn without serious discomfort. It leaves a clear view over a wide angle and can thus be used to study eye movements of a car driver or air pilot. In the form

used it is not sensitive enough for small movements but an increase
of sensitivity would appear to be possible (see footnote to § 2.19).

2.17. Reflection at the limbus

Rashbass (1960) has used a method in which the difference between
the light scattering efficiency of the sclera and of the cornea is used
to control the position of a cathode-ray tube spot so that its image is

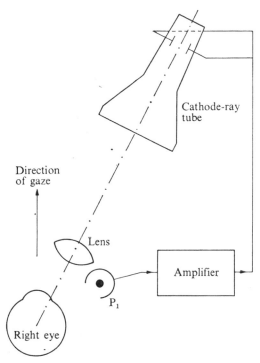

FIG. 2.6. Apparatus used by Rashbass (1960).

kept focussed on the limbus. The movements of the spot then follow
the movements of the eye. Figure 2.6 is a schematic diagram of his
apparatus. The cathode-ray tube and lens are adjusted so that when
the subject is looking straight forward and the spot is central on
the tube face its image falls on the limbus. A photomultiplier P_1 is
placed fairly near the eye and picks up the scattered light. If the eye
turns to the left the spot falls on the sclera and the amount of
scattered light increases. Conversely when it turns to the right the
spot falls on the cornea and the scattered light decreases. These

changes in the signal received by the photomultiplier are used to move the spot so as to return its image to the limbus.

A second photomultiplier P_2 (not shown) is needed to monitor changes in the intensity of the spot on the cathode-ray tube. The feed-back loop must be designed so that it does not 'hunt' unduly, but returns the spot to the desired stable position rapidly. The method is

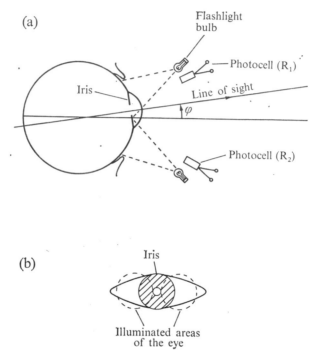

FIG. 2.7. Apparatus used by Stark, Vossius, and Young (1962).

used only for horizontal movements of the eye. Measurements on photographs of the display indicate that there is a noise level of about 5′. The time resolution is about 5 ms or better. The apparatus is thus suitable for recording the larger saccades but is not sensitive enough for examination of the smaller saccades or the tremor. It has been used for experiments on conjugate and disjunctive eye-movements (Rashbass 1961*a*; Rashbass and Westheimer 1961*a*) and for an examination of the relationship between saccadic and smooth pursuit movements (Rashbass 1961*b*).

2.18. Another reflection method has been used by Stark, Vossius, and Young (1962). Two flashlight bulbs are used to illuminate the sclera as shown in Fig. 2.7, and two photo-transistors R_1 and R_2

mounted on goggles worn by the subject receive the scattered light (from the region of the limbus), which alters when the eye rotates. Calibration was made by asking the subject to fixate a series of marks separated by known visual angles. The photo-transistors had a time-lag of 2 ms. They had a bandwidth of 10 Hz at high illumination and less at low illumination. It appears that the method is capable of detecting movements of about 30′. Wheeles *et al.* (1966) have developed a method in which an image of the eye is projected on a screen (Fig. 2.9), and photo-transistors observe the position of the boundary. H-rotations of about 3′ are detected but errors due to head movements (§ 2.15) are not completely eliminated.

2.19. Television method

A method in which the corneal reflex is viewed by a television camera has been developed by Mackworth and Mackworth (1958).† A schematic diagram of the apparatus is shown in Fig. 2.8. A standard Pye television camera is placed at eye-level, 2 in from the eye and at 45° to the line of regard. This receives the corneal reflection of a pointolite bulb which is 20 in away. A second television camera views the scene which the subject sees. The outputs are mixed so that a spot showing the direction of regard is super-posed on the scene. A cine photograph of this display can be made. The electronic circuits can be adjusted so as to give reasonably accurate superposition over a considerable area. The subject's head is fixed by a dental bite and cheek supports. The smallest detectable movement is about 1°. The method is not suitable for recording small eye-movements without further development.‡ It has many possibilities in relation to automation and control. We shall describe some of these in the next paragraph.

2.20. Llewellyn-Thomas, Mackworth, and Howat (1960) developed a variation of the preceding method in which the corneal reflection is used to control the spot on a television tube as before, but this tube is now viewed by a matrix of photocells. These can be made to control a teletype machine which prints out a record of the changing eye-movements. It is also possible to make the subject view a television

---

† See also Llewellyn-Thomas and Mackworth (1960).

‡ A Japanese commercial instrument made by Nac, Tokio is basically similar in principle. The whole camera system is carried on the subjects head. Movements of a few minutes can be detected. Rutley (1972) describes an instrument which is a substantial modification of one made by Polymetric Co. New Jersey, U.S.A.

tube presentation which is controlled by the signals received from the photocells. For example, the presentation may be blacked out in the region to which the subject turns his regard, thus creating a kind of artificial central scotoma. Alternatively, the presentation may be made to move in response to the eye-movements. The lack of sensitivity and speed makes it impossible to apply this method directly to problems involving small eye-movements. However, some of its features could be associated with other more sensitive methods.

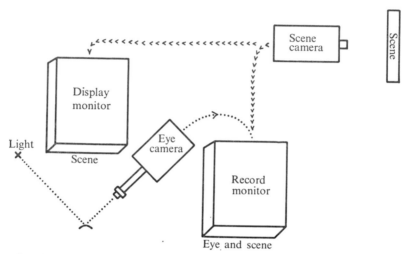

FIG. 2.8. Schematic diagram of arrangement used by J. F. Mackworth and N. H. Mackworth (1958). Scene is viewed by subject directly.

2.21. Scleral observation method

In this method the movement of either a natural mark such as a scleral blood-vessel or an artificial mark (e.g. a minute drop of mercury or a flake of chinese white) is observed. As with the corneal reflection method, there are three groups of methods employing direct visual observations, photography, or photo-electric recording. Suppose that the eye rotates through an angle θ about an axis which is in Listing's plane and at the same time there is a translation d_2 in a direction in Listing's plane and perpendicular to this axis. Then the total movement observed is

$$d = d_2 + d_\theta = d_2 + A\theta, \tag{2.10}$$

where $A = 13 \cdot 9$ mm.

If θ_m is in min.arc and the distances in millimetres we obtain

$$d = d_2 + 4 \cdot 1 \times 10^{-3} \, \theta_m. \tag{2.11}$$

Thus a rotation of 1′ causes a movement of 4μm, and a head translation of 10 μm causes an error of 2′. The method is thus only slightly less sensitive to head movements than the corneal reflection method (§ 2.13).

2.22. Effect of torsional movements

Unfortunately, torsional rotations are confused with rotations about axes in Listing's plane. Consider, for example, the situation shown in Fig. 2.9. The eye is initially in the primary position (Fig.

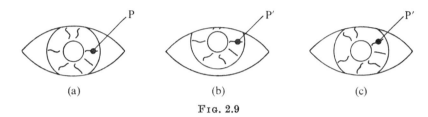

(a)   (b)   (c)

FIG. 2.9

2.9(a)) and the marked spot P moves a distance d in a vertical direction (to the position shown in Fig. 2.9(b)). This movement may be due to any one of the following causes:

(a) a translation of the head through a distance d,
(b) a V-rotation $\theta = d/A$ (as shown in Fig. 2.9(b)),
(c) a torsional movement $\psi = d/B$ (as shown in Fig. 2.9(c)),

where B is the distance from the optic axis to the marked point. This is usually placed a few millimetres outside the cornea whose width is about 11 mm. Thus B is 8 mm to 11 mm and more than 0·5 A. A torsional movement ψ is equivalent to a rotation θ in Listing's plane of more than 0·5 ψ. This error may be avoided by observing more than one marked point.

2.23. Barlow's experiment

Accounts of experiments by visual observations and early photographic methods are reviewed by Lord and Wright (1950) and by Carmichael and Dearborn (1948). We shall describe the experimental arrangement of Barlow (1952) who brought the photographic recording version of this method to its highest sensitivity. The apparatus is shown in Fig. 2.10. The subject was supine. Droplets of mercury about 0·1 mm in diameter were placed on the edge of the cornea.

The subject held his eyelids open to prevent blinking but lacrimation usually ended an experiment after 3–5 min. The following optical arrangement was used. Light from a small ophthalmoscope lamp A reflected by the drop C was collected by the microscope objective B and refocussed as shown. The mirror D and the viewing system F are used for aligning the apparatus and the mirror is swung to one side

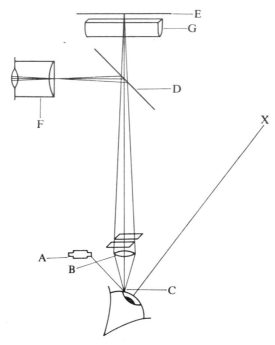

Fɪɢ. 2.10. Apparatus for photographic recording of scleral reflection. (After Barlow 1952.)

for recording. The usual drum camera arrangement is employed. The film moved continuously at 25 mm s^{-1} and the image was photographed at a magnification of 35.

2.24. Fixing the head

Barlow took extreme precautions to fix the head. The subject's head rested on a stone slab let into the wall. A rigid iron frame fitted round the head and wedges were driven in on one side. The teeth were fixed by a dental impression. The movements of a small drop of mercury placed on the forehead were recorded, but it was not possible to be sure how far these movements were affected by skin twitching. A small movement periodic with the pulse was observed, in agreement with the findings of Lord (1948) and Findlay (1969a). The method of fixing the head is very uncomfortable for the subjects and the early records showed movements of the eye which were probably associated with the discomfort. When the discomfort had been reduced, and the subjects had become used to the apparatus, results agreed with those of other experimenters. The records were measured under a tenfold enlargement on which 1 mm represented 4 ms in time. It was estimated that the deflection could be measured to 0·2 mm, which was equivalent to 0·2′ in eye rotation. The method thus has a good frequency range and sufficient sensitivity to detect the tremor, but not sufficient to measure it accurately. With the techniques now available the discomfort could probably be reduced while retaining the advantages of this method.

2.25. Photography of scleral blood vessels

A method similar in principle to that used by Barlow has been employed by Higgins and Stultz (1953). They photographed the subject's eye and then selected a suitable scleral blood vessel to be photographed under higher magnification and on moving film. A vessel whose main direction is horizontal gives a record of V-rotations and one whose direction is vertical may be used for H-rotations. They used a dental impression to fix the head but do not appear to have employed any auxiliary constraints. From the data given it appears that they could resolve times of order 3 ms. The effect of residual head movements is not mentioned in the paper but must almost certainly have been appreciable.

2.26. Separation of rotation and translation

If two suitable signals are received it is, in principle, possible to calculate the rotation of the eye, and the translation—including both translations of the head and translations of the eye in its orbit. In practice it may be difficult to do this with sufficient accuracy without flooding the eye with light. Consider the arrangement shown in Fig. 2.11 which represents a view from above. Suppose that the eye is illuminated by a parallel beam of radiation using a point source and a beam-splitter S. A lens forms an image at QQ′ of an identifiable region on the surface of the eye (such as the edge of the iris). The anterior surface of the cornea, regarded as a spherical mirror, forms an image of the source at its focus F, and the lens L forms an image of F at D. Now suppose that the head is translated, in a direction perpendicular to the incident beam of light, through a distance Y_T. Then P, P', and F' all move through the same distance Y_T. If the eye rotates through a small angle θ (about an axis through I and perpendicular to the plane of the diagram), F moves through a distance $Y_1 = (A - r/2)\theta$ in a direction parallel to PP'. This rotation also causes a movement of P or P' which has a component $Y_2 = (A' \cos \phi)\theta$ along the same direction. When translation and rotation occur simultaneously, the

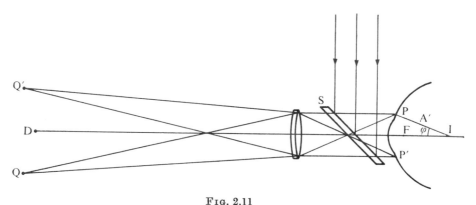

Fɪɢ. 2.11

movements of F and P are

$$d_F = Y_T + (A - r/2)\theta \tag{2.12}$$

and

$$d_P = Y_T + (A' \cos \phi)\theta. \tag{2.13}$$

2.27. Thus the effect of translation is eliminated by measuring $d_P - d_F$ which is the movement of F with respect to P. This difference may be deduced from measurements of the movements of Q and D. These may be made photographically or, more accurately, by an electronic scanning technique (§ 2.28). Thus two suitable data can be combined to measure rotation when small movements of the head are present. Some errors are eliminated by using the mean position of two points such as P and P' as one datum. Unfortunately, the accuracy of measurement required to attain an accuracy of 1' or better, is high, and it is difficult to find sufficiently well defined marks on the eyeball. This method, in the form described, has never been used.

2.28. Two data were measured by Rashbass and Westheimer (1961*a*) in an attempt to eliminate the effect of translations of the head. Their apparatus is shown in Fig. 2.12. A vertical line is made to scan the cathode-ray tube horizontally, and light is received by two photo-multipliers P_1 and P_2. The former receives light scattered from the cornea and sclera, and the amount of light changes sharply when the scanning line crosses the limbus. The other cell is placed to receive

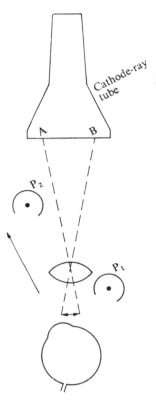

FIG. 2.12. Apparatus used by Rashbass and Westheimer (1961a). The spot on the cathode-ray oscilloscope is scanned between A and B. Dash lines represent two extreme positions of central ray from the spot to the eye.

the corneal reflection at a certain angle. The signals are combined to produce the display shown in Fig. 2.13. The sharp drop on the left represents the passage over the limbus and the peak on the right is the corneal reflection. The authors state that the marked difference y measures rotation. They do not give the results of any tests on translational and rotational movements of artificial eyes, but state that the system is ten times less sensitive to translations than the corneal reflection method. The noise level is about 5′, and the frequency response is estimated to be good up to 30 Hz. Probably the noise

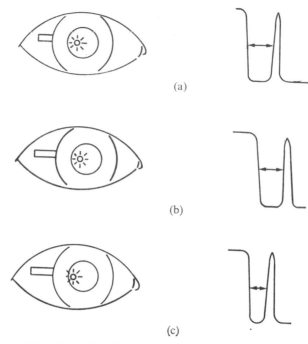

FIG. 2.13. After Rashbass and Westheimer (1961a).

level can be reduced and the frequency response improved, but a reduction of noise to 0·1′ to 0·2′ and an increase of frequency response to 150 Hz (required to record and analyse small movements of fixation) would be very difficult to achieve.

2.29. Portable apparatus

An apparatus for photographing the eyes of an air pilot has been developed by Melville Jones and Free (1960). The whole apparatus, including a cine camera and weighing about 5 lb, is carried on a flying helmet. Cine photographs are taken at 16, 32, or 64 frames per second. A special instrument for measuring the positions of several marked features on the sclera was also made, and H-, V-, and T-movements are separated. It is estimated that accuracies of ±0·5° for H- and V- and 1° for T-movements are obtained. Hartridge and Thomson (1948) have used an apparatus which is essentially a low-power microscope attached to a plastic cap worn by the subject. Photographs are taken by a camera which is not attached to the head.

2.30. Corneo-retinal potential measurements

It is found that there are electrical potentials within the eye such that the eyeball may be regarded as a small battery with a positive pole in the retina and a negative pole in the cornea. The true corneo-retinal potential can be measured only in a recently excised eye, but the corneo-retinal potential leads to certain differences in potential between electrodes placed in contact with the skin at suitable positions in the neighbourhood of the orbit. Variations in these potentials have been used to measure eye-movements. Unfortunately the method suffers from a number of artifacts. The measured potentials include components of E.E.G. potentials, of muscle potentials, and skin responses. The measured potential for stationary eyes varies greatly from subject to subject and from one time to another. Shackel (1960), Shackel and Davis (1960), and Kris (1958) have studied these movements with a view to finding methods of detecting the artifacts and making corrections. A study of the method by Byford (1961) shows that while observations of large eye-movements may be made by this method, it is not suitable for observation of the small movements in which we are interested.

2.31. Observation of the optic disc

The method which will now be described has the unique feature that it directly measures movements of a retinal image relative to marks on the retina formed by retinal blood vessels. Movements of the eye can be inferred by calculation. The method, as used by Cornsweet (1958), measures H-rotations only, and is applicable only to subjects who have a sufficient length of vertical blood vessel crossing the optic disc. Fig. 2.14 shows a drawing of part of the optic disc of one subject.† A small bright spot of light is scanned across the region shown. The optic disc is covered by myelinated nerve fibres which reflect light well, and the blood vessel is a dark shadow. Figure 2.15 shows the variation of signal due to the light reflected from the fundus, which is allowed to fall on a photo-multiplier. A differentiating circuit is used to produce a signal which passes through zero when the scanning spot is on one of the maxima. This point is

† See also Fig. 1.15.

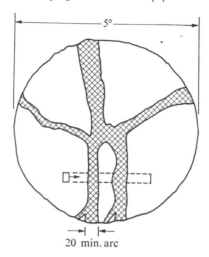

FIG. 2.14. After Cornsweet (1958).

less likely to be affected by changes in the blood vessel due to pulse than a measurement using one of the edges of the blood vessel.

When the scanning spot is in a certain position (to the left of the blood vessel in Fig. 2.15), the scan of a cathode-ray tube is started. The spot on the cathode-ray tube becomes bright when the differentiated signal becomes zero. The position of the bright spot on the cathode-ray tube thus depends on the distance of the retinal blood vessel from the position of the retinal image when the scan is started. The image on the cathode-ray tube is shifted vertically between scans and a record is obtained by photography.

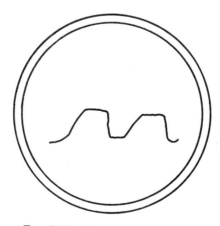

FIG. 2.15. After Cornsweet (1958).

2.32. Sensitivity and frequency response

The noise level corresponds to an error of about 0·2′. Each scan lasts only 20 μs but the repetition rate is only 10 s^{-1}. The spot of light falls on the blind spot but the glare is appreciable. Eye-movements up to 3° can be measured. It is difficult to find vessels suitable for measuring V-rotations, but it might be possible to infer V-rotations from measurements of H-rotations and of rotations at about half-way between H and V provided that T-rotations can be neglected. If T-rotations are to be measured, then a second spot of light on an area of the retina remote from the blind spot would be needed.

The sensitivity at present available is about four times too small and the upper frequency limit is about fifteen times too low for accurate measurement of the smallest eye-movements. Some improvement of these characteristics may be obtained but the limitations due to photon noise will prevent a very large improvement unless information from a considerable region of the retina is used. § 5.30 describes a development based on this method.

2.33. Electronic velocimeter and accelerometer

Bengi and Thomas (1968*a*) give three methods of recording eye-movements. One of these is described in § 3.20. The other two, which do not involve attachments to the eye, will now be described. In both of these methods, apparatus is attached to the head by a face mask and head band. In the first method, the probe forms one plate of a capacitor. The globe forms the ground electrode. The plate is near the junction of cornea and sclera. Rotation of the globe alters the capacity because the cornea sticks out from the sphere of which the sclera is part. Alteration of the capacity changes the frequency of an oscillatory circuit and this change is detected by a modified F-M radio-receiver. The change of frequency is proportional to the amplitude of the movement (for small movements), but this signal is differentiated so that the output is proportional to the angular velocity.

In the second device, a metal probe covered with rubber touches the sclera, and its movements are transferred to a piezo-electric transducer. The signal is differentiated to yield an output proportional to the angular acceleration.

2.34. For a given r.m.s. amplitude of sinusoidal motion (of frequency ν), the r.m.s. velocity is proportional to ν and the acceleration to ν^2.

This is obviously of advantage in recording the saccades and the high-frequency components of the tremor movement (§ 2.4). The records are not affected by movements of the head. Unfortunately, they are extremely sensitive to translations of the measuring system relative to the eye. Such translations may arise in three ways. First, minute twitches of the skin may move the apparatus relative to the skull. Second, the globe may move relative to the skull, either in the direction of the visual axis or perpendicular to it (§§ 1.13 and 2.15). Third, the apparatus itself may not be sufficiently stable, particularly in the mount of the probe. The last of these may be eliminated by careful design, but the others present formidable problems. In the scleral observation methods a translation of 10 μm is equivalent to an angular error of 2′ (§ 2.21). The accelerometer probe amplitude is subject to an equal error. The velocimeter probe is subject to an equal error in respect of translations in a direction tangential to the sclera (in the region of the probe). It is much more sensitive (perhaps by a factor of 10 or more) to translations in a radial direction. These estimates apply to displacements. The position in regard to velocity is more favourable. For this reason both instruments are adequate to record the saccades which have very high velocities and accelerations (§ 4.4). It is unlikely that satisfactory records of tremor can be obtained with the velocimeter. The r.m.s. tremor amplitude corresponding to a band width of 5 Hz at 30 Hz is about 0·1′ (§ 4.11). The corresponding r.m.s. velocity is only about 10′ s^{-1}. Radial translation at the low speed of 1 μ s^{-1} would produce 10 per cent error. The accelerometer may be suitable for recording tremor.

3

Methods of recording eye-movements (2)

3.1. Introduction

In this chapter we shall describe methods involving an attachment to the eye-ball. Most of these methods use a contact lens on which a small mirror is mounted. Assessment of the accuracy and frequency response of any of these methods falls into two parts; (a) estimation of the characteristics of a physical system which measures the rotations of the mirror and (b) a study of the fidelity with which rotations of the eye are reproduced by the beam of light reflected from the mirror.

The physical systems have followed a normal process of development. The characteristics of the early systems, which involved photographic recording, were not as good as those described in specification (1) of § 2.7, though rather better than the characteristics of the methods described in Chapter 2. However, by the use of photo-electric detection and modern electronic techniques it is possible to measure the rotation of a small mirror to much better than 0·01′, and to obtain a good frequency response from 0 Hz to 200 Hz. In this chapter we shall describe various methods and assess the characteristics of the physical measuring systems, so far as these may be deduced from the published data. The fidelity with which the mirror follows movements of the eye is considered in the Appendix. The effect of imperfect following on the measurement of small eye-movements is almost certainly unimportant, e.g. the error in saccade magnitude due to slip is less than the difference between median values for different subjects, or even between median values for the same subject on different days. As the analysis becomes more elaborate, special consideration will have to be given to this source of error in relation to, (i) magnitude of overshoot for saccades (§ 4.5) and (ii) frequency spectrum of the tremor (§ 4.11).

3.2. Early methods

Orchansky (1899) used a metal or glass shell made to fit over the cornea. A mirror was attached to the shell and there was a small central hole for the pupil. Light from a small source was reflected on to a moving film by the mirror. No results were published and it is not possible to estimate the sensitivity. A similar method was used by Marx and Trendelenburg (1911), who constructed a thin aluminium shell to fit over sclera and cornea. H- and V-rotations were both measured, but not simultaneously. Head movements (rotations) were recorded simultaneously by light reflected from a mirror mounted on a frame which was securely attached to the nose. Movements of about 1′ could be detected and the saccadic movements during fixation were observed.

3.3. Mirror resting on the eyeball

Adler and Fliegelman (1934) used a small thin mirror 3 mm in diameter. The eye was anesthetized using a drug which has no effect on the size of the pupil and does not dry the cornea. The mirror was placed on the eyeball at the temporal limbus. It adhered so firmly that recordings could be made with the subject sitting in an erect posture. The subject prevented lid closure with one finger but took care not to press on the globe. The target was at 2 m from the subject and the drum camera at about 1·5 m (see Fig. 3.1). Only H-rotations of the

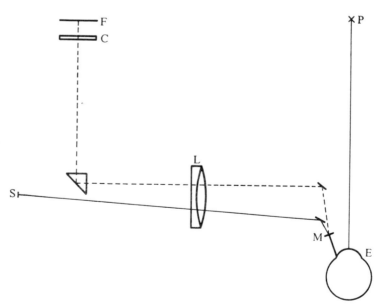

Fɪɢ. 3.1. Diagrammatic representation of apparatus used by Adler and Fliegelman (1934). Mirror M rests on eye; C is a cylindrical lens which focusses beam on to film F.

eye were recorded. The head was fixed in a head-and-chin rest. The film moved at about 5 cm s^{-1} so that 0·5 mm represented 0·01 s, and frequencies up to 100 Hz could be recorded. Assuming that deflections of 0·1 mm could be measured, the sensitivity would be about 0·1′. It is probable that the head was fixed to better than 1·0 mm, but not to 0·1 mm. A movement of 0·25 mm would move the retinal image by about 0·5′ but would not alter the position of the trace on the record. Ratliff and Riggs (1950) suggested that Adler and Fliegelman made a mistake in calculating the rotation of the eye from measurements on the trace, and it is almost certain that their values of angular movements should be divided by a factor slightly greater than two.

3.4. Ratliff and Riggs (1950) also made records with a mirror resting on the sclera, though their main results were obtained with the contact lens method which will be described later (§ 3.5). They used a 2 mm mirror attached by a thin layer of wax to a 6 mm disc of absorbent tissue. This was placed on the sclera clear of the cornea, and no anesthetic was required. The lids had to be taped apart and this caused drying of the cornea followed by lacrimation after a few minutes—so that only short records could be obtained. A similar experiment in which the mirror was attached to the sclera by methyl cellulose was carried out by Riggs, Armington, and Ratliff (1954).

3.5. Contact lens methods

Several experimenters have used a mirror attached to a close-fitting contact lens. Ratliff and Riggs (1950), and Ditchburn and Ginsborg (1953) independently worked out methods which differed only in minor technical details. Fender (1956) introduced photoelectric recording and also made some other important improvements. An apparatus designed for measuring torsion was devised by Davies and Merton (1957), and one which could be used for recording eye-movements when the subject was under rapid acceleration was developed by Byford (1959). The contact lens method has recently been used by Boyce (1967) as part of a method of recording eye-movements on magnetic tape for later analysis by a digital computer. The general advantages of the contact lens method are obvious. It measures eye-rotations directly, and if the target is sufficiently far from the subject conversion to retinal image movements is simple and unambiguous. The disadvantages are the cost of supplying each subject with a well-fitting lens, and the possibility that the lens does not follow the eye exactly.

6

3.6. The apparatus used by Ditchburn and Ginsborg (1953) is shown in Fig. 3.2. A flat of 3 mm diameter was worked on the temporal edge of the corneal portion of the contact lens at about 35° to the visual axis. The first lens was of glass, but the lenses used for most of the records were moulded plastic contact lenses. The flats were accurately worked. The lenses included a correction for refractive

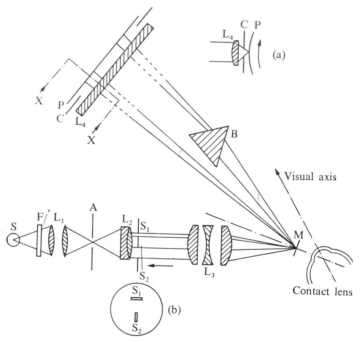

Fig. 3.2. Apparatus used by Ditchburn and Ginsborg (1953). Mirror M is on contact lens. Inset (a) shows section on X–X in main diagram. Inset (b) shows view of slits seen in direction of arrow.

errors. A strongly reflecting rhodium film was deposited by vacuum evaporation (Ginsborg and Heavens 1951). Rhodium films are much more resistant to the tear fluids than aluminium films. A medical examination chair was used to provide support for the back. The subject bit on a metal dental impression made in two parts. The upper section fitted the front upper teeth and carried a mirror for recording head movements. The lower section was fixed to a pillar secured to the table containing the optical components, and locked both the lower teeth and the upper section of the impression. Two identical optical systems, of which one is shown in Fig. 3.2, allowed four data to be recorded simultaneously. These could be either (a) two components of rotations of one eye and two head rotations or (b) two components of eye-rotations for each eye.

3.7. The arrangement permits H-rotations and V-rotations to be recorded on the same drum camera, by the use of a horizontal slit S_1 and a vertical slit S_2, as shown. B is a right-angle prism with its base at 45° to the horizontal. The V-component of rotation then causes a sideways movement of the spot of light derived from S_2. The lenses L_2 and L_3 focus the pinhole A on the mirror M, and L_3 also focuses S_1 and S_2 on L_4, which is a cylindrical lens. L_4 focuses both spots onto the recording paper. Paper speeds of up to 16 cm s^{-1} were used, and time calibration was obtained by running one source on alternating current so that one trace was interrupted at intervals of 0·01 s.

If R is the distance of the paper from the mirror, and D_H is the deflection of the horizontal beam then

$$2R\theta_H = D_H. \tag{3.1}$$

If D_V is the deflection of the vertical beam, α is the angle between the normal to M and the incident recording beam, and β is the angle between the visual axis and the normal to the mirror, then

$$2R\theta_V \cos\alpha \cos\beta = D_V. \tag{3.2}$$

Translational movements of the mirror do not affect the value of θ_H or θ_V. Torsional rotations of the eyeball cause deflections which must be regarded as errors in θ_H and θ_V since no method of separation is available. For light incident parallel to the optic axis ($\alpha = 0$), the errors in θ_H and θ_V due to a *small* torsional rotation θ_T are approximately

$$\Delta\theta_H = \beta(1-\cos\theta_T) = \beta\theta_T^2/2, \tag{3.3}$$

$$\Delta\theta_V = \beta\sin\theta_T = \beta\theta_T. \tag{3.4}$$

Thus the error $\Delta\theta_H$ is zero to first order but there is a first-order error in θ_V if θ_T and θ_V are of the same order of magnitude.

The fixation mark was at 4·5 m from the subject so that movement of the head through 0·1 mm would involve a change in direction of fixation of 0·06′. The smallest rotation which could be detected under the best conditions was about 0·15′, but blurring of the record, due to grease and moisture on the mirror, usually gave somewhat lower sensitivity. When the steady source was used the frequency response should be linear up to several hundred Hertz. A fixed mirror was attached to the pillar supporting the head and its movements were recorded while the subject was biting on the dental impression. The mirror was found to be stationary, showing that the optical system was free from vibration.

3.8. The apparatus used by Ratliff and Riggs (1950) differed from that just described in the following ways.

(a) A 5 mm hole was drilled in the scleral portion of the contact lens, and a good quality mirror was cemented in.

(b) Head movements were recorded by means of a mirror attached to a pair of goggles (with the glass removed).

(c) A collimator provided a fixation mark at infinity—so that translation of the head made no difference to the direction of fixation.

A record obtained by Ditchburn and Ginsborg is reproduced in Fig. 4.14. The records obtained by Adler and Fliegelman and by Ratliff and Riggs are of similar quality.

3.9. Contact lens with stalk

Several important improvements to the contact lens method of recording were introduced by Fender (1956). The first of these was the use of a stalk on the contact lens as shown in Fig. 3.3. In this arrangement the beam of light is reflected from a good optical surface which is not contaminated by tear fluids or grease from the eyelids. It is also an important advantage to be able to set the mirror normal to the optic axis, because this enables H- and V-rotations to be measured without any error due to T-rotations. Fender (1955a) was able to record the T-rotations by the addition of a second mirror as shown in Fig. 3.4. The two incandescent balls of an alternating current pointolite lamp were used as independent sources to give beams A and B. Part of the beam A and part of the beam B were rotated through a right-angle by

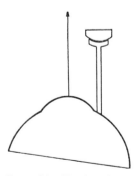

Fɪɢ. 3.3. Mirror on stalk used by Fender 1956, modified by West 1968a.

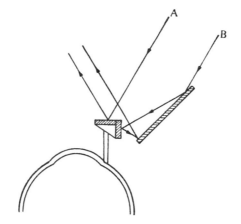

Fig. 3.4. Mirrors on stalk used by Fender 1955a.

a Dove-prism. The two parts of a beam A record H- and V-rotations and the two parts of beam B record H- and T-rotations. A specimen record is shown in Fig. 3.5. The second H-rotation record is not reproduced in this figure.

3.10. Stalk-assembly

In order to obtain the full advantages of a method involving the use of a contact lens with stalk, the following requirements must be satisfied.

(a) The stalk must be firmly cemented to the scleral portion of the lens and placed so that the lids can close around it without disturbing the lens; the junction between stalk and lens must be smooth to avoid irritation (§ A.7).

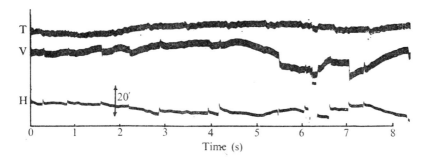

Fig. 3.5. Record of H-, V-, T-components.

(b) To ensure adequate stiffness, the stalk should be at least 4 mm in diameter; a plastic rod or a thin tube of duralumin may be used (§ A.6).

(c) The mirror must be at least 6 mm in diameter and flat, to within $0\cdot1\lambda$, over the central 5 mm (§ A.2).

(d) The mirror must be adjusted so that it is normal to the visual axis within $1°$ (§ A.3).

All these requirements can be met without serious difficulty, but some care is required. Technical details are given in the Appendix.

3.11. Photo-electric transducer

The records obtained by Adler and Fliegelman, Ratliff and Riggs, Ditchburn and Ginsborg, and others all showed the presence of a fine tremor of amplitude about $0\cdot5'$. It appeared to be an irregular motion with components in the frequency range 30–80 Hz. Fender (1956) used the apparatus shown in Fig. 3.6 to study this tremor. A grid G_1 is placed in the projection system, and after the light has been reflected at the eye mirror, it is refocussed so that the image of G_1 falls on a

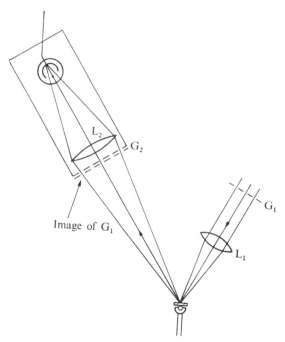

FIG. 3.6. Apparatus for recording tremor. (After Fender 1956.)

similar grid G_2. Light which passes through G_2 is focussed on the photo-
multiplier P. The spacing between the bars of G_2 is made a little greater
than the maximum amplitude of tremor motion so that each bar contributes to the signal due to tremor motion, and total output of this signal
is proportional to the number of bars.

This arrangement makes the low-frequency drift movements and the
high-frequency tremor movement yield signals of about the same amplitude. The circuit also provides further discrimination against signals
of frequency 0–5 Hz as compared with signals of frequencies about 20

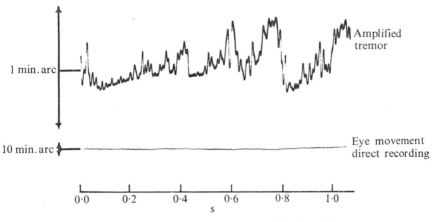

FIG. 3.7. Record of tremor. (From Fender 1956.)

Hz. The tube of the cathode-ray oscilloscope is photographed and a
portion of one record is shown in Fig. 3.7.

3.12. A different kind of photo-transducer for eye-movements was
designed by Byford (1959 and 1962*a*). The principle is shown in Fig.
3.8, in which C is a small medical lamp carried on a stalk attached to a
contact lens. The stops D, E, F, G are so placed that movements of the
lamp cause changes in the light received by the photo-multiplier.
Byford showed by calculation, and by tests with an artificial eye, that
these changes are linearly proportional to the rotation of the eye for
movements up to about 10°. Byford made one form of this transducer
in which the photo-multiplier and slits were mounted on a bench, and
the subject's head was fixed by a dental bite and by supports. Most of
the work, however, was done with a model in which the whole apparatus
was mounted on a dental impression so that it could be carried by the
subject. We call this the *subject-held model.*

3.13. The bench-mounted instrument was capable of recording H-
rotations and V-rotations, but the subject-held instrument measured

only one component. This device has two sources of error which do not arise in the mirror system. First, the apparatus is sensitive to translational movements of the head and of the eye in its orbit, and secondly, the T-rotations cause an error in the H-rotation or V-rotation (whichever is being measured) unless the lamp is placed on the axis of vision. The stalk used by Byford was about 2·5 cm long so that the lamp was approximately 4 cm from the instantaneous centre of rotation. The sensitivity to head-movements is thus about three times less than the sensitivity of methods in which the movement of a marked point on the sclera is used, and seven times less than that of corneal reflection methods. Byford showed that the spurious signals, due to shaking the

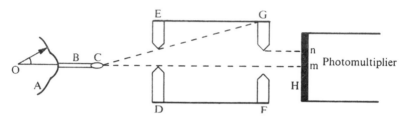

FIG. 3.8. Photo-electric transducer. (From Byford 1962*a*.)

head violently or tapping the apparatus with a spanner, were small, and concluded that only negligibly small errors occurred when the apparatus was in normal use. If the lamp is placed on a horizontal meridian, the torsional movements cause no first-order error in measurement of H-rotations. The error in measurement of V-rotation due to a torsional rotation θ_T is approximately $r\theta_T/40$ where r is the distance (in millimetres) of the lamp from the visual axis. If r is 20 the error is $\frac{1}{2}\theta_T$ and since torsional movements are considerably smaller than the H- and T-rotations, the percentage error is fairly small. The response of the mechanical part of this system is good for frequencies up to at least 200 Hz, and the electrical system can be designed to match this response.

3.14. Polarized light method for T-rotations

Davies and Merton (1957) obtained a record of T-rotations by attaching a piece of birefringent mica to the eye and measuring its effect on polarized infra-red radiation. The apparatus is shown in Fig. 3.9. A stalk, attached to a small corneal contact lens, carries a mica plate. Polarized light passes through the plate and is reflected by the partially silvered mirror M. It then passes to an analyser. Rotation of the mica plate (which should be approximately a quarter-wave plate) alters the plane of polarization of the reflected light and hence the current received by the photocell. The subject sees the bright fixation mark through the partially silvered mirror and the mica plate. In the form described by Davies and Merton, the method appears to be capable of detecting T-rotations of about 20′ and is thus not sensitive enough to measure the torsional components of small eye-movements. However, photoelectric methods of detecting changes of polarization azimuth

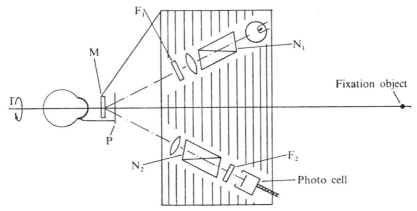

F ɪ ɢ. 3.9. Apparatus for measuring T-component (from Davies and Merton 1957). N_1 and N_2 are nicol prisms, P is a mica plate attached to the contact lens. M is a 90 per cent reflector supported independently of the head. F_1 and F_2 are infra-red filters.

of a few seconds of arc are well known and the rotation of the plane of polarization is nearly four times the T-component of eye rotation. The method can probably be made sensitive enough for the measurement of small eye-movements. It is less simple than the mirror-reflection method Its main advantage is the extremely small weight of the attachment to the eye.

3.15. Recording on magnetic tape

Any of the methods which produce an electrical signal may be associated with a recording system involving the use of magnetic tape moving at fairly high speed. The tape may be played back at reduced speed into a digitizer whose output punches paper tape for analysis by a computer. A well-designed system of this kind accepts and uses information much more rapidly than any system which depends on reading from a record on photographic paper or on a pen-recorder. If, however, there were no record that could be visually inspected, some aspect of the phenomenon might be overlooked because the appropriate analysis had not been included in any of the computer programs. It is therefore desirable that, at least part of the time, a visible record is available. It is possible both to arrange for a visible record to appear during the experiment, so that the experimenter may adjust experimental conditions if he wishes, and also for a visible record on a penrecorder to be produced from tape which has been stored. The recording system† used by Boyce (1967) is shown in Fig. 3.10. The light reflected

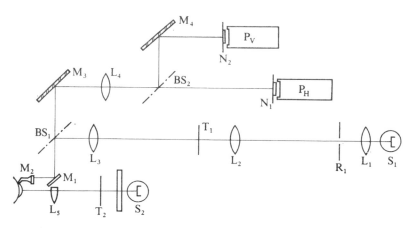

FⅰG. 3.10. Photo-electric transducer for recording H and V components: $L_1 \ldots L_4$ compound lenses, L_5 portion of spectacle lens, $M_1 \ldots M_4$ mirrors, BS_1 and BS_2 beam splitters, S_1 and S_2 strip-filament lamps, N_1 and N_2 masks. T_1 is a target whose image falls on the photo-multipliers, and T_2 is a fixation mark viewed by the subject through the lens L_5.
(After Boyce 1967.)

from the mirror on the contact lens is divided into two parts which fall on photo-multipliers P_H and P_V. Masks are placed in the optical system so that H-components of the eye-rotations produce a change in the light falling on P_H, and V-rotations alter the amount of light falling on P_V. With reasonable attention to details of design, the variation in output from P_H and P_V are proportional to the H- and V-components of eye-rotations within certain ranges. The limits are determined by the angle corresponding to, (a) the light passing entirely on to the dark region, and (b) the light filling the clear region of the masks. The useful range can be set at any desired value, but the accuracy of measurement is inversely proportional to the range. In many experiments the range was 30′ and the smallest movement which could be detected was about

† St. Cyr and Fender (1969*a*, *b*, *c*) used the method described in § 3.12, together with an analogue recording system followed by an A-D converter, to produce a digital signal. This subsequently was analysed by computer. H- and V-data for two eyes were accepted simultaneously.

0·3′. This is satisfactory for saccades, but a narrower range would be needed for analysis of tremor.

3.16. The output from one of the photo-multipliers is passed through a low-pass filter (to remove noise above about 1000 Hz) and then to an F-M tape recorder. A train of periodic pulses (interval 10·4 ms) was simultaneously recorded on a separate channel. The replay signal is generated by comparing the frequency recorded on the tape with that produced by a local oscillator. The analogue thus produced is sampled at intervals of 10 ms, the command for each sample being derived from the recorded pulses. The samples are digitized and passed to the printer or the tape punch. When the samples for one component have all been treated, the tape is run back and the process is repeated with the other component. The command pulses ensure that corresponding parts of the two records are used.

3.17. Analysis of results

The data for the computer consists of two tapes containing the H- and V-components respectively. The first step is to combine these components so as that all future analysis can be done on vector displacements from a mean position. The program sorts the data into blocks within which the signals remained with the limits of linear response. It corrects an occasional mispunch by replacing the mispunched value by the mean of the preceding and following values. If the blocks are too short, or if there are many mispunches, the set of data is rejected.

Following the above recoding, sorting, and correcting program, the computer may be used to produce a variety of data such as median saccade magnitudes, distribution of directions of saccades and drifts, correlations between saccades and following drifts, etc. For most of these it is necessary to identify saccades. This is done by means of a program† which compares the readings of successive samples with a 'template' which picks out a movement whose velocity and acceleration exceed certain preset values. This accepts saccades whose magnitude exceeds a certain value (2′). Smaller saccades cannot be unambiguously distinguished from the tremor.

3.18. Method using magnetic search coil

Robinson (1963) measured eye-movements by recording the voltage generated by a search coil embedded in the scleral portion of a contact

† For details see Boyce (1965*a*, 1967).

lens. The head of the subject was in a uniform alternating magnetic field. Let us first consider the measurement of the V-component of eye-movements. A coil of N turns, each of area A is situated in a plane normal to the visual axis, i.e. in a vertical plane when the eye is in the primary position. The magnetic field $H_z \cos \omega t$ is in a vertical direction. When the eye is tilted upwards through an angle ϕ from the primary position, the voltage induced is

$$e_\phi = 10^{-8}\, \omega N A H_z \sin \phi \sin \omega t. \qquad (3.5)$$

In the arrangement used $N = 10$, $A = 2\!\cdot\!55\ \mathrm{cm^2}$, $\omega = 3 \times 10^4$, and $H_z = 2\!\cdot\!2\ \mathrm{G}$. When $\phi = 10°$, the induced voltage (e_ϕ) was $2\!\cdot\!2\ \mathrm{mV}$ (r.m.s.). The noise level of the amplifier was about $2\ \mu\mathrm{V}$, so that an accuracy of about $0\!\cdot\!01°$, or about $1'$, was obtained. This accuracy can be improved by comparing the voltage from the search coil with that generated by a fixed coil in the same magnetic field. N and H_z can be increased to give a sensitivity of about $10''$ if this is required. An upper limit to the magnetic field is set by the appearance of phosgenes at about $200\ \mathrm{G}$.

3.19. The H-component of eye-movements may be recorded by using a second magnetic field which is in the direction of the visual axis when the eye is in the primary position. This field ($H_x \cos \omega t$) is in quadrature with the vertical field and gives a signal proportional to $\sin \theta \cos \phi \cos \omega t$ when the H-component of rotation is θ and the V-component is ϕ. Phase-sensitive amplifiers distinguish the two signals. The T-component may be recorded if a second search coil (as nearly as possible at right-angles to the first) is embedded in the contact lens.

Tests showed that the system is capable of recording frequencies up to about 1000 Hz. It is thus quite fast enough to record both saccades and tremor. The weight of the coils is only about 15 per cent of the weight of the contact lens. A linear output of the three components may be obtained by digitizing the voltages to form an input for a computer.

3.20. Accelerometer method

Records of eye-movements may be obtained by attaching a sensitive strain-gauge of suitable frequency-response to a stalk mounted on a contact lens. The stalk is loaded sufficiently to bend slightly when the eye makes saccadic movements. Alternatively, a piezo-electric accelerometer may be attached to a contact lens. This method was used by Thomas (1961), Bengi and Thomas (1967 and 1968a), and by West and Boyce (1968). This apparatus is very convenient for recording the distribution of saccade intervals and for obtaining statistics on saccade magnitudes. It is also sensitive to the high frequency components of tremor. If a device of this kind is used for detailed records of acceleration during the progress of a saccade, or for tremor analysis, it is necessary to test for resonance and damping. The requirements are somewhat more severe than those stated in § 2.7 for devices which record displacements.

4

Kinematic description of small eye-movements

4.1. Introduction

This chapter gives a description of the small eye-movements, i.e. the small rotations of the eye in its orbit, which remain when a subject fixes his gaze as accurately as he can upon a well-defined fixation mark. In normal vision these rotations involve corresponding movements of the retinal image. Other movements of parts of the retinal image are produced by movements of objects in the visual field. We shall later be concerned with three important questions:

(a) To what extent are eye-movements controlled, and how does the control operate?

(b) Have the movements of the retinal image any important function in visual perception?

(c) How does a subject distinguish between movement of the retinal image due to rotation of the eyes, and movement of the retinal image due to movement of an object in the external world?

Discussion of these matters requires both a description of eye-movements and also of the loss of vision which occurs when the retinal image is stabilized (Chapter 6–13). The main treatment is therefore postponed to Chapters 12–16, but it is desirable to keep these problems in mind when considering the kinematic description of eye-movements.

4.2. Different types of movement

A photographic record of the H-, V-, and T-components is reproduced in Fig. 3.5. Each of the components includes the following:

(a) Periods of fairly slow movement (called *drifts*).

(b) Occasional sharp movements, usually of several minutes of arc (called *saccades* or *flicks*).

Examination of the original records reveals a third type of movement (called *tremor*). This is

(c) An irregular oscillatory movement having characteristics rather like random 'noise'. Frequencies of up to 150 Hz are present though most of the 'power' is in the lower frequency range (Fig. 3.7). The amplitude of the retinal image movement due to tremor is about equal to the smallest intercone distance.

All three types of eye-movement have been studied in detail using methods involving contact lenses and similar attachments to the eye, but the existence of each of them has also been demonstrated by experimenters who used no attachment to the eye, including Barlow (1952), Riggs, Armington, and Ratliff (1954), and Bengi and Thomas (1968a). This shows that none of these components is an artifact due to irritation of the eye by tight-fitting contact lenses or due to slip by badly fitting lenses. The possibility that the movements are increased or decreased by the attachment is not excluded (§ 4.11). In this chapter we are mainly concerned with the H- and V-components of the drifts and the saccades. These components determine the accuracy of fixation, since they produce movements of the retinal image which are much larger than the movements due to tremor or to small T-components. The effect of tremor is discussed in § 4.11 and of torsion in § 4.29.

4.3. Saccadic movements

A record of one component of an involuntary saccade, obtained by Byford (1962a), is reproduced in Fig. 4.1. There is an *initial movement* of magnitude M_i, and a small *final movement* of magnitude M_f which will be discussed in § 4.5. These two movements give a *resultant saccade* of magnitude M_s. For involuntary saccades† occurring during fixation, M_s is usually less than 10′ and very seldom greater than 30′. The saccade shown in Fig. 4.1 is abnormally large, but there is no reason to believe that it is not typical in regard to the variation (with time) of displacement, speed, and acceleration. For involuntary saccades of magnitude up to 40′, the *duration* t_i of the initial movement is nearly constant for any one subject, and the difference between subjects is not very large. Most experimenters obtain values between 25 ms and 30 ms. The extreme range of values reported is from 20 ms to 40 ms, but the highest values probably include experimental error due to the inadequate high-frequency response of some recording systems (§ 2.7).

† Much larger involuntary saccades occur in pathological conditions of nystagmus.

4.4. Westheimer (1954*a*), Robinson (1964) and Yarbus† have shown that, for large voluntary saccades, t_i varies linearly with M_i. Extrapolation of the lines obtained by these experimenters (Fig. 4.2) predicts a nearly constant value of t_i when M_i is less than 60′. This value is in the range 20 ms to 30 ms in agreement with the measured value for involuntary saccades (§ 4.3).

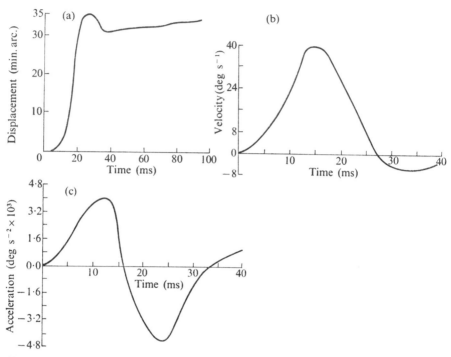

Fɪɢ. 4.1. Record of saccade (Byford 1962*a*); (a) displacement versus time, (b) velocity versus time, and (c) acceleration versus time.

If t_i is nearly constant, then the maximum speed S_m attained during the initial movement is roughly proportional to M_i (Fig. 3 of Ginsborg 1953). This conclusion is supported by Gliem and Günther (1965) who measured speeds for saccades of magnitudes 6′ to 100′. They also found no significant difference between the speeds for persons with normal vision and for patients at an eye-clinic. Fig. 4.1 gives a maximum speed S_m of 2400 min.arc s^{-1} when $M_i = 35′$, corresponding to the formula $S_m = 70\,M_i$. This is in reasonably good agreement with an estimate of 600 min.arc s^{-1} for a saccade for which $M_i = 10′$ (Ditchburn and Ginsborg 1953). The acceleration should be proportional to M_i^2. Byford's curve gives a *maximum* of $2 \cdot 5 \times 10^6$ min.arc s^{-2} for $M_i = 35′$.

† Reproduced in Yarbus (1967), Fig. 79.

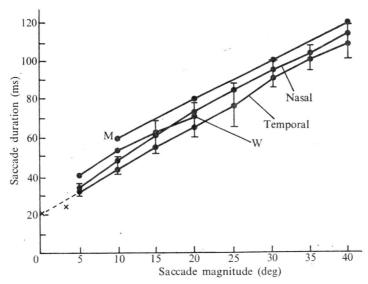

FIG. 4.2. Saccade duration versus saccade magnitude for voluntary saccades. W, data from Westheimer (1964a); M, data from Mackensen (1958); points × ... × from Ginsborg (1953); data for nasal and temporal saccades from Robinson (1964).

4.5. The final movement of a saccade

Ginsborg (1953) showed that, in voluntary saccades of about 3°, the initial movement sometimes falls short of target and sometimes overshoots it (§ 15.3). The final movement may be regarded as a correction. Boyce (1965a) found that, in the small involuntary saccades of fixation, the final movement does not in general return exactly along the direction of the initial movement, but always has a substantial component in this direction. An obvious possibility is that the recorded overshoot is an artifact due to the inertia of the lens, causing it to slip when the eye decelerates. The lens would then move further than the eye and return later to its equilibrium position (Appendix § A.12). It is likely that, with some lenses, a part of the recorded overshoot is produced by slip, but the whole effect cannot be explained in this way. The overshoot has been observed by many experimenters, including some who did not use any attachment to the eye (Westheimer 1954a; Barlow 1952; Lord and Wright 1948; Rashbass 1960; Higgins and Stultz 1953). Slip of the contact lens would vary with the acceleration and magnitude of the primary movement. Boyce (1965a), using a moderately well-fitting contact lens, obtained an overshoot which varied with the deflection M_s produced by the saccade. When the lens

7

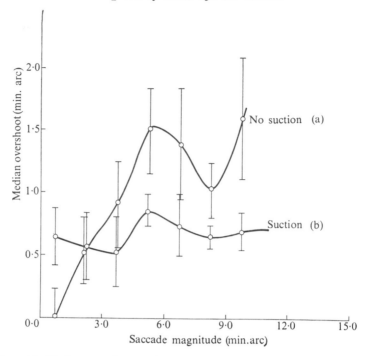

FIG. 4.3. Median overshoot against saccade deflection. (from Boyce, 1965*a*.)

was made to adhere more closely by suction the overshoot magnitude became constant at about $(0.6' \pm 0.1')$ when M_i varied from 1′ to 12′ (Fig. 4.3). Byford (1962*b*) found a constant overshoot of about 3′ when M_i varied from 5′ to 15′. The difference between the values for the constant overshoot found by Boyce and by Byford may be an inter-subject difference. Although the overshoot is important in relation to the dynamics of eye-movements (§§ 15.29–15.34), the over-all displacement M_s is the significant parameter in relation to accuracy of fixation.

4.6. Intersaccadic interval

The eye moves with a relatively low speed during the interval T_{is} between two saccades. This speed varies a good deal from one interval to another for any one subject, and the mean value (or median value) varies considerably from one subject to another. Different experimenters have recorded speeds of from 0 to 20 min.arc s^{-1} for individual intersaccadic intervals. Nye (1962) obtained median drift speeds of $1\cdot5$ min.arc s^{-1} and $3\cdot6$ min.arc s^{-1} for two subjects. A rough estimate of mean speed is obtained by dividing the mean values of M_d in Table 4.1 by the corresponding mean values of T_{is}. The range of mean speeds, calculated in this way, varies from 2 min.arc s^{-1} to 8 min.arc s^{-1}.

The movement of the eye during any one intersaccadic interval usually looks like a linear movement plus a small irregularity (the tremor). For purposes of measurement it is convenient to define the *drift magnitude* M_d to be the distance between the positions of the eye at the beginning and at the end of the intersaccadic interval. The drift is then linear by definition, and any 'wavering' is regarded as part of the oscillatory movement.

4.7. Median values

Table 4.1 gives median values (and, in a few cases, mean values) obtained by various experimenters. The table includes two results on each of four subjects, the eye-movements being recorded on two different days (Boyce 1965*a* and 1967). There is an appreciable difference between the results given by one subject on two different days, but a considerably larger difference between subjects in respect of M_s and also T_{is}. The variations between subjects in respect of M_d are fairly small. Boyce (1965*a*) showed that the median values of the parameters M_s, M_d, and T_{is}, were not significantly altered when the adherence of the lens was improved by suction. It is thus unlikely that any important error is introduced by slip of the contact lens. Nachmias (1959 and 1961) measured M_s for two subjects and repeated the measurement on the same subjects after about two years. The results are in good agreement.

4.8. Range of variation of the parameters

The ranges of variation (for four subjects) of M_s, M_d, and T_{is} are shown in Table 4.2. Histograms of M_s and M_d, obtained by Boyce (1965), are shown in Figs. 4.4 and 4.5. Histograms of T_{is} for two subjects, obtained by Ginsborg (1953), are shown in Fig. 4.6. The distributions for all three parameters (M_d, M_s, T_{is}) are skew. The mean values (with one exception) exceed the median values, because very large values of the parameters, although fairly rare, occur more frequently than would be predicted from a normal curve fitted to the lower three-quarters of the population.

TABLE 4.1†
Value of M_s, M_d, and T_{is}

Experimenter	Subject	Median			Mean			Notes
		M_s	M_d	T_{is}	M_s	M_d	T_{is}	
Adler and Fliegelman (1934)		5·6		0·7	8		1·0	Median values from mean.
Ratliff and Riggs (1950)		3·9			5·6			Mean M_s is average of 5 subjects. Median values from mean.
Lord (1950)	W.D.W.			0·3			0·45	
	W.D.W.			0·9			1·3 (Supine)	Median
	M.P.L.			0·5			0·7	values
	M.P.L.			1·6			2·3 (Supine	from
	R.W.G.H.			0·6			0·86	
	R.W.G.H.			0·6			0·86 (Supine)	means.
	R.N.W.			0·7			0·94	
	L.C.T.			3·6			5·2	
	P.B.W.			3·7			5·3	
	E.S.L.			8·4			12·0	
Ginsborg (1953)	B.L.G.	4·3		0·50	6·1		0·71	Median values from means.
	D.M.M.	4·1		0·78	5·8		1·11	
Fender (1956)	R.W.D.	19·0	2·8	0·6	20·9	4·1	1·08	Vector values obtained from H-components.
	D.H.F.	7·8	5·7	0·97	8·3	9·0	1·05	
	S.M.	22·8	3·2	1·0	28·1	4·7	2·0	
	R.M.P.	4·2	2·8	0·28	8·8	3·0	0·35	
Cornsweet (1956)	L.A.R.	3·6		0·8	4·5		1·2	Mean M_s from graph of saccade magnitude as function of eye-ball position. Median values from means.
	C.R.C.			0·5			0·7	
Nachmias (1959)	V.N.	2·0	1·5	0·35			0·45	M_s and M_d estimated as mean of medians of polar plot. M_d from 0·2 s samples with median T_{is}.
Yarbus (1957 and 1965)		8·0		0·5				Over-all averages for 1000 saccades for 4 subjects.

TABLE 4.1 (*Continued*)

Experimenter	Subject	Median			Mean		T_{is}	Notes
		M_s	M_d	T_{is}	M_s	M_d		
Clowes (1959)	M.B.C.	6·4			9·2			Mean values from H- and V- components. Median value from means.
Krauskopf, Cornsweet, and Riggs (1960)	J.K.(LE)	2·5						LE = Left eye. RE = Right eye. Vector values from H-components.
	J.K.(RE)	3·8						
	LAR(LE)	3·5						
	LAR(RE)	5·6						
Nachmias (1961)	V.N.	1·2	0·8		1·7	1·2		Median values from means. Drift estimate from polar plot.
	J.A.	3·4	1·1		4·8	1·6		
Nye (1962)	P.N.		2·8	0·8			1·1	Median T_{is} obtained from mean T_{is}. Median M_d from median drift velocity and median T_{is}.
	E.N.		1·5	1·0			1·4	
Fiorentini and Ercoles (1963)	A.F.			1·7			2·4	Median values from means.
	A.M.A.			17·5			25·0	
Steinman (1965)	R.S.		2.3	0·35			0·5	T_{is} (mean) from mean saccade frequency. Median T_{is} values from means. Median M_d from 0·2 s drift magnitudes with median T_{is}.
	M.H.		4·5	0·5			0·7	
Boyce (1965)	D.C.W.	3·7	1·5	0·42			0·62	
	D.C.W.	5·5	3·0	0·5			0·72	
	P.R.B.	8·4	3·7	0·31			0·44	
	P.R.B.	5·9	2·4	0·18			0·26	Median T_{is}
	H.R.P.	6·0	2·1	0·17			0·24	
	H.R.P.	6·1	2·2	0·20			0·28	obtained from
	D.F.B.		1·5	0·14			0·20	
	D.F.B.	9·0	1·5	0·15			0·22	mean T_{is}

† (a) Where median values have been obtained from mean values a conversion factor of 0·7 has been assumed.

(b) Where vectors have been obtained from horizontal components a conversion factor of $\sqrt{2}$ has been assumed.

(c) Where two different values for any given subject are given, the arithmetic mean has been used to produce histograms, but left and right eyes are treated separately and so are supine and upright positions.

TABLE 4.2

Range of variation of M_s, M_d, and T_{ls} for four subjects (after Fender 1956)

	M_s				M_d				T_{ls}			
	RWD	DHF	SM	RMP	RWD	DHF	SM	RMP	RWD	DHF	SM	RMP
Mean	14·8	5·9	19·9	6·2	2·9	6·4	3·3	2·1	1·08	1·05	2·0	0·35
Median	13·5	5·5	16·2	3·0	2·0	4·0	2·3	2·0	0·6	0·97	1·0	0·28
Maximum	39·0	24·0	57·8	28·0	13·0	23·0	12·2	8·0	4·2	2·06	14·6	1·1
Minimum	2·0	0	1·2	0	0	0	0	0	0·02	0·30	0·03	0·03

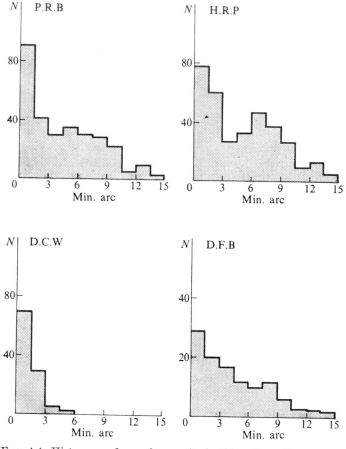

FIG. 4.4. Histogram of saccade magnitude (M_s). (From Boyce 1967.)

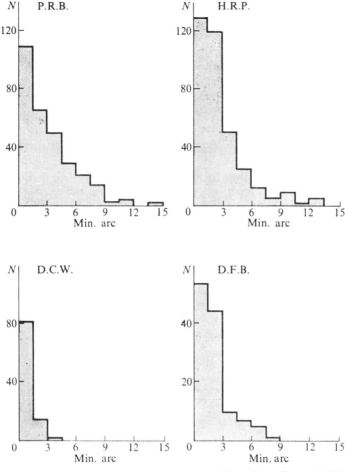

F I G. 4.5. Histogram of drift magnitude (M_d). (From Boyce 1967.)

Histograms of M_s and M_d for four subjects are shown in Figs. 4.4 and 4.5. No subject shows any significant indication of a bimodal distribution. Fig. 4.6 shows histograms of T_{is} for two subjects. The range of variation between subjects, shown in Table 4.1, is large. Histograms of inter-subject variation of the median values M_s, M_d, and T_{is} are shown in Fig. 4.7(a), (b), and (c), (Ditchburn and Foley-Fisher 1967). The histograms shown in Fig. 4.7 are based on rather small numbers, but are sufficient to give a general indication of the way in which these parameters vary among subjects with normal vision. Some of the extreme values may be due to variation of experimental conditions (§ 4.9). Median values for distribution of medians between subjects are:

(a) Saccade magnitude M_s—4·5′ (50 per cent of subjects in the range 3·0′ to 6·0′).

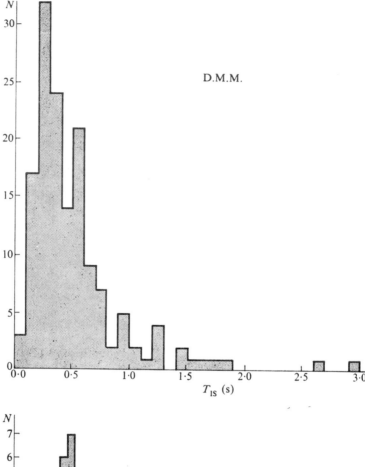

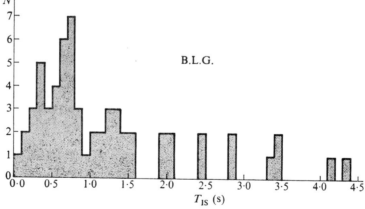

FIG. 4.6. Histogram of intersaccadic intervals. (From Ginsborg 1953*b*.)

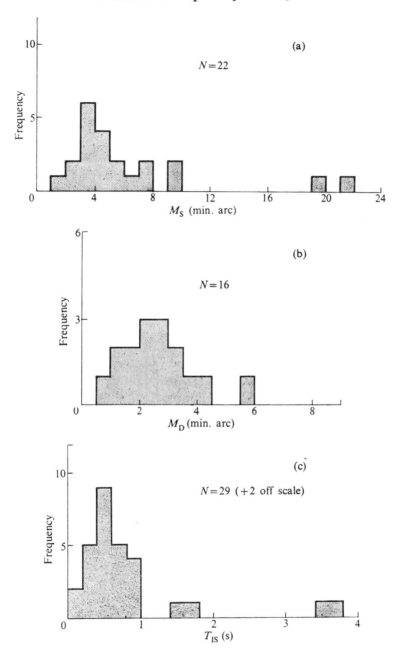

FIG. 4.7. Intersubject variations of (a) median saccade magnitude M_s, (b) median drift magnitude (M_d), and (c) intersaccadic interval T_{is}. (From Ditchburn and Foley–Fisher 1967.)

(b) Drift   magnitude $M_d - 2\cdot5'$ (50   per   cent   in the range $1\cdot7'$ to $3\cdot2'$).

(c) Intersaccadic interval $T_{is} - 0\cdot58$ s. (50 per cent in the range $0\cdot3$ s to $0\cdot7$ s).

(d) Saccade frequency $(1/T_{is}) - 1\cdot6$ s^{-1}.

4.9. Variation of intersaccadic interval with experimental conditions

Barlow (1952) found that the mean intersaccadic interval depended on the degree of attention to the visual task. Immediately after the subject was asked to change to a new fixation task there was a decrease in intersaccadic interval. There was an increase in intersaccadic interval (fewer saccades) when the subject did mental arithmetic while fixating. Clowes (1959, 1961) found that some subjects could learn to 'relax' in such a way that the mean intersaccadic interval was greatly increased. When this happened the target became less clearly seen. The subject could learn to accept this loss and not make a sharp movement to restore good vision. Fiorentini and Ercoles (1966) found that one of two observers could suppress saccades completely for periods up to about 30 s (§ 14.10). Steinman *et al.* (1967) found that experienced subjects could suppress saccades for about 10 s, without much loss of visual performance. Lord (1950), who used no attachment to the eye, obtained four of the five highest values for T_{is} ($2\cdot3$, $5\cdot2$, $5\cdot3$, and $12\cdot0$ s), but the longest time (25 s) was obtained by Fiorentini and Ercoles (1963) who used contact lenses (Table 4.1). This suggests that, although irritation due to an uncomfortable contact lens may increase the saccade rate, a well-adjusted contact lens has no significant effect. Other variations of eye-movements with experimental conditions are described in §§ 4.20–4.25 and in Chapter 14.

4.10. Frequency analysis of small eye-movements

Separation of eye-movements into saccades, drifts and tremor, and measurement of median values, constitutes one method of extracting the general behaviour of eye-movements from measurements of a limited number of short records. Frequency analysis is another method which is of considerable interest in relation to the tremor. Any 'signal' $f(t)$, defined for all values of t (and subject to certain mathematical conditions) may be associated with a Fourier frequency spectrum defined by

$$A(\nu) = a\exp(i\varepsilon) = \frac{1}{2\pi}\int_{-\infty}^{\infty} f(t)\exp(2\pi i\nu t)\,dt, \qquad (4.1)$$

where a and ε are both functions of the temporal frequency ν.

The power spectrum† is defined as

$$W(\nu) = A(\nu)A^*(\nu) = a^2. \qquad (4.2)$$

Eye-movements do not form a determinate signal. We cannot use a record of eye-movements over a finite time to predict, *in detail*, the future course of eye-movements. However, many of the methods of Fourier analysis can be applied to signals which, although not determinate, are stochastic and stationary. A stochastic signal is one for which the probability distribution for the value at any instant is defined (and also the probability contingent on a previous value). A stationary signal is one for which these probabilities remain constant with time. Eye-movements are stochastic, and they are stationary to the extent to which we can ignore fatigue and effects of training.

4.11. Findlay (1967) developed a method of investigating a signal which consists of impulsive signals superimposed on random 'noise', in connection with the analysis of radio 'whistles'. In this method the power due to the noise is unambiguously separated from the power due to the impulses. He applied this method to the analysis of eye-movement records obtained with the apparatus described in §§ 3.15–3.17 (Findlay 1971). His results for saccades and tremor are shown in Fig. 4.8. The spectral amplitude a, i.e. $W^{\frac{1}{2}}$, is shown as a function of ν. For a second subject, the spectrum of the tremor was nearly the same. The saccade spectrum was similar in form, but larger. This subject has about the same average size of saccade but a higher saccade frequency.

In the curves of Fig. 4.8, both spectral densities fall smoothly from the lowest frequency measured (5·0 Hz) to a point where the power due to the signal cannot be distinguished from 'noise' in the measuring system. Several of the earlier workers who observed tremor thought that the spectral density reached a subsidiary maximum at some frequency about 80–100 Hz (Fender 1956; Yarbus‡ 1956), but these observations were not based on a long series of experiments. Fender and Nye (1961) obtained a curve generally similar to that of Findlay. Bengi and Thomas (1968*b*) show a velocity spectrum in which there is a sharp maximum at 40 Hz and a weak one at 80 Hz. It is possible that the accelerometer has a better spectral resolution than the apparatus used by Findlay. It is also possible that the maxima are artifacts due to a resonance of the measuring system at a subharmonic of the basic frequency. Boyce (1965*a*) found strong subharmonic resonances at

---

† See Ditchburn (1963, pp. 115–16).
‡ Yarbus (1967, p. 115).

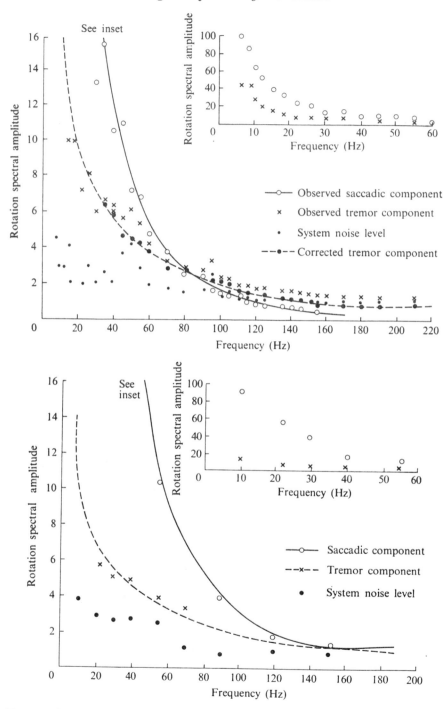

Fɪɢ. 4.8. Rotational spectral amplitude versus frequency for saccadic and tremor components of eye-movements (a) subject J.M.F. (b) subject H.R.P. (From Findlay 1971.)

similar frequencies in certain contact lens assemblies. He took considerable care to eliminate them in the apparatus which was subsequently
used by Findlay.

4.12. Accuracy of fixation—contour map

For many purposes it is desirable to find a measure of the extent to
which the visual axis wanders when a subject is fixating. One measure
of this 'wandering' is a contour map which can, in principle, be prepared
in the following way. Imagine that the beam reflected at near-normal
incidence from a mirror on a contact lens is reflected onto a square
array of detectors. Each detector is connected to a clock which records
the time for which the spot of light falls on it. A diagram showing the
time spent in different areas can then be prepared (Fig. 4.9), and different densities of shading may be used to give a contour map. The
apparatus required for this method would be expensive. The same information can be obtained by analysis of records of H- and V-components, preferably by computer. Another method which is less
laborious than calculation from H- and V-records is to make a cine-film

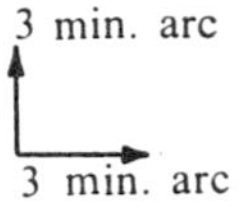

3 min. arc

3 min. arc

10	80	60				
100	10	200				
10	10	140	10	10		
	110	210	130	70	230	
	430	1940	340	180	520	
	430	1000	510	650	390	
10	640	680	200	120	130	
	10	180	90		10	

FIG. 4.9. Data for two-dimensional histogram. Figures give time in milliseconds for
which visual axis point in directions represented by squares. Total time = 10 s. (From
Boyce 1967.)

of the position of the spot on the screen. This film is then projected at reduced speed on to a screen with a square grid, and the number of frames for which the spot is within any given square is counted. This method allows the actual path of the spot to be plotted to give a sequential map (§ 14.7). Fig. 4.10 shows two contour maps obtained by Bennet-Clark (1964). Yet another method is to allow the spot to fall on a photographic plate. The density of the plate in a given area depends

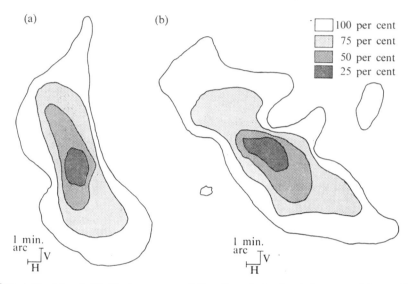

Fig. 4.10. (a) and (b). Contour maps of direction of visual axis for two subjects. (From Bennet-Clark 1964.)

upon the total time the spot has spent in this area. After calibration and measurement with a microdensitometer, contours of equal density can be expressed as contours of equal time. This method was used by Nye (1962) and Bennet-Clark (1964).

4.13. In preparing a contour map the experimenter must choose, (a) the total time T over which the eye movements are observed, and (b) the size of the small area A into which the visual field is subdivided. The average time t which the eye spends in a given area is proportional to TA and we should expect a statistical fluctuation roughly proportional to $(TA)^{\frac{1}{2}}$. Thus, if the product TA is too small, the statistical fluctuation will be proportionately large.† On the other hand if T is too large the subject may change his criterion of fixation, or he may suffer from fatigue so that the overall accuracy of fixation is much less

† It will always be large in relation to any region where the eye spends a small time.

than that obtained with small T. Also, certain artifacts are more likely to appear when T is long. It is thus necessary to choose T and A with care; the value appropriate in one context may not be appropriate in another. It is also necessary to take into account the fact that some subjects fatigue more rapidly than others. Boyce (1965*a*) found some evidence that fatigue became important after about 20 s and he made $T = 10$ s. In order to keep TA reasonably large he used a rather coarse grid for which $A = 9$ min.arc² ($TA = 90$ min.arc² s). Fender (1956) made $T = 120$ s and $A = 2.25$ min.arc² ($TA = 250$ min. arc² s). Fender and Julesz (1967) made records of both eyes and calculated horizontal and vertical disparities of the directions of the visual axes. They made $T = 120$ s and $A = 1$ min.arc² ($TA = 120$ min.arc² s). Consideration of the two patterns suggests that for many purposes it would be desirable to work with intermediate values. e.g. $T = 40$ s (or more for some subjects) and $A = 4$ min.arc² ($TA = 160$ min.arc² s). In the photographic method, the effective size of the element of the grid is determined not by the grain of the plate but by the size of the spot of light. If this is made too small the time required to build up a suitable photographic density imposes an excessively high value of T. It is necessary to use a very bright source and a fairly fast type of photographic material in order to be able to obtain a satisfactory method with reasonable values of A and T. The duration of record used in a single sample was about 10 ms for Boyce, 30 ms for Fender, 20 ms for Fender and Julesz, and 60 ms for the cinematic record used by Bennet-Clark.

4.14. Accuracy of fixation—bivariate normal distribution

Nachmias (1959) recorded H- and V-components of eye-movements over periods of 30 s and calculated the direction of gaze at intervals of 0·2 s. He obtained the distribution shown in Fig. 4.11. Steinman (1965) recorded the last 20 s of 30 s periods of fixation. He calculated the direction of gaze at intervals of 2 s. He used 150 records to obtain mean distributions but analysed them so as to obtain the mean variation of position during any one period of fixation, i.e. variance due to change of the mean direction of gaze between observation periods was eliminated. A distribution of positions obtained this way can be examined to see if it forms a bivariate normal distribution (analogous to the normal distribution of a quantity related to one variable). Both Nachmias and Steinman made statistical tests and concluded that the observed distributions were near to a normal distribution (though Steinman found that the small deviations from a normal distribution were statistically significant at the 0·001 level). They therefore determined the constants of the bivariate normal distribution which most nearly fitted their results. Nachmias observed eye-movements with the target at a great distance (relaxed accommodation), and also with a target at 30 cm. In Table 4.1 the results for relaxed accommodation are used. Steinman made observations with targets of different size, colour, and luminance. The results for small targets (10′ in diameter)

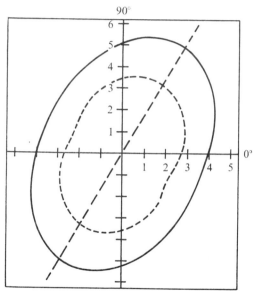

Fɪɢ. 4.11. Distribution of directions of the visual axis showing approximate bivariate normal distribution: – – – direction of major axis of distribution ellipses. Abscissae and ordinates in min-arc. (From Nachmias 1959.)

and white light, and high luminance are used in Table 4.1. Other results obtained by Nachmias and by Steinman are discussed in § 4.16.

4.15. If the measured positions of the eye are assumed to have a bivariate normal distribution, the dispersion can be represented by a series of ellipses whose areas are given by the following expression:

$$A(P) = 2k\pi\sigma_H\sigma_V(1-\rho^2)^{\frac{1}{2}}, \qquad (4.1)$$

where σ_H and σ_V are the standard deviations of components of position along two meridians, and ρ is the product moment of correlation of these two position moments. P is the probability of an observation falling within the ellipse of area $A(P)$ expressed as a percentage. k is connected to P by the relation

$$P = 100(1-e^{-k}). \qquad (4.2)$$

If $k = 1$ then $P = 63$ per cent. The results of Nachmias (1959), Bennet-Clark (1964), and Steinman (1965) all show distributions in which σ_H differs from σ_V. It follows that ρ is not equal to zero. Nevertheless, a moderately good estimate of the accuracy of fixation is obtained by replacing the ellipse for which $P = 63$ per cent by a circle of equal area, i.e. by putting

$$\sigma^2 = \sigma_H \sigma_V \tag{4.3}$$

and

$$\rho = 0, \tag{4.4}$$

so that eqn (4.1) reduces to

$$A(63) = 2\pi\sigma^2. \tag{4.5}$$

Nachmias measured $A(68)$ in steradians. This is converted to $A(63)$ in (min.arc)^2 using the relations $A(68) = 1 \cdot 13\, A(63)$ (obtained from eqn (4.2)) and 1 steradian $= 1 \cdot 8 \times 10^7$ (min.arc)^2. Boyce[†] measured the median value of the radius-vector from the mean position. It may be shown that this is equal to $1 \cdot 178\sigma$. The results of Nye (1962) yield a lower limit for the median distance between two sample points chosen at random. This is equal to $1 \cdot 666\sigma$. The measurements of Bennet-Clark (1964) give estimates of $A(75)$ and $A(50)$ from which a value of $A(63)$ may be obtained by interpolation. Boyce (1965) and Fender (1963) give distributions in the form of a square array from which σ_H and σ_V, and hence σ, have been calculated. Ditchburn and Ginsborg (1953) made records of 10 periods of fixation (each 5 s long) and separated by 300 s. The 'extreme deviation' from the mean position is 10′. If we assume that this is 2σ the figures in Table 4.3 are obtained.

4.16. Results

The results obtained by different experimenters are summarized in Table 4.3. The results of Boyce, Steinman, and Nachmias, and of Krauskopf, Cornsweet and Riggs are directly comparable. The remaining values are derived from necessarily inaccurate estimates of areas of contour maps reproduced on a small scale.[‡] There is an inter-subject variation in σ of about 2:1. There is also an indication that σ increases substantially when T exceeds 30 s.

[†] Table 5.3, p. 11 of Boyce (1965a).
[‡] St. Cyr and Fender (1969a) give equiprobability ellipses for right and left eyes of two subjects. The scale is so small that only rough estimates of area can be made. From such estimates it appears that σ for the eye which fixated best, is about 3′, and for the eye which had worst fixation is about 6′. These estimates refer to monocular viewing, and to fixation of the eye which sees the target.

TABLE 4.3

Values of σ and A(68) monocular vision

Reference	Subject	$T^\dagger$	σ	A(68)	Original datum and notes
Steinman (1965)	M.H.	20	3·2	72	log A(63).
	R.S.	20	2·2	35	log A(63).
	J.A.(R)	30	3·1	68	A(68) R = Right eye.
	V.N.(R)	30	3·15	70	A(68) L = Left eye.
Nachmias (1959)	V.N.(L)	30	2·4	40	A(68)
	J.A.(R)	30	4·3	132	A(68) Fixation at 30 cm.
	V.N.(L)	30	2·5	45	A(68) Fixation at 30 cm.
Bennet-Clark	H.C.B.-C.	10	1·95	27	A(50) and A(75)
(1964)	D.C.W.	10	1·90	26	A(50) and A(75)
Boyce (1965a)	D.C.W.	10	1·4	14	Median displacement from
	H.R.P.	10	2·65	50	mean = 1·178σ.
	P.R.B.	10	3·05	66	
Nye (1962)	P.N.	2·5	2·65	50	Median difference of two
	E.N.	2·5	1·92	26	samples = 1·67σ.
Krauskopf,	L.A.R.(R)	2	1·78	22·5	
Cornsweet,	L.A.R.(L)	2	1·78	22·5	Median horizontal
and Riggs	J.K.(R)	60	3·16	71	displacement from
(1960)	J.K.(L)	60	2·44	43	mean = 0·674σ.
	L.A.R.(R)	60	3·03	66	
	L.A.R.(L)	60	2·62	49	
Fender (1963)	—	120	4·5	140	Rough estimate of A(68).
Ditchburn and	B.G.	(3000)	5	180	Rough estimate see § 4.15.
Ginsborg					
(1953)					
Rattle (1969)	J.F.	∼10	1·65	20	σ.
	M.W.	∼10	4·7	160	σ.

† T is defined in § 4.12.

4.17. Rate of displacement

Riggs, Armington, and Ratliff (1954) and Nye† (1962) measured the median displacement $\Delta\theta$ of the direction of the visual axis in a short time Δt, the initial time being chosen at random. Nye used the following procedure. The components V_t and H_t of displacement from an arbitrary zero were measured at times $t = 0$, δ_0, $2\delta_0$, $3\delta_0$, ... 374, where δ was the smallest resolvable time interval. δ was approximately 27 ms so that the whole time of observation was 10 s.

† See also Fender and Nye (1963).

A computer was programmed

(a) to calculate $R_{t\delta}^2 = (A_{t+\delta}-H_t)^2+(V_{t+\delta}-V_t)^2$ for $t = \delta_0,\ 2\delta_0,$ $3\delta_0$, etc. and for $\delta = \delta_0$,
(b) to form a histogram of $R_{t\delta}^2$, to extract the median value and to calculate its square root $R_{\delta_0}(\text{med})$, and
(c) to repeat for $\delta = 2\delta_0,\ 3\delta_0$ up to $75\delta_0$.

The procedure used by Riggs, Armington, and Ratliff was equivalent. Since their calculations were made without a computer, the data used

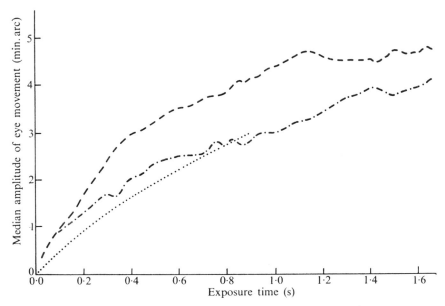

Fɪɢ. 4.12. Median displacement of visual axis from initial position as a function of time: subject E.N. $-\cdot-\cdot-$; subject P.N. $----$; measurement of Riggs *et al.* ..... (After Nye 1962 and Riggs *et al.* 1954.)

was less. The results are shown in Fig. 4.12. For small times the displacement $R(\text{med})$ is nearly proportional to the time t. For long times $R(\text{med})$ should asymptotically approach a value R_m equal to the difference between two random samples of the position of the eye. This constant value is, of course, subject to an irregular fluctuation due to sampling errors. This difference should be equal to $1\cdot666\sigma$. Nye's calculations do not extend far enough to give the asymptote with certainty and the values calculated for σ (inserted in Table 4.2) must be regarded as lower limits (§ 4.15).

4.18. Effect of size of target on accuracy of fixation

Steinman (1965) measured the variation of $A(63)$ with the diameter D of a small bright circular spot which was used as fixation mark. For a variation from 2′ to 28′, one subject showed a small increase of $A(63)$ with D, and the other a small decrease. Both showed a considerable increase (about 50 per cent in one case and 100 per cent in the other) when D was further increased to 87′. Both subjects showed irregular changes of the order of 1′ to 4′ in the mean direction of fixation for

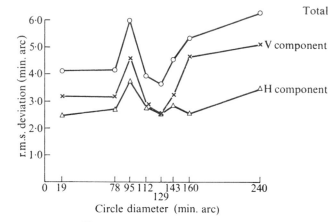

Fig. 4.13. (After Rattle 1969.)

targets of different diameter. Rattle (1968b) made similar measurements with circular targets of diameters 4′ to 240′. He took particular care to ensure that the targets were free from any small light or dark spot or other blemish which the subject might use as a fixation mark. Results for one subject are shown in Fig. 4.13. When the diameter is 95′, σ is larger (i.e. fixation is less accurate) than it is for target diameters of 78′ and 112′. A second subject gave similar results with the maximum value of σ at 112′. Boyce (1965a) used circular targets of diameters 1′, 4′, and 10′ to test the hypothesis of an insensitive circular zone of about 7′ (§ 13.12). From this hypothesis he predicted that the target of diameter 4′ would be more difficult to fixate than either the 1′ target or the 10′ target. His results for each of two subjects show that median saccade magnitude and median drift magnitude are significantly greater for 4′ than for 1′ or 10′ targets.

4.19. Effects of luminance and hue on accuracy and direction of fixation

Steinman (1965) found no variation of A(63) when the luminance of the test spot was increased from 10 cd m^{-2} to 100 cd m^{-2}. The saccade frequency was also unchanged. Boyce (1967) found no significant differences in median saccade magnitude, drift magnitude, or saccade frequency for two subjects when the background luminance was altered from 27 cd m^{-2} to 270 cd m^{-2} and then to 2700 cd m^{-2}. Since all these luminances are within the photopic range, we should expect little variation. Gliem (1967) found that saccade magnitude was four times larger at a luminance of 3×10^{-3} cd m^{-2} than it was at 5×10^{-1} cd m^{-2}. The higher value is at the lower end of the range of transition from photopic to scotopic vision. Steinman and Cunitz (1968) studied eye-movements when subjects fixated a target consisting of a circle 5·4′ in diameter seen against a dark ground. When the luminance of the target was 0·7 cd m^{-2} the pattern of eye-movements was similar to that observed at higher luminance. The accuracy of fixation was less; σ was 3·6′ whereas the same subject had given the value 2·2′ in experiments in the luminance range 10–100 cd m^{-2} (Table 4.2). When the target luminance was reduced to 0·3 cd m^{-2} it was no longer seen when viewed directly, in foveal vision. The pattern of eye-movements then changed. The target drifted into the centre where it disappeared. A saccade then moved it, in a random direction, into a position where it could be seen. In agreement with Gliem, it was found that both saccades and drifts were much larger than those observed at higher luminance.

4.20. Eye-movements in total darkness

Ditchburn and Ginsborg (1953) made observations on the accuracy of fixation when a subject attempted to maintain the direction of the visual axis, after the target had been extinguished, leaving complete darkness. Both saccades and drifts increased in magnitude and the deviation of the eyes during 5 s was about 60′. Cornsweet (1956), Nachmias (1961), Fiorentini and Ercoles (1966), and Matin and Pearce (1969) also examined movements during brief periods in the dark following fixation (Fig. 4.13). Skavenski and Steinman (1970) made observations over longer periods. The eye remained within 120′ of the primary position for 2 min. It tended to drift slowly away and to be returned by saccades. This indicates the existence of some extra-retinal signal (§§ 14.11–14.12).

4.21. Subjects with defective vision

Gliem and Gunther (1965) measured saccades for subjects with defective vision but without recognized pathological nystagmus. They found that saccade magnitude was not significantly different in the range 1·0 normal to 0·25 normal acuity. For lower visual acuity, saccade magnitude increased steeply.

4.22. Accuracy of fixation for different colours

Both Steinman (1965) and Boyce (1967) investigated fixation with targets of white, red, and blue colours. Steinman found no significant difference in $A(63)$ or in drift magnitude, saccade magnitude, and saccade frequency for one subject. Another subject gave reduced saccades and drifts with blue, as compared with white light, but it is doubtful whether the difference is significant. These results are surprising in view of many reports of 'blue-blindness of the fovea' (Thomson and Wright 1947), and the results of Brindley (1954), which indicate that the interconnections of blue receptors in the fovea range over 7' (§§ 9.11 and 9.14). These suggest a possibility that the accuracy of fixation might be much worse for blue than for other colours, yet the above experiments show that it is not (§ 14.25).

4.23. Mean direction of fixation for different colours

Fender (1955b) observed a displacement of the *mean* direction of fixation for red light of 12·0' in a temporal (horizontal) direction, and 3·7' in a vertical direction, as compared with the mean direction for green. The direction for white was the same as for green, and the direction for blue was not significantly different. Steinman (1965) found a difference of 4' between red and white fixation directions for one eye of one subject. Other differences between fixation direction for white, red, and blue were not significant (tests on three eyes). Fender attributed his result to chromatic aberrations.

4.24. Fixation in directions other than primary position

Fender (1956) found that for one subject the intersaccadic interval was 2·0 s when fixating in the primary position, and 1·0 s when the target was situated so that the eye had to be turned 18° (temporal) from the primary position in order to fixate. The median saccade magnitude increased from 16′ to 24′, and the median drift from 2·3′ to 2·9′. There were much larger increases in the maximum saccade (58′ to 113′) and drift (12′ to 51′). Nachmias (1961) found large differences for one subject in *vertical* components of saccades and drifts when the eye was turned in a horizontal direction. This subject showed no difference in *horizontal* components. A second subject showed large differences in horizontal components and very little in *vertical* components.

4.25. Variation of accommodation

Nachmias (1959) found that, for one subject, $A(68)$ was 59 min. arc^2 when fixating on a distant target, and 132 min.arc^2 when the target was at 30 cm. A second subject showed only about 10 per cent increase in $A(68)$ when required to fixate at 30 cm. The first subject gave a 50 per cent increase in drift magnitude and the second no difference when changing from a distant target to one at 30 cm. The intersaccadic interval was unchanged for both subjects. Possibly the first subject was accommodating with difficulty and was unable to give undivided attention to the fixation task. It seems reasonable to expect that there should be no change in accuracy of fixation with accommodation as long as the subject is able to focus the target easily, and a significant loss of accurate fixation when there is difficulty in accommodation.

4.26. Binocular fixation

Records of horizontal components of movements of the two eyes were made by Lord (1950), Riggs and Ratliff (1951), Ditchburn and Ginsborg† (1953), and Krauskopf, Cornsweet, and Riggs‡ (1960). Ditchburn and Ginsborg also recorded vertical components.§ All experimenters are agreed that saccades occur simultaneously in the two eyes (K.C.R. found no exception in 4000 saccades). It is also agreed that horizontal components in the two eyes are usually, but not always in the same sense (K.C.R. found this true for all except 2 per cent of saccades; D.G. found rather more exceptions). K.C.R. found high correlations (0·76 to 0·91) between magnitudes of horizontal components in the two eyes. D.G. observed that vertical components are nearly always in

† Referred to as D.G.
‡ Referred to as K.C.R.
§ Later work by St. Cyr and Fender (1969*a*) is discussed in § 15.19.

TABLE 4.4

Median standard deviations of horizontal components
(monocular and binocular vision)

Fixation condition	Subject	Separate eyes		Both eyes (convergence)
		Left	Right	
Binocular (near)	J.K.	1·46	1·98	1·87
	L.A.R.	1·78	2·64	2·45
Binocular (far)	J.K.	2·32	2·06	2·04
	L.A.R.	2·05	1·72	2·20
Monocular	J.K.	1·64	2·13	...
	L.A.R.	1·77	2·04	

the same sense and of about the same magnitude. These results imply that saccades in the two eyes are not under independent control; there must be a central action which controls both direction and magnitude (§ 15.18ff).

4.27. Fixation in monocular and binocular vision

The accuracy of fixation in monocular and binocular vision are compared in Table 4.4 (due to K.C.R.). This table refers to the horizontal component, whereas Table 4.3 refers to the radius vector. In all experiments, the fixation point was seen with relaxed accommodation. For 'far vision', the required convergence is zero. For 'near vision', it is appropriate to a target distance of 55 cm. There is no significant difference of accuracy of fixation between any of the three conditions, binocular (far), binocular (near), and monocular vision. The standard deviation of convergence is more than 2' whereas the accuracy with which angular convergence can be estimated in stereo rangefinders is better than 0·1'. This was also found by Riggs and Ratliff (1951), and by D.G. Fender and Julesz (1967) made records of the disparity of H- and V-components of the two eyes over periods of 120 s. Treating the results as a bivariate normal distribution they obtained standard deviations of 8' for H- and 7' for V-components of the disparity. It is possible that fatigue contributes to these values, and that standard deviations for shorter periods would be significantly lower.

4.28. Eye-movements in binocular vision

Riggs and Ratliff (1951) found no correlation between the tremor in the two eyes, and K.C.R. found no correlation between drifts. This would be expected if tremor and drift are essentially due to oculo-motor instability (§ 14.4). D.G. find some evidence of convergence/divergence waves (Fig. 4.14). These may be associated with micro-fluctuations in accommodation reported† by Arnulf, Dupuy, and Flamant (1951). Since the drifts in the 'waves' are more often opposed than together, negative correlation would be obtained from samples in which accommodation was fluctuating. K.C.R. found correlations of −0·46, −0·22, −0·03, +0·09, +0·26, and +0·63. These results, considered over all, do not show significant correlation, but they suggest

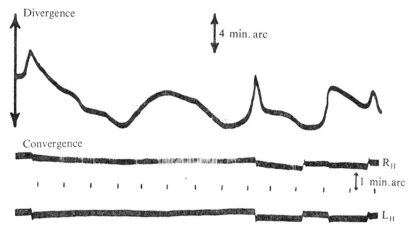

F IG. 4.14. Record of H-components for right eye R_H and for left eye L_H. Top curve shows variation of horizontal disparity on an enlarged scale. Time markers 0·1 s.

that examination of many records might show that there are conditions which lead to a negative correlation and others which give a positive correlation.

K.C.R. found that, for two subjects, the number of saccades in a given time was nearly 40 per cent more when the subject was fixating with both eyes than the average for the right and the left eye when viewing monocularly. For both their subjects the average saccade magnitude for the two eyes was larger when viewing binocularly than when viewing monocularly. For one subject all the relevant differences are significant ($P < 0·002$). The other gave much smaller differences which are not all statistically significant.

4.29. Torsional movements

Fender (1955a and 1956) investigated torsional movements associated with small H- and V-rotations. A record of torsional components

†Arnulf, Dupuy, and Flamant (1955); Arnulf and Dupuy (1960)

is included in Fig. 3.8. T-rotations are about one-third of the H- and V-components. The absolute magnitudes are small but very much larger than the normal torsion calculated from eqn (1.13). Even if we take the most favourable case (when the horizontal and vertical components are equal and tan $\alpha = 1$), the normal torsion is less than 0·01' when H- and V-components are each equal to 10'. We have seen in § 1.22 that normal torsion is produced when the superior and inferior recti exert about 1·9 times as large an effect as the obliques. Fender suggested that, in the small involuntary movements, the ratio of the movement θ (due to the recti) and the movement ϕ (due to the obliques) was equal to a constant (A), which might be different from 1·9. Substituting this constant in eqn (1.14) and eqn (1.15) and also inserting the values of sines and cosines for $\psi = 51°$ and $\chi = 23°$ we obtain

$$ R = \frac{T}{V} = \frac{0·78A - 0·39}{0·63A + 0·92} . \tag{4.6} $$

He measured the T- and V-components at 25 points and obtained a regression line with a slope of about 1:3. This leads to a value of $A = 0·1$, indicating that the effect of the obliques is very small and may be zero.

4.30. This result was not considered satisfactory because the correlation coefficient was only 0·58 and there is about a 6 per cent probability of obtaining this correlation by chance. Fender therefore examined torsional movements associated with small *voluntary* movements up to about 13 min.arc. He obtained torsional components up to about 3·0 min.arc., whereas normal torsion would only be about 0·01'. These voluntary movements, made while following a target, included saccades, and Fender measured the V- and T-components of these saccades and obtained a correlation coefficient of 0·93 between these components. The ratio R was 2·48 ± 0·18. The value of A, calculated from eqn (4.6) is numerically less than 0·04. It may be either positive or negative, i.e. the effect of the obliques is not significantly different from zero. Only two subjects were used in the experiment described in § 4.23 and one in the extension reported in this paragraph. The conclusion that small eye-movements are predominantly due to the four recti is therefore not necessarily valid for all subjects.

4.31. The torsion discussed in §§ 4.29 and 4.30 may be regarded as a small 'error' superposed on normal torsion. Measurements of normal torsion associated with large movements of the eyes have been made to an accuracy of about a degree, and an 'error' of a few minutes of arc would not be detected. It is only in a situation where normal torsion is very small that this small additional effect is of interest. It should be remembered that in the above discussion we have assumed that each pair of muscles acts in the simplest possible way—like two fine threads attached to opposite ends of a diameter of a sphere. The insertion of the opposed muscles are, in fact, not exactly opposite to one another.† Also, each muscle is a fairly wide band which probably does not always operate exactly as a whole. If the upper part of the lateral rectus were to slacken slightly, without any corresponding change in the medial rectus, a small torsional movement would be produced. There are thus several ways in which torsional components of the observed magnitude may be caused.

† Duke-Elder (1961). *System of Ophthalmology.* Vol. 2, pp. 420–23.

5

Apparatus for producing a stabilized retinal image

5.1. Historical

The wide use of servo-controlled systems in the second world war suggested to several people the idea of using a signal derived from the eye-movements to move a target, so as to keep its image always on the same part of the retina. The most common proposal was to make the eye-movements generate electrical signals which would control the movements of a spot on the screen of a cathode-ray tube. No results of early experiments with this method have been published (as far as the author knows). It is difficult to generate a signal which follows the saccadic eye-movements with sufficient fidelity without using an attachment to the eye. Young and Stark (1963) used a system in which signals derived from the eye (without an attachment) controlled the position of a spot on a cathode-ray tube. For their purposes the required accuracy was about 100 times less than that needed for studying vision with a stabilized image. All of the studies of stabilized images have been obtained by the use of the optical devices, developed in the period 1950–60. Recently Kelly, Crane, Hill, and Cornsweet (1969) have designed an electrical system using a signal obtained by fundus reflection. This project has made considerable progress but formidable technical problems remain unsolved (§ 5.30).

5.2. The optical lever method

The same methods of producing a stabilized image, with variations of design, were devised independently and described about the same time by Ditchburn and Ginsborg (1952), and Riggs, Ratliff, Cornsweet, and Cornsweet, (1953). The methods are shown schematically in Fig.

5.1 and Fig. 5.2 respectively. In both methods a beam of light is reflected from a mirror M_1 on a contact lens. When the eye turns through an angle θ_H in a horizontal plane, the reflected beam turns through $2\theta_H$ and the target moves through a distance $2l\theta_H$ on the screen S. The subject views this screen through a system of mirrors so as to see it at a distance $2l$, and thus the angular movement in the visual field is θ_H, i.e. is equal to the angular movement of the eye. The system shown in Fig. 5.2 is easier to adjust, and that shown in Fig. 5.1 gives a somewhat larger field. Riggs and co-workers introduced an unstabilized annulus by inserting a thin piece of microscope glass in the compensating path as a fixation mark. The appearance of the field was as shown in Fig. 5.2(a). Ditchburn and Ginsborg used the edge of the screen for the same purpose but this was at a much greater distance from the axis of vision than the annulus. The movements of the eye requiring compensation are then appreciably larger than when the annulus is used. Both experimenters produced an unstabilized image, for comparison, by introducing a small plane mirror in front of the eye-mirror.

5.3. Both systems, in principle, give complete compensation for H-rotations. They can also be adjusted by varying the distances between the mirrors to give exact compensation for V-rotations, but they cannot be made to compensate H-rotations and V-rotations simultaneously because the mirror is not normal to the axis of vision. This introduces a factor $\cos \theta$ into the calculation of the pathlength required to give exact compensation in respect of V-rotations (where θ is the angle between the visual axis and the normal to the mirror on the contact lens). This angle was 35° in the apparatus shown in Fig. 5.1 and 30° in the apparatus shown in Fig. 5.2. Thus when H-rotations are completely compensated, the movements of the retinal image in a vertical plane are about 15 per cent of those which would be produced normally by V-rotations.† Both sets of experimenters adjusted their apparatus to give accurate compensation for H-rotations. Ditchburn and Ginsborg checked the adjustment by replacing the eye with a telescope which had a small mirror attached to the object glass. If the adjustment is correct the position on the image is unaltered (with respect to crosswires in the telescope) when the telescope is rotated in a horizontal plane. By using a suitable magnification (about ×10), it is easily possible to detect

† In 1945 the author constructed a more elaborate system which included two weak cylindrical lenses. These produced an anamorphic magnification of the angular movements of the beam reflected from the contact lens. Tests with a telescope showed that compensation in respect to both planes could be obtained simultaneously. Some of the phenomena now accepted as associated with the stabilized image were noticed. The experiments had to be discontinued (owing to the movement of the author from Dublin to Reading) before any results considered suitable for publication were obtained.

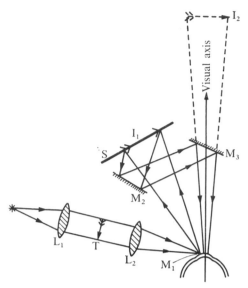

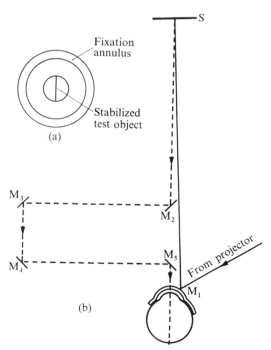

Fɪɢ. 5.1. An image I_1 of the target T is formed on the screen S by the lens L_2. S is viewed by reflection in the mirrors M_2 and M_3 so that the subject sees a virtual image at I_2. (From Ditchburn and Ginsborg 1952.)

Fɪɢ. 5.2. The image of the target formed on the screen S is viewed by light reflected at M_2, M_3, M_4, and M_5. Inset (a): target surrounded by fixation annulus. (From Riggs *et al.* 1953.)

movements of less than 1 per cent of the rotations of the telescope. A high quality telescope will permit a much more accurate check (§ 5.22).

5.4. Neither of the above systems compensates with respect to head-movements. The optical path from eye to screen was about 600 mm in each apparatus. The head was fixed with a dental bite and auxiliary supports. Residual head movements were almost certainly less than 0·03 mm (§ 2.15), i.e. the retinal image movements due to movements of the head were less than 0·1'. Slow movements of this magnitude almost certainly have no effect on vision (Chapter 10). The above systems also do not compensate for T-components of eye-movements. The effect of T-components in respect of retinal images is almost certainly negligible for points near the centre of the field (§ 5.17).

5.5. Direct-attachment systems

The main optical alternative to the optical-lever method is an apparatus in which the whole optical system, including the target, is mounted on a contact lens or rubber suction device (Figs. 5.3–5.9). If the apparatus functions perfectly, the image remains on the same part of the retina. All three components of eye rotations, and all three components of translational movements of eye or head, are compensated. Residual movements can arise from (a) imperfect following of the eye by the contact lens or suction device, (b) imperfect rigidity of the system, and (c) possible internal changes in the eye, including change of shape of the eye, accommodation, pupil-reflex, etc. These limitations will be discussed later. In the following paragraphs it is assumed that if the subject has a refractive error, it has been corrected by working a suitable power on the contact lens so as to give clear vision of distant objects. The apparatus shown in Fig. 5.5, where the correction is adjusted for near-vision, is the only exception.

5.6. A direct attachment device was constructed by the author in 1945. A brass tube, about 7 mm long, was glued to the contact lens, and a rice paper tube 25 cm long was slipped over the contact lens. The target was a fine tungsten wire stretched across the tube. No permanent disappearance of the wire was observed, and the apparatus was considered to have failed owing to insufficient rigidity of the tube. Devices employing direct attachment were described by Ditchburn and Pritchard (1956) and by Yarbus† (1956). Similar devices have since been used by

† The paper quoted is the first of a series by Yarbus. The English translation of his book (Yarbus 1967) gives detailed description of various devices which he used, and of methods of construction.

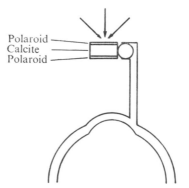

Polaroid
Calcite
Polaroid

Fɪɢ. 5.3. Direct attachment system: polaroid–calcite–polaroid unit.

other workers. The polaroid-calcite-polaroid unit (Fig. 5.3) used by Ditchburn and Pritchard produces a pattern of rings and brushes† (Fig. 5.4). The unit is illuminated with a convergent beam of light which is focussed onto the pupil of the eye. If the size of the beam in the plane of the eye-pupil is about the same size as the pupil then the pupil alternately expands and contracts. This oscillation of pupil area is avoided if the beam diameter is either (a) smaller or (b) about 50 per cent larger than the diameter of eye-pupil. The latter arrangement is preferable (§ 5.16). The pattern of rings and brushes is focussed on the retina by the unaccommodated eye. The location of the centre of the pattern on the retina is determined by the angle between the optic axis of the crystal and the visual axis. This location is fixed so long as the crystal rotates with the eye.

5.7. The variety of patterns which can be produced this way is restricted, and none of them has sharp boundaries with high contrast. Sharper patterns were produced by substituting a thin parallel-sided piece of mica (partially silvered on both sides) for the polaroid–calcite unit. Fabry–Pérot fringes are seen‡ if the system is illuminated with monochromatic light (e.g. mercury green (546 nm) from a low-pressure source). They, too, are focussed with relaxed accommodation. Either of these arrangements gives an angular field of 20° very easily, and larger fields can be obtained. This method could now be improved using the highly coherent light of a gas laser.

5.8. A much wider variety of patterns can be viewed as stabilized images if a lens of power about 25D is added either to the contact lens

† See Ditchburn, *Light*. Blackie, London, for coloured photographs of the rings and brushes (Plate IV), and for an account of the relevant theory (Chap. 16).

‡ See Ditchburn, *Light*. Blackie, London, for colour photographs of the Fabry–Pérot fringes (Plate 1) and for theory (Chap. 5).

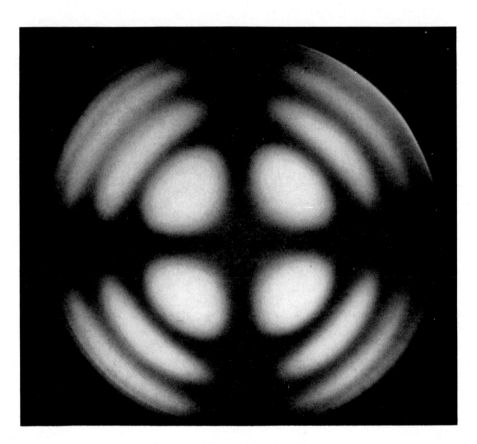

Fig. 5.4. Ring and brush pattern.

as shown in Fig. 5.5, or separately as shown in Fig. 5.6(*a*). The weight is
rather less in the former apparatus but the latter makes it possible to
use a cemented doublet corrected for spherical aberration and chromatic
aberration. This gives an image of much higher optical quality. The
arrangement with the central tube (Fig. 5.6(b)) is very rigid, excludes
stray light, and prevents clouding due to lacrimation or to wax from
the eye. Since the tube is usually touching the eyelids, the lens must
fit very tightly to avoid destabilization due to incipient blinks. If the
distance of the focal plane from the lens is accurately measured the
tube length may be adjusted so that the image is focussed on the retina
by the unaccommodated eye. The target may be a photograph on 8
mm or 16 mm film and, in a rather simple way, its position can be
adjusted to bring any desired part into the centre of the field of view
(Bennett-Clark and Ditchburn, 1963). In order to obtain a strong adhesion of the lens to the eye Evans (1964) and Pritchard (private
communication) have used a modified fundus lens. This has a higher
curvature than either cornea or sclera and seats on a small circular area
of the sclera (see Fig. A.5). It is pushed onto the eye to create suction.
Evans found an anaesthetic necessary, but Pritchard used no anaesthetic. Neither worker taped back the eyelids.

5.9. A device described by Yarbus† (1956) is shown in Fig. 5.7. A
rubber sucker of outer diameter 13 mm seats in the region of the
limbus. A hollow bulb B is attached to the body of the sucker and
connected with the cavity. A glass plate P is attached to the sucker,
and a lens L of focal length 3 cm is cemented to this plate with canada
balsam. A cylindrical tube of duralumin, with a diaphragm D (0·8 mm
in diameter), is also fixed to the glass plate. An outer tube slides tele-
scopically on this cylinder and carries the target with a piece of matt
glass behind it. The matt glass was illuminated with a tungsten bulb
and the illuminance was 5000 cd m⁻². The angular size of the retinal
image varied between 1° and 15°. Adjustment of the telescopic tubing
enabled the target to be sharply focussed. Coloured objects were obtained by inserting pieces of painted gelatine. A single colour background was produced by the use of external colour filters. The diaphragm reduces the effect of spherical aberration and of fluctuations in
the accommodation of the eye. In order to prevent condensation on
the inner surface of the glass plate, the sucker was warmed to a few
degrees above body temperature. A few drops of an anaesthetic
(dicaine) were instilled before placing the device on the eye. The eyelids
were taped back. Air was expelled from the bulb B, and the sucker

† Yarbus (1967). In his book Yarbus describes 8 devices (called caps) labelled P_1 to P_8
Fig. 5.7 and 5.8b represent P_7 and P_6 respectively. Fig. 5.8a represents an earlier device.

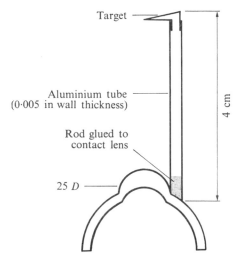

F ɪɢ. 5.5. Direct attachment system with high power contact lens. (From Clowes and Ditchburn (1959).)

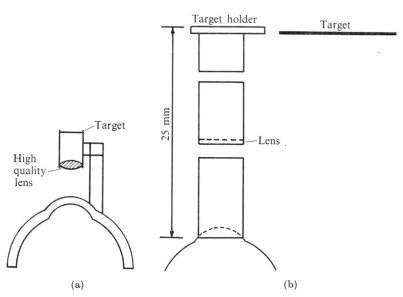

F ɪɢ. 5.6. Direct attachment system with external contact lens. (a) Mounted on stalk; (b) mounted on central tube. (b) is an 'exploded' view: the three tubes slide in a tight telescopic fit; the target, shown to the right, slides into the holder at the top of the third tube. (After Evans 1965b.)

gently touched onto the eyeball. The suction gave a firm fit to the eye. The device could be released from the eye by squeezing the bulb. Experiments never exceeded 10 min. The other eye was occluded. The suction pressure cannot be measured directly in this apparatus. It may be roughly estimated from the relative volumes and is probably at least 10 cm Hg, very much larger than that recommended for use with a contact lens (§ A.9).

5.10. Yarbus† (1957a) describes another suction device which is shown in Fig. 5.8(a). The outer diameter of the cap is 13 mm as before. It is made of plastic, and Yarbus states that 'when the cap had to be very light, it is advantageous to make the body of thin (0·1 mm) duralumin with a thicker (0·5 mm) and lightly goffered edge. Since the cap was without inertia, the retinal image of the screens could be kept quite stationary'. A small mirror M was attached to the cap to enable eye-movements to be recorded. The tube was not used and the target was mounted on a frame of four steel wires W. This enabled the subject to see an unstabilized background as well as the stabilized image. A shield was used to control how much of the visual field was occupied by the unstabilized image.

Fig. 5.8(b) shows a third arrangement used by Yarbus† (1960a). This is made of goffered duralumin. The diaphragm D constitutes an artificial pupil of 1·5 mm. The target is seen after reflection in the mirror M, and is illuminated from the side as shown, in order to control the amount of light entering the eye through the sclera. Yarbus states that the lightest of his devices weighs only 100 mg. This presumably does not include the weight of the target and attachments.

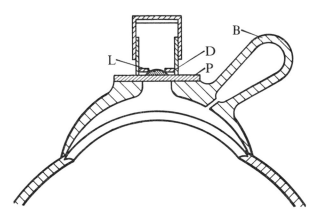

FIG. 5.7. Rubber suction device (After Yarbus 1965).

† See also Yarbus (1967).

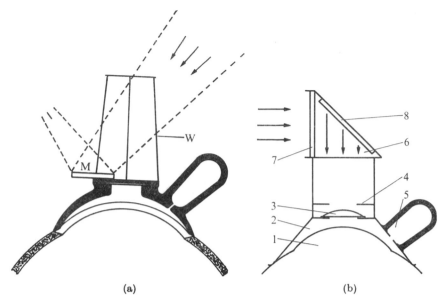

Fɪɢ. 5.8. (a) Rubber suction device. (b) Duralumin device with rubber suction attachment. (From Yarbus 1965).

5.11. Barlow (1963) made the attachment device, shown in Fig. 5.9, by spinning aluminium sheet (0·1 mm thick). It seated near the limbus. Amethococaine was used as an anaesthetic. He states that if the anaesthetic is not used 'a mildly unpleasant sensation occurs when the lens seats near the limbus, and this increases to distinct pain when suction is applied. This would be quite easily bearable, but accidental

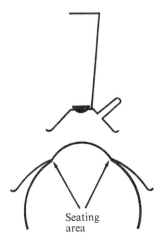

Fɪɢ. 5.9. Aluminium suction device. (From Barlow 1963.)

jarring of the lens and attempts to blink are exceedingly painful...corneal abrasions have resulted from accidental jolting of suck-on lenses, particularly those with sharp edges. They heal rapidly'. Probably this damage is avoided, or at least reduced, by the thickened and smoothed edge used by Yarbus.

5.12. Development of the optical lever system

Although the direct attachment methods involve only rather simple apparatus and are capable of producing accurate stabilization, the range of experiments which can conveniently be carried out is somewhat restricted. It is difficult to introduce a variable contrast, bipartite field or a colour-mixing system into a direct attachment device. It is also very difficult to produce an image of very high optical quality, with very sharp boundaries, using the simple lenses which can be mounted on a direct attachement. For these, and other reasons, development of the optical lever method to its fullest capacity is important. An improved optical lever system is shown in Fig. 5.10. The projector system forms an image of the pointolite source on the eye-mirror and an image of the target at I_1. The lens L_3 refocuses this image

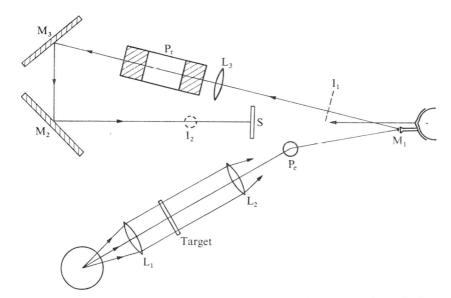

Fig. 5.10. Improved optical lever system: for convenience the target projector is above the plane of the rest of the apparatus and the periscope P_e lowers the beam to the correct height; P_r is a Dove prism required to give the correct direction of displacement. I_2 is the image of the pointolite ball; Maxwellian view is obtained by replacing S by a lens which, focuses I_2 on the subject's pupil. (From Fender, 1956.)

on the ground-glass screen S. The lens L_3 reverses the movements of the image with respect to the eye but this is corrected by the reflections. It may be shown that the system is stabilized if $D = 2d - r$, where D is the distance of the screen from the first nodal point of the eye, d is the distance from M_1 to I_1, and r is the distance from the second nodal point of the eye to it's centre of rotation. Since D is not known accurately the adjustment must be made empirically as described by Ditchburn and Fender (1955).

5.13. The most important new feature of this apparatus was the use of a mirror with its normal parallel to the visual axis, enabling compensation for H-rotations and V-rotations to be obtained simultaneously. The illuminance of the image (80 cd m^{-2}) was much higher than that obtained in earlier apparatus using the optical lever. Still higher illuminance can be obtained by substituting a field lens for the screen, so as to obtain Maxwellian view. Fender considered that the direct view of the screen was a substantial advantage, giving the subject an approach to the psychological conditions of normal vision. This system was used in the experiments described in §§ 10.5–10.10. It is superseded by the telescopic systems described in § 5.15.

5.14. Stabilization conditions

In order that all receptors should receive constant stimuli it is necessary to have both the following.

(a) *geometrical stabilization*, i.e. an image which remains on the same part of the retina when the eye rotates or the head is translated. and

(b) *illumination stabilization*. Constant illumination of the retinal image under the above conditions. Illumination stabilization implies that the exit pupil of the system must not move relative to the pupil of the eye sufficiently to alter the amount of light entering the eye. Also there must be no significant amount of vignetting (giving a change of illumination over part of the field) due to movement of the exit pupil.

The required accuracy of geometrical stabilization is discussed in § 5.31 and of illumination stabilization in § 5.33. In each case there is a time element in the situation; movements of the retinal image of considerable amplitude, or changes of illumination by a considerable factor, have no effect on vision if they are made smoothly and at a sufficiently slow rate.

5.15. Telescopic system

An arrangement shown in Fig. 5.11 was suggested by Clowes and Ditchburn (1959) as a basic scheme to fulfill these requirements. P is a projector system similar to a lantern projector. The target (which may be a lantern slide) is at the focus of lens L_p. This lens gives a parallel beam corresponding to any point A on the target, and also focusses the

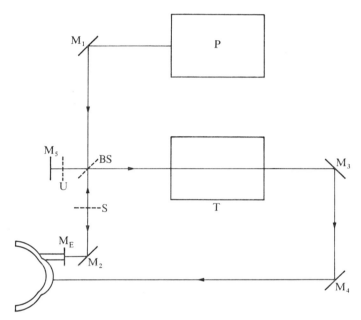

F IG. 5.11. Telescopic system (schematic diagram). BS is a beam splitter. Source, target and L_P are in the unit P. Shutter S is opened to view the stabilized image and shutter U to view the unstabilized image.

source of light on the eye-mirror M_E. The axis of the small cone of light which falls on M_E is normal to the mirror which is, itself, normal to the direction of the visual axis. After reflection, the light passes through the beam-splitter into the telescope T, whose magnification is M. The light from any point A on the target emerges from T as a parallel beam and is focussed onto the retina by the unaccommodated eye. When the eye rotates (about any axis in Listing's plane) through an angle θ, the beam entering the telescope rotates through 2θ, and the beam entering the eye rotates through $2M\theta$. Thus the rotation relative to the eye is $F\theta$, where $F = 1 - 2M$. If $M = \frac{1}{2}$ then $F = 0$, and the system provides geometrical stabilization against H- and V-rotations

The retinal image is stabilized against small movements of the head parallel to the visual axis because the light from A is incident as a parallel beam on the mirror M_E, and against similar movements in any direction at right angles to the visual axis, because the target is seen at infinity. In this system, an unstabilized image of the target may be produced by inserting the mirror M_5 at the position shown. Shutters placed at S and U enable either the stabilized, or the unstabilized, image to be occluded.

5.16. Exit-pupil of the system

The telescope T contains a field lens, which focusses an image of the spot of light on the eye-mirror M_E, on the eye-pupil. This image consitutes the exit-pupil of the stabilization system. The amount of light entering the eye is not affected by a small rotation or translation of the eye provided that the exit-pupil of the system is either, (a) considerably smaller than the eye-pupil, or (b) considerably larger than the eye-pupil. With the former there are the following disadvantages.

(i) The use of a very small pupil makes the light more coherent. This increases diffraction effects and also shows up any corneal irregularities.

(ii) Movements of the exit-pupil across the eye-pupil cause a change in apparent brightness owing to the Stiles–Crawford effect.

5.17. This system is not stabilized against T-rotations of the eye. The effect of T-rotations is zero in the centre of the field of view. It increases linearly from the centre outwards, but the spacing of the cones in the fovea also increases in the outer part of the fovea, and in the peripheral retina the size of receptor fields increases. The T-rotations which occur during fixation are too small to produce any appreciable effect. Consider, for example, the situation 30′ from the centre of the fovea, using data given in Table 1.1, p. 5. A torsional movement of 8′ (which is larger than most of the torsional saccades) moves the retinal image by about 0·4 μm, equivalent to a visual angle of 0·1′. This is less than 0·1 times the intercone spacing in this region.

5.18. Various secondary effects are avoided by using normal incidence on the eye-mirror M_E. If the mirror is normal to a direction corresponding to a given point R (on the retina), then there is no movement due to torsion at this point. It is usual to choose R to be as near as possible to the centre of the fovea, i.e. to set the mirror normal to the visual axis. If the field seen by the subject has an angular *diameter* ϕ, then the cone incident on the mirror M_E must be of semi-angle ϕ (i.e. of angular diameter 2ϕ). This allows for the reduction by $\frac{1}{2}$ in the telescope T. An expression for the magnitude of image-movements in the outer parts of the field usually includes a factor $(1-\cos\phi)$. This factor is approximately 5×10^{-4} for a field of 2° which covers the fovea. If a field of 10° is used, the factor is 25 times greater, but the size of the receptor fields has increased, so that the image-movement is still too small to produce any effect on vision.

5.19. Fluctuation of accommodation

There are two effects of fluctuation of accommodation: (a) to defocus the image and (b) to move it across the retina. The movement is approximately in a horizontal direction. It arises because the visual axis and the central pupillary line of the eye do not coincide (§ 1.8). For small objects, subtending less than 5°, the effect (b) is the larger. According to Gullstrand (Table 1.2, p. 10) a change of 12D in accommodation moves the nodal point by 0·48 mm, or 40 μm per dioptre. This has to be multiplied by the angle (in radians) between the visual axis and the central pupillary line to obtain the resulting movement of the retinal image. This is 4 μm per dioptre. Fender (1956) measured the change of apparent angular size of the blind spot when the accommodation was altered, and obtained the considerably larger value of 17 μm per dioptre. Using this larger value, the microfluctuations of order 0·02D, reported by Arnulf, Dupuy, and Flamant (1951), are still negligible, and much larger fluctuations would not produce significant effects. Since this movement is approximately in a horizontal direction its effect on vision may be almost completely eliminated when it is possible to use a target whose critical boundaries are all horizontal. A bipartite field, a black bar, and a grating are all examples of targets whose critical boundaries can be set in a horizontal direction.

5.20. Telescopic system (practical details)

An experimental realization of the scheme described above is shown in Fig. 5.12. L_5 and L_7 are separated by the sum of their focal lengths, and form the telescope T of Fig. 5.11. If they alone were used we should require $f_7 = 2f_5$, but, in order to obtain a larger field, it is necessary to introduce two more lenses L_4 and L_5. These are of approximately equal focal lengths. They are separated by the sum of their focal lengths to form a telescope of nearly unit magnification. The condition for stabilization is then:

$$f_4 f_7 = 2f_5 f_3. \tag{5.1}$$

Intermediate images of the target are focussed at I_1 and I_2. The lens L_6 is a field lens and, when placed in the plane I_2, exerts no effect on magnification and focus of the image. Its focal length is chosen so that an image of the eye-mirror is formed on the pupil of the eye, and the subject sees the target in Maxwellian view.

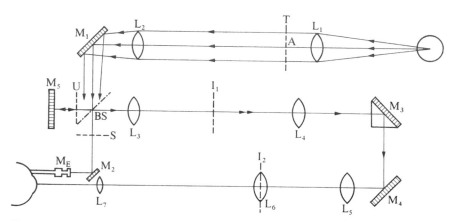

FIG. 5.12. Telescopic system (practical diagram) (from Clowes and Ditchburn 1959).

5.21. L_3, L_4, and L_5 are high quality $f/2\cdot9$ lenses by Dallmeyer, of focal lengths approximately 20 cm, and L_6 is an achromatic combination of focal length 50 cm. L_7, which is used at very low aperture, is a combination of an achromatic lens and a weak spectacle lens. The over-all magnification is first adjusted by altering the separation of these two components. A fine adjustment may be made by displacing L_6 from the position shown. A movement Z_0 of L_6, changes the magnification by $100\ Z_0/f_6$ per cent. This movement causes the image to move from infinity to a point distant $f_7^2 f_6/Z_0^2$ from the eye. Thus, a displacement of 1 cm changes the magnification by 2 per cent while moving the image into a point 800 m distant. The carriage which carries L_6 is moved by a micrometer screw reading to 0·01 mm so that a change of magnification of 0·002 per cent can be made.†

5.22. The complete apparatus includes provision for

(a) projection of a bipartite field,
(b) projection of an unstabilized comparison image,

† This method of using the field lens was suggested by Professor H. H. Hopkins.

(c) projection of a fixation annulus,
(d) projection of an adapting field,
(e) colour mixing in the target,
(f) recording of eye-movements while viewing the stabilized image.

Working diagrams are included in the original paper (§ 5.15). The apparatus was tested using a telescope reading angles to 0·2′. It was found that considerable care in alignment is needed. It was possible to adjust the apparatus so that 99·5 per cent of the H- and V-rotations are compensated over a field of approximately 2° diameter. No movement of the image could be detected when the telescope was translated either horizontally or vertically. Outside this region the error of stabilization increases. It is roughly proportional to the square of the distance from the centre of the field, e.g. at 6° from the centre 95 per cent of the H- and T-rotations are compensated. In the outer part of the field there is also some interaction between horizontal and vertical movements, i.e. a horizontal movement of the eye causes some vertical movement of the image.

5.23. Simplified telescopic system

The system described in the preceding paragraphs can be adapted to meet almost any requirement of experiments on vision with the stabilized image. It is, however, unnecessarily elaborate for many experiments. Its complexity makes it expensive and difficult to construct. The very large number of components makes it difficult to eliminate veiling glare. The telescopic system shown in Fig. 5.13 is more compact

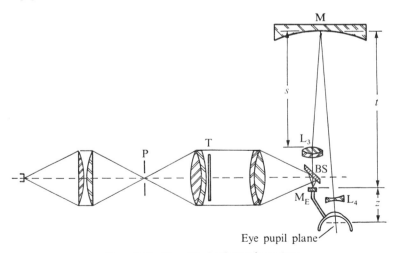

Fig. 5.13. Simplified telescopic system.

and uses many fewer components (Ditchburn 1963). It has a better light transmission, better image contrast, and a wider angular field. The stabilization and image sharpness are not as good as that obtained with the more elaborate apparatus, but it is fairly easily adjusted to give better than 98 per cent stabilization. This performance is sufficient for many experiments (§§ 5.31 and 10.13).

5.24. In this system, the lens L_3, the mirror M, and the lens L_4 form a telescope which must (a) have angular magnification $\frac{1}{2}$ and (b) focus the eye-mirror M_E on the eye-pupil. These conditions require

$$f_3 = \frac{(s+t)f_M - st}{3f_M - t} ,$$

(5.2)

and

$$f_4 = \frac{2tf_3}{3f_3 - s} ,$$

(5.3)

where s and t are distances marked on the diagram, f_M is the focal length of the mirror, and f_3 and f_4 are the focal lengths of the lenses.

From eqn (5.3) it may be seen that if $s = 3f_3$ then f_4 is infinite, i.e. the lens L_4 is not required. If this lens is omitted, there is no latitude of adjustment, and no tolerance in regard to the relation of the remaining components. It is therefore advantageous not to make $3f_3$ exactly equal to s, and to use a weak spectacle lens L_4 to make the final adjustment. The lens L_3 must be a good achromatic doublet. In this design the chief ray is incident normally on M_E and the concave mirror, M, is used nearly on axis. Details of the design and instructions for adjusting the apparatus are given in the paper quoted in § 5.23.

5.25. Semi-telescopic system

A stabilization system described by Keesey† (1960) is shown in Fig. 5.14. This is a modification of a system previously used by Riggs and Tulunay (1959). Target material at T is at the focus of the lens L_3 so that from any point on the target parallel light is incident on the eye-mirror M_E. The light reflected from this mirror is focussed at L_4, and viewed by the observer through the mirrors M_5, M_6, and M_7. Maxwellian view is obtained by the use of a field lens at L_4. In this system the lens L_3 functions like the objective of a telescope and L_4 as the field lens, but the eye-lens is omitted. The system is stabilized against translations of the head in the direction of the visual axis but not against translations in directions perpendicular to this axis. Since the

† Mrs. U. Tulunay Keesey née Tulunay.

viewing distance is about a metre, a movement of the head of 0·1 mm corresponds to a retinal image movement of about 0·3′, so the system is fairly insensitive to the transverse head movements. It could be completely stabilized against head movements by the insertion of a spectacle lens of focal length twice that of L_3 at a suitable point between M_6 and M_5. This system would then be optically equivalent to the one shown in Fig. 5.13. As between these two systems, that shown in Fig. 5.13 gives a larger field of view, a higher luminance, and a more direct

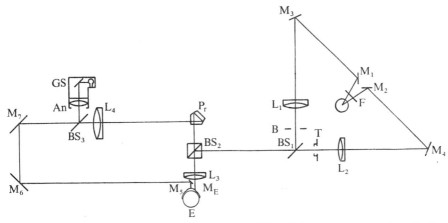

F ɪ ɢ. 5.14. Semi-telescopic system. Target material at T is seen superposed on background illumination from B. An unstabilized fixation mark is provided by GS. (From Riggs and Tulunay 1960.)

view of the target, while that shown in Fig. 5.14 is probably easier to adjust and may be more convenient in regard to introduction of fixation annulus or adapting fields. The balance of advantage between the two systems must depend on details of optical design and on the particular problem under study. The field of view given by the system shown in Fig. 5.14 is adequate for the study of foveal vision.

5.26. The components to the right of BS_2, in Fig. 5.14 enable two sets of target material (placed at T and B), which are each effectively in the focal plane of L_3, to be seen together. Since one lamp illuminates both T and B, the relative luminance of the two parts is unaffected by small fluctuations in the intensity of the lamp. This arrangement is especially suitable for experiments on contrast in a bipartite field. The components above BS_3 are provided for the insertion of a fixation annulus. Another semi-telescopic stabilization system which also provides a bipartite field is described by Krauskopf (1957). A very compact optical lever stabilization system was used by Riggs and Whittle (1967).

5.27. Binocular stabilization

It is possible to obtain stabilized images in both eyes by the use of two direct attachment systems. This method was used by Ditchburn and Pritchard (1960). The method does not provide for accurate alignment of target images on corresponding areas of the visual fields of the two eyes. This requires a double optical lever system. Fig. 5.15 shows a system for binocular stabilization used by Shortess and Krauskopf

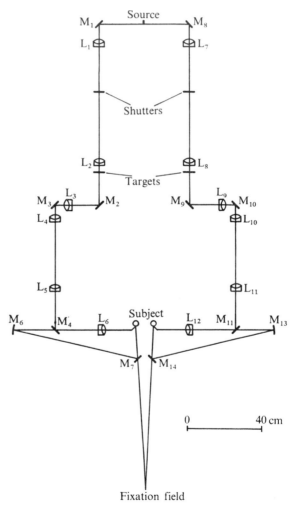

Fig. 5.15. Binocular stabilization system. (From Shortess and Krauskopf 1961.)

(1961). This system is essentially two semi-telescopic systems placed side by side with devices providing for accurate alignment of the targets on corresponding retinal areas. Stabilization is provided in respect only of H-rotations. Fender and Julesz (1967) used two systems, each similar to that shown in Fig. 5.11, to study binocular stabilization (§ 13.18).

5.28. Stabilized image of the iris

All the systems so far described require the subject to wear a close-fitting contact lens. This restricts the number of subjects available and it is desirable that at least some of the qualitative reports should be checked by a large number of observers. It is therefore desirable to produce a stabilized image without using any attachments to the eye. Since the eye must control the movements of the target, and a sufficiently good control cannot be obtained from the corneal reflex, it is necessary to use some part of the eye as the target. The apparatus shown in Fig. 5.16 was devised for use at an exhibition of the *Physical Society* (Ditchburn, Fender, Mayne, and Pritchard 1956). It produces a stabilized image of the iris. In order that the image be stabilized, it is necessary that the magnification of the final image shall be $+L/d$ where d and L respectively are the distances of the iris and of the final image from the centre of rotation of the eyeball. The position of the centre of rotation varies from subject to subject so that there is an uncertainty in d in the range 11 mm to 13 mm. The variation in L, which must be fixed at some value greater than the shortest distance of distinct vision, is negligible. L was fixed at 30 cm so that a magnification of about 25, with provision for ± 10 per cent variation, was needed. In the apparatus shown, the lens L_1 forms a real magnified image of the

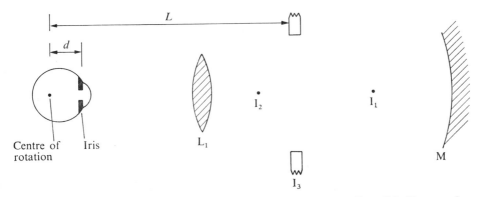

FIG. 5.16. Apparatus for producing a stabilized image of the iris. (From Ditchburn *et al.* 1956.)

iris at I_1, the concave mirror forms a further magnified real image of I_1 at I_2, and after the light has passed again through L_1 the subject sees a virtual image at I_3. The magnification is about $\times 3$ in each stage. Small variations in positions of the components enable focus to be maintained while the magnification is altered. The apparatus is not stabilized against head movements. A head band and chin rest were provided. About 300 persons attempted to view an image of the iris and about half of these were able to 'find the image'. 95 per cent of those who did locate the image reported some of the effects which will be described in Chapter 6.

5.29. Other methods

If the action of the extraocular muscles could be inhibited, then a subject viewing a distant scene would have a stationary retinal image. Adequate clamping of the eyeball without producing pressure effects on vision is probably not possible. The injection of drugs has been proposed but not, so far as the writer knows, the typical effects associated with a stabilized image have never been obtained in this way. It would be difficult to be quite sure that there were no side-effects on the visual system when all action of the extraocular muscles was prevented in this way. The use of Haidinger's brushes and other entoptic phenomena to produce images which are stationary with respect to the retina are described in §§ 6.19–6.21. Cornsweet (1962a) has reported experiments on a stabilized image of the retinal structure.

5.30. Fundus-reflection method

The method for measuring eye-movements by fundus-reflection, devised by Cornsweet (§§ 2.31–2.32), has been developed with a view to providing a method of stabilizing the retinal image (Kelly, Crane, Hill, and Cornsweet 1969; Kelly and Crane 1970). A small spot of blue light is imaged on the fundus and scanned round the optic disc at high speed. Variations in the intensity of the reflected light are produced as the spot passes over the numerous blood vessels which cover this part of the retina. These are detected by a photo-multiplier. The signal is digitized and passed to an on-line computer. A selected frame of this signal is stored in a magnetic-core array. Correlation with subsequent frames generates information about H-, V-, and T-components of eye-movements. This information is used to produce signals which move mirrors in such a way as to restore the track of the moving spot to the same part of the retina. Tests on an early version of this device indicated a tracking accuracy of 0·5′, and there was hope of further improvement by scanning a larger area of the fundus. Unfortunately, further work has revealed serious technical difficulties in the serveo-system, and development is in abeyance. Analysis reported by Cornsweet (1966) shows that any device of this kind must work rather close to the signal/noise limits which are set by the maximum amount of light which can be tolerated by the eye.

5.31. Required accuracy of geometrical stabilization

Experiments reported in § 10.5 indicate that slow movements of the retinal image at speeds of 1′ s⁻¹ produce little or no effect on vision with a stabilized image. Thus compensation of 80 per cent of the normal drift movements is sufficient. Saccadic movements of 1·0′ produce an effect if the target has a very sharp boundary which falls on the central fovea of a subject with high visual acuity. It is thus necessary for a stabilization apparatus to compensate for the saccadic components of eye-movements so well that the residual movements are less than 0·5′. Any apparatus which does this is almost certain to be satisfactory in respect of compensation for drift and tremor. Since the velocity may rise to 1000′ s⁻¹ during a saccade there must be no time lag in excess of 0·5 ms.

Residual movements θ_R may be expressed in the form

$$\theta_R = F\theta_e + P\dot{\theta}_e + \theta_s + \theta_0, \tag{5.4}$$

where θ_e is the angular movement of the eye and $\dot{\theta}_e$ is its angular velocity. If the stabilization apparatus is perfectly adjusted then $F = 0$, and the first term vanishes. The second arises if the compensation follows a saccadic movement of the eye with a short time lag. θ_s represents the effect of slip of the contact lens, or any similar defect in the apparatus, and θ_0 represents residual movements of the retinal image due to imperfect rigidity of the dioptric system of the eye (§ 10.17).

5.32. Since it is not always possible to make F and P exactly zero, it is desirable to reduce θ_e (and hence $\dot{\theta}_e$) as far as possible by providing conditions in which saccades greater than 10′ are rare. For this purpose, the lens must not be very uncomfortable. If necessary, an anaesthetic must be used despite the objections stated in § A.1. The subject must have a good fixation mark which is not stabilized. When only one eye is

10

viewing the stabilized image, the other may view the fixation mark. Alternatively, one eye may view the stabilized image surrounded by an unstabilized annulus (Fig. 5.2(a)). It is easy to make $F < 0.03$, so that, if θ_e is less than $10'$, then $F\theta_e$ is less than $0.3'$. The term depending on $\dot{\theta}_e$, i.e. upon the velocity of eye-movements, is effectively zero provided that the apparatus is sufficiently rigid and that only optical elements are involved. The only method involving non-optical elements is the fundus-reflection method. In this method, the time involved in computing corrections when following a saccade must be very short.

The experiments of Riggs and Schick (§ A.12) indicate that, with a very good lens, the term $F\theta_e$ can be reduced to less than $0.3'$. Those of Boyce (§ 4.5 and § A.14) indicate that the same effect may be produced by applying suction to a lens which is fairly good. No reliable estimate can be made of retinal image movements due to imperfect rigidity of the dioptric system. The high acuity of the visual system indicates that these movements cannot cause significant blurring of the retinal image in normal vision. The fundus-reflection apparatus compensates for these movements.

5.33. Required accuracy of illumination stabilization

Yarbus (§ 11.7) has shown that vision is affected when the illuminance of a retinal image is changed by 30 per cent in one second. A higher rate of change would be needed if the change operated for a shorter time. A smaller rate of change would not produce any effect even if it operated for a considerably longer time. It is not difficult to design a stabilization system so that its exit pupil coincides with the eye pupil (§§ 5.17–5.25). The residual variation of illuminance should then be very much less than 30 per cent per second. It is thus much easier to achieve adequate pupil stabilization than it is to obtain adequate geometrical stabilization, provided that both are considered in the optical design. Yarbus (1967) has shown that, if no precautions are taken, a significant amount of light may enter the eye through the sclera. Fluctuations of this light, associated with movements of the eyes (or of the eyelids), may be sufficient to prevent fading of the retinal image. This effect may be large when a rigid stabilization system is used without Maxwellian illumination. If the room as a whole is not darkened, it is then desirable to shade the sclera. In experiments with the telescopic systems (§§ 5.15–5.24), the target is seen strongly illuminated in Maxwellian view, and the room is generally dark. Under these conditions, scleral light is almost certainly negligible.

6

Vision with stationary images—general description

6.1. Introduction

This chapter summarizes a number of qualitative descriptions of appearances reported by subjects who have viewed a stabilized image. Some of the phenomena have been further investigated by methods leading to numerical results, and these more detailed studies will be reported in later chapters. The total number of people who have systematically viewed stabilized images is small (probably less than 50). The number who have acted as subjects in a series of experiments, and are therefore able to compare one kind of situation with another, is smaller. Since it is necessary to use the reports of a rather small number of people, the author has included his own observations, as a subject. This chapter includes some reference to images, other than stabilized images, which are stationary on the retina (§ 6.16 ff).

6.2. The pattern of rings and brushes shown in Fig. 5.4 was observed by Ditchburn and Pritchard (1956) using the apparatus shown in Fig. 5.3. This pattern covers a region of the retina out to about 10° from the central fovea. There are no sharp edges or strong contrasts in the field. The sequence of events was described as follows: 'When the subject first looks, the fringes are clearly seen, but they fade in a period of from 1 s to 5 s leaving a grey field, which sometimes goes black. This fade-out persists for about 10 s, after which the eye makes a sharp and uncontrollable movement, and the fringes are seen very clearly. Sometimes the fringes re-appear less clearly, and over only part of the field, without any violent movement of the eye. The fade-out has been observed at the very high brightness obtained by allowing the subject to view a bright cloud through the unit. With light interrupted at a suitable frequency, the image does not fade-out'.

6.3. The following types of visual appearance mentioned above have been confirmed by independent observations of several people:

Type I   Sharp and clear as in normal vision.

Type II   Loss of pattern perception leaving a grey field, or a field which is faintly coloured.

Type III Total loss of visual perception leaving a black field.

Type IV   Intermittent and partial loss of pattern perception—a condition in which the clearness of the picture fluctuates as a whole, and also locally. Most commonly some features of the target are seen hazily and others not at all. Occasionally some features are seen clearly while others are not seen at all.

This division is arbitrary. Type II might be regarded as an extreme form of type IV, or type III might be regarded as associated with type II. The scheme given above is chosen for convenience of reference.

6.4. Barlow (1963) gives detailed descriptions which are in general agreement with the above description of type IV and with similar reports recorded in theses by Fender (1956), Pritchard (1958a), and Clowes (1959). Barlow also describes an appearance which can be identified with type II above. In his experiments, the type IV appearances are obtained a few seconds after the first presentation of the target, but the reappearances gradually become weaker leaving a grey field (type II). This condition is reached after about a minute or longer, and it persists until stabilization is disturbed. Yarbus (1956b, 1957a, 1959a, 1960, and 1967) describes only one appearance which he calls an 'empty field'. This is obtained only after 2–3 s and remains 'permanently', i.e. for at least 2–3 min, which appears to be the time of a single experiment (Yarbus 1957b). Yarbus (1957a, b) states that the empty field has a faint colouration derived from the target, but he never reports any trace of the target structure which was reported by others mentioned above, including Barlow.† It appears probable that the 'empty field' is, in general, to be identified with the appearance we have called type II, and that the differences in description are due to differences in the targets used and in minor details of experimental conditions (§ 9.30). However, the phrase 'blacker than night' which he uses in one paper (Yarbus 1959a) suggest that on some occasions he observed the appearance we have called type III. We shall now discuss the different types in more detail.

† Barlow (1963) p. 48.

6.5. Type I. Clear vision

The appearance obtained when any target is illuminated with a flash of light of less than 0·1 s is nearly the same in normal vision and in vision with a stabilized image. Riggs, Ratliff, Cornsweet, and Cornsweet (1953) obtained slightly better visual acuity (measured in terms of the reciprocal of the width of a fine line which was visible 50 per cent of the time) with a stabilized image than with normal vision. Keesey (1960) found no significant difference between normal vision and vision with stabilized images (presented for times less than 0·2 s) in respect of acuity (measured as before), vernier acuity, and discrimination of the structure of a grating test object. These results will be discussed in Chapter 12; for the present we accept the result that vision is substantially the same as in normal vision when the period of exposure is 0·1 s or less. This sharp appearance is not obtained with after-images (Ditchburn and Drysdale 1973). The characteristic sharp image is also obtained if the illuminance of a target producing a stabilized image is suddenly increased, and also if a target which has disappeared (in whole or in part) is suddenly moved through a visual angle of 2′ or more (§ 10.8).

6.6. Type II. Hazy field

Barlow (1963) describes 'a stable appearance of a fog or grey sky with ill-defined dark and light clouds in it corresponding to black and white parts of the original image'. He says, 'this final state, a very blurred low contrast version of the original image, seems to persist without fluctuation for as long as conditions are unchanged. When it has disappeared the cornea has been found to be misted or the lens surface smeared'. The initial parts of this description agree well with appearances observed by Pritchard and myself when viewing the ring-and-brush patterns. The field appeared grey and cloudy. No trace of the structure of the original pattern remained but this was probably because the target contained an intricate pattern of low contrast (Fig. 5.4). The colour of the remaining field did, in a vague way, represent the colour of the target. White illumination left a grey or grey-brown haze, red illumination left a slight suggestion of orange-yellow, and blue or green illumination left a grey which could be described as 'bluish'. Yarbus (1957c) also mentions a slight colouration (derived from the target) in the 'empty field'. Gerrits *et al.* (1966) report that when the image begins to fade an area *outside* the target seems bright for a short time.

Appearances obtained with the stabilized image are not *exactly* like anything seen in normal vision. Since the words used to describe the appearances are necessarily drawn from normal visual experience they are not adequate to describe the essentially new features of a different visual experience. This applies especially to a description of colour (hue). The appearance of a hazy field when the target is blue or green may be described as a very unsaturated and rather dim field of a hue similar to that corresponding to 500 nm, but it is not identical with any appearance seen in normal vision.

6.7. Type III. Black field

In this condition the whole visual field goes black. This condition seldom occurs without an intervening period corresponding to appearance type II (or possibly type IV). When it occurs, weak unstabilized stimuli in the outer field disappear. Unstabilized weak stimuli in the other eye also disappear. When stabilized images are presented to both eyes, type II or type IV appearances may occur in one eye at one time and in the other eye at another time. But, whenever the black field (Type III) appears, it does so in both eyes (§ 13.17). It also terminates simultaneously in the two eyes. This behaviour almost certainly implies the intervention of a central action.

6.8. In the black field no trace of the original target remains, either in form or in colour. On one occasion when the black field appeared, the subject thought that the experimenter had extinguished the light, although no change had been made. Subjects state that the black field is not a purely negative experience and is not the same as darkness. One subject described it as 'more black than black', and several others have said that this is a good description of what they see. Yarbus uses the expression 'blacker than night' (§ 6.4). Subjects recognize a difference between the black field and total darkness and yet find great difficulty in describing what it is. Possibly the loss of perception of the weak 'retinal light', due to suppression of the resting discharge (§ 7.24), is being observed. No one who had seen the 'black field' would describe it as 'hazy' or 'grey'.

6.9. Type IV. Fluctuating clearness

When a stabilized image is first presented, it is seen clearly (type I). After a period of 2–10 s the details of the target disappear leaving a grey field (type II). If conditions are not suitable for the type III appearance, a regime (which we call type IV) is established in which the target is seen intermittently but not, as a rule, very clearly. Appearance and disappearance alternate with a period of 2–3 s. The whole target may re-appear at once, but hazily, or sections of the target may re-appear while others remain invisible. The parts which re-appear are not of necessity the sharpest or most prominent features. However, the parts which re-appear are not selected by an entirely random process (Chapter 13).

6.10. The following conditions favour the observation of the black field (type III) rather than the grey field (type II) or the fluctuating regime (type IV):

(a) target with low contrast and no sharp boundaries;
(b) target large enough to include a large area of the extra-foveal retina;
(c) good stabilization;
(d) comfort of the subject, and absence of non-visual stimuli such as noise (§ 6.25).

All these conditions were satisfied when the apparatus shown in Fig. 5.3 was used to produce a ring-and-brush pattern, and the black field was frequently obtained with this apparatus. It is frequently observed with the suction devices (Figs. 5.7 and 5.9) used by Yarbus and by Barlow, and less frequently with the optical lever method of stabilization. This is probably because, (1) suction improves adherence to the eye (this together with the rigidity of the simple system helps to give good stabilization), and (2) the optical system is not of sufficiently high quality to produce retinal images with very sharp boundaries. Optical lever systems, if made with good optical components, give sharp images but are more difficult to adjust for very good stabilization.

6.11. Recently it has been possible to obtain the black field in a controlled way. I have observed a target which consists of a circular bright patch of 5°, or more, seen against a dark ground. The circular boundary is stabilized. When this is centred so that the whole of this boundary is in the parafoveal region, the black field is easily and repeatedly obtained. When it is not centred, the black field appears less often. When a little simple structure (e.g. a black line) is introduced into the central area, the black field is still obtained—especially if the structure is not very sharply focussed. This happens even when a small amount of unstabilized structure is introduced (§ 9.30). When, however, a very sharp 'picture' with a good deal of structure is shown in the central region, the black field seldom appears. In these experiments, the accuracy of stabilization was the same throughout and observation of the black field depended entirely on the target. This does not exclude the possibility that, for any given target, observation of the black field may depend on the accuracy of stabilization (§ 10.13 and 10.18).

6.12. It is important to distinguish between (a) reappearances in which the whole target is seen very clearly and (b) reappearances in which

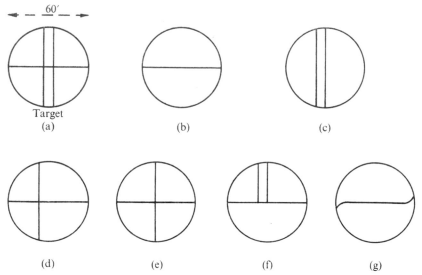

Fɪɢ. 6.1. Target (a) and various appearances seen when retinal image is stabilized. (g) is mentioned in § 6.13.

only part of the target is seen, or the whole is seen indistinctly. When only part of the target is seen, it is usually indistinct, but occasionally a part is seen very clearly. In my experience, the reappearances which follow a deliberate disturbance of the lens always cover the whole field and are very clear. It is probable that all reappearances of this kind are produced by mechanical destabilization. The other type of reappearance, (b), is not associated in any simple way with movements of the eye, and there is strong evidence that this type is not associated with movement of the retinal image (§§ 6.23–6.28). Figure 6.1 shows a fairly simple target (a) and some of the fragments which I observed when it was viewed as a stabilized image; (b) might be explained by a vertical displacement of the retinal image leading to the appearance of horizontal lines; similarly, (c) might be due to a horizontal displacement of the image leading to reappearance of vertical lines; (d), (e), and (f) cannot be explained by any movements of the retinal image.

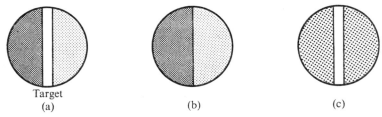

Target
(a)   (b)   (c)

Fɪɢ. 6.2. Target (a) and two appearances seen when retinal image is stabilized.

Fender displayed a bipartite field in which the two parts were separated by a light region as shown in Fig. 6.2(a). Sometimes the central line disappeared, leaving the contrast between the two outer parts still visible (Fig. 6.2(b)). On other occasions, the central line could be clearly seen, but the areas on the two sides of it appeared to be equally bright (Fig. 6.2(c)). Barlow (1963) reports an essentially similar difference between the behaviour of the long-range and short-range 'structure' in the image (i.e. low and high spatial frequencies).

When a transparent colour reproduction of one of the Isihara plates is shown as target, using the apparatus shown in Fig. 5.6(a), the outlines of the circles do not always disappear when the hue differences have become invisible (Beeler, Fender, Nobel, and Evans 1964). This indicates that the effect of retinal image movements on the hue detectors is not the same as the effect on the pattern detectors of the visual system.

The successive stages of disappearance of a stabilized image are often interesting. The target shown in Fig. 6.3(a) goes rapidly through the

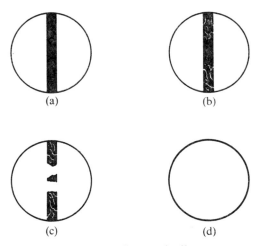

(a)   (b)

(c)   (d)

Fɪɢ. 6.3. Target (a) and stages in disappearance.

stages (b), (c), and (d) before disappearing. The fine white lines may be due to retinal blood vessels (§ 9.12).

6.13. Sometimes a target may be seen with distortions. I have seen the horizontal line of the target shown in Fig. 6.1(a) appear to have curved ends as shown in Fig. 6.1(g). When the ring-and-brush pattern is shown, the brushes sometimes appear to invade the rings and distort the pattern. Sometimes the stabilized image is seen as a complete figure when the target contains an incomplete figure (§ 6.17). Barlow (1963) has pointed out that when a black square on a white ground disappears the apparent luminance in the region occupied by the square is higher in the stabilized image than in the target. In this situation it is not strictly correct to speak of the target as 'fading' or 'fading out'. It is better to speak of disappearance of structure or contrast.

Even very bright targets disappear and the rate or frequency or disappearance does not vary very rapidly with luminance from 0·3 cd m⁻² upwards. The ring-and-brush pattern viewed against a bright cloud (with a luminance of perhaps 10 000 cd m⁻²) disappeared in a few seconds (§ 6.2). Yarbus (1960b) mounted a small medical lamp on a suction device and observed the filament directly. The image disappeared in 2–3 s and did not reappear. Fender (1956) observed that the threshold luminance for seeing a small spot of light in a stabilized image was about 40 times higher than the normal threshold for foveal vision.

6.14. Restoration of vision by imposed movement

It has been found by several workers that vision may be restored by tapping one of the components of an optical lever system (e.g. one of the mirrors in Figs. 5.10 or 5.11). This effect has been systematically explored and will be further discussed in Chapter 10. Sharp saccadic movements of 2 min. arc are effective in restoring vision. Very rapid oscillatory movements have an adverse effect and very slow movements simulating the natural drift have little effect by themselves. Oscillatory movement of frequencies about 8 Hz are effective if the amplitude is sufficient. Campbell and Robson (1961), and Barlow (1963), find that repeated small regular movements have a decreasing effect (§ 6.20).

6.15. Restoration by intermittent illumination

It has been shown by several observers that vision is partially restored by intermittent or modulated illumination of the field. The effect is complicated (Chapter 11), and results with square-top modulation are not related in a simple way to those obtained with sine-wave modulation. A very large number of parameters (wave-form, frequency, depth of modulation, colour, area of retina) can be varied, and much work remains to be done in this field. Campbell and Robson (1961), Barlow (1963), and Sharpe (1972) find that in certain situations the effect of modulation decreases with time (§ 6.20).

6.16. Stationary images

We shall use the term *stationary retinal image* to include any image which remains on the same part of the retina even when the eye moves. Stabilized images, produced by use of special apparatus for stabilization against the effect of eye-movements and head movements, are thus considered as one class of stationary retinal images. Other stationary images include

(a) after-images;
(b) shadows of the retinal blood vessels;
(c) Maxwell's colour spot (under suitable conditions);
(d) Haidinger's Brushes (under suitable conditions).

All stationary retinal images have one property in common—their fixed position on the retina. They also show certain features in common. There are, however, important differences which must be expected in view of the differences in conditions which produce them. Stabilized images produce a constant photo-chemical state of each part of the retina if the stimulating light is kept constant for a sufficient time. In this situation an equilibrium should be reached, when the rate of breakdown of photo-labile substances is equal to the rate of regeneration. When after-images are seen, the stimulus is in the past and the chemical balance is changing. The shadows of retinal blood vessels are permanent and it is reasonable to suppose that in normal conditions the visual system is able to 'compensate' for them as it compensates for the very much larger 'blind' spot. With these similarities and differences in mind we will now consider some qualitative observations on stationary images—other than stabilized images.

6.17. After-images

After-images appear and disappear at intervals like the stabilized image of type IV. Bennet-Clark and Evans (1963) have observed partial reappearances in sharp after-images produced by flash-illumination of well-defined patterns. Non-random pattern fragmentation is observed both in stabilized images and in after-images (§ 13.4). An incomplete pattern may sometimes be seen completed, e.g. an incomplete circle may be seen as a complete circle (§ 13.8). Negative after-images are obtained by first looking at a bright target and then at an illuminated white screen. Barlow and Sparrock (1964) have observed negative stabilized images in a similar situation. Some after-images become much stronger and sharper when the field is illuminated with light modulated at a few cycles per second. This is sometimes called 'development' of the after-image. It is tempting to draw an analogy between the fading of the after-image (even though 'development' is maintained) and the fading of a stabilized image, but the time-scales of the two phenomena are quite different. The decay of an after-image may take 5 min or more (Alpern and Barr 1962; Brindley 1962). With the stabilized image, disappearance occurs in times of a few seconds even when the retinal illumination is very strong (§ 6.13), and although the photo-chemical stimulus is maintained. Some other reason must therefore be assigned for the fading of the stabilized image.

6.18. Haidinger's brushes

If a suitable screen is illuminated with polarized light whose plane is slowly rotated at about 1 Hz, an observer sees a rather vague pattern which spreads like brushes from any point on the screen which is fixated. The brushes rotate with the plane of polarization. The effect is seen most clearly in fairly deep blue light and can be demonstrated to a large audience.† The brushes are due to the crystalline properties of the optic media immediately in front of the retinal receptors. If the rotation of the plane of polarization is stopped the rings become stationary on the retina; they then disappear in less than a second and do not reappear as long as the polaroid is not rotated. The very rapid disappearance is probably mainly due to the small absolute difference of luminance between rings and background and the very small gradient of luminance at their boundaries (Chapter 9).

6.19. Shadows of the retinal blood vessels

The shadows of the retinal blood vessels are not seen under normal conditions. This is not because they are too small or insufficiently

---

† A piece of polaroid on the outer side of the main lens of a projection lantern is rotated. The beam of light falls on a white metallized screen which does not produce too much depolarization. A blue filter is used.

opaque. The vessels of another person's eye are easily seen in an opthal-moscope, and it is possible to arrange to see one's own retinal blood vessels at unit magnification (Cornsweet 1962). It has long been known that they are made visible by suddenly illuminating the retina with light coming from one side. Lettvin† constructed a simple apparatus for demonstrating this effect using two small medical lamps which are switched on and off at a frequency of 1–2 Hz and in opposite phase (so that one is on whenever the other is off). If the lamps are placed on the upper and lower lids of the closed eyes, the subject sees the hori-zontal blood vessels clearly outlined. The shadows are moving with a small amplitude as they fall alternately on parts of the retina above and below the region immediately under the vessels. If the lamps are transferred to suitable positions at the sides of the eyes, the vertical parts of the vessels are seen. There is a tendency for the effect to de-crease with time, provided that the lamps are fixed relative to the eyes and not pressed strongly against them.

6.20. Fatigue effect‡

Campbell and Robson (1961) used a cathode-ray tube to produce a small high-luminance source whose image could be scanned over the plane of the pupil of the eye. The amplitude, frequency, and contrast of the light scan were separately controlled, and the spot could be moved either horizontally or in one meridian. When the diameter of the beam was less than 0·2 mm in the pupil plane, and it was moved at optimum¶ amplitude and frequency, a detailed shadow of the capillaries was perceived. If the spot was stopped so as to produce a stationary shadow on the retina, the image disappeared very rapidly and could not be made to reappear by modulating the intensity of the light. It reappeared for a much longer period if the spot was moved (at suitable amplitude and frequency), but even the moving shadow ultimately disappeared and did not reappear spontaneously. These experiments have been extended by Sharpe (1972). His results are described in § 10.20–10.22.

Since none of the shadows of retinal blood vessels appear in the central fovea an additional experiment was made on the shadow of the yellow (minus-blue) macular pigment. This can be perceived by presenting alternatively, a green and a purple (minus-green) light of

---

† Private communication.
‡ See note at the end of § 10.22.
¶ The authors do not state what amplitude and frequency were 'optimum'.

equal luminance with a suitable frequency of interchange. It is observed that if the two-colour beam is brought to a fine focus in the pupil, a mottled appearance is seen in the centre of the field, and the rather vague Maxwell colour shadow is also seen. This disappears after a short time like the shadows of the retinal blood-vessels. It should be noted that the pattern seen in the central fovea is of very low contrast and has no sharp edges. The retinal blood vessels offer a higher contrast (when illuminated with blue light) and have sharper boundaries, but they are seen extra-foveally, using a region of the retina which has a much lower visual acuity.

6.21. Fixation effects

It has long been known that if a subject fixates carefully, there is a pronounced loss of visual discrimination in the peripheral field: this is known as the Troxler effect (Troxler 1804). This effect has been investigated with modern techniques by Clarke (1957). His results indicate some similarities with the effects observed in the fovea using stabilized images. The low resolving power of the peripheral retina makes the residual eye-movements of fixation insufficient to maintain full visual performance. Many observers can learn to suppress saccades (§ 4.9). Some of them fixate sufficiently well to lose the finer details of a foveal image and certain other visual discriminations. It is particularly easy to lose discrimination between adjacent blue and green, or orange and red patches whose luminance is not very different.

These effects produced by fixation are always less than the effects obtained with stabilized images—except that objects in the extreme periphery of the visual field disappear almost equally quickly in fixated and in stabilized vision. It is important that observations on stabilized images made by a few observers are confirmed qualitatively by observations which can be made by larger numbers of people. Nevertheless, the physiological study of the function of eye-movements requires an experimental arrangement in which the uncontrolled normal movements are removed by accurate stabilization in order that the effect of controlled movements may be studied.

6.22. E.E.G. records

In most subjects, α-rhythm is found in E.E.G. records taken from the occipital region when the subject is in the dark, or is viewing a ganzfeld. It is partially or completely suppressed when a pattern is viewed in normal vision (Adrian and Matthews 1934). E.E.G. records together with records of the appearance and disappearance of the stabilized image were made by Pritchard.† He estimated that the α-rhythm was present about 5 times as much when the target was not seen as it was during periods when the target was seen. Keesey and Nichols (1967) gave about 3:1 for this ratio. Lehmann, Beeler, and Fender (1965a) made a statistical analysis and found a significant correlation ($P < 0.002$) between disappearance of the target and presence of the α-rhythm. Evans and Smith (1964) found a correlation between intermittent disappearances of an after-image (printed on the retina by a short flash of light) and the α-rhythm. In this case the correlation applied to the period after the strong disturbance of the α-rhythm by the flash had subsided.

When a subject views a ganzfeld there are 'perceptual blanks', and several workers (e.g. Tepas 1962) have noted that these blanks coincide with increased α-rhythm. It is also found that when a structured target in normal vision is near the threshold of visibility, there are fluctuations in the extent to which it is perceived. Failure of perception is correlated with strong α-rhythm.

6.23. The experiments mentioned in the preceding paragraph are consistent with either of the following hypotheses:

(a) fluctuating signals, sent by the retina to the cortex, control the α-rhythm activity, or

(b) fluctuating changes of activity at a central level cause variations in perception of a structured target even when a constant input is received from the retina.

A decision between these hypotheses may be made by recording in detail the time relations between the rise and fall of the α-rhythm and visibility of the target. Observations of this type have been made by Lehmann *et al.* (1965b), and by Keesey and Nichols (1967). They both find that the α-rhythm rises about 0·7 s *before* the subject reports the disappearance of target structure (by pressing a key). The α-rhythm is suppressed about 1 s *before* the reappearance is reported. This result is inconsistent with hypothesis (a) unless it be assumed that there is an abnormally long delay in reporting appearance and disappearance of the stabilized image. Subsidiary experiments showed that the delay is not abnormally long. The results thus indicate that the main part of fluctuations in perception, obtained when viewing a stabilized image, are due to changes in cortical activity and not to changes at retinal level.

† Pritchard (1958a (p. 146), 1961a).

6.24. This result does not exclude the possibility that, on some occasions, reappearance of the image is due to slip of the contact lens. Examination of the histograms of time delays reveals minor peaks corresponding to a small number of reappearances in which the above time relation is reversed. It is probable that these are due to the slip of the contact lens.

Barlow and Sparrock (1964) measured the apparent luminance of an after-image in relation to that of a stabilized image on an adjacent part of the retina (§ 8.17). The consistency of their results suggests that both apparent luminances increase and decrease together—as would be expected if the fluctuations are controlled by the same central process.

6.25. Effect of auditory stimulation on visibility

Observations of the percentage of time for which a stabilized image is seen, are subject to considerable random fluctuations between the results of successive trials. Several experimenters have found that variation in noise level is one cause of these fluctuations. Pritchard (1958*a*) investigated the effect of sound on the percentage (V) of time for which a certain target was visible. He used the apparatus shown in Fig. 5.3 to view the pattern of rings and brushes. His experimental sessions lasted up to one hour. Observation periods of 120 s alternated with rest periods during which the subject saw a blank field of about the same average luminance (15 cd m^{-2}) as the test field.

With a trained subject in a moderately well soundproofed room, in an isolated building, V fell rapidly from a value of 50 or more to less than 10, and fluctuated about this value for the remainder of the session. Fig. 6.4 is a record of a session in which continuous noise (at about 70 dB above threshold) was started 15 min after the beginning of the session and maintained at a steady level for the remainder. When the noise started, V rose sharply, but after ten minutes began to fall again, and by the end of the session had reached the value which would have been obtained in a session without noise.

6.26. Further experiments were carried out with monotones at 1000 Hz and 400 Hz at roughly 70 dB above threshold. When quiet periods, and periods with sound at 1000 Hz, were alternated, the value of V for periods with sound was between 40 per cent and 50 per cent, and the value for the quiet periods was 20 per cent, as compared with 10 per cent for a session which included only quiet periods. When 'quiet', 400 Hz and 1000 Hz were presented in successive periods of 60 s for

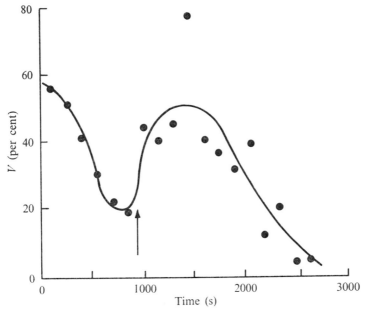

FIG. 6.4. Effect of noise on visibility of stabilized image. Noise started at time marked ↑. (From Pritchard 1958a.)

25 min, the value of V for the periods with sound was greater than that obtained in the neighbouring quiet periods by 10–20 per cent. There was considerable irregular fluctuation, but no systematic variation with time. No effect was produced by sound which was only a little above threshold for audibility.

6.27. It is thus shown that

(a) sound produces an effect which does not decay instantaneously when the sound is removed;

(b) a steady sound produces habituation, i.e. the effect is reduced to about half the initial effect in 500–1000 s, and no effect can be detected after about 2000 s;

(c) habituation is prevented if either (1) 120 s sound is alternated with 120 s quiet or (2) sounds of two different frequencies are alternated; and

(d) the effect depends on the intensity of the sound rather than on the information conveyed by it.

Magoun studied some effects of sound on E.E.G. records from sleeping cats. The sound produced 'arousal', and there were habituation

11

effects very similar to those described above. These results were interpreted in terms of stimulation of the reticular formation of the brain stem.

6.28. It has been suggested that the effect of sound might be to increase eye-movements, and to produce destabilization effects by slip of the contact lens. However, Krauskopf and Coleman (1956) found no change in saccade amplitude or inter-saccadic interval due to binaural stimulation at 80 dB above threshold. Significant, but still fairly small, effects were produced by stimulation at the much higher level of 137 dB. It is nearly certain that changes of eye-movements are not significant in Pritchard's experiments. It is probable that the effect of the auditory stimuli is to maintain 'attention'. This probably involves producing or maintaining the type of brain activity which favours perception of weak stimuli (§ 6.23). Unfortunately Pritchard then had no facilities for making E.E.G. records in order to test the correlation with his other data.

6.29. Effect of reversed movements of the retinal image

In normal vision, when the eye turns towards the right, the retinal image moves across the retina towards the right. Using the telescopic stabilization system described in § 5.15, and making $M = 1$, gives $F = -1$. When the eye moves to the right, the retinal image then moves to the left with respect to the retina. The magnitude of the movement is the same as in normal vision. Clowes (1961) found that in this situation, the appearance of the target was indistinguishable from its appearance in normal vision. The subject correctly identified the brighter half of a bipartite field, and the difference of luminance appeared to be about the same as with normal vision. This implies that the signals which enable a subject to say which side of a boundary is dark, are not reversed when the relation between eye-movement and retinal-image movement is reversed. Thus this discrimination is not made by using the variation of visual signals from receptors near the boundary, together with information about the phase of the oscillatory movement or the direction of drifts or saccades. In view of the results described in § 7.33, it would be of interest to perform the same experiment with a boundary between red and green areas of equal luminance. This test was not made.

7

The visual system

7.1. Introduction

This chapter is concerned with those aspects of the physiology of the visual system which are relevant to experiments on eye-movements and on vision with stabilized retinal images. It is inevitably a selection of a small fraction from a large body of knowledge. In writing an account of this type it is difficult to avoid giving the impression that the biological system is much less complicated than it really is. Analogies with physical systems fit the prototype at certain points but not at others. In general, the biological system is much richer in its adaptive possibilities than the analogous physical system which has some of its properties. The theory of information channels derived from the study of electrical signals passing along transmission lines is directly applicable to the processes of transmission of information along nerve fibres, yet the process of nervous conduction involves both chemical and physical effects and is more complicated than the process of conduction along a submarine cable. A brain does not differ from a large computer only in having a larger number of 'circuit elements'. Its units are themselves much more complicated in their action than the resistors, transistors, etc. from which a computer is built. Physical and chemical principles are applicable to biological material but we are far from being able to understand their application in detail. We therefore use simplified models to guide our thinking and to suggest fruitful experiments. These models are useful within limited ranges.†

7.2. Neurons

The basic unit of the nervous system is the neuron. Each neuron (Fig. 7.1) consists of:

(a) the cell body (called the *soma*) containing a nucleus;
(b) a number of *dendrites* which are thin fibres growing out of the cell body and which receive stimuli;

† For more general accounts of the physiology of vision see Davson (1962), Brindley (1960), Granit (1947, 1962), and Adler (1965).

(c) an *axon* or nerve-fibre: this is a single cylindrical fibre which emerges from the cell body and transmits electrical impulses carrying information about the stimulus. The axon ends in a ramification of branches having terminal knobs (called *telendrons*) which make connection with other neurons.

Within this general description, neurons differ greatly in the size of the various parts and in the details of connections to other neurons or to muscle fibres. In the retina there are neurons whose largest linear dimension is only a few micrometres. At the other extreme there are neurons whose axons extend from the foot up to the spinal cord. There is also a wide range in the diameters of nerve-fibres. Most of those with which we are concerned are in the range 1 μm to 3 μm, but recent work with the electron microscope (Pedler 1965; Dowling and Boycott 1966) has revealed a multitude of much finer connections within the retina.

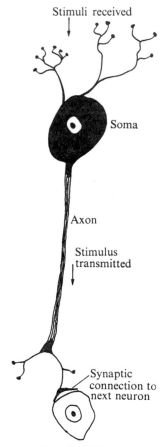

FIG. 7.1. Neuron.

7.3. Conduction in nerve-fibres

The interior of a fibre contains liquid and is separated from an exterior liquid by a thin membrane. Both the interior and exterior fluids contain K^+, Na^+, and Cl^- ions to which the membrane is permeable. When any given part of a fibre is resting (i.e. not stimulated) the membrane is much more permeable to K^+ and Cl^- than to the Na^+ ion. A certain metabolic process (known as the 'sodium pump') removes Na^+ from the interior so that the exterior concentration is about 10

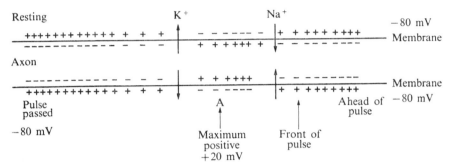

Fig. 7.2. Distribution of charge as pulse passes from left to right. The point A corresponds with A on Fig. 7.3.

times the interior concentration. This makes the interior negative with respect to the exterior by a resting potential E_r of about 80 mV. The ion K^+ is then under a field driving it inwards, and its concentration within the fibre rises until the number of ions reaching the fibre wall from within (with sufficient energy to get out) is equal to the number which the field is driving in (Donnan equilibrium). This happens when the concentration inside is about 30 times the concentration outside. The situation shown on the left-hand side of Fig. 7.2 is thus established. When one end of the fibre is stimulated, either by a small electrical potential opposed to E_r, or by the arrival of a minute quantity of certain chemical compounds, the wall suddenly becomes much more permeable to sodium ions. These rush into the fibre so rapidly that in about 0·5 ms the inside of the fibre becomes positive with respect to the outside (right-hand side of Fig. 7.2). This, in turn, produces a neutralizing outward flow of potassium ions. Finally, the sodium pump restores the resting equilibrium. The whole variation of potential is over in about 0·5–1·0 ms (Fig. 7.3). This variation is called a *spike* or *pulse*.

7.4. The rise of potential within the fibre produces a potential opposed to E_r immediately ahead of the region in which the action described in

the preceding paragraph is taking place. The wall thus becomes permeable ahead of the stimulus and the whole action is propagated along
the fibre. For any one kind of nerve-fibre there is a minimum stimulus
which will initiate a propagated potential change. Provided this minimum is exceeded, the magnitude of the spike and its duration are
determined, not by the stimulus, but by the properties of the fibre.
The spikes carried by any one nerve-fibre are indistinguishable in

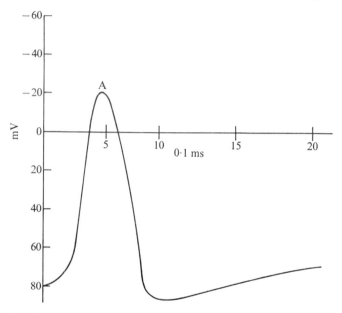

FIG. 7.3. Variation of potential inside fibre (with respect to potential outside) during
passage of a 'spike'.

magnitude or shape. There is a propagation velocity which is characteristic of the fibre. The optic nerve-fibres show a bimodal distribution of velocities with peaks at 20 m s^{-1} and 40 m s^{-1}. The larger
velocities are obtained with the fibres of greater diameter.

There is a *refractory period*, usually about 0·5 to 1·0 ms, immediately
after a spike. At the beginning of this period a renewed stimulus does
not initiate a spike; at a later time a spike can be initiated but the
threshold is higher than normal. Sometimes this is followed by a period
when the threshold is less than normal. After about 1·0 ms the system
returns to the equilibrium resting state.

7.5. Small and large stimuli

If a chemical stimulus is so weak that only the minimum quantity
of the chemical compound is available, there will be only one spike.

If, however, several times the minimum quantity is available there may be sufficient left at the end of the refractory period to initiate a second spike and, in general, a large stimulus will initiate a group of spikes. The number of spikes is not proportional to the size of the stimulus. In the retina it is more nearly proportional to the logarithm of the stimulus. The refractory period of 0·5 ms implies that no fibre can carry more than 2000 spikes s^{-1}. For very short periods spikes can be transmitted at this rate but other considerations reduce the maximum steady rate of transmission to about 150 s^{-1}.

7.6. Recruitment

In some situations receptors of differing sensitivity are available. A weak stimulus then stimulates only the most sensitive receptors. If the stimulus is increased, more and more receptors respond and spikes appear in the associated nerve-fibres. This process, which is known as *recruitment*, extends the dynamic range† of the system. There is no direct evidence that recruitment is effective in relation to the fibres of the optic nerve but it offers a simple explanation of certain phenomena, e.g. the increase of foveal acuity with luminance over a certain part of the range.

7.7. Myelinated fibres

The type of nerve-fibre described in §§ 7.3–7.5 has a wall-resistance per unit length, an internal resistance, etc., like a submarine cable. These constants can be measured, and the velocity of propagation calculated from them agrees with that found by direct experiment. Partly because the fibre is very thin and partly because the insulation resistance of the wall is low, signals would decay to a small fraction of the input value in less than a millimetre if the losses were not made good by energy derived from the metabolic process. In all the nerves with which we are concerned, losses are reduced by the presence of a sheath of insulating material called myelin. This covers the axon except at certain 'nodes', occurring at intervals of 0·5–2 mm, where it becomes thin enough for ions to be transmitted through the walls as described in §§ 7.3–7.4. At each node the spike is restored to its original size.

7.8. Synapses

The connections between neurons are called *synapses*. In the simplest kind of synaptic coupling the telendrons of a first-stage neuron make

---

† The dynamic range may be defined as the logarithm of the ratio of the largest signal which can be accepted to the smallest which can be detected in a reasonable time.

contact with the dendrites of a second-stage neuron. The arrival of a pulse at the end of the first-stage neuron stimulates the second-stage neuron so that a spike runs out along its axon towards the third-stage neuron. Transmission across a synapse involves a delay of less than 1·0 ms. This transmission of a pulse is operationally similar to the passage of a pulse across a condenser in an electrical circuit, but the action is not primarily electrical. The arrival of the pulse at the end of the first-stage neuron causes the production of a minute amount of certain chemical substances in the second-stage neuron. This, in turn, produces changes of potential which are eventually propagated along the axon of the second neuron. The chemical stage in this process makes possible more complicated kinds of synaptic interaction, some of which are described in § 7.9.

7.9. Ganglion cells

In the central nervous system, information is not only received and transmitted, it is also analyzed and recorded. One basic unit which enables this to be done is the ganglion cell (Fig. 7.4). This type of cell is found in the brain and spinal cord and in the output stage of the retina (Figs. 7.5 and 7.6). A typical retinal ganglion cell is connected by nerve fibres to a number of preceding neurons (bipolar cells and horizontal cells). These fibres penetrate the ganglion cell. When the preceding neuron of which they are part carries a pulse, they produce small

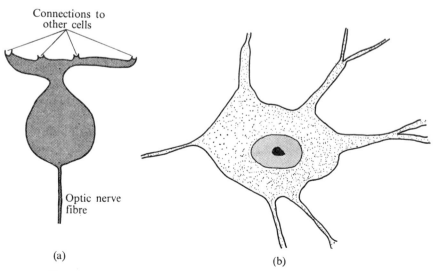

Connections to other cells

Optic nerve fibre

(a)

(b)

FIG. 7.4. Ganglion cells. (a) retinal (b) type considered in § 7.14.

amounts of a chemical compound within the ganglion cell. Some produce substances which cause potential changes tending to excite the cell; others have an inhibitory action. It is rare for a cell to fire (i.e. to send a pulse or series of pulses along its axon) as a result of the action of one preceding neuron. In general a ganglion cell fires when the excess of excitatory over inhibitory signals exceeds a certain threshold. This threshold depends on the previous state of the cell, and on the fluid outside. In some kinds of tissue, it is continuously adjustable. When the threshold is passed the ganglion cell sends a burst of spikes along its axon—the number in the burst depending on the excess of excitatory over inhibitory signals received.

A ganglion cell in the visual pathway, or in the visual cortex, may also receive fibres from sources other than photoreceptors. These may make it easier for the visual signals to make the cell fire, and this action is called *facilitation*. There may also be *inhibition* from non-visual sources or from other receptors. This may be local or at a higher level; the latter is called *central inhibition*.

7.10. The visual pathways

The main visual pathway is shown in Fig. 7.5(a). The receptors have synaptic junctions with the bipolar cells which form the bodies of the second-stage neurons. The bipolars in turn are synaptically connected to the retinal ganglion cells whose axons are the fibres of the optic nerve. These make synaptic connections at the lateral geniculate body (L.G.B.) to the neurons which run to the visual cortex. The bipolars, ganglion cells and L.G.B. are relay stations at which information is analysed, filtered, and recoded. In a nervous pathway the number of fibres at a higher stage may be greater than that at a lower stage, in which case the path is said to show *divergence:* if it is less, the path is said to show *convergence*. The central fovea has less than 10^4 cones, and is connected to an area of the cortex which contains 10^6 cells in the initial sub-layer and many more in underlying layers; thus there is an overall divergence of more than 100:1. The rest of the retina contains about 10^8 rods and 10^6 cones, and it has about 10^6 fibres going from ganglion cells to the L.G.B. There is thus a strong convergence between the extra-foveal receptors and the ganglion cells.

Connections from the right-hand (temporal) side of the right eye and from the right-hand (nasal) side of the left eye go to the right-hand side of the visual cortical area. In a corresponding way, connections from the left-hand sides of both retinas go to the left-hand side of the visual cortical area. The region in which the fibres cross over is called the *optic chiasma* (Fig. 7.5(b)).

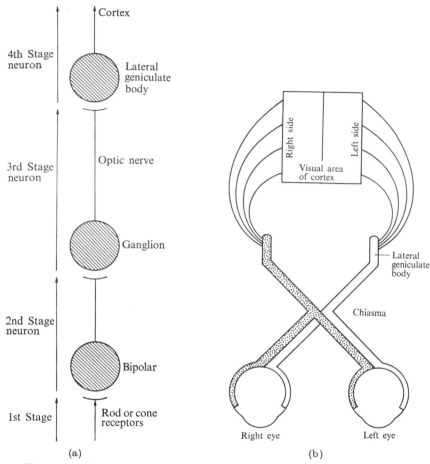

Fɪɢ. 7.5. Schematic diagrams of: (a) main visual pathway; (b) the chiasma.

7.11. Connections within the retina

Some of the connections within the retina are shown schematically in Fig. 7.6 (Dowling and Boycott 1966). This is based on electron-microscopic examination of the retina. The primary process of vision is the absorption of a photon by a molecule of pigment in one of the receptors. This changes† the permeability of the cell wall and produces

† In vertebrate retinae the change is a *decrease*, and the flow of ions is in the opposite direction to that described in § 7.3. The receptors are not just volumes containing pigment. They have a complicated structure including transverse 'plates'. For details of their action see the account of a symposium on the physiology of photo-receptors, presented to the Federation of American Societies for Experimental Biology (*Federation Proceedings*. (1971). Vol. 30, No. 1—including Worthington 1971; Baylor and O'Bryan 1971; Hagins and Rüppel 1971).

a potential change (§ 7.3). This leads to the chemical transfer of a signal across the synapse to a bipolar cell. The bipolar cell receives also signals which may be either of the same or of opposite sign from horizontal cells. These signals depend on the illuminance of other receptors in the immediate vicinity, and to a lesser extent of more distant receptors. It passes on a signal which is a function of the

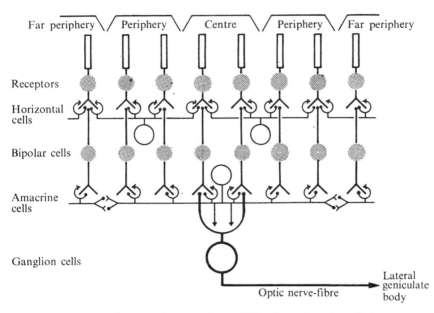

FIG. 7.6. Schematic diagram of connections within the retina. ⋏ excitatory synapse; ↓ inhibitory synapse; the connections between horizontal cells and receptors and also between amacrine cells and bipolars are two-way contacts. (From Dowling and Boycott 1966.)

difference between the illuminance of the receptor, or receptors, to which it is directly linked and illuminance of a surrounding region of the retina. This provides for detection of a boundary between light and dark areas, provided certain conditions are fulfilled (§ 8.2).

7.12. Receptor fields

A retinal ganglion cell receives signals from one or more bipolars, and also has complicated lateral connections (Fig. 7.6). It can be stimulated by light falling on any region within a certain small area of the retina. This area is called the *receptor field* of the ganglion cell. In higher vertebrates (e.g. cat and monkey) the receptor fields have a small central region and a larger periphery. These transmit opposed signals to the ganglion cell. Receptor fields of neighbouring ganglion cells overlap so that one receptor may send positive signals to one ganglion cell and inhibitory signals to another. An individual cell in the L.G.B. is usually connected to more than one ganglion cell, and hence to a considerable number of retinal receptors which constitute its receptor field. In general, spatial location becomes less precise at each higher level, while analysis becomes more sharply defined. This relation between retina and cortex is very different from the rather simple idea of point-by-point mapping of the retina in the cortex which was formerly accepted. Nevertheless, the ability of the fovea to resolve pinpoints of light whose angular separation is roughly equal to the intercone distance does imply a certain kind of point-to-point representation of at least the central 20′ of the retina at the highest level, i.e. there must be individual cells at cortical level whose response is dominated, though not entirely controlled, by the difference between the illuminance of one central cone and its neighbours (§§ 7.29 and 12.29).

The way in which information is analysed in the retina is not understood in detail. In the receptors and bipolars there is continuous variation of potentials, associated with continuous changes of chemical balance. Spikes first appear in the ganglions, and it is at this level that the propagated spikes begin.

7.13. Spatial summation

A flash of light falling on a small area of the retina can be perceived, provided that the subject is dark-adapted, when the energy per unit retinal area is so low that no one receptor can have absorbed more than one photon (Pirenne† 1962b). Thus a change of one molecule in one rod receptor can initiate a signal, but one such signal does not lead to perception of light for reasons discussed in § 7.18. However, when a very small number of photons (not more than 10 at most and possibly as low as 5) is absorbed within a small area and within a short time, a flash of light is perceived. The fact that a number of sub-threshold signals may co-operate in this way is known as *spatial summation*. The existence of lateral connections and of receptor fields provides a way in which this summation can occur. Spatial summation is obtained at the expense of spatial resolution. It is therefore advantageous to have small receptor fields when the luminance is high and to

† *The eye* (ed. Davson). Vol. 2. p. 134.

alter the connections so as to enlarge the receptor fields as the luminance falls (§ 7.28).

7.14. Temporal summation

The chemical substances associated with excitation and inhibition at
synapses are formed and decay very rapidly. The associated post-
synaptic potentials leak away in less than a millisecond. Thus signals
which summate in the most simple way in a single ganglion cell must
reach the cell within one or two milliseconds. Visual signals summate
over times of 30 ms and more, as is shown by studies of flicker fusion
(§ 11.2), so that some other action must occur. Groups of ganglion
cells are interconnected to form *ganglion pools*. When one ganglion cell
is excited, potential pulses spread to other cells in the pool.† Pulses
travel to and fro in a small region, and the excitation lasts for much
more than a millisecond. This kind of process extends the period over
which effects may summate. It also reduces the temporal resolution
of the system. As with spatial summation, it is advantageous to change
from extensive summation at low luminance to shorter-period summation (and good time resolution) at high luminance.

7.15. Adaptation

When the eye has been kept in darkness, or exposed to a steady level
of illumination for a sufficient period, it acquires properties determined
by this prevailing level. At high luminance, visual acuity, colour vision,
and temporal resolution are good, but sensitivity (i.e. the ability to
discriminate small additional visual stimuli, such as a weak flash of
light) falls. As the luminance is reduced, visual acuity and temporal
resolution become weaker and colour vision is lost. The process by which
the eye adjusts to a new level of luminance is called *adaptation*.

When a subject is transferred from bright daylight to darkness,
adaptation takes place in two stages (Fig. 7.7). In the first stage, the
sensitivity to weak flashes of light increases by a factor of about 100
in about 7 min. In the second stage, which is first manifest after about
10 minutes, a further increase of sensitivity by a factor of 300 occurs in
about 20 min. At the end of this period (i.e. half an hour after going
into the dark) adaptation is nearly complete though a small increase in
sensitivity is obtained by further adaptation for 20 hours. The first stage

† Burns (1968) includes a statistical theory of this kind of excitation.

of adaptation is associated with cone vision and the second with rod vision. This is shown by many experiments, but most clearly by experiments on night-blind persons (who have no rod function) and on rod monochromats (who have no cone function). Cone vision (or *photopic vision*) prevails when the eye is adapted to a retinal illuminance of more than about 1·0 td and rod vision (or *scotopic vision*) when it is adapted

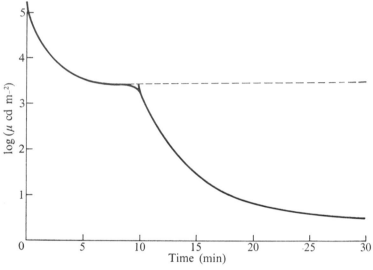

FIG. 7.7. Dark adaptation following light adaptation to about 10^4 cd m^{-2}. Full line: parafoveal adaptation, white light. – – – – –: foveal adaptation, red light. The absolute magnitude depends on shape, precise retinal location, colour, etc. The general course of adaptation is similar for yellow, green or white light, and for many sizes and shapes of target.

to a retinal illuminance of less than 0·1 td. If a subject who is adapted to a low level of retinal illuminance (or to darkness) is exposed to daylight, he is dazzled for a short period. This effect falls rapidly during a few seconds and, after about 2 min, the subject is well adapted to the higher luminance.

7.16. Sensitivity of the retinal receptors†

A flash of green light (507 nm) such that about 100 photons (or 4×10^{-4} ergs) are incident on the pupil of a dark-adapted eye, may be perceived provided that the retinal area and the duration are small enough for effectively complete spatial and temporal summation.

† Pirenne (1962*b*).

Rushton‡ (1956a) has determined the absorption spectrum of the rod pigment (*rhodopsin*) *in vivo*. The sensitivity of the dark-adapted eye, regarded as a photon detector, varies with wave-length in accordance with expectation based on this absorption spectrum. It is a maximum at about 507 nm. At this wave-length, dark-adapted rods absorb nearly 30 per cent of the light incident upon them. This is rather less than 10 per cent of the light incident on the pupil because some is lost by reflection and absorption in the dioptric media, and some falls on the gaps between the rods. Thus 100 photons at the pupil are needed for 5 to 10 photons to be absorbed. The minimum number of photons for perception in cone vision is about 2×10^3 incident on the pupil, or 500 on the retina (Miller 1959). This reduced sensitivity, compared with the rods, is partly due to lower absorption by the cones, but mainly to the lower spatial and temporal integration. It is nearly certain that absorption of a single photon in a cone is enough to initiate a signal. There is also evidence that, for extremely small areas and times, rods and cones have equal sensitivity (Arden and Weale 1954). The lower absorption and small spatial and temporal integration of the cone system are associated with its colour discrimination, high visual acuity, and good temporal resolution.

7.17. Vision at high luminance

The visual system can discriminate signals over a range of luminance from about 10^{-6} cd m^{2} to 10^5 cd m^{-2}. At 10^3 cd m^{-2} light adaptation is not complete, but this level may be taken as typical of high luminance. Crawford (1937) determined the luminance of a flash which is just visible against a background to which the subject is adapted, as a function of the luminance of the background. The reciprocal of this liminal increment measures the sensitivity of the eye as a function of the luminance to which it is adapted. By this test, the fovea is about 400 times and the parafovea about 50 000 times less sensitive when adapted to 10^3 cd m^{-2} than when adapted to total darkness. The visual system adapts to high luminance by

(a) reduction of the pupil area by a factor of about 10,
(b) reduction of spatial and temporal summation, and
(c) reduction of the available number of unbleached pigment molecules because a significant fraction are bleached.

(a) accounts for only a small part of the reduction of sensitivity; (c) does not become important until the luminance is very high. Rushton

‡ See also Rushton (1965).

(1958) shows that, at 10^3 cd m^{-2} (or 5×10^3 td) only about 10 per cent of the cone pigment is bleached so that 90 per cent of the pigment is still available, but the retinal sensitivity is only about 1 per cent of the cone sensitivity of the dark-adapted retina. There is thus some additional cause of reduced sensitivity, probably associated with (b) (§ 7.19).

7.18. Photon fluctuations

When a succession of weak flashes of light are all produced in the same way and allowed to fall on a photon-detector, the number of photons recorded is subject to a statistical fluctuation about an average value. The probable value of the fluctuation is about $n^{\frac{1}{2}}$ when the average number of recorded photons is n. It is thus a fraction $n^{-\frac{1}{2}}$ of the number of photons recorded, i.e. 0·1 per cent when n is 10^6, but 10 per cent when n is 100. Thus when the average number of photons absorbed by a flash of light is 5, then sometimes the actual number absorbed is 4 or 6 and, less frequently, 7 or 3. The probability of deviations of any size can be calculated. Flashes of nominal value corresponding to the absorption of from 1 to 10 photons, were presented in random order in experiments by Hecht, Shlaer, and Pirenne (1942) and by Baumgardt (1959). The frequency of seeing was measured as a function of the average number of photons which should have been absorbed. It was found that the results (for one subject) were compatible with the conclusion that 5 absorbed photons or more were always perceived, and 4 or less were never perceived, i.e. the whole variation in frequency of seeing could be assigned to the purely physical cause of photon fluctuations. However, the results are equally consistent with the view that the average number required is greater than 5 and that parts of the variation, represented by the frequency of seeing curve, is due to 'biological variation', i.e. that the number of signals required for perception varies a little from one test to the next.

7.19. Signal: noise ratio†

There have been a number of attempts (e.g. Rose 1942, 1947) to show that all visual discriminations are determined by photon fluctuations. For example, it is suggested that, if under a given condition, a luminance difference of about 1 per cent is perceptible, this indicates

† A bibliography (up to 1962) is given by Pirenne (loc. cit. § 7.13).

that spatial and temporal summation are such that about 10^4 absorbed photons are used, and the fluctuation is 100, or about 1 per cent. It is certain that photon fluctuations set limits to the performance of the eye under any prescribed conditions. It is probable that, at low luminance, this limit is approached within a factor of 2 or 3. At higher luminances the performance falls more and more below that predicted from photon fluctuations acting alone and in the most simple way. Some other kind of fluctuation must be involved (Aguilar and Stiles 1954; Barlow 1958 and 1962). It has been suggested (Rushton 1965) that when receptors contain some bleached molecules, certain ganglion pools continually receive signals from these receptors. These signals are not perceived as light because they are constant spatially and temporally so that they are like the signals derived from stabilized images. The number of spikes in one of these signals is subject to a statistical fluctuation which constitutes noise, and a fresh signal, due to an additional stimulus, is certain to be perceived only if it produces signals in the ganglion cells much larger than the average value of this 'noise'. When the additional stimulus produces signals about equal to the noise, it is seen on some occasions and not on others, and a frequency-of-seeing curve can be measured. In this way a very small fraction of bleached molecules can alter the sensitivity by a considerable factor. This scheme, in its simplest form, does not agree quantitatively with measurements of the variation of flash threshold with area and duration and with the background illuminance against which it is displayed (Rushton 1965). Fuortes and Hodgkin (1964) give an account of electrophysiological measurements on signals in the visual system of *Limulus*. Their results are in accordance with values calculated from a model in which the primary signals are subject to attenuation, and the attenuation factor is determined by the signals from bleached molecules. This model is analogous to the a.v.c. system of a radio-receiver. Rushton (1965) applies this model to the human visual system and obtains quantitative agreement with a range of experimental data. Crawford (1937, 1947) has measured the thresholds for flashes of different sizes, duration, and retinal location for a subject in the dark, but not dark-adapted. He finds that, at any given time, the eye behaves as though a certain amount of light were present. This 'equivalent background light' is the same for different areas and durations of the test flash. This 'background' is believed to be associated with signals from the bleached pigment. When a subject is completely dark-adapted a small 'equivalent background' remains. This 'retinal light' (or 'eigengrau') may be associated with fluctuations in the resting discharge of some cells in the visual pathways (§ 7.24). The relation of the background light to stationary images is discussed in §§ 8.16–8.18.

12

7.20. Subsidiary pathways

The optic nerve includes the following subsidiary pathways:

(a) Fibres controlling pupil reflex, movement of eyelids in response to a flash, and probably some eye-movements,
(b) Fibres going to parts of the brain other than the visual cortex,
(c) Fibres capable of carrying signals from the cortex to the retina (efferent signals): these are called centrifugal fibres (Granit 1962),
(d) Fibres from one retina to the other (called inter-retinal fibres).

The nerve divides, after leaving the chiasma, so that some fibres go to the pretectal region and some to the superior colliculus. The pretectal region is associated with the pupil reflex. The superior colliculus is possibly associated with movement of head and eyes when a bright light is seen.

It is difficult to understand why about 20 per cent of the 10^6 fibres of the optic nerve go to the superior colliculus and pretectal region since the information required for their functions (see (a) above) appears to be so simple that it could be carried by less than 100 fibres. Possibly they have some additional function not yet understood, but, on the other hand, their organization may be a relic of an earlier state of evolution which preceded the development of the visual cortex (Brindley 1960, pp. 89–92). The inter-retinal fibres do not, in any obvious way, assist binocular vision. The centrifugal fibres from mid-brain to retina may affect the sensitivity of the appropriate part of the retina when interest in one region in the visual field has been aroused.

7.21. Reaction time for eye-muscle response to visual signals

The distance from eye to cortex is about 10 cm, and the velocity of spikes in the optic nerve is about 30 ms^{-1} (§ 7.4). The transit time is therefore about 3 ms. This value is confirmed by direct measurement (Fischer 1932; Malis and Kruger 1956). After allowing 5 ms for delays at synapses, the total transit time, retina to cortex and back to the eye-muscles, is not more than 15 ms. The reaction time for movement of the eyes in response to unpredicted movement of a target is at least 150 ms (Chapter 15). The main part of this reaction time must thus be associated with processes in the cortex by which the magnitude and direction of movement is decided (§§ 15.3 and 15.12–15.14).

7.22. On-off signals in the visual system

Experiments on electrical signals in the optic nerve due to stimulation of visual receptors were carried out by Adrian and Matthews (1927, 1928). They recorded signals from electrodes placed on the optic nerve of the conger eel. Illumination of the retina produced a strong burst of spikes soon after the light was switched on, and another soon after it was switched off. There was a much slower rate of discharge when the illumination was maintained at steady level. Strong signals were received when illumination was changed, and weak ones when it was steady. The signals increased, though not in direct proportion, when the change of illumination was increased. They thus carry information about the time and amount of any change of retinal illuminance. Parallel results were obtained with other sensory responses. Subsequent research has shown that this kind of on-off response is basic to visual processes in general (Granit 1933, 1955, and 1962). It is desirable to consider next some results obtained in relation to visual systems whose lateral interactions are fairly simple.

7.23. Signals from individual receptors—*Limulus*

Hartline and Graham (1932) studied the horseshoe crab (*Limulus*),[†] whose eye consists of comparatively large units (ommatidia). Nerve-fibres extend from each of these units for several centimetres without the intervention of synapses or ganglion cells—though there are some horizontal connections. The optic nerve was dissected until electrodes connected to the remaining part gave spikes which were almost certainly from one ommatidium. When this ommatidium was illuminated there was a strong burst of spikes followed by a steady stream at a much lower rate (Fig. 7.8). The frequency in the initial burst was approximately proportional to the logarithm of the illuminance up to a maximum of about 100 spikes per second. The rate of steady firing was about a tenth of the initial rate. It increased with the illuminance but not according to any simple law. For flashes of up to about a second in duration the reciprocity law of Bunsen and Roscoe (that the response is proportional to the product of intensity and time) was valid. The course of light and dark adaptation and a threshold uncertainty related to photon fluctuations (§ 7.17 ff), were also observed.

† Hartline (1968) gives a summary of experiments on records from single nerve-fibres in the horseshoe crab and in the frog.

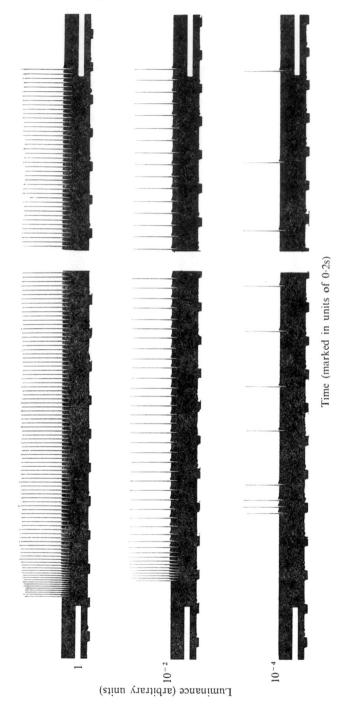

Time (marked in units of 0·2s)

Luminance (arbitrary units)

FIG. 7.8. Electrical response in optic nerve of Limulus to different levels of illumination (marked at left in arbitrary units). Time marker at intervals of 0·2 s. Termination of horizontal white line indicates onset of illumination. (From Hartline 1932.)

7.24. Vertebrate responses (frog)

Hartline (1938, 1940) observed responses in single nerve fibres of the frog. All fibres show a weak background of spikes at irregular intervals when there is no illumination. There are three types of responses to illumination.

(a) A sharp burst of spikes at 'on', and a steady stream, at a much lower rate, which persists as long as constant illumination is maintained.

(b) At 'on' the background discharge is extinguished; at 'off' there is a burst of spikes which decays in about 2 s leaving the background discharge.

(c) A burst of spikes at 'on' and a similar discharge at 'off'; the background discharge is maintained all the time.

These responses are shown diagrammatically in Fig. 7.9. Other responses are occasionally observed. All the effects, including the discharges at 'off', increase with the magnitude of the stimulus so that any one of them constitutes a 'signal' from which the magnitude of the illuminance could be inferred. The fibres which show response (c) respond strongly to small changes of illuminance and also to small movements of a spot of light on the retina.

These results indicate that retinal ganglion cells in the frog do not all have the same connections to the receptors, and that horizontal connections, which are numerous, play an important role. It is desirable to consider next some rather more simple kinds of interaction found in *Limulus*.

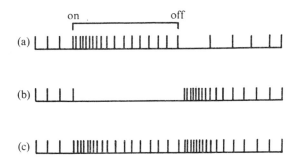

Fig. 7.9. Responses to onset and termination of illumination (frog). (a) On-fibre; (b) off-fibre; (c) 'on-off' fibre. (After Granit 1955.)

7.25. Lateral interaction in *Limulus*†

In *Limulus* each nerve fibre from which records are made cannot be traced unambiguously to an individual ommatidium. Nevertheless the fibres pass through a plexus of nerve tissue near to the receptors. If connection is made further from the receptor than this tissue, interaction between signals from neighbouring ommatidia can be observed, provided that this tissue is left intact. The first observation of this type was that two adjacent ommatidia exert a mutual inhibitory action. The rate of discharge in each, when both are stimulated, might be 20 per cent less than that obtained in one which is stimulated with the same illuminance, the other being in darkness. This *lateral inhibition* extends over a wide area around any given receptor, though the mutual interaction of two receptor-systems decreases as their separation increases. Lateral inhibition applies to the whole action of a receptor— including its ability to inhibit neighbouring receptors. Illumination of a receptor C (which is so far from A that its inhibitory effect on A is negligible) may inhibit a receptor B, which is nearer to A. The inhibitory effect of B on A is reduced, and signals in the fibre associated with A may be *increased* by illuminating C.

7.26. Synthetic effects in *Limulus*

The effects which have been described in the preceding paragraph have a time variation. Thus if a receptor A is steadily illuminated and a neighbouring receptor B, which has been in darkness, is suddenly illuminated, there is a sharp fall in the rate of firing from A after about 100 ms. This is followed by a partial recovery to a steady rate which is lower than that which was obtained when A alone was illuminated. If the illumination of B is suddenly removed, then the rate in A in-increases sharply to above normal after about 200 ms and then settles down to the normal rate. Taking these time relations into account, Ratliff and Mueller (1957) were able to find experimental conditions in which appropriate areas were illuminated for appropriate times so as to produce an 'on' signal in some nerve fibres, an 'off' in others, and an 'on-off' in yet others. In this way some of the phenomena which Hartline observed in the nerve fibres of the frog were simulated, at least qualitatively.

† The observations described are due to Hartline and a number of co-workers: Hartline (1949); Hartline, Wagner, and Ratliff (1956); Hartline and Ratliff (1957, 1958); Ratliff, Miller, and Hartline (1958). Summaries are given by Hartline (1968) and by Ratliff (1965).

In order to study the effect of lateral interaction on ability to make useful discriminations in the visual field, Ratliff and Hartline (1959) observed the response when the following two kinds of patterns were projected on to the eye of *Limulus*:

(a) a pattern containing a light area and a dark area separated by a sharp straight line boundary (Fig. 7.10(a));

(b) a pattern similar to (a) but with a graded boundary between the dark and the light areas (see Fig. 7.10(b)).

The pattern was moved, and the response in one receptor was measured when it was at different distances from the edge. The results are shown in Fig. 7.10(a) and (b). It may be seen from Fig. 7.10(a) that the effect

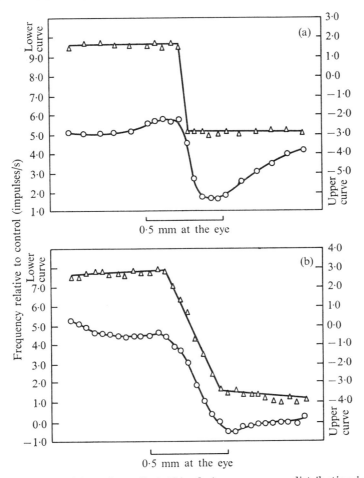

Fig. 7.10. Simulated boundary effect (*Limulus*): upper curve, distribution in target; lower curve, response, (from Ratliff and Hartline 1959); cf. Fig. 12.9.

of the mutual interactions is to emphasize the edge while *decreasing* the difference of signals between large areas (remote from the boundary) which have very different illumination. With the graded boundary (Fig. 7.10(b)) there are fringes, similar to the Mach bands, which are seen when a human subject views a graded boundary (§§ 12.26–12.32).

The effects observed in *Limulus* are only qualitatively similar to those obtained with vertebrates. They do not necessarily form part of the normal visual process in *Limulus*. Nevertheless it is important that a relatively simple type of interaction can produce these effects.

7.27. Organization of receptor fields

A ganglion cell gives the highest rate of firing in response to a small spot of light when the spot is in a certain position which is regarded as the centre of the receptor field. The response falls sharply as the spot is

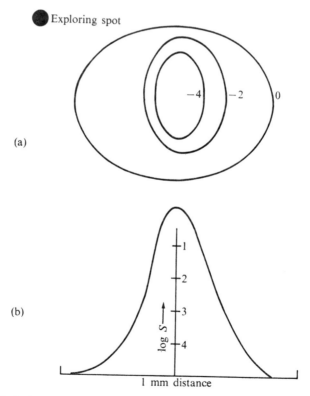

FIG. 7.11. Variation of sensitivity *S* (i.e. number of spikes per unit time) within a receptor field: (a) contour map, (b) log *S* vs distance. (From Hartline 1938.)

moved from this point in any direction. Hartline (1938) measured the threshold illumination required to produce a definite response, as a function of position, of the spot on the retina of a frog, and obtained contour maps (Fig. 7.11(a)). The variation of sensitivity is shown in (Fig. 7.11(b)).

7.28. Kuffler (1953) found that some ganglion cells in the cat retina gave an 'on' response to a spot of light in the centre of the receptive

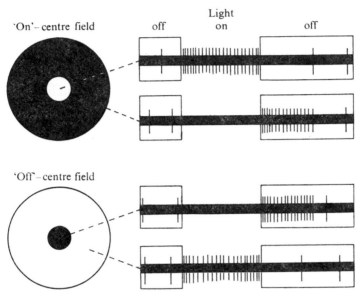

FIG. 7.12. On-centre and off-centre receptive fields. Effect of illumination of centre and periphery shown on right for cat retina. (Results obtained by Kuffler (1953). Figure reproduced from article by Hubel in Scientific American (1963) **209**(5), 57. © Scientific American 1963.)

field, and an 'off' response to one in a peripheral area. Other ganglion cells gave an 'off' response to central stimulation and an 'on' response to stimulation by a small spot of light in the periphery of the field (Fig. 7.12). In each case stimulation of the outer part of the field tended to inhibit the response to a stimulus in the centre. These are called 'on-centre' and 'off-centre' cells respectively. Barlow, Fitzhugh, and Kuffler (1957*a*, *b*) measured thresholds in various conditions of light and dark adaptation, and for spots of different sizes, colour, and duration. In the absence of a flash stimulus, there is a maintained discharge in any stage of adaptation. This is temporarily suppressed by illuminating the 'off-region' of the appropriate receptor field but returns, after five minutes, to a value which is not very different whether the eye is in

Receptive field of on-centre unit

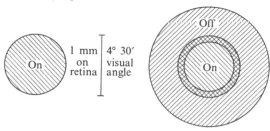

Dark-adapted   Light-adapted

FIG. 7.13. Change in organization of receptor field with dark adaptation (cat). (From Barlow, Fitzhugh, and Kuffler 1957*b*.)

steady light or in darkness, and does not depend strongly on the state of dark adaptation. The 'threshold' was defined as the minimum flash illumination which caused the rate or pattern of nerve impulses to differ from the maintained discharge by an amount which was recognized by the experimenter. It was found:

(a) that 'on-centre' and 'off-centre' ganglion cells were about equally abundant, had about the same threshold, and dark adapted in a similar way;

(b) that the threshold fell by more than 4 log units during dark adaptation which took 3 hours;

(c) towards the end of dark adaptation the opposed outer parts of the receptor fields ceased to function, the cells becoming simple 'on-units' or 'off-units' of the type found by Hartline in the frog (Fig. 7.13). This change is not a simple cone–rod transition.

7.29. Effect of spots of different sizes

One way of studying the organization of the receptor field is to start with a small spot which is moved until it gives maximum response from the cell under study. The variation of threshold illuminance when the diameter of the spot is increased is then measured. Complete spatial summation would require that this threshold should be inversely proportional to the area. When the spot is less than a millimetre in diameter the variation is not very different from this. However, above this size the threshold ceases to fall and then begins to increase, because part of the light falls on the outer part of the receptor field which is opposed to the centre. When the whole field is illuminated the response is small.

Wiesel (1960) made records from 82 cells in a cat retina. The cat has no fovea with very high resolution but there is an 'area centralis'. The range of lateral interaction was about 3° in this area and 6° in the periphery. The majority of the centres of the fields were about 1° in diameter. The area of the whole field was about 10 times as large as the area of the centre. Hubel and Wiesel (1960) made a similar investigation on the spider monkey (*Ateles*). This animal has a well-defined fovea. Spikes were observed from single nerve-fibres corresponding to receptive

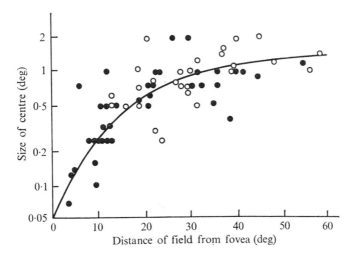

FIG. 7.14. Variation of size of centre of receptive field with distance from centre of fovea for cat retina. (From Hubel and Wiesel 1960.)

fields with centres situated at 4° to 60° from the centre of the fovea. Within this range the diameter of the centre of the receptor field varied from 5′ to 2° in a fairly regular way (Fig. 7.14). For technical reasons no records were obtained from the fovea itself. Extrapolation of the curve suggests that the diameters of centres of the receptor fields in the central fovea are about the same as the inter-cone distance.

7.30. Moving objects

The organization of the retina into receptive fields, in the way described above, is obviously capable of producing a time sequence of signals containing information about movement. For example, suppose that a black circular object is moved across the 'on-centre' of a receptive field, the diameter of the object being about equal to that of the on-central part of the field. Then the response will include, first a reduction in firing rate as the object blocks the 'on-centre', and then a sudden increase when it is again uncovered. There will be less important effects due to covering and uncovering of a small part of the off-surround, but the general pattern of response will be that shown in Fig. 7.15. For this object the response is the same no matter in which direction the movement takes place. Objects of different shape and size would give different patterns of response. For a small object the pattern will depend on whether the path lies exactly across the centre. Responses of this kind for a variety of objects and for different rates of movement† have been obtained by Kozak, Rodieck, and Bishop (1965).

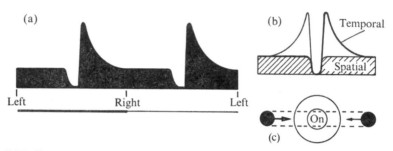

Fig. 7.15. Response to passage of black disc across on-centre receptive field. (a) Average response histogram for movement from left to right and back again as shown in (c). Thick and thin lines correspond to movements to left and right respectively. (b) Spatial and temporal variation of response. (After Kozack, Rodieck, and Bishop.)

7.31. Movement detectors

Barlow and Levick‡ (1965) have found ganglion cells in the retinae of rabbits which respond to movement in a different way. These cells give signals that do not depend very much on the shape or size of the object (provided it is fairly small) but respond to movement rather than to the object moved. The movement must have a component along a given axis and in a preferred direction (for any one of these cells). This kind of function cannot be predicted from the map of the receptive field obtained with static objects. It nearly certainly involves connection of at least two receptors to another cell (probably a bipolar) with a relative time delay. One possibility is shown in Fig. 7.16 in which the preferred direction is ABC. It is suggested that when the object moves in this direction, its arrival at A sends forward a signal which reaches the 'and' gate after a time interval Δt so that it passes the signal which it

† These results refer to records from cells in the L.G.B. (cat) but are qualitatively similar to less detailed records from retinal ganglion cells.
‡ See also Barlow, Hill, and Levick (1964).

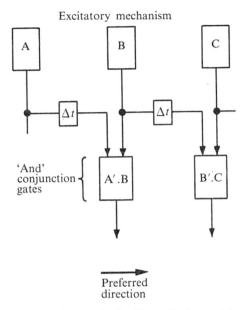

FIG. 7.16. Movement-detector logic. (From Barlow and Levick 1965.)

receives from B, i.e. *facilitation* occurs with a suitable time delay. A somewhat similar scheme involving *inhibition* (with a time delay) is also possible, and certain experiments favour this second scheme. The movement-detectors operate over distances which are very much smaller than the size of the detector field obtained by 'static' methods.

7.32. Colour discrimination at retinal level

A large number of experiments on colour matching in bipartite fields leave little doubt that, for human beings, the primary information about colour is that postulated by the trichromatic theory. The information content, under optimum conditions, is the same as that which would be obtained by three photo-cells with different variations of sensitivity with wavelength. This has led to a search for three kinds of retinal receptors each characterized by a different spectral sensitivity. Recently microspectrophotometry has revealed cones with three distinct absorption spectra (Wald 1964).

The trichromatic theory is concerned with the information content of the signals required to make the discriminations of luminance, hue, and saturation found in bipartite field experiments. It says nothing about the way in which this information is encoded before it reaches the level of perception. A considerable number of observations, chiefly on simultaneous contrast, support the idea (suggested by Hering 1875) that the main information involved in visual colour is encoded in three signals:

(a) the difference between white and black (i.e. total luminance);
(b) the difference between the amount of red light and the amount of green;
(c) the difference between the amount of yellow and the amount of blue.

This 'opponent-colour' theory is not an alternative to the trichromatic theory. The two theories are complementary since one deals with information content and the other with a particular way of encoding. In the next paragraph we shall describe evidence that the opponent-colour method of encoding is used in the visual system of some animals.

7.33. Opponent-colour encoding

Receptor fields of retinal ganglion cells of goldfish have been studied by Wagner, MacNichol, and Wolbarsht (1960). They first used white light stimuli and found, as expected from earlier work, some cells which gave typical 'on' responses, some which gave 'off', and some of the 'on-off' type. When this last type was illuminated with monochromatic light a dramatic wavelength dependence of the pattern was obtained. A pure 'on' response was obtained for wavelengths from 400 nm to 550 nm, and a pure 'off' response for wavelengths from 600 to 700 nm (Fig. 7.17). The long wavelengths showed the usual strong inhibitory influence on the resting discharge. Further work showed that the 'on' and 'off' action had different sensitivities which varied with wavelength as shown in Fig. 7.18, so that a sufficiently strong stimulus in the range 530–600 nm excited both effects and gave the 'on-off' response. It was also shown that for one wavelength a receptor field with 'on-centre' and 'off-periphery' and an intermediate 'on-off' region was obtained. These observations have later been considerably extended to show the existence of a complicated organization (Wagner, MacNichol, and Wolbarsht 1963; Daw 1968; and Hammond 1971).

Hubel and Wiesel (1960) have shown that a similar kind of discrimination exists in the retina of the spider-monkey. De Valois (1960 and 1964) and collaborators have shown that in the L.G.B. of the monkey (*Macaca mulatta*) there are cells which relay signals of the type which we have just described. There are other cells which respond to

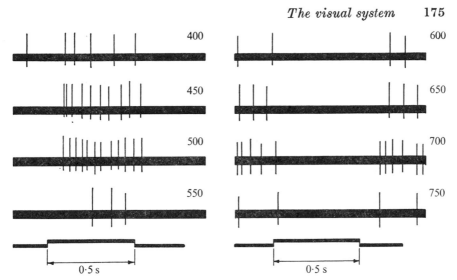

FIG. 7.17. Opponent responses to flash lasting 0·5 s: wavelengths in nanometres. (From Wagner, MacNichol, and Wolbarsht 1960.)

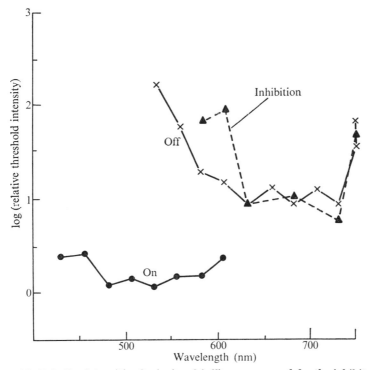

FIG. 7.18. Relative intensities for 'on' and 'off' responses and for the inhibitory action as functions of wavelength. (From Wagner *et al.* 1960.)

narrow bands in the spectrum (Sperling and Harwerth 1971). This last system is reminiscent of the earlier researches of Granit (1955) which led to his 'dominator and modulators' theory. It suggests that the higher vertebrates use more than one system of coding information about hue.

7.34. Analysis of information in the retina

We shall now summarize some of the results described in §§ 7.27–7.33 on the signals which go from the retina to L.G.B. and cortex. The following important features have been described:

(a) a large response to changes of illumination, and a smaller response to steady illumination,

(b) receptor fields with opposed centre and periphery—the receptor fields of different ganglion cells overlap,

(c) special movement detectors,

(d) cells which give mainly 'on-responses' to light at one end of the spectrum and 'off-responses' to light of other wavelengths.

7.35. The response of one ganglion cell in any one condition is a resultant or 'mixture' of signals from all the receptors in its field. In this mixture each receptor has a 'weighting factor' which may be positive or negative. A resultant of many signals contains less information than the individual observations from which it is derived. However, each receptor is connected to many ganglion cells (with different weighting factors) so the loss is not as great as if it were connected to one only. Even so, there is a large over-all loss of information, partly because (except in foveae) there is a convergence from receptors to ganglion cells. The analysis appears to preserve, and indeed to emphasize: (a) changes occurring in the visual field, especially local flashes of light or movements of objects; (b) boundaries between areas of different illuminance, and to a lesser extent, between areas of different hue. There is some evidence (McIlwain 1964) of a weak interaction of very wide range, possibly over the whole retina.† Also there are some signals in the optic nerve which relate to changes in the average illumination of the whole retina (Enroth-Cugell and Jones 1963). Burns and Webb (1970) found a widespread excitation in response to meaningful visual stimuli which was not evoked by meaningless patterns. This kind of signal is needed to provide a background against which the more

† Kuffler, Fitzhugh, and Barlow (1956) found a maintained activity in retinal ganglion cells, dependent only on local illuminance, but this may be used only for control of the pupil diameter (§ 8.21).

specific receptor-field system can operate by giving differences which are 'local' either in space or in time.

7.36. The lateral geniculate body (L.G.B.)

Work on the L.G.B. is reviewed by Granit (1962). Since then receptor field organization has been explored in greater detail. Some cells have fields similar to those of the retinal ganglion cells but with a sharper organization—e.g. a more precise balance between centre and opposed periphery (Hubel 1960). Some fields have an asymmetrical organization (Arden 1963a,b; Kozack, Rodieck, and Bishop 1965) like that of certain cortical cells (§ 7.39). There is a considerable difference between species in regard to the complexity of analysis carried out in the L.G.B. There are connections to other parts of the brain as well as to the visual cortex. In the L.G.B. signals from other senses (e.g. sound) may modify the visual analysis so as to emphasize certain parts of the visual field or certain aspects of the visual situation in the signals passed to the cortex—in psychological terms to direct attention to features of interest. Signals can pass from the L.G.B. to the recticular formation in the brain stem, and from the reticular formation to the visual cortex and to other parts of the brain. These signals may control 'arousal' in general, and 'visual attention' in particular† (Moruzzi and Magoun 1949). The existence of the appropriate connections is certain but their function is not.

7.37. Projection of visual field in the striate cortex

There is a topographical representation of the retina in the striate cortex in the sense that cortical cells have receptor fields. Areas in the cortical map are not proportional to the corresponding retinal areas. In man the fovea has a larger cortical representation than the whole of the extra-foveal retina even though it constitutes only about one ten-thousandth of the whole retinal area. Talbot and Marshall (1941) found (in monkeys) that the cortical distance corresponding to 1' in the foveal field was about 500 μm, i.e. 100 times the retinal distance. This implies an area magnification of 10^4:1. This magnification, coupled with the small size of foveal fields, makes possible high resolution of point sources together with a large number of pattern distinctions.

† See also *Brain mechanisms and consciousness* (Ed. Delafresnaye), Blackwell, Oxford (1954).

The crossing of fibres at the chiasma (§ 7.10) implies that each cerebral hemisphere receives information mainly from the contra-lateral half of the visual fields of *both* eyes (Fig. 7.5b). This brings to-gether information from corresponding areas of the two retinae, and makes possible the accurate comparisons which are needed for bi-nocular vision.

7.38. Multiple representation of visual fields in the cortex

Marshall and Talbot (1941) found two topographical representations of the visual field in the cat. One was in the striate cortex and another in an adjacent area. Hubel and Wiesel (1965) háve greatly extended these observations and have found a third area in which there is a different kind of topographical representation.† In a certain sense, each of these areas contains a multiple representation which may be explored by passing a probe downwards through the cortex to the underlying layers of cells. A hierarchy of cells was found; four ranks in this hier-archy were recognized. These were called

   (a) simple cells,
   (b) complex cells,
   (c) lower-order hyper-complex cells,
   (d) higher-order hypercomplex cells.

We shall refer to these as C_1, C_2, C_3, and C_4 cells respectively. A C_1 cell receives information several retinal ganglion cells, and thus from many receptors. Each other kind of cell receives information from at least two, and usually more, cells of the next lower rank. The stimulus required to excite a response becomes more sharply defined at each stage, and absolute location in the visual field (as opposed to loca-tion relative to another stimulus) becomes less well defined.

7.39. Simple cells (C_1)

The receptor fields of these cells are not circular, and they are larger than those of retinal ganglion cells. The cancellation of centre and surround is so precise that no change from the resting discharge is produced by diffuse illumination. A typical shape is shown in Fig. 7.19(a). This cell has an inhibitory centre and will detect a vertical black bar, up to 1° wide, which will give a strong positive signal as it crosses the centre. Cells of this shape with 'on' centres will similarly detect a slit of light. Cells whose fields had horizontal and vertical axes

† The paper quoted gives reference to earlier work of the same authors.

and several intermediate directions were found. A number of cells have fields like that shown in Fig. 7.19(b)—a small but very strong centre and an asymmetrically placed opposed region. These would accurately locate one edge (e.g. in a bipartite field) as the eye-movements moved its image across the centre (§ 8.1).

In one set of experiments (Hubel and Wiesel 1959) 9 units out of 45 examined were found which could be driven independently from homologous parts of the two retinae. The field geometry was the same

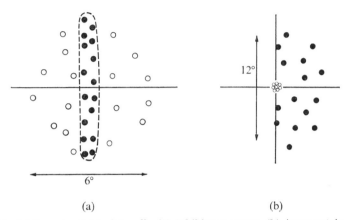

(a)   (b)

Fɪɢ. 7.19. (a) Receptor field of C_1 cell with inhibitory centre. (b) Asymmetric field with excitatory centre. (Excitatory regions marked ○; inhibitory regions marked ●.) (From Hubel and Wiesel 1959.)

for the two eyes and excitatory and inhibitory effects summated, algebraically so that illumination of an excitatory area in one eye and an inhibitory in the other gave nearly no response. A suitable moving object which is imaged on exactly corresponding areas of the two retinae will give a very different response from one which is imaged on areas which do not quite correspond.† This suggests that these cells may play some part in depth perception. The existence of 36 cells which respond only to one eye is interesting in relation to the results reported in § 13.17–13.20.

7.40. C_2, C_3, and C_4 cells

C_2 cells respond to a more precisely defined 'preferred stimulus' than C_1 cells, and ignore its exact position provided it is within the receptive

† In later experiments, cells were found which responded when images were displaced relative to corresponding positions, in a horizontal direction. These cells form 'depth-detectors'.

field. They give little response to small spots of light, and cannot be mapped into 'on' and 'off' areas. If the preferred stimulus is a slit, then there is an optimum width and an optimum rate of movement as well as optimum orientation. The effect increases with length until the slit straddles the field and then remains constant.

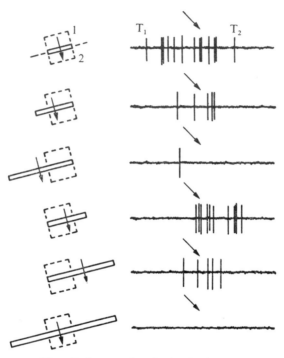

Fig. 7.20. Responses of C_2 cell whose preferred stimulus is a slit of well-defined length. Nerve impulses on the right between times T_1 and T_2 are recorded as slit passes from 1 to 2 across the field. Slits are all 8' wide and rate of movement is $3°$ s^{-1}. (After Hubel and Wiesel 1965.)

The receptor fields of C_3 cells are divided into parts which are antagonistic but in a different sense from the opposition found in cells of lower rank. A moving stimulus in one part of the field activates the cell. The same stimulus in another part reduces it. This has the effect that, for a slit stimulus there is an optimum length as well as width, orientation, and rate of movement (Fig. 7.20). This kind of behaviour is consistent with the hypothesis that the cell has positive connection to one C_2 cell (or group of C_2 cells) and negative connection to another. The C_4 cells have an even more precisely defined stimulus, which is usually quite small, but may be introduced in any part of a large field. Fig. 7.21(a) and (b) shows the behaviour of a cell which responds to a narrow tongue introduced from either of two perpendicular directions and in any part of the field. It gives little response to a wider tongue. The response of these cells combines information derived from many receptors so as to identify pattern-units (§ 13.9). There can be little doubt that these cells are samples of an extensive hierarchy in which geometrical aspects of the visual world are analysed to produce identifications of value to the animal (§ 7.44).

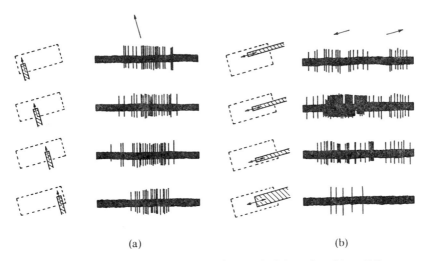

(a)   (b)

Fig. 7.21. (a) Response of C_4 cell to bar of suitable width introduced into different parts of the receptor field; (b) Response of same cell to bar of same width introduced into different parts of field and much weaker response to wider bar. (From Hubel and Wiesel 1965.)

7.41. Fatigue effect

The cell described in the preceding paragraph showed the following 'fatigue' effect: if the optimum stimulus (a tongue $\frac{1}{2}°$ wide) was repeatedly introduced into the same part of the receptor field at intervals of 2 s the response became less and less. After 7 trials it could scarcely be detected. It recovered completely when an interval of 10 s was left before repeating the stimulus. This 'fatigue effect' was obtained only when the stimulus was introduced repeatedly *into the same part of the receptor field*. If the cell was repeatedly stimulated by introducing the stimulus into different parts of the receptor field the response was maintained. This last observation suggests that the fatigue, or accommodation, occurs at a much lower level, possibly at retinal level. This effect is of interest in regard to the results reported in § 6.20.

7.42. Cortical signals related to contrast discrimination

Burns, Heron, and Pritchard (1962) investigated responses of cells in the visual cortex of the cat to a single straight boundary which was oscillated in a direction perpendicular to the boundary. All the cells that responded to retinal excitation were in a state of continuous activity when no visual stimulus was presented. The mean-frequency (measured over about 200 ms) fluctuated over a range of about 2:1. 'On-off' signals were observed when the boundary was oscillated in a suitable part of the receptor field, but the mean frequency (over about a minute) was very little affected by repetitive stimuli because, following a burst of spikes, there was a period in which the rate fell below the average rate when resting. They therefore divided a minute's record into short-time segments, and measured the mean frequency during each interval obtaining values f_1, f_2, etc., and computed

$$\frac{x^2}{\bar{f}} = \frac{1}{\bar{f}^2} \sum (f_1 - \bar{f})^2 \qquad (7.1)$$

where $\bar{f}$ is the mean-frequency over the whole minute. x^2 is a measure of the extent to which the stimulus drives the cell away from its mean frequency.

By this sensitive criterion, pattern movement of 2' to 5' (roughly corresponding to the inter-cone distance) could be detected, but there was no response to a stationary pattern with constant illumination. The effect of varying frequency and amplitude are shown in Figures

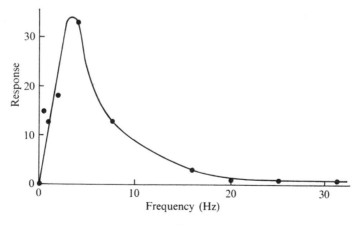

FIG. 7.22. Variation of response $(x^2/\bar{f})$ with frequency of oscillation; (From Burns, Heron, and Pritchard 1962.)

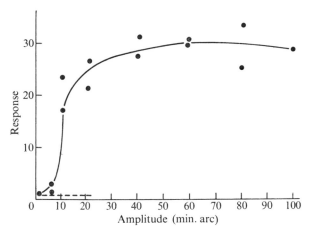

F I G. 7.23. Variation of response with amplitude of oscillation; – – – – – response to stationary stimulus. (From Burns, Heron, and Pritchard 1962.)

7.22 and 7.23, (compare with Figs. 10.3–10.5). The optimum frequency was about 3Hz and the optimum amplitude was 50′, implying an average speed of about $500' \, s^{-1}$. The eye-movements of the cat (recorded by Pritchard and Heron (1960) and Hebbard and Marg (1960)) include a drift at $30' \, s^{-1}$ and a tremor of median amplitude 0·3′. Saccadic movements are rare. The optimum movements are thus much faster than the natural movements, and it is possible that the cells studied are used to detect rapidly moving prey.

7.43. Burns and Pritchard (1964) carried out experiments with the boundary located at about 1° from the centre of the receptive field, in the preferred orientation, and oscillated at optimum frequency and amplitude. They compared results obtained when the centre was on the light side of the boundary with those obtained when it was on the dark side. In the former situation there were many more short intervals between spikes than on the light side. This difference depends more on luminance difference (i.e. on contrast) than on absolute luminance. This is one way in which the visual system can distinguish the light and dark sides of a boundary without using detailed information about eye-movements (§ 6.29).

Burns and Webb (1971) examined the responses to an oscillatory bright line, (a) when it was in an otherwise dark field, and (b) when it was near to, but on the dark side of, a parallel light-dark boundary (Fig. 7.24). There was considerable difference between these responses. Thus the stationary boundary which, by itself, caused no measurable change in the discharge of any of the cells, produced a substantial

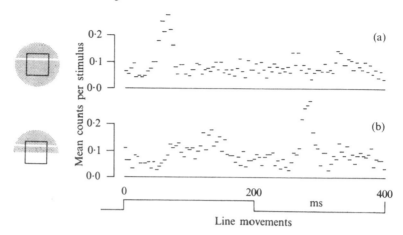

Fig. 7.24. Averaged responses of a cell in cat's visual cortex to oscillation of a white line; (a) field otherwise dark, and (b) placed near to, but on the dark side, of a stationary boundary. The insets at the side show the stimulus patterns superimposed on the receptive field, whose limits are indicated by the black square. (From Burns and Webb 1971.)

change in their response to another stimulus. This effect was also obtained when the stationary pattern was viewed by one eye, and the oscillating stimulus was in the appropriate part of the other retina.

7.44. Functional analysis of visual information

The experiments described in §§ 7.22–7.42 all have essentially the same objective—to understand the basic logical analysis of signals from the retinal receptors, as far as possible. A somewhat different approach is to look for some relation between responses to appropriate artificial stimuli and detection of prey or avoidance of predators.[†] Barlow (1953) suggested that the frog's visual analysis should contain a fly-detector. Maturana, Lettvin, McCullough, and Pitts[‡] (1960) investigated this in detail.

There is a well-defined point-to-point representation of the retina in the *Colliculi* (Gaze 1958). The ganglion cells form five natural types according to their function with respect to analysis of visual information, and the ends of the axons from three types each end in separate layers in the tectum. The two remaining types end in one stratum.

† An interesting research, to some extent of this type, on the beetle *Chlorophanus* was made by Reichardt (1957).

‡ See also Lettvin *et al.* (1959).

There are thus four strata each containing a map of the retina in respect of some function. The different types of ganglion cells respond in the following ways:

type I to an edge which moves into the field and remains there (spikes are observed after the edge has stopped moving);
type II to an edge of suitable convexity which is moving into the field;
type III to changes of contrast;
type IV to reduction of general illumination;
type V to total darkness (inhibited by light).

It is suggested that types IV and V enable the frog to place itself in a suitable shady spot where it is not too conspicuous either to an attacker or to its prey, and types I to III, taken together, constitute the 'fly-detector'.

7.45. Autrum (1959) showed that the frog has no permanent eye-movements like those found in man (and in some other animals). Thus, when the frog has found a suitable shady spot, the eyes are fixed —'on-off' action ceases—and the visual field becomes hazy. The entrance into the field of an object with edges of suitable curvature (i.e. about the size and shape of a fly) activates cells of types I to III, and it is assumed that there are cells which respond only when ganglions of types I to III are operating simultaneously. These higher cells must, at least crudely, represent the visual field because they 'command' the attack.

7.46. This 'functional' approach to visual perception in the frog has yielded results of great interest, yet there is a danger that something may be overlooked in this process of interpretation. *One* way in which the information in the five classes of cells can be usefully combined has been found, but there may be many more. For example, rate of movement may be used to distinguish one kind of moving object from another of similar shape. Some criteria which distinguish common enemies from other large moving objects may also exist. In this kind of analysis, we may stop too soon because we forget that the real frog is more complicated than the frog which an engineer would design.

7.47. The electroretinogram

When light falls on the retina there is a change in potential difference between an electrode placed on the cornea and one placed on the forehead. A record of this potential difference is called an *electroretinogram*

(E.R.G.). This potential can be recorded without discomfort to a human subject by using a contact lens with an embedded metal electrode whose end is flush with the inner surface of the lens. It has been shown by means of experiments (on excized eyes and on animals) with electrodes placed within the eye, that the potential arises in the retina. The E.R.G. experiments constitute the only way in which the electrical process associated with neural action in the human retina can be objectively studied. The E.R.G. forms a link between results obtained on animals with microelectrodes inserted in the visual pathway, and psychophysical experiments on human vision. Granit (1947) has reviewed his own extensive studies and related work of others on human and animal E.R.G. More recent critical reviews have been made by Brindley (1960 and 1971) and Granit (1962).

7.48. The electroretinogram may be recorded as a response to a brief flash of light or to modulated illumination. It is also evoked by the following display which does not involve any change in the total light incident. The subject views a square-wave grating of alternate light and dark bars. The grating is moved rapidly so as to interchange the black and white regions of the retinal image. In a modification of this display, the subject views a grating whose alternate bars are illuminated by light of two different wavelengths but of the same luminance. When the two wavelengths are interchanged an E.R.G. response is evoked even though there is no change of luminance in any part of the retina.

7.49. Gross potentials and micropotentials

The potentials recorded in the E.R.G. measure the over-all activity of the retina. They are resultants of a large number of vertical (and horizontal) signals in the visual pathway within the retina, but they do not yield any information about the activity of any one cell or even of a fairly large group of cells. In a similar way, the electroencephalograph (E.E.G.) can record, from suitably placed electrodes, information about changes in cortical activity associated with the receipt and processing of visual information, but once again the gross potential gives no data in relation to the potential spikes, directly associated with visual information. Records of fluctuations of total current in intercontinental cables may indicate that a financial or political crisis has led to a large increase in the number of messages, but convey nothing about the information in the messages. Psychophysical observations on stabilized images are largely concerned with vision, or failure of vision of targets (or of target details), which cover only a small part of the retina. Many observations can be understood in relation to signals similar to those described in §§ 7.22–7.43. There are a few points at which experiments on eye-movements and on vision with stabilized images can be related to the E.R.G. (§ 16.9) or to the E.E.G. (§§ 6.23–6.25, and § 16.10). These points of contact are, however, less numerous than might have been expected in view of the importance of E.R.G. and E.E.G. records in electrophysiology.

8

Theory of stabilized images

8.1. Introduction

The observations on vision with stationary images show that movements of the retinal image have an important function in normal visual perception. Before proceeding to more detailed experiments, it is desirable to consider this function in relation to the physiological experiments described in Chapter 7. Only general qualitative relations can be expected at this stage but these may be useful in suggesting further experiments.

8.2. Visual signals in normal vision

Consider the situation shown in Fig. 8.1 where the dots represent an idealized system of retinal receptors, and the line represents the boundary between a light and a dark region in the retinal image. Suppose that the low-frequency components of the eye-movements cause the boundary to oscillate so that the receptors shown in Fig. 8.2 are sometimes on the lighter side and sometimes on the darker side. Strong 'on-off' signals are then transmitted by these receptors, and these outline the boundary. If the eye-movements were simply oscillations about a mean position, these signals would decrease and possibly cease in a few seconds because some part of the neural system would accommodate (§ 7.41 and §§ 6.19–6.20). The drift component of the eye-movements retards this fade-out by transferring the mean position of the boundary to a new set of receptors. However, the drift movement may not be sufficient, by itself, for this function. Also if it continued unchecked in one direction (or with random changes of direction) it would move the point of interest away from the centre of the fovea. The saccades have two functions.

(a) to compensate the drift motion to some extent, and
(b) to change the centre of fixation (§§ 14.15–14.18) sufficiently to maintain the visual signals (§ 7.41).

This description in terms of 'on-off' signals does not take account of the structure of receptor fields. The electrophysiological results indicate that movement of a boundary to-and-fro across a receptor field must generate strong signals in the associated cell. The organization of fields described in § 7.38 ff. show how this movement may be used to

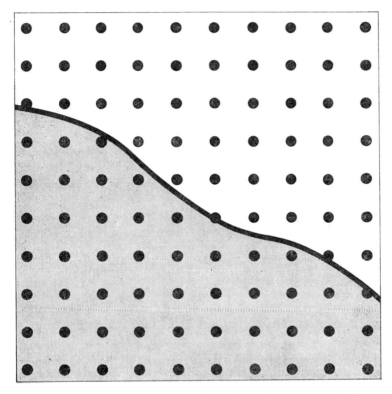

FIG. 8.1. Light-dark boundary superposed on schematic array of retinal receptors.

identify different pattern units. Some details of this process will be considered later. Here, it is important to note that all these actions depend on movements of the retinal image.

8.3. The experiment on reversed movements of the retinal image (§ 6.29) shows that some signal not associated with the direction of the eye-movements must exist to give information about which side of a light-dark boundary is darker. This may be an area signal of the type found by Enroth-Cugell and Jones (§ 7.35), or a more local interaction between signals from cells near to, but on opposite sides of, the boundary (§ 7.43). Probably a similar signal is used to discriminate which

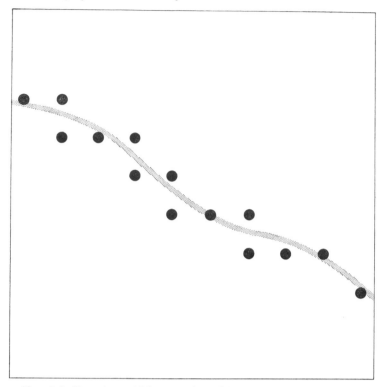

F IG. 8.2. Receptors which are activated by oscillation of boundary.

side of a red–green boundary is red, though this is not quite certain (§ 6.29).

With this general description we may now discuss what happens when the basic 'on-off' signals associated with boundaries are cut off, or greatly reduced, by the stabilized image technique or by the use of other stationary, or nearly stationary, retinal images.

8.4. Visual stimuli

The following kinds of visual display will now be considered.

1(a) *Ganzfeld with steady illumination.* The whole retina is illuminated so that, as nearly as possible, the illuminance has the same value at all points on the retina, and this value is also constant with time.

(b) *Ganzfeld with varying illumination.* The retinal illuminance varies with time but is the same for all retinal areas at any given time.

2(a) *Stationary image with steady illumination.* The illuminance varies with position on the retina but remains constant with time.

(b) *Stationary image with varying illumination.* The illuminance varies with time but relative values at different points on the retina remain unchanged.

3(a) *Moving images.* The whole image moves together owing to eye-movements or to imposed movements of a stabilized image.

(b) *Moving images.* Movement of part of the retinal image due to movement of an object within the field.

Normal visual situations include both movements of the retinal image as a whole and movements of images of objects moving within the field of vision. In normal vision these two kinds of movement can be distinguished in most situations (§§ 16.1–16.2).

8.5. Ganzfeld (steady illuminance) (1(a))

With stimulus 1(a), the 'on-off' responses are not stimulated. Any signal at cortical level must depend on the small differences between the pattern of spikes in the resting discharge of retinal ganglion cells and a pattern which represents steady, uniform illuminance. Specific pattern detectors (§§ 7.39–7.40) are not stimulated, but it is possible that some other cortical cells show an increase—or possibly a decrease—in the number of short intervals between spikes (§ 7.43). At retinal ganglion level, the effect of uniform illumination may be to reduce the resting discharge (§ 7.24). The ganzfeld may be regarded as a more extreme condition than a pattern stabilized image in which different areas of the retina receive different, though constant, amounts of light. Yet, although a ganzfeld does darken considerably, the black field appearance is obtained with the stabilized image but not with the ganzfeld. Most experimental arrangements for producing a ganzfeld give a decrease of illuminance towards the periphery of the retina. Also, if the pupil reflex has not been paralysed, there are slow fluctuations of retinal illuminance with time. It is possible that these residual effects prevent the development of the black field.

8.6. Ganzfeld (fluctuating illuminance) (1(b))

In condition 1(b) 'on-off' signals should be stimulated at receptor level, but since all receptor fields are uniformly illuminated the compensation at cortical level, in the cells whose responses were investigated by Hubel and Wiesel (§ 7.39), should be very precise. The type of signal reported by Enroth-Cugell and Jones (§7.35) should remain, and this may enable the variation of retinal illuminance to be perceived. However, these signals are weak. Some estimate of their effect may be obtained by experiments on the smallest perceived change and rate of change of illuminance in a ganzfeld (§ 11.9), and with a stabilized image (§ 11.7).

8.7. Stabilized images—steady illumination

Situation 2(a) is the normal condition for experiments on stabilized retinal images if stabilization is perfect. Those cells which detect light in the constant ganzfeld, situation 1(a), may be expected to operate, but only in proportion to the area of the retina which is stimulated. Since the ganzfeld experiments indicate that these signals are weak, even when the whole retina is illuminated, and since most stabilized images are confined to fairly small regions of the retina, very little contribution to visual perception may be expected from this kind of signal. Any boundary between areas of different illuminance is likely to intersect the receptor fields of many retinal ganglion cells and a pattern of lateral interaction will be established. When the boundary cuts through a receptor field there may be signals which depend on whether the centre is within the illuminated area and on the fraction of the opposed periphery which is illuminated. In most of the electrophysiological experiments, receptor fields have been explored with brief flashes of light and 'initial response' has been measured. The stabilized image produces steady illumination for all receptor fields, and the initial burst of spikes should be over in a few milliseconds leaving only weak signals. It is therefore not remarkable that the field should go dark and hazy after 2–3 s. Indeed, if we consider only effects at receptor level we should expect the field to become hazy in about 0·1 second. However, it is reasonable to suppose that, after the signals from the retinal ganglion cells have ceased, time is required for activity to decay in linked groups of cells at cortical level. The existence of a 'memory' of this type extending over a few seconds is shown by the 'waterfall effect' (§ 16.13).

Vision may be expected to depend critically on conditions at the boundaries between light and dark areas. If the boundaries are so sharp that they effectively divide through the on- and off-parts of the receptor fields, response should be very different from that obtained with gradients of illuminance which are so slow that any one receptor field has nearly uniform illuminance (Fig. 9.1). Experiments on the effect of varying the sharpness of the change from a light to a dark area are suggested. It is also desirable to have tests on boundaries between opponent colours (§§ 7.32–7.33). Experiments on sharpness of boundary are reported in §§ 9.11–9.16, and on colour in § 9.18.

8.8. Stabilized images with varying illumination (situation 2(b))

In this situation, the 'on-off' action is stimulated by a continuous change of illumination if the variation is rapid enough. A continuous variation of illuminance should therefore make it possible to see stabilized images more clearly. Yarbus has found a rapid continuous variation of luminance does have this effect (§§ 11.7–11.8). Very complicated effects are obtained in experiments on flicker fusion in normal vision. The parameters which can be varied are numerous. They include

(i) mean luminance of target,
(ii) amplitude of fluctuation,
(iii) frequency of fluctuation,
(iv) wave form,
(v) colour (hue and saturation).

In this situation it is not easy to design experiments on stabilized images in fluctuating light whose results have simple and unambiguous interpretations. However, the situation with flickering stabilized images is a little less complicated than that obtained with normal vision. The effect of uncontrolled image-movement in modulating the illuminance on any retinal receptor is absent. Movement detectors which depend on a time delay (§ 7.31) will not operate. A number of experiments on stabilized images with periodic fluctuation of illumination are described in § 11.11ff.

8.9. Moving images (situation 3(a) and (b))

Normal vision involves moving retinal images, but the retinal image movements are then very complicated. The stabilized image technique enables controlled movements to be used in order to find out what parts of the natural movements are important. It is also possible to study the effects of movements which do not lie in the normal range (§ 9.5). One important aim of experiments on vision with controlled movements of the retinal image should be to find movements which differentiate between visual discriminations. If, for example, a regime could be established in which shape was clear, but not colour, then important deductions concerning colour discrimination could be made. Experiments on controlled movements are described in Chapter 10. There is considerable progress towards understanding which movements are useful and some indication that all kinds of visual discrimination are not equally affected by saccadic movements (§§ 9.28 and 11.22–11.23).

8.10. Stabilized images—type I

Now consider the four types of appearance of stabilized images described in §§ 6.3–6.12. The clear picture seen when a stabilized image is first displayed, or when it is suddenly moved to a neighbouring region of the retina, presents no difficulty. The initial display gives strong 'on' signals in appropriate receptors and these carry the information needed for a sharply-defined image to be perceived (§§ 12.1–12.12 and 12.18). Movement of the image by a distance which is a substantial fraction of a linear dimension of a receptor field should stimulate signals in a new set of pathways. Modulation of the luminance stimulates 'on-off' signals over a large part of the visual field and thus supplies the information needed for a clear picture. Thus, in all the situations in which a sharp image is seen, suitable signals are generated by processes which have been extensively investigated by electrophysiologists.

8.11. Type II. Hazy field

The hazy field is observed in situations where 'on-off' signals are not operative. Thus both luminance boundaries (between light and dark areas) and hue boundaries (between areas of different hue) become ill defined. What remains must be perceived by means of signals which do not depend on eye-movements. Signals of this kind have been detected (§§ 7.35 and 7.43) but they are much weaker than those generated by movement of a suitable target across the receptor field associated with a cortical cell. Some experiments indicate that some signals associated with boundaries continue when the retinal image is stabilized, but these signals are of a lower order of magnitude than the signals which operate when eye-movements are present (§ 9.16).

8.12. Local adaptation

When a stabilized image is displayed for some minutes each part of the retina becomes adapted to the light which it receives. This adaptation reduces the difference between signals from regions which receive light of different illuminance and hue. It seems probable that this process would produce a hazy field after a few minutes, but in fact the hazy field appears in a few seconds. At this stage only a small part of the photo-chemical adaptation has taken place. By testing with small spots of light superimposed on the stabilized image, it has been shown that adaptation continues long after the image has disappeared or become very hazy (§§ 9.33–9.34). The establishment of a hazy field (and of appearances III and IV) must be due to a more rapid process than photo-chemical adaptation.

8.13. Type IV. Fluctuation

When the signals from the retina have been weakened in the way described in the preceding paragraphs, cells at cortical level which respond to specific pattern stimuli, may receive signals that do not greatly exceed the fluctuations of their resting discharge. The visual system has then a 'threshold signal' concerning a certain element of pattern in a certain area of the visual field. It is well known that, in all sensory experiments, when the signal is near 'threshold' the subject gives some positive responses and some negative responses. Thus, when the appropriate cortical cell is receiving weak stimuli, sometimes the pattern element is seen and sometimes it is not. If the fluctuations in signals in different cortical cells are uncorrelated, then the different pattern elements do not affect one another. Occasionally several elements may give positive responses simultaneously in favour of parts of a certain well-known pattern. The visual system may then give a positive signal in respect of the pattern as a whole—even when the pattern displayed is incomplete (§§ 6.17 and 13.8). In other circumstances the negative responses of a large number of cells belonging to sections of a given pattern may override positive signals from some elements (§§ 9.12 and 9.23).

8.14. Type III. Black field

On some occasions the hazy field is succeeded by a 'black field' which remains until stabilization is disturbed, and there is strong evidence that action at a central level is involved. The following is a tentative theory of this effect. When the hazy field occurs, most of the specific pattern detectors are not giving clear signals. The hue-detectors are giving only feeble signals. Thus there are weak signals that some visual stimulus is displayed but all specific signals needed to identify it are zero or very abnormal. All the signals associated with meaningful patterns are confused. This leads to a reduction of those signals which control visual attention, possibly through the reticular formation. This loss of awareness leads to a further loss of intelligible visual information which in turn further reduces visual attention. By this kind of 'vicious circle', or positive feed-back, the whole visual perception system becomes inoperative and the field goes black. A strong external stimulus—visual or non-visual—is needed to restore vision when this regime has been established.

8.15. This situation is not likely to occur unless the subject is free from all stimuli which are recognized as uncomfortable. It is more likely to occur when an anaesthetic has been used in connection with a device attached to the eye (provided the anaesthetic is strong enough) than with a tight-fitting contact lens without an anaesthetic. A necessary condition is the establishment of stabilization which is so good that residual movements of the retinal image are not large enough to produce clear signals in any of the specific detectors. This implies that the demands on accuracy of stabilization increase when sharp boundaries are present in the foveal part of the retinal image. Thus type IV rather than type III is likely to be observed when the target boundaries are mainly in the periphery and when any boundaries in the foveal region are not sharp (§§ 6.11 and 9.12). When type III fluctuations are observed, the pattern elements which are seen cannot be related to possible directions of small movements of the retinal image due to destabilization. It remains possible that, for any given target, accuracy of stabilization is one factor which affects visual attention and hence determines whether type II or type III or type IV appearance are seen during one particular experimental session. It is, however, probable that once reasonably good stabilization has been established, the comfort of the subject and the kind of target displayed, have more effect than a further improvement of stabilization (§ 10.13).

8.16. After-images

Barlow and Sparrock (1964) have given the following discussion of the relation between after-images and stabilized images. They start with the concept of 'equivalent background light', introduced by Crawford (1937, 1947), in presenting his results on dark-adaptation (§ 7.19). This supports the concept of an 'intrinsic background noise' derived from fluctuations in the photo-chemical state of receptors and leading to a fluctuating state of excitation in some ganglion pools (Rushton 1965).

In the first few minutes of dark adaptation (following exposure to a moderately high retinal illuminance of 10^3 to 3×10^4 td) the equivalent background derived from Crawford's measurements on the parafovea is fairly strong. The same amount and distribution of light derived from an external illuminated screen would be seen as a moderately strong and clear image. In fact, after about 10 s, only a weak and hazy after-image is perceived with some difficulty.† Barlow and Sparrock suggest that these after-images appear weak and hazy because they are stationary on the retina. They cover the area which received the original strong stimulus, and this area does not move in response to eye-movements. The appearance is, indeed, very similar to the type-II appearance of a stationary image.

8.17. Direct measurement of equivalent background

Barlow and Sparrock consider that previous attempts to measure the equivalent retinal illuminance of after-images by comparison with small screens of known luminance have given irregular and conflicting results because the after-image is stationary on the retina and the comparison patch is not. On the view that it is necessary to compare like with like, it should be possible to derive the equivalent retinal illuminance of the 'background light' by measuring the luminance of targets which, when viewed as stabilized images, appear to match the after-image. This comparison was made at different stages during the course of dark-adaptation. The values of equivalent light obtained this way agreed with those obtained by Crawford's method within an error of a few tenths of a log unit in most conditions.

If stabilized images and after-images are similar in the above way it should be possible to produce negative stabilized images analogous to negative after-images. This was done by superimposing a general field with unstabilized edges upon a stabilized image. The stabilized area becomes darker than the surround although it receives more light. Also, if two stabilized images are derived from targets of different luminance, the one which is brighter when seen as a positive stabilized image is darker when seen as a negative image. This happens because the extra light in the stabilized area bleaches pigment, reducing the sensitivity of the retina to the background light. Other experiments related to this effect are described in §§ 9.33–9.35.

---

† After-images imprinted by very strong flashes (near the damage threshold) remain strong and clear much longer.

8.18. Differences between stabilized images and after-images

The above experiments were made with targets which had extra-foveal boundaries. Even with these, Barlow and Sparrock did not find complete equivalence. Initially there was a colour difference between the stabilized and unstabilized image. Also, although it was usually possible to find a match between a stabilized image and an after-image which was valid when they were viewed as positive images or as negative images (by superimposing the same unstabilized background on both), this was not always so. The match failed in early stages of adaptation, and also near the rod–cone transition. Brindley (1959), in the course of observations on extra-foveal after-images, which were produced by strong flashes of light, observed a similarity between after-images viewed more than 15 s after the stimulus and stabilized images. During the first 15 s complicated colour changes are observed in the after-images. Brindley ascribes these to rearrangement of neural interactions. No similar phenomena are observed with stabilized images.

8.19. Foveal after-images

A sharp image may be imprinted on the retina by a target illuminated with a fairly strong flash of light of duration up to a few milliseconds. If the image is on the fovea, the target is seen as a strong, clear, positive after-image at about 1–3 s after a flash, whose integrated retinal illuminance is about 10^3 to 10^4 td–s. The image remains positive, but gradually becomes less sharp until it disappears at about 10 s after the flash. Subsequently it appears as a hazy image which looks very like a stabilized image (type III).

A stabilized retinal image is seen clearly if the retinal illuminance is varied rapidly (§ 11.7). This suggests that the clear positive after-image may be associated with a rapid variation of the equivalent background light during the period immediately after the flash. The results of Crawford (1947) show that for a variety of conditions, the equivalent background light is approximately proportional to t^{-n} from about 3 s to 100 s after a flash. n varies a little with experimental conditions, but within the range 1·7 to 2·5. The rate of change of equivalent illuminance (using the definition given in § 11.7) is n/t. A stabilized image is very clear when this rate is 1·0, and is seen when it is 0·3. On this basis the after-image should be very clear at about 2 s and should disappear at about 8 s. These times are approximately correct but measurements under a wider range of conditions are needed to test adequately the hypothesis that the observed phenomena of the positive after-image are associated with variation of the equivalent background.

8.20. The foregoing discussion may be summarized as follows. After-images following a flash go through 3 stages.

(a) An initial phase (which lasts about 1 s for foveal after-images but much longer for after-images in the parafovea and periphery). In this phase colour and apparent luminance change rapidly. This phase is probably associated with overload of the visual system and re-arrangement of neural connections.

(b) A second phase, which lasts about 10 s, for foveal after-images following moderately strong flashes. In this the after-image is like a stabilized image with rapidly changing illumination.

(c) A third phase in which the after-image is hazy, and structure is seen intermittently. The after-image is then like a stabilized image with steady illumination.

8.21. Pupil reflex

Gerrits, de Haan, and Vendrik (1966) measured the diameter of the pupil (by flash photography), when the subject was viewing a stabilized image which had faded so that little or no light was perceived. The size of the pupil is the same, within experimental error, as it is when the same retinal illuminance is viewed as an unstabilized image. This shows that the signals which go from the retina to the superior colliculus or pretectal region (§ 7.20) are not affected by eye-movements in the way described in § 8.1. They depend on the photo-chemical state of the receptors which fall within a certain area of the retina, rather than on the signals from a boundary. If the pupil reflex is to assist in protecting the retina from strong light, the signal which controls it must not be cancelled when the whole of the receptor fields of many retinal ganglions are uniformly illuminated. This constitutes one reason why area signals (§ 7.35) must exist, and why the balance between centre and periphery of a receptor field is less precise at the retinal ganglion level than at the L.G.B. or cortex (§ 7.36).

The experiment of Gerrits *et al.* was carried out under conditions which probably produced a hazy field (§ 6.6). It is not certain that the same result would be obtained when the black field was present (§ 6.7).

9

Discrimination of luminance and hue

9.1. Boundaries in relation to receptor fields

This chapter is mainly concerned with experiments on the differences between contrast-discrimination in normal vision and in vision with stabilized images. Before describing the experiments, it is desirable to extend the dynamical theory of normal vision which has been outlined in § 8.1. Suppose that Fig. 9.1 represents a set of receptor fields with 'on-centres' and 'off-surrounds'. This is simpler than the retina because we are not representing the overlapping of receptor fields and are not including any fields with 'off-centres' and 'on-surrounds'. These features are not needed for our present purposes and it is also unnecessary to specify whether the fields belong to retinal ganglion cells or to cortical cells.

Suppose that a visual target consisting of a circular patch of light on a dark area is suddenly exposed. Then receptor fields which lie wholly within the lighted area transmit weak signals because their 'on-regions' and 'off-regions' mutually inhibit each other (§ 7.28). Fields wholly within the dark region transmit only their 'resting' discharge (§ 7.42). Fields which are intersected by the boundary contribute signals because the portions illuminated do not, in general, balance. Thus a static boundary is perceived when it is first exposed. After a few seconds, signals become weaker. The boundary either disappears or becomes hazy like an after-image. If the boundary oscillates, so that sometimes it crosses the small centres of the receptor fields, then strong signals will be generated by the processes described in §§ 7.39–7.40. Even these die out after a fairly short time, but vision may be maintained by moving the boundary to new receptor fields (§ 7.41).

9.2. This account of normal vision implies that conditions at and near the boundary are of critical importance. For a target which contains light and dark areas, visual perception depends almost entirely on those receptors which are close to the mean position of the boundaries, i.e. within the dashed lines in Fig. 9.1. In this region conditions are far from simple. Oscillation of the boundary alters the photochemical state of these receptors and also continually changes the lateral interactions. Detailed study of conditions near the boundary, by direct measurement of pigment density or by other physiological methods, is very difficult. It is, however, possible to study the effects of variations of sharpness (and of other conditions at the boundary) on the perception of contrast. These psychophysical experiments cannot give precise information on

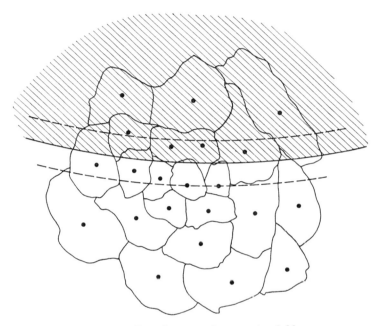

Fɪɢ. 9.1. Boundary crossing receptor fields.

physiological conditions, but they do provide fairly definite evidence about the range of lateral interaction for different regions of the retina and for different hues. They also suggest that there are at least two 'signals' involved in visual perception. These have different ranges of interaction and depend in different ways on eye-movements.

9.3. The bipartite field

Many experiments on discrimination of luminance and hue have been carried out with a circular target divided into two parts by a diameter (Fig. 9.2). The two parts differ in luminance, or in hue, and the difference is reduced until the subject has difficulty in perceiving it. The percentage V of observing time for which the subject can perceive the difference is then used to establish a threshold. V is called the *visibility*. This quantity is used as a measure of visual perception. It is not suggested that there is a linear relation between V, or log V, and any physiological signal. It is assumed that, when V is large, the signal associated with visual perception is large enough to be readily distinguished from background noise. A small value for V indicates that the signal/noise ratio is so low that the subject has difficulty in deciding whether a signal is present or not.

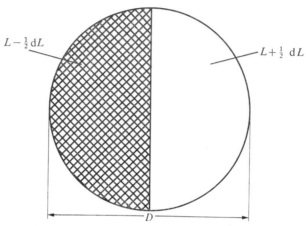

Fig. 9.2. Bipartite field: $L = \log$ (luminance).

It is also not necessary, for most of the interpretation, to know whether the residual vision obtained with the stabilized image is due to imperfect stabilization or to processes analogous to those which maintain perception of after-images. The differences between perception of contrast with the stabilized image and perception in normal vision are certainly due to elimination of a large part of the eye-movements of fixation. These differences are very large and we are concerned with the existence of differences and not with quantitative measurement against a well-defined scale.

9.4. The experiments described in §§ 9.5–9.17 refer only to differences of luminance (and not differences of hue) between the two halves of the field. $L - \frac{1}{2}\mathrm{d}L$ and $L + \frac{1}{2}\mathrm{d}L$ are logarithms (to base 10) of the luminances in cd m^{-2}. We shall describe experiments on the effects of varying

(a) the logarithmic difference $\mathrm{d}L$ (i.e. the logarithm of the ratio of the two luminances),

(b) the mean value of L,

(c) the size of the target (measured by the visual angle D subtended by a diameter),

(d) the sharpness of the boundary, and

(e) the eccentricity, i.e. the visual angle ε between the direction of the centre of the target and the axis of fixation.

It is found that these factors interact in a rather complicated way, but most of the results can be described in terms of a lateral interaction related to sizes of receptor fields similar to those which have been found in experiments on animals (§§ 7.28 and 7.29), or on human beings (Hallett 1963; Baumgardt and Hillman 1961).

In the experiments to be described in §§ 9.6–9.10, the boundary between the two parts of the target is very sharp. The boundary between the two parts of the retinal image is less sharp owing to passage through the stabilizing system and also through the dioptric system of the eye. The sharpness of the retinal image is discussed in § 9.10.

9.5. Effect of varying dL (white light)

The curve shown in Fig. 9.3 represents the variation of V with dL for white light. It incorporates data for 7 subjects obtained by four experimenters (Fender 1956; Clowes 1961; Riggs and Tulunay 1959; West 1965 and 1967). For $V = 50$, dL is about 0·3. This may be compared with a value of d$L = 0\cdot005$ for $v = 50$ with normal vision. Some subjects show a steeper sigmoid curve. The steepest part of the curve occurs at a different value of dL for each subject. Thus the mean curve, shown in Fig. 9.3, is less steep than many of the curves obtained for single subjects.

Clowes (1961) made observations under the following conditions.

(i) Normal vision—subject encouraged to move his eye so as to obtain best vision.

(ii) Normal vision—subject asked to fixate the boundary as accurately as he could.

(iii) Stabilized retinal image.

(iv) Subject fixating as in (ii) but normal retinal image movements of fixation exaggerated.

The apparatus shown in Figs. 5.11 and 5.12 was used. Condition (iv) was obtained by making the magnification of the telescope T equal to $-\frac{1}{2}$, so that $F = -2$ (§ 5.15). The results are shown in Fig. 9.4. For condition (i) the subject can perceive a difference between the two parts of the field nearly all the time, provided dL is greater than about 0·01

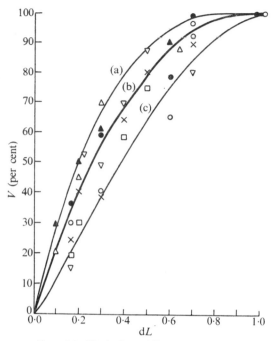

FIG. 9.3. Variation of V with dL (white light).

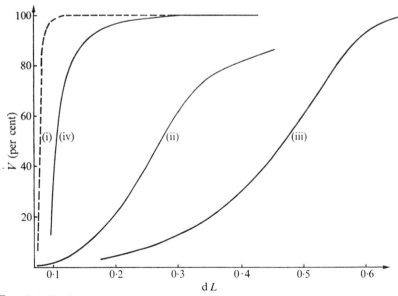

FIG. 9.4. Variation of V with dL; (i) Normal vision; (ii) unstabilized target but subject fixating boundary; (iii) stabilized retinal image; (iv) exaggerated movements of fixation. (From Clowes 1961.)

(the corresponding ratio of two sides is 100:97). V falls sharply when dL is reduced beyond this point. For normal vision with fixation (condition (ii)), the results are variable, since they depend very much on how accurately the subject succeeds in fixating during any one trial. The mean values of dL (for $V = 50$) are ~0·005 for normal vision without fixation, 0·28 for normal vision with fixation, 0·5 for stabilized vision, and 0·11 when the normal movements of fixation are exaggerated.

9.6. An interesting feature of these results is the very large difference between normal vision with fixation and normal vision without fixation. A similar large difference is found in colour matching. Differences of hue, which are easily perceived when eye-movements are not restricted, quickly disappear if the boundary is fixated. Thus the residual movements of fixation are not sufficient to maintain the most sensitive judgements of contrast, and need to be supplemented by semi-voluntary movements. It is therefore of considerable practical importance that observers using instruments, such as polarimeters and colorimeters, in which two halves of a bipartite field have to be adjusted to equality, should be instructed *not* to fixate the boundary. The most accurate judgement is obtained by looking into the instrument intermittently and accepting the first impression. Similarly, when comparing fabrics, it is best to look away from the samples at a neutral ground and then look back, briefly, at the juxtaposed samples.

9.7. Variation with dL (red, green, blue)

The variation with dL when both sides of the field are illuminated with red light is similar to that obtained with white light (West 1967). For blue and green, some subjects give about the same result as with white light, but others show a much slower increase of V with dL (Fig. 9.5). The reason for this difference is not known. In later experiments on bipartite fields, with the same hue (but different luminances) on the two sides of the boundary, it was found that results obtained with white, red, and green light were similar, provided that the green filter cut out all light of wavelength below about 500 nm. Attention was therefore concentrated on three conditions: (a) white (b) blue (produced by inserting an Ilford 306 filter, which transmits wavelengths *below* 480 nm), and (c) minus-blue (produced by inserting an Ilford 110 filter, which transmits wavelengths *above* 520 nm). In a few experiments Chance OR1 and OGr1 filters were used to produce red and green light, respectively.

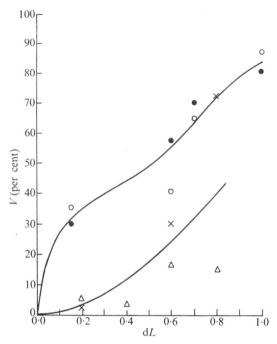

FIG. 9.5. Variation of V with dL for green light. Upper curve for subjects D.C.W., ●; D.F.B., ○; and M.B.C., ×. Lower curve for subjects L.A.R., △; and M.B.C., ×. (After West 1967.)

9.8. Variation with mean luminance (L)

West (1967) included experiments on variation of luminance in a series of experiments in which all the parameters (a) to (e), mentioned in § 9.4, were varied. Different hues were also used. For any one hue, L was varied by 2·5 (i.e. the luminance was changed by a factor of 300). The maximum available luminances were 14 000 cd m⁻² for white, 10 000 cd m⁻² for minus-blue, 650 cd m⁻² for red, 800 cd m⁻² for green, and 100 cd m⁻² for blue. Statistical analysis showed that the variance associated with L did not significantly differ from zero. Fender (1956), in a smaller number of experiments, also found no significant dependence of V with L when a bipartite field was used.

The above results do not, of course, exclude a small variation of V with L. Tests on other targets (Fender 1956 and Evans 1965b) show a small increase of V when L is increased. Since the variation of V with L (within the photopic range) is small, accurate adjustment of L is not necessary in most experiments with stabilized images (§ 13.11).

9.9. Effect of eccentricity

The variation of V with eccentricity (§ 9.4) for a bipartite field of 90′ diameter and a sharp boundary was investigated. It was found that, when the target was outside the fovea, it frequently disappeared as a whole. In Fig. 9.6, V_A is the percentage of time for which some part of the target could be seen and V_B is the percentage for which the difference between the two parts could be seen. Two colours, blue and minus-blue, were used with $\mathscr{L}$ about 100 cd m⁻². For both colours, (a) total disappearance does not occur until ε exceeds 1°, and (b) for eccentricities greater than 4°, luminance discrimination is very poor. Clarke (1957) used a target which was steadily fixed and obtained a qualitatively similar (but smaller) effect. The more frequent disappearance when the

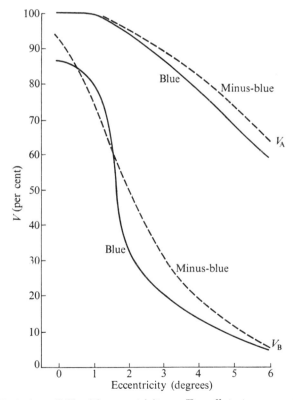

FIG. 9.6. Variation of V with eccentricity ε. For all tests: mean target luminance 100 cd m⁻², retinal illumination = 800 td, dL = 0·5, dθ < 0·5′. Results are shown for blue light, results for minus-blue are similar. (From West 1967.)

target is in the periphery is probably due to the larger area of receptor fields in this region. Small residual movements of the retinal image then have less effect.

9.10. Sharpness of boundary

A bipartite field with a sharp boundary may be prepared by photographing a black and white drawing with a good camera. Bipartite fields with blurred boundaries may be produced by defocussing the lens

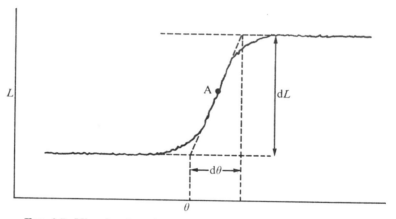

F ɪ ɢ. 9.7. Microdensitometer trace across boundary. (From West 1967.)

and processing the negative in a suitable way. Fig. 9.7 represents a microdensitometer trace across such a boundary. The logarithm L of the luminance falls linearly across most of the boundary and the width $d\theta$ is defined to be the angular distance between points where the extrapolated line of maximum slope meets the horizontal lines. The width of the boundary of the corresponding retinal image ($d\theta_R$) is always greater than $d\theta$ because of diffraction and aberration in the dioptric system (§§ 1.25–1.32). When the target is perfectly sharp ($d\theta = 0$) and the pupil is 2·43 mm, diffraction alone will produce a gradient over a region corresponding to $d\theta_R = 1\cdot0'$ approximately (Byram 1944; Fry 1969; Gubisch 1967). The effects of spherical and chromatic aberrations may be taken into account by a calculation based on the measurements of Campbell and Gubisch (1966). The calculation due to Gubisch (1967) indicates that the minimum value for the range over which dL changes by 0·5 (i.e. the illuminance of the retina changes by a factor of 3) is about 1·5′. The geometrical aberrations together with scattering in the optic media, will also spread the 'tails' of the diffuse boundary and so cause a reduction of effective contrast. This effect is probably very small in red light but may be significant when blue light is used. For monochromatic light the boundaries should be a little sharper than for white light. Minus-blue should be intermediate between white and monochromatic light. When $d\theta = 0.5'$, the target appears perfectly sharp to the observer; $d\theta_R$ is then less than $2.0'$ whereas $d\theta_R$ for a perfectly sharp boundary ($d\theta = 0$) is a little more than $1.5'$. The average distance between the centres of foveal cones is $0.6'$ (Table 1.3). The sharpest possible boundary is blurred enough to extend across three cones. The illuminance of these are in the ratio $8:5:3$ (approximately) when the middle of the boundary coincides with the centre of one cone. A movement of the boundary by $1'$ alters the illuminance of the central cone by a factor of about 2.

9.11. Effect of sharpness of boundary (foveal vision)

Measurements of V were made with $D = 1°$, $\varepsilon = 0$, $\mathscr{L} = 100$ cd m^{-2}, and $dL = 0.27$, and with values of $d\theta$ equal to $0.5'$, $2.2'$, $6.5'$, and $16'$. It is estimated that the corresponding values of $d\theta_R$ are $2.0'$, $3.5'$, $8'$, and $17'$. Fig. 9.8 shows results for blue and for minus-blue light. The curve for minus-blue falls smoothly as $d\theta_R$ increases. That for blue shows little change until $d\theta_R$ exceeds $8'$, after which it falls sharply. It is probable that V starts to fall when $d\theta_R$ exceeds the range of some interaction process. If this is so then, in the fovea, the range for minus-blue is not more than $2'$ while the range for blue is about $7'$. These values agree with estimates based on measurements of summation areas (Hallett 1963).

9.12. Variation with diameter of field (white light)

The variation of V with D for white light ($\mathscr{L} = 1400$ cd m^{-2}) and a sharp boundary ($d\theta = 0.5'$) is shown in Fig. 9.9. Within the range $D = 0.5°$ to $5°$, V falls as D increases, rapidly at first and then more slowly. Other data show that the decrease continues to $8°$ and that there is no significant further change out to $14°$. This result is somewhat unexpected. Vision with large targets is usually better than with small targets. The long boundary in a $4°$ bipartite field might be expected to give a stronger signal than that obtained with a $0.5°$ field and so make it easier to detect the difference of luminance.

The subjective appearances of the target (Fig. 9.10) enable us to understand what happens. The boundary usually fades in the outer region

15

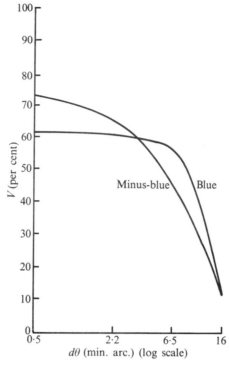

FIG. 9.8. Variation of V with width of boundary ($d\theta$). For all tests $D = 1°$ and $dL = 0\cdot27$. Retinal illuminance $= 850$ td for blue and 700 td for minus-blue. (From West 1967.)

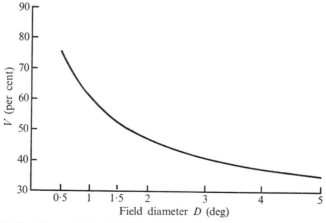

FIG. 9.9. Variation of V with diameter D of field. Target luminance 1400 cd m^{-2}, white light, $dL = 0\cdot15$, $d\theta < 0\cdot5'$. (From West 1967.)

first (as would be expected from Fig. 9.6). This leaves an illogical percept. The subject can see a boundary along the line PQ (Fig. 9.10(c)$_1$)
between two areas of different subjective brightness but there is no
distinguishable outer boundary for the two areas. Going from X to Y
along the dotted line the luminance has changed but there is no distinguishable boundary or gradation of luminance. The perceptual

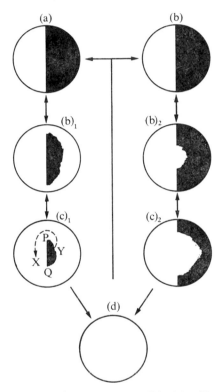

F I G. 9.10. Target (a) and successive appearances (b)$_1$, (c)$_1$, (d) or (b)$_2$, (c)$_2$, (d). (From
West 1967.)

system resolves this difficulty either (a) by extending the observed
boundary to the edge of the circle, or (b) by deciding that there is no
boundary, even in the centre.

It appears that (b) occurs much more often than (a) and therefore V
falls as D increases. This explanation may be tested by inserting an
annulus to separate the central and outer parts of the field as shown in
Fig. 9.11(a). It is found that the central and outer parts of the boundary
now operate independently so that the appearances shown in Figs.
9.11(b), (c), and (d) are all seen. The central boundary vanishes as often
as it would if only a small circle ($D = 0.75°$) were presented alone.

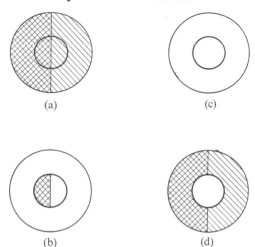

(a)   (c)

(b)   (d)

FIG. 9.11. Target (a) and possible appearances (b), (c), (d). (From West 1967.)

It is found in other experiments with stabilized images that a bright patch in the field (either in the same eye or in the corresponding part of the other eye) close to a stabilized image *increases* the value of V (§ 13.17). This positive 'field effect', which presumably operates by maintaining attention, is not inconsistent with the effect shown in Fig. 9.10.

9.13. Variation with diameter and sharpness (white light)

Fig. 9.12 shows the variation of V with D for, (a) $d\theta = 0.5'$ (sharp boundary), (b) $d\theta = 6.5'$ (intermediate), and (c) $d\theta = 16'$ (diffuse boundary) for white light. With the diffuse boundary, the small receptor fields in the fovea offer no advantage and V shows the expected *increase* of V with D at low values of D, changing to a slow fall for higher values of D. For a sharp boundary V *decreases* as D increases throughout. The boundary of intermediate sharpness (curve b) shows very little variation of V with D. These results suggest that there are two opposed effects (i) the induced fading described in the preceding paragraph, and (ii) an increase of signal with size of target. For $d\theta = 0.5'$, the first effect predominates; for $d\theta = 6.5'$ the two effects nearly cancel out. For $d\theta = 16'$ the second effect predominates when $D < 1.5°$, and the first effect predominates when $D > 1.5°$. This would be expected if, in the parafovea, receptor fields are so large that the targets with sharp

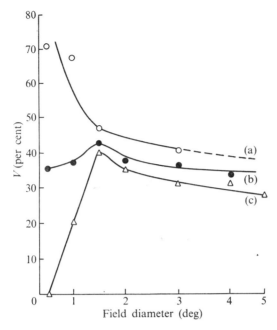

F IG. 9.12. Variation of V with D: (a) sharp; (b) intermediate, and (c) diffuse boundary
White light. (After West 1967.)

boundaries produce signals which differ very little from those obtained
with diffuse boundaries.

9.14. Variation with diameter and sharpness (blue and minus-blue light)

A comparison of results obtained with blue and minus-blue light is
shown in Fig. 9.13. The curves (c) and (d) for minus-blue are very
similar to those shown in Fig. 9.12 (a) and (c), for white light. For the
very diffuse boundary ($d\theta = 16'$), the curve (b) for blue light is only a
little different from the curve (d) for minus-blue. The curve (a) for a
sharp boundary seen in blue light differs a great deal from the curve (c)
for a sharp boundary and minus-blue light. It is indeed closer to curve
(d) for minus-blue and a diffuse boundary. This suggests that the receptor fields for blue are much larger than the fields for minus-blue, so
that the system for observing a boundary in blue always 'sees' a diffuse
boundary. The results are consistent with a range of interaction of $2'$
or less for minus-blue and of about $7'$ for blue.

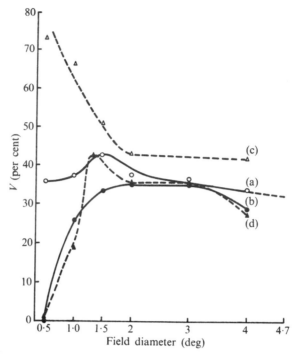

F IG. 9.13. Variation V with D for diffuse boundary ((b) and (d)) and sharp boundary ((a) and (c)); for blue light ((a) and (b)) and minus-blue light ((c) and (d)). (After West 1967.)

9.15. Effect of interposed dark or light bar

If the information leading to perception of contrast is derived mainly from receptors very near the boundary, it should be possible to learn something about the process by interposing a dark or light bar to separate the two parts of the field whose luminances are compared. Clowes (1961) made experiments with dark bars of width 1′ upwards. Results obtained by West (1967) are shown in Fig. 9.14, for a 1° field with d$L = 0.5$, and $\mathscr{L} = 100$ cd m^{-2}. As would be expected, V decreases as the width of the bar (W) increases from 0.5′ to 9′, but V is slightly better for $W = 0.5′$ than for no bar. This applies both to dark and to light bars. It seems probable that the very narrow bar serves to maintain signals in the region of the boundary. This effect is stronger with blue light but the results are complicated because the blue target often disappears as a whole. Le Grand (1933) found that accuracy of photometric matching (with normal vision) was *reduced* when a dark bar of 1′ was introduced into the bipartite field.

9.16. Lateral signal for a stabilized boundary

The results shown in Figs. 9.13 and 9.14, together with those obtained by Clowes (1961), imply that when the fields are juxtaposed ($W = 0$), a contrast of d$L = 0.5$ can be perceived 50 per cent of the time. A

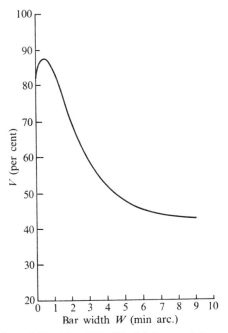

FIG. 9.14. Variation of V with width W of interposed bar; minus-blue light. (After West 1967.)

corresponding level for perception in normal vision, without restriction on eye-movements, is about 50 or 100 times lower. Thus the 'signal' which allows perception when the boundary is stabilized, is very weak. It also behaves in a different way from the normal signal generated by eye-movements, both in regard to separation of fields, and in regard to time. Clowes (1961) found that if d$L = 0.6$ the difference of luminance was always seen ($V = 100$) in normal vision, even when the fields were widely separated ($W = 15′$). In stabilized vision, V fell from 0.95 for juxtaposed fields to 0.3 with widely separated fields ($W = 15′$). Also, with the stabilized image, the visibility decreased slowly with time over a period of 90 s. The signal generated by eye-movements decays in 2–3 s when the image is stabilized (§§ 6.2–6.4). Thus there appears to be evidence for the existence of a weak signal which maintains hazy vision when the retinal image is stationary.

9.17. Foveal threshold with stabilized images

Fender (1956) described observations on the course of dark adaptation with stabilized images. The stabilizing system described in § 5.12 (Fig. 5.10) was used. The target was a circular patch ($D = 1°$) placed as accurately as possible on the fovea. An unstabilized fixation annulus (4° in diameter and 0·25° in width) was provided. It was dimmed as the experiment proceeded, so that at every stage it was just visible. After adaptation to 10 cd m^{-2}, the test patch was shown. The subject turned a piece of polaroid (to reduce the luminance) until a threshold was reached below which the target was not seen at all in stabilized vision. The adaptation curve obtained with white light was smooth, but the threshold was higher (30 times for one subject, and 3 times for another) than the corresponding threshold for normal vision. The ratio of the threshold for red to that for blue varied little when the image was stabilized, but showed a large change when the target was not stabilized (Fig. 9.15). This change may be due to the subject not

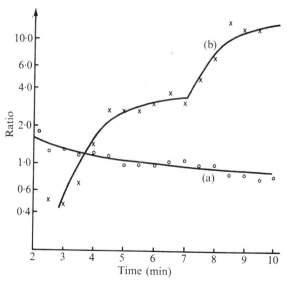

F IG. 9.15. Variation of ratio of threshold for red to that for blue in dark adaptation for (a) stabilized and (b) unstabilized target continuously exposed. (From Fender 1956.)

succeeding in holding the fixation accurately enough to keep the image on the central fovea when it was unstabilized. The results, taken over-all, show no evidence for 'blue-blindness of the fovea'.

9.18. Hue discrimination

We shall now describe observations made when two colours are pre-sented side by side in a bipartite field which is stabilized. Three things happen at the same time, though not usually at the same rate. These are:

(a) desaturation of all hues;
(b) colour fusion;
(c) a general tendency for the whole field to fade out.

The second of these requires further explanation. McCree (1960) has shown that steady fixation of a bipartite field induces a loss of hue discrimination. This happens most readily in the peripheral field and when the luminance is not too high. The effect is observed in the fovea using a stabilized image (Ditchburn 1957). The effect is seen most strongly when the luminance difference is small. Discrimination be-tween blue and green becomes very weak, and discrimination between red and orange is also weak, though not as weak as that between blue and green. Discrimination between red and green is still comparatively good. Thus the remaining discriminations are somewhat similar to those of a tritanope. This loss of hue discrimination is very much more pronounced with a stabilized image. It is easy to observe the two halves of a moderately well-stabilized bipartite field (centred on the fovea) 'fuse' into a single circular patch. This happens rapidly when one half is illuminated with bright green light and the other with a deep blue light. The central line disappears, the outer boundary remaining fairly clear. The whole patch appears grey with a faint suggestion of blue or green.

9.19. Effect of eye-movements

Clowes (1962) recorded the eye-movements made by a subject who was able to obtain colour fusion fairly well in normal vision. He found that, when the colours were fused, the saccadic movements had been greatly reduced. Hue discrimination was normal when the subject was asked to move his fixation direction to-and-fro about the field. Colour fusion was almost completely inhibited when the apparatus shown in

Fig. 5.12 was used to produce exaggerated movements. It was sometimes found that, when the retinal image was moved sharply through a small distance, the hue difference was perceived, for a short time, but only in the region near the boundary. These tests establish beyond doubt the importance of eye-movements in hue discrimination.

9.20. Stages in failure of the discrimination

The three effects described in § 9.18 do not always occur in the same order. When the two sides of the bipartite field are blue and green, and of about equal luminance, the usual sequence is (i) considerable desaturation of the blue side in 1–2 s, accompanied by slightly slower desaturation of the green side, (ii) fusion of the two greyish patches after about 3 s, and (iii) disappearance of the whole field very soon after. On some occasions, however, the whole field disappears so quickly that it is difficult to distinguish the other stages. Bipartite fields with yellow and white, or red and orange, follow much the same sequence except that red desaturates less. When red and green are juxtaposed, colour fusion is rarely observed. Usually green desaturates and then the green half of the field disappears, leaving a red semi-circle. This disappears after, at most, a few seconds. When a bipartite field with red and blue sides is displayed as target, the blue appears to spread over the red giving a magenta colour, Later, the whole target disappears without colour fusion and without much desaturation of the red side of the field.

9.21. Test fields with some stabilized and some unstabilized boundaries

Yarbus† (1957c) carried out a different series of experiments on hue discrimination. He used the apparatus shown in Fig. 5.7 to provide targets which were entirely stabilized. With the apparatus shown in Fig. 5.8(b) he was able to produce test fields in which the stabilized target was seen against a background containing unstabilized boundaries. As a preliminary to the main experiments he carried out experiments with test fields of very wide angle and stabilized boundaries using a considerable range of luminance and hue. The 'empty field' always appeared after a short interval (1–3 s). If the other eye was occluded the field appeared dark grey. If the other eye was illuminated with

† See alternatively Yarbus (1967, p. 79).

diffused light, then the test field acquired a tinge of the same hue as the light seen by the other eye.

9.22. Inner boundary stabilized

In the next series of experiments the target was as shown in Fig. 9.16. The inner and outer boundaries of the annulus were stabilized. The outer boundaries of the field were not. The hue in the annulus (whose boundary is stabilized) was, in general, different from that of

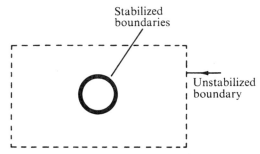

Fig. 9.16. Target with unstabilized outer boundary. (From Yarbus 1965.)

the area outside the annulus. The central region assumed the luminance and hue of the outer region. No information is available from its boundaries, and it assumes the colour of its background. In some respects it behaves like the blind spot of the retina.

9.23. Field with small unstabilized areas

In a further series of experiments by Yarbus, part of the field was stabilized, but small coloured areas with unstabilized boundaries were present. It was found that

(a) if the stabilized target was larger than any of the unstabilized areas, it appeared grey when the other eye was occluded; when the other eye viewed a uniform coloured field, the stabilized image took this colour;

(b) if the stabilized target was about the same size as one of the small uniformly illuminated areas, it was sometimes seen to fuse with the background;

(c) if the stabilized target was so small that it was seen entirely within one of the coloured areas, complete fusion was obtained.

9.24. Experiments were carried out using the test field shown in Fig. 9.17. A and a were stabilized. The rectangular boundaries of B_1 and B_2 were unstabilized. The range of eye-movements was such that A was always seen against B_1 (which was of variegated colour), and a against B_2 (which was of uniform colour). It was found that A and a each behaved as if the other were not there. A (which was larger than the patches of B_1) became grey or else assumed the colour presented to the other eye, and a fused with the uniform colour of B_2. This independent action is exactly what would be expected if information is obtained entirely from boundaries. Yarbus concluded that when a

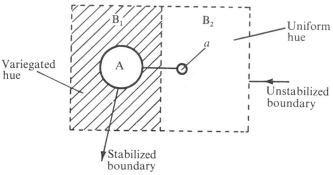

Fᴵɢ. 9.17. Target with some stabilized and some unstabilized boundaries. (From Yarbus 1967.)

large uniformly coloured area is viewed (in normal vision) the centre of the area is essentially an 'empty field'. It gives no information. 'It is as if we perceive the colour at the edges and extrapolate it to the centre'.

9.25. Colour discrimination—annulus with outer boundary unstabilized

Using the apparatus described in § 5.25 Krauskopf (1963) presented a stimulus shown in Fig. 9.18. A disc of one colour is surrounded by an annulus of another colour. The inner boundary is stabilized while the outer boundary is not. Wratten filters, with peak transmissions at 493 nm, 529 nm, 593 nm, and 640 nm, were used to produce blue, green, yellow, and red stimuli. Whenever fusion was observed the whole field assumed the hue of the annulus, in agreement with the results of Yarbus. This effect has also been observed by the author and by Gerrits *et al.* (1970*b*).

Krauskopf measured the percentage of time for which a difference of hue was perceived, as a function of the ratio of luminance of the disc to luminance of the annulus. The latter was fixed at approximately 170 cd m^{-2} for all colours. The luminance ratios for different hues were calculated from the spectral transmissions of the filters using the C.I.E. photopic visibility factors. The points of equal luminance as judged by the observers in heterochromatic photometry are marked by arrows.

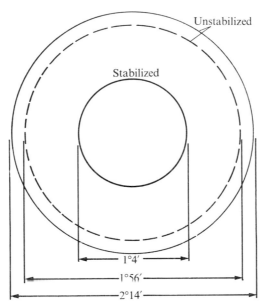

Fɪɢ. 9.18. Target with inner boundary stabilized and outer annulus with unstabilized edge. (From Krauskopf 1963.)

The results obtained when the inner boundary is stabilized are shown in Fig. 9.19. In a control experiment with normal fixation, but with both boundaries unstabilized, there was extremely little fusion, and when it was reported (always with some doubt) it lasted less than a second.

9.26. Under the conditions of Krauskopf's experiment, fusion is a function of luminance difference. When a definite minimum is obtained, it corresponds to a disc-luminance *a little lower than the annulus-luminance*. The difference of the logarithms is usually 0·3 or less, but there are larger differences when the minima are not well defined. The difference of 0·3 (or less) is probably due to the geometrical asymmetry of the photometric fields and may be compared with a mean difference of 0·11 log units found by Barlow and Sparrock (1964) when making

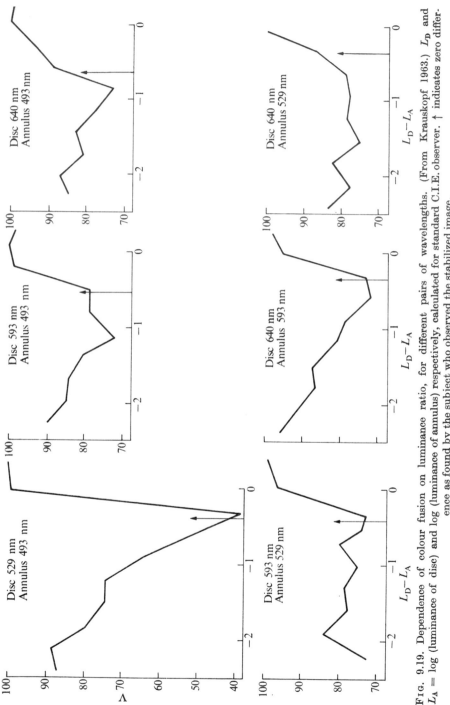

FIG. 9.19. Dependence of colour fusion on luminance ratio, for different pairs of wavelengths. (From Krauskopf 1963.) L_D and L_A = log (luminance of disc) and log (luminance of annulus) respectively, calculated for standard C.I.E. observer. ↑ indicates zero difference as found by the subject who observed the stabilized image.

photometric comparisons in white light between two stabilized images. One was a central patch of 5° and the other was an annulus between circles of diameters 7° and 28°. Pairs of graphs with the same hues (e.g. red disc/green annulus and green disc/red annulus) are generally similar, indicating that the information derived from the inner boundary depends on the two hues displayed and very little on which one is outside. Fusion is most marked between blue and green, and next between red and orange-yellow (640 nm and 593 nm). Fusion occurs about 20 per cent of the time between red and green or red and blue

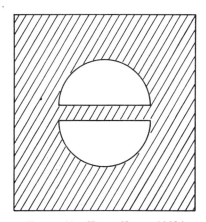

Fig. 9.20. (From Clowes 1962.)

(i.e. pairs of wavelengths of which are on opposite sides of 580 nm). Using the bipartite field (two semi-circles of different hue and with all boundaries stabilized) Fender (1956) and Clowes (1962) did not observe colour fusion under this condition because the patch of wavelength less than 580 nm usually desaturated and disappeared before fusion could be observed. In the arrangement used by Yarbus and by Krauskopf, the unstabilized outer boundary prevents disappearance and desaturation of the annulus.

9.27. Clowes (1962) examined the effect of separating two semi-circular patches (of different hue) by a dark band. The patches were seen against a dark ground as shown in Fig. 9.20. All boundaries were stabilized. When the two parts of the field were separated by 10′ to 15′, subjects reported that the two patches desaturated and disappeared. They were not seen as exactly the same in hue at any stage. When red and blue semi-circular patches were closer together the blue appeared to spread into the red area, giving it a magenta tinge. Later the blue disappeared. In a similar way blue 'spread over' a green area, then both parts of the field desaturated and appeared the same. This spreading was observed only with blue, i.e. red and green did not interact in this way, nor did red appear to spread into the blue area. One subject saw this spreading of blue into green in normal vision, and a separation of 30′ was needed to inhibit it. This subject had normal colour vision by an Isihara test. Chromatic aberration would account for only about 4′ of spread at most. It is possible that this effect is due to preferential small angle scattering of blue light by the lens and other optic media. It is more likely that it is due to spread of blue light within the retina itself, or to horizontal neural connections of that part of the receptor system which signals the presence of blue light. The existence of this spread implies that little advantage would be gained if the refractive system of the eye were more accurately corrected for chromatic aberration at the blue end of the spectrum.

9.28. The apparatus shown in Fig. 5.6(b) has been used to study visual discriminations when viewing coloured transparencies of outdoor scenes (Beeler, Fender, Nobel, and Evans 1964). Subjects reported areas of rapid desaturation and also intermittent loss of pattern perception in some areas (e.g. a house, or a group of people disappeared and re-appeared). The most interesting feature of these experiments (in which 6 subjects gave similar reports) was that areas of desaturation did not normally coincide with areas of loss of pattern-perception. Further observations were made with 5 subjects. They were first tested with Isihara plates (unstabilized) and were all found to have normal colour vision by this test. The Isihara plates were photographed on Koda-chrome high-resolution film at reduced size (about 20:1). The detail and colour rendering were not perfect but were surprisingly good considering the size reduction. The targets produced in this way were viewed in the stabilization apparatus. They were centrally fixated and subtended approximately 5°. The following observations were reported.

(1) Disappearance was slower than with black and white patterns.
(2) The coloured numerals desaturated to the point where their shape could not be perceived. The residual image had a vaguely defined hue which bore some relation to the card from which it was derived. It was found that:

(a) card 1 (orange figures on a blue ground), card 6 (blue-green figures on a reddish ground), and card 14 (multicoloured), all appeared to be brown (sometimes qualified 'greenish-brown', or 'yellowish-brown', or 'tan'); (b) card 10 (red-brown figures on a blue-green background) appeared to be green; (c) card 22 (red on grey) appeared to be grey.

(3) Desaturation of the whole field sometimes occurred leaving the circles still visible so that a whole plate was seen as a set of uniformly bright monochromatic circles.

9.29. Interruption of the light for 0·5 s produced regeneration of colour, but only for a short time. Deliberate mechanical destabilization to produce a sharp movement of the retinal image produced a similar brief restoration of hue discrimination. Experiments with three subjects confirmed the above findings. It was also found that flicker at 4–8 Hz produced a marked reduction in desaturation. However, oscillation of the target over 2' at a frequency of 4–8 Hz did not produce any large effect (§ 10.9).

9.30. Target with stabilized outer boundary

The results of the above experiments indicate that signals from a boundary between two closed areas carry the information which enables differences of hue and of luminance to be perceived. This view has been developed by Land (1971). If signals from boundaries give only differences, some additional signal is needed to fix absolute values, e.g. to decide which area, in a complicated scene, is white. One possibility is that the outside edge of the retina constitutes a sort of 'zero'. The colour of an area at the centre of the field is then measured by integrating from the outside inwards, i.e. by adding differences across the various boundaries which lie between the central area and the edge of the retina. The following experiment was carried out to test this hypothesis.

The subject wore a contact lens which carried a black shield. This had a central circular hole, subtending about 10°. The circular boundary was stabilized. If the subject viewed a card which was uniformly illuminated, with white or coloured light, the whole field went black and remained black. This result was also obtained when a little unstabilized structure was introduced into the central area. When more structure was present, part of the structure was seen, and the rest of the field appeared grey. When, however, the subject viewed a scene containing much detail and some moving objects, then all features were seen, as clearly as in normal vision. Minor differences of hue (e.g. between two slightly different shades of green) were clearly perceived. In this situation, all signals from the outside boundary of the field are cut off. It follows that the signals from inner boundaries must determine hue and not just differences of hue. It should, however, be noted that although the visual system can detect small differences of luminance and hue, absolute judgements are very imprecise.

16

9.31. After-image following a target which is not perceived

There are a number of experiments which show that the photo-chemical state of the retina is, as one would expect, determined by the light received rather than the light perceived. Craik (1940) obstructed the blood supply to the eye, making it temporarily blind. Part of the retina was illuminated. No light was perceived but an after-image was observed after release of pressure. This implies that information leading to perception of after-images is stored photochemically in the retina rather than as a 'memory' at a higher level.

9.32. Phenomena following extinction of stabilized image

When the light illuminating a stabilized image which has faded, is extinguished, an after-image is obtained. Details of structure which are never visible in the stabilized image, after it first faded, are seen in the after-image. Yarbus (1967) found that, when the illumination was very bright (850 cd m^{-2}), there was a brief flash of light ($\sim$0·1 s) immediately after the light was extinguished. This was followed by a brief dark interval, and then the after-image appeared.† The speed of this effect suggests an electrical action, and it seems probable that a burst of spikes constituting an 'off-signal' is produced. In normal vision this signal is superposed upon the signals connected with perception of the image, and is correctly associated with extinction of the light. In the abnormal situation where a stabilized image (or a ganz-feld) has faded, this signal is initially interpreted as an 'on-signal' i.e. the subject perceives an *increase* of illumination. When the further signals which would be associated with a permanent increase of light in normal vision are not received, a 'correction' is made, and the perceived field goes black. At a slightly later stage, the 'shock' has passed and a normal after-image is seen.

9.33. Adaptation to a steady light

In the experiments described above, adaptation of the retina (by a stimulus which is not perceived) is demonstrated qualitatively.

† A similar effect has also been observed by the author. One eye is occluded and the other closed, and the face is turned towards the sun on a bright day—thus producing a strongly illuminated ganzfeld. After about 10 s the field darkens appreciably. On cutting off the light suddenly, after about 30 s, the bright flash followed by brief darkness and a vague after-image are seen.

Sparrock (1969) investigated this adaptation quantitatively. He tested the state of adaptation of the retina by measuring the liminal brightness increment when a short flash of light is superimposed (a) in the centre of a large illuminated area using an unstabilized image and (b) in the centre of a similar area of a stabilized image which has faded. It is found that when all relevant conditions are the same, the luminance of the test spot which is seen 50 per cent of the time is the same for conditions (b) and (a). In these two conditions the photochemical state of the region of the retina to which the test stimulus is presented is the same. The perceptual situation is quite different, since in (a) the background light is perceived and in (b) it is not perceived (or appears very weak) because the signals at the boundary are not operative. Thus these experiments indicate that the liminal brightness increment depends on the photochemical balance and not on what is perceived.†

9.34. Progressive adaptation

The experiments described in the previous paragraph refer to adaptation which has proceeded until equilibrium is reached. Yarbus carried out a series of experiments which show that the photochemical state of the retina continues to change after a stabilized image has faded. These experiments are described in detail, with several coloured plates to show the appearances of test fields, by Yarbus (1967). We shall describe one typical experiment. A large area of the retina was covered by a stabilized image illuminated with red light. Within the stabilized image was an unstabilized, small, circular, white spot. At first the spot appeared white on a red ground. Then after 2–3 s the stabilized red field vanished, and the spot was seen white on the empty field. After 20 s the spot was seen pale blue on a slightly different part of the field (because it moves with the eye). After 40 s it appeared to be dark blue. This sequence occurs because increasing amounts of the red pigment (erytholabe) are bleached as photochemical equilibrium proceeds.

9.35. Yarbus also describes a somewhat different effect. A small stabilized spot was first viewed against a red, unstabilized background. The spot disappeared against the background so that the whole area appeared red. The background was then changed to blue. The spot was first seen as red on blue. Then in 2–3 s it disappeared and the whole area was blue. If the colour of the background was alternated at about 2 Hz, the apparent colour of the stabilized spot could no longer follow

† Nachmias referred to some similar results in a lecture to the Optical Society of America (April 1965).

the changes. It was seen all the time, and appeared as a red-blue mixture. In this experiment, the final steady appearances can be explained in terms of the photochemical adaptation of the retina. The delay in changing colour must be associated with neural processes. Yarbus suggests that these processes are essentially the same as those which control the time required for initial fading of a stabilized image.

9.36. Gerrits and Vendrik (1970a) describe an experiment in which the subject viewed a brightly-illuminated, central, circular disc, surrounded by an annulus which was less brightly illuminated, and then by a dark field (Fig. 9.18). Both circular boundaries were stabilized and green light was used. When the target had faded, the illumination of the annulus was suddenly altered, that of the centre remaining constant. When the illumination of the annulus was decreased or switched off, the annulus appeared purple and the centre appeared bright green. Also, a green halo appeared outside the annulus. The image faded again in a few seconds. In this experiment the reduction of green light in the region of the annulus which has faded is interpreted as a purple (i.e. minus-green) stimulus. The absence of corresponding change, both inside and outside the annulus, is interpreted as a green stimulus. However, the halo extends only a short distance outside the annulus (into the dark surround), whereas the centre where green is present is seen as a homogeneous green disc. When the experiment was repeated with a black central disc, the green colour did not significantly spread into the centre. This experiment shows that the 'filling in' effects in stabilized targets are not as simple as the result of the experiments described in § 9.22 would suggest.

Effect of imposed movements of the retinal image

10.1. Artificial stimulation of 'on-off' signals

In normal vision, receptors near the boundaries between light and dark regions in the retinal image are subject to fluctuating illumination due to movements of the image (§ 8.1). These fluctuations may be expected to give rise to 'on-off' signals which carry information about the positions of the boundaries. It has been assumed as a working hypothesis, that the loss of these signals is the primary cause of the failure of visual perception when the retinal image is stabilized. If this is so, it should be possible to stimulate 'on-off' signals and so restore visual perception, to some extent, either by small imposed movements of the target or by fluctuating illumination of the whole field. Early experiments showed that visual discrimination could be improved by either of these methods. Once this is established, it is desirable to study the details of the restoration of perception by different kinds of imposed movement, and by modulating the illumination at different frequencies and amplitudes. Experiments on imposed movements are reported in this chapter, and those on modulated illumination in Chapter 11.

10.2. Imposed unidirectional movements

The effect of unidirectional movements was investigated by Yarbus† (1959a). The apparatus, shown in Fig. 10.1, was mounted on the suction device shown in Fig. 5.8(b). A capillary containing alcohol, coloured black, was viewed against an opal screen C which subtended a visual angle of 45°. The meniscus was made to move along the capillary by evaporation of alcohol from cotton-wool placed in the space A. The velocity of the meniscus could be varied from $3'$ s^{-1} to $300'$ s^{-1}, by altering the rate of evaporation. The internal diameter of the capillary was only 0·03 mm so that saccadic movements of the eye did not affect

† Also Yarbus (1967), p. 86.

the steady movement of the meniscus. In most experiments an air-bubble was trapped in the fluid so as to form a moving bright object as shown in Fig. 10.2(a). The visual angle subtended by this object was about $10° \times 0·5°$.

10.3. The following observations were made.

(a) A few seconds after presentation of the target the boundaries disappeared leaving an 'empty field'. When the bubble moved, the subject saw a bright 'comet' moving through the field at the leading edge of the bubble, and a dark 'comet' at the trailing edge (Fig. 10.2(b)).

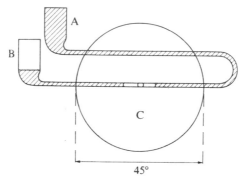

FIG. 10.1. Apparatus for studying imposed movement. (From Yarbus 1967.)

These were called the *'on-comet'* and the *'off-comet'* respectively. If some part of the capillary was marked with a black transverse band, each comet was split into two isolated parts as it passed over the band. Neither the 'on-comet' nor the 'off-comet' was altered in length as the dark band was traversed. Small objects (angular diameter about 5°) of different hue and luminance were moved about in the region of the comets. These moving objects were seen, but they produced no obvious changes in the length and appearance of the comets, except when a coloured object was actually behind a comet. The comet then assumed the hue of the unstabilized object.

(b) The length of each comet was roughly proportional to the velocity of the meniscus.

(c) The leading portion of each comet appeared uniform in brightness and hue. Yarbus considers that this indicates that the process initiated by the moving edge operates unchanged for a certain period after the edge has passed. This period is from 1 s to 3 s. The length of the tail of the comet is such that extinction takes place in 5 s to 8 s from the time when the edge passes a certain point. Judgement of where a comet terminates is necessarily not very precise.

(d) The lengths of both the 'on-comet' and the 'off-comet' were least when the image of the meniscus crossed the fovea, and greatest when it was in the region of highest rod-density.

(e) The comets were seen only when the meniscus attained a certain minimum velocity. With a screen luminance of about 140 cd m^{-2} and good contrast (produced by excluding light from the sclera) the minimum velocity was about 4' s^{-1}. When light was allowed to fall on the sclera (giving a lower contrast) the minimum velocity increased to about 20' s^{-1}.

(f) The length of the comet was not noticeably affected by altering the colour of the incident light.

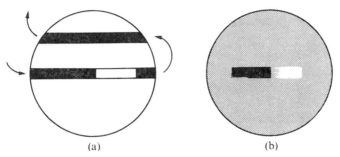

Fɪɢ. 10.2. 'Comets' at boundaries of moving targets. (From Yarbus, 1967.)

(g) Increasing the amount of light incident on the opal glass by a factor of 10^2 or 10^3 led to an increase in the length of the comet by a factor of 1·5 to 2.

(h) If the illumination of the eye was suddenly increased (but by an amount which did not cause the whole target to re-appear) the comets became fainter and sometimes disappeared.

The comets have also been observed by Gerrits, de Haan, and Vendrik (1966).

10.4. Yarbus considers that the time required for disappearance of the 'comet', after the leading edge has passed, is a measure of the decay of a 'fast process', and that this process is identical with the one associated with the initial disappearance of a stationary image (§ 6.4). In the author's opinion, the two processes are not identical, though the decay of 'memory' of information is an important common factor, both in the disappearance of the stabilized image and in the termination of the comet. However, in Yarbus's experiment, the edge moves steadily through a distance which is large compared with the distance between retinal receptors and with movements of the retinal image due to the drift component of eye-movements. The eye-movements produce irregular movements of the retinal image, whose direction is frequently changed, but the above experiment involves a unidirectional movement. In this situation the moving edge may bring specific movement detectors (§ 7.31) into operation. These have a 'memory' (§ 16.14), and the extinction of the comet may depend partly on decay of the signals which constitute this memory. The time required for complete extinction of the comet (5–8 s), as against 1–3 s for decay of the stabilized image, does suggest that the two processes are not the same. Also the author finds that stabilized images disappear more quickly in blue light than in red or green and more quickly in the periphery than in the fovea. The comet is the same length for all colours and is *longer* in the periphery than in the fovea.

10.5. Imposed slow movements (foveal vision)

The effect of imposed slow movements on foveal vision has been studied by giving the target an oscillatory movement of fairly large amplitude and of period comparable with the interval between saccades in normal vision (Ditchburn, Fender, and Mayne 1959). The apparatus shown in Fig. 5.10 was modified by placing the mirror M_2 on a pivoted mount and oscillating it. Considerable care was taken to ensure that the mirror moved smoothly, and without tremor. The target was a vertical black line 5' in diameter seen against a circular patch 60' in diameter, and of luminance 50 cd m^{-2}. The movement was perpendicular to the direction of the black line. The visibility factor V, i.e. the percentage of the time for which the target was seen (§ 9.3) was measured alternately for the moving and for the stationary retinal image (V_M and V_0 respectively). In order to compensate for day-to-day variation in the subject's performance, all values of V_M were reduced to a common value of V_0 (equal to its average over a longer period).† The reduced average value of V_M is called V_R. The oscillation was at a constant frequency of 0·55 Hz and the amplitude‡ was varied. The results are shown in Fig. 10.3. It may be seen that although V_R increases with amplitude (and hence with velocity), the increase at a velocity corresponding to the *median* drift velocity for this subject in normal vision does not produce an important effect. It thus appears that the drift movements *by themselves* are not capable of maintaining normal vision.

---

† Reference should be made to the paper quoted in the text for details of experimental arrangement, reduction formula, test of reliability, etc.

‡ The term 'amplitude' has its usual meaning—i.e. it is the maximum deviation from the main position. The 'peak to peak' excursus is twice the amplitude.

10.6. These results cannot be expected to agree precisely with those of Yarbus, since his moving object was a 'light' target. However, it may be noted that, for foveal vision, he was able to detect comets when the velocity of the target was 3′ to 5′ s⁻¹, and that, according to Fig. 10.3, V_R is 55 for an average velocity of 3′ s⁻¹ and 75 for an average velocity of 5′ s⁻¹, as compared with 37 for V_0, i.e. the rate of movement at which Yarbus is able to see the comets with a bright target is sufficient to

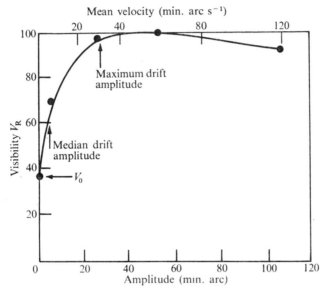

Fɪɢ. 10.3. Visibility related to (a) excursus (= 2 × amplitude) of slow movement and (b) mean velocity. The vertical arrows show median drift magnitude and maximum drift magnitude (for this subject) during fixation. (From Ditchburn, Fender, and Mayne 1959.)

produce a significant increase in the probability of seeing the black line. The subject was aware of the slow movement within a few seconds after it started.

10.7. Imposed saccadic movements

Using the apparatus described above, with a black bar 3′ in width, and with a field luminance of 50 cd m⁻², the effect of saccadic movements, with displacements varying from 2·5′ to 25′, was measured. The saccadic movement was produced in the following way. The black bar was an image of a fine wire which was placed between the poles of an electromagnet, as in an Eindhoven string galvanometer. On depressing a key, current flowed through the wire which was sharply displaced by the magnetic force. The wire was critically damped so that there was no overshoot as in a natural saccadic movement (Fig. 4.1). The final position was reached in about a millisecond, as compared with about 30 ms for the main movement of a natural saccade.

10.8. The following experimental procedure was used. The subject at first saw the target clearly. As soon as it began to disappear, the key was pressed, moving the target to the right. The key was released when it

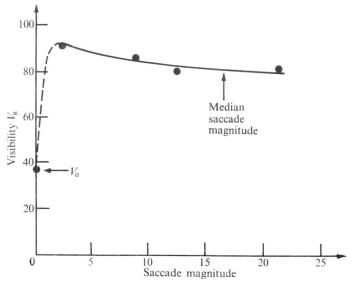

FIG. 10.4. Visibility related to saccade magnitude. Arrow shows median saccade magnitude (for this subject) during fixation. (From Ditchburn, Fender, and Mayne 1959.)

began to disappear again, and the target then jumped back to the original position. The results obtained with different amounts of movement are displayed in Fig. 10.4 which shows that even the smallest displacement used (2·5′) was sufficient to cause immediate regeneration of the image. The movement of the wire could always be seen by the subject who reported that this procedure 'gave a *very sharp* image', i.e. sharper than that normally observed after spontaneous regeneration. Some experiments at Reading (which were not completed) suggest that a displacement of 1′ causes regeneration, but that one of 0·5′ does not.

10.9. Sinusoidal movements

The above apparatus was used to produce sinusoidal movements of the bar by passing alternating currents through the wire. The movement of the wire was recorded photographically on a magnified scale, and the amplitude was measured on the record. Experiments were performed with amplitudes as low as 0·1′. Such movements are significant only if the apparatus is free from parasitic vibration, and stringent precautions were taken against stray vibrations. The target was a bar 2·75′ wide seen against a field of luminance 150 cd m⁻². Fig. 10.5 shows the value of V_R as a function of amplitude for different frequencies.

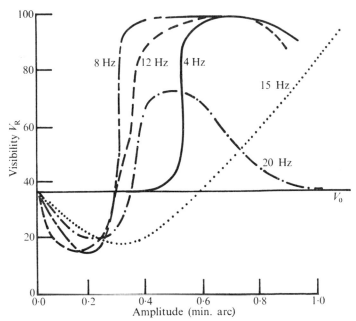

F I G. 10.5. Visibility for oscillatory movements of various frequencies and amplitudes. 4 Hz ———, 8 Hz – — –, 12 Hz – – –, 15 Hz . . . ., 20 Hz —·—· (From Ditchburn, Fender, and Mayne 1959.)

The whole range of results is displayed in Fig. 10.6 which is a contour map. The dashed lines represent extensions of the observations based on the assumption that at low frequencies and large amplitudes the effect depends solely on the velocity of the movement. The contour map includes an area, shown dotted in Fig. 10.6, corresponding to movements for which the target is seen *less* often than it is with the stabilized image. The adverse effect is large for frequencies of 15 Hz upwards, and for amplitudes of about 0·3′. This kind of movement blurs the edges of targets, owing to persistence of vision, so causing a reduction in the visibility. The amplitude is apparently insufficient to activate the 'on-off' mechanism. There is another area, lightly shaded in Fig. 10.6, in which movements do not produce any significant effect. This includes movements at frequencies below 3 Hz with amplitudes less than 0·3′.

10.10. Figs. 10.5 and 10.6 show that, for frequencies in the range 4–12 Hz, there is a sudden improvement in vision when the amplitude exceeds 0·3′. This amplitude gives a peak-to-peak movement of 0·6′, roughly equal to the intercone spacing. For amplitudes greater than 1·0′ the effect decreases, possibly because the peak-to-peak movement is nearly equal to the width of the line. In this situation some receptors

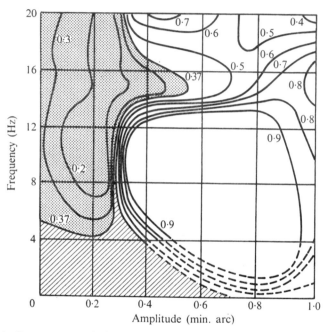

F ɪ ɢ. 10.6. Contour map of visibility as a function of frequency and amplitude. (From Ditchburn, Fender, and Mayne 1959.)

'see' a fluctuation at twice the nominal frequency, and this may reduce the favourable effect. When the retinal image of the bar was vibrating at 4 Hz (and at higher frequencies) the subject could not perceive the movement of the wire, nor could any degradation of the boundaries (more than that usually associated with a stabilized image) be observed. When a similar movement was observed with normal vision, the degradation of the sharp edge was obvious.

10.11. Experiments by Krauskopf

Experiments on the effect of sinusoidal movements were also made by Krauskopf (1957). He used four different targets consisting of *bright bars* 0·17′, 1′, 4′, and 8′ in width on a *dark field*. The contrast at which each target was visible for 50 per cent of the time was measured for five different frequencies and four different amplitudes of movement, i.e. 24 conditions (including zero movement) in all. The number of conditions is rather large in relation to the number of observations, and this accounts for some irregularity in the results. Conclusions must be drawn from the general trend of the results rather than from individual points. The points which lie within the plateau of the contour map of Fig. 10.6 (amplitudes of 0·5′ and 1′ and frequencies of 5 Hz and 10 Hz) give a significant improvement in vision (i.e. a reduction in the contrast which is visible 50 per cent of the time). The remaining results for the 4′ bar correspond to conditions outside the range included in the contour map, but the improvement in vision at 1 Hz, 2 Hz, 5 Hz, and 10 Hz for 2′ amplitude, and the loss at 20 Hz and 50 Hz for amplitudes 0·5′, 1·0′, and 2·0′ are in agreement with the general tendency of the contour map. The results of the two sets of experiments (described in §§ 10.9–10.11) agree about as well as can be expected in view of the differences of targets. The over-all conclusions are that sinusoidal movements of moderately low frequencies (4–8 Hz) with amplitudes 0·3′ to 1′ have a favourable effect, and that high frequency movements (over 15 Hz) have an unfavourable effect.

10.12. Effect of fatigue

Campbell and Robson (1961), using entoptic images in the parafovea and periphery of the retina, reported that the effect of small movements decreased rapidly with time (§ 6.20). Sharpe (1972) extended these observations (§§ 10.20–10.21). Barlow (1963) also described a 'fatigue effect'. Repeated small movements acting on an otherwise completely stationary retinal image will produce 'on-off' signals, but always in the same pathways of the optic tract. These may produce a constant signal at some place in the cortex and accommodation may cause the constant signal to be ignored after a few seconds (§ 7.41). This effect was not reported in the experiments of Ditchburn, Fender, and Mayne and of Krauskopf. This may be due to occasional destabilization due to small movements of the lens (equivalent to small saccadic movements of the retinal image) which transfer the 'on-off' signals to other pathways in the optic nerve, and thus maintain vision. Also, in both these experiments individual observations covered short periods, and a decrease in visibility towards the ends of these periods might not be noticed when averages were calculated. It is also possible that the fatigue effect does not operate in foveal vision. The existence of the 'fatigue' effect supports the view that normal vision is maintained by a *combination* of the irregular vibrations (chiefly in the frequency range 2–10 Hz) and the saccadic movements,† possibly with some assistance from the drifts. These movements acting together prevent the loss of signals found by Hubel and Wiesel when an object was oscillated in exactly the same part of a receptor field (§ 7.41). No experiments are available on the effect of imposed movements for targets of different colours. The results of such experiments would be of considerable interest.

10.13. Effect of fractions of the natural movements

Riggs and Tulunay (1959) investigated vision with eye-movements which were known fractions of the natural eye-movements. The apparatus was similar to that shown in Fig. 5.14, except that the mirrors M_6 and M_7 were replaced by a single reflecting prism P. The value of F, i.e. the fraction of the normal movements allowed to remain (§ 5.15), was varied by moving P. Normal vision corresponds to $F = 1$, and stabilized vision to $F = 0$. The target was a circular bipartite field (Fig. 9.2). Logarithmic differences (§ 9.4) of 0·63, 0·3, 0·21, and 0·1 were used. There was an unstabilized fixation annulus. The value of F could be altered from 1·15 to −0·25, and steps of 0·03 could be used. When F was varied the angular diameter of the target varied from 140′ to 45′. It is unlikely that this undesired complication had any important effect on the conclusions stated below.

10.14. In one series of experiments, F was varied only in respect of movements normal to the diametral boundary of the bipartite field. For directions parallel to the boundary F was equal to 1. Results are shown in Fig. 10.7. In these tests F was varied in steps of 0·15, and the value of V for $F = 0·2$ is significantly more than that for $F = 0$. In a second series of experiments F was varied by smaller steps from +0·15 to −0·02. No significant difference of V was observed. In this second series F was the same for both H- and V-movements. It is concluded that when F is within the range −0·1 to +0·1, vision is the same, i.e. the image is effectively stabilized.

10.15. Eye-movements were not recorded. In general, subjects in vision experiments tend to adopt any policy which improves visual performance, unless this policy is counter to an instruction. In this experiment,

† Ditchburn and Fender (1955).

visual performance would be improved by increasing the eye-move-ments (so as to make the retinal image movements more nearly normal) as F is reduced. However, the unstabilized fixation annulus would restrain this action to some extent.

From the data given in §§ 10.2–10.11, it appears that 20 per cent of the normal drift or tremor movements would have little effect on V. Therefore the increase of V when $F = 0.2$ (as compared with the value when $F = 0$) is probably due to saccades. If under the conditions of

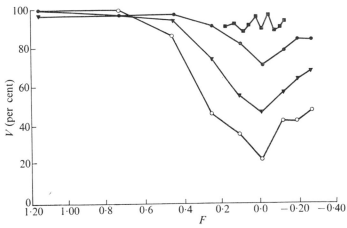

Fɪɢ. 10.7. Visibility related to stabilization ratio F for bipartite field: $dL = 0.62$ ■; 0.3 ●; 0.21 ▲; 0.10 ○. (After Riggs and Tulunay 1960.)

these experiments saccades of $10'$ were occurring, then the residual image movements would be saccades of $2'$, and these would be expected to have a significant effect (§ 10.8).

10.16. Most of the above experiments were carried out with a low contrast target. Fender (1956) using a dark bar $5'$ wide on a dark ground found that the visibility fell rapidly to zero at some value of F near to $F = 0$. Changes of F by less than 0.01 made a significant differ-ence. This result was repeated with the same subject but has not been obtained in any other experiment. Clowes and Ditchburn using the apparatus shown in Fig. 5.12 varied F by very small steps but did not find any sharp variation of V when F is near zero.

10.17. What value of F gives minimum visibility?

It has usually been assumed that the most accurate stabilization will be obtained when $F = 0$, the value of F being obtained from calcula-tions based on the optics of a telescopic system and confirmed by measurements with a telescope (§ 5.22). This is almost certainly true in respect of slow movements of the eyeball but it is possible that, in saccadic movements, the lens of the eye lags a little behind, subsequently resuming its normal relation to the eyeball.† In this situation, no system which accepts signals from the position of the eyeball will give exact dynamic compensation for all components of eye-movements, and it is possible that the best compensation would occur for a value of F near to, but not exactly equal to, zero. The value of F giving maximum difference from normal vision would probably be positive and less than 0·1. Complete stabilization, even if the optical system of the eye is not rigid should, in principle, be obtainable by the fundus-reflection method (§ 5.30).

10.18. Movements of extra-foveal stabilized images

Experiments on imposed movements have been made by Gerrits and Vendrik (1970). Most of their observations refer to the extra-foveal region of the retina. They used a small electric motor, mounted on a suction device, to produce the movements. The motor rotated at 50 revolutions s^{-1}. In order to produce slower apparent oscillation, stroboscopic illumination was used. This, of course, is a situation somewhat different from that involved in normal vision since the target is moving rapidly and is subject to intermittent illumination. The weight of the motor is also larger than that of attachments to the contact lens used by other experimenters. Some amount of mechanical destabilization due to this cause is likely. However, movements of a few minutes of arc (due to movement of the suction device) would not be very important since imposed retinal image movements of about 3° were used. Saccadic movements of 3° restored vision but the image faded again in a few seconds. This effect is similar to that described in §§ 10.7–10.8 for foveal images. Larger movements are needed to restore vision in the extra-foveal region than in the fovea because of the lower spatial resolution associated with larger receptor fields. However, the smallest saccade required to restore the image was not measured and may be much smaller than 3°.

10.19. When a target consisting of a dark circular patch was oscillated, with an amplitude of 1·5° and a frequency of 0·2 Hz, two arcs appeared. These are probably essentially similar to the comets observed by Yarbus (§ 10.3). At 2 Hz the whole of the circular disc was seen. At

† A small change in shape of the lens arising from inertia would produce the same effect.

4 Hz the image broke up. These oscillations involve velocities of the retinal image very much higher than the velocities due to the drift components of eye-movements, and amplitudes much larger than those associated with the oscillatory movements. These observations show that large movements in the extra-foveal region produce results similar to those obtained in the foveal region with small movements. Detailed comparison with the results of other experimenters is unprofitable because of the difference in method and approach.

10.20. Movements of the retinal blood vessels

Sharpe (1972) made detailed measurements on the visibility of the retinal blood vessels when a spot of light is moved across the expanded pupil of the eye, extending the work of Campbell and Robson (§§ 6.20 and 10.12). The retinal illuminance is not stated, but since the deep blue colour of the field was easily seen, photopic vision is involved. The larger blood vessels were seen when the light falling on them was temporally modulated, but movement of the shadows from one cone receptor to another was necessary to make the smaller vessels visible. The spot was made to oscillate in a linear path at a frequency in the range 2–20 Hz. The displacement required to make the vessels visible was smallest at about 10 Hz. If the spot was continuously scanned at the same frequency, the shadows became more difficult to see, and disappeared in times which varied with the size of vessel and the frequency. For frequencies of 10–20 Hz the shadows disappeared in 3–5 s—a time not much longer than that required for initial fading of a stabilized retinal image. For a frequency of 5 Hz, the times for disappearance ranged from 20 s for small vessels to 60 s for larger vessels. This suggests that still larger targets might not disappear at all.

10.21. Calculation of the magnitude of the movement of the shadows corresponding to a given movement of the spot on the pupil is difficult because the distance d of the blood vessels from the receptor varies a good deal. Some anatomists state that the vessels are in two or three layers (Duke-Elder (1961), Vol. II, Figs. 449 and 450). Others state that capillaries anastomose through all the retinal layers (Toussant, Kuwabara, and Cogan 1961), implying that d ranges from near zero to over 0·4 mm. Sharpe measured the movement of shadows for some of his own vessels and deduced $d = 0·12$ mm with a standard deviation of 0·03 mm. Other workers have obtained values from 0·19 to 0·36. Apart from the difficulty of this measurement, the results cannot be compared quantitatively with those described in §§ 10.5–10.11 because the region of the retina is different. Sharpe attempted to simulate the normal eye-movements of fixation, and found that the movements he used did not maintain good vision. This is in accordance with the observation that, when a subject fixates, vision in the periphery is lost, vision in the parafoveal region becomes less distinct, and some subjects experience partial fading even in the fovea. To some extent, the fatigue effect is transferred from one eye to another. This, together with other evidence, indicates that perceptual fading is controlled centrally (§§ 13.15–13.20).

10.22. Filling-in of scotomas

In normal vision the blind spot is not noticed and many patients are unaware of additional small blind regions due to pathological conditions. The visual system accepts the fact that no signals are received from certain parts of the visual field. It completes the pattern which it deduces from other regions by interpolation through the blind region. This is shown by the visual illusions produced by displaying targets which present to the blind regions target details (or omissions) which cannot be deduced by interpolation. With stabilized images patterns are occasionally completed, but this completion is intermittent and unstable except in a few situations, e.g. when the missing part is a small part of a circle. The boundaries of the blind spot, or of a small retinal scotoma, are stationary on the retina, and this explains why these boundaries are not seen. The completion of pattern is, however, much stronger than any similar phenomenon observed with stationary images. The visual processors have become adapted to the lack of information from certain areas and are thus accustomed to interpolate more extensively and for a wider range of patterns.

It is possible that the shadows of the blood vessels are essentially extensions of the blind spot. The visual system has learnt to offset signals from these areas, including signals associated with *small* changes of the direction of illumination or of colour. The vessels are not perfectly stabilized, owing to effects of the pulse which may be seen in an ophthalmoscope, or, in some circumstances, entoptically. (Friedman 1931; Adler 1965; Cornsweet 1970.) Thus the process which suppresses signals (or lack of signals) associated with the blood vessels may not be identical with that which suppresses a stabilized image of another retina (Cornsweet 1962). This can only be tested by further experiments on imposed movements of retinal images in the extrafoveal parts of the retina.

If the shadows of the retinal blood vessels are suppressed by an interpolation process as suggested above, then the experiments on moving shadows are of great interest as a unique way of investigating this process, but they do not give information about stabilized images. The fatigue effect may be much smaller for the movements of retinal images of external targets. So far, none of the experimenters on imposed movements has found a fatigue effect.

Stabilized images with fluctuating luminance

11.1. Perception of flicker

A great deal of work has been done on the perception of flicker when a subject views, in normal vision, a target whose luminance† $\mathcal{L}$ is made to fluctuate about a mean value $\mathcal{L}_0$. One condition, which has often been used, is obtained by interrupting the source of light so as to give equal periods of light and darkness (Fig. 11.1(c)). Flicker is perceived when the frequency of interruption f is less than some critical value f_c which is called the *critical fusion frequency* (CFF). It is found that f_c increases with $\mathcal{L}_0$; the curve of f_c versus log $\mathcal{L}_0$ is nearly linear (Fery-Porter law).

A new way of studying the way in which information about flicker is processed in the visual system was developed by de Lange (1957, 1958a and b), and extensively used by Kelly (1959, 1964). Suppose that only part of the light illuminating the target is interrupted so that there are alternate periods of luminance $\mathcal{L}_0(1+a/200)$ and $\mathcal{L}_0(1-a/200)$ as shown in Fig. 11.1(b). The quantity a then measures the difference between the extremes as a percentage of the mean. Since the total light cannot ever be negative, a is limited to the range 0–200. The case $a = 200$ is shown in Fig. 11.1(c). It is now possible to measure the value of a, when flicker is just perceived, as a function of frequency. This yields curves similar to those shown in Fig. 11.2.

11.2. Linearity of the system

A simple sinusoidal fluctuation of luminance (Fig. 11.1(a)) may be represented by

$$\mathcal{L} = \mathcal{L}_0\{1+A \sin(2\pi ft+\delta)\}, \tag{11.1a}$$

where $\mathcal{L}_0$ is the amplitude, f is the frequency of the fluctuating component, and δ is a phase constant. The relative amplitude A cannot

---

† $\mathcal{L}$ stands for the luminance, measured in cd m⁻². The symbol L, used in certain other chapters, stands for $\log_{10} \mathcal{L}$ i.e. for the logarithm (to base 10) of the luminance.

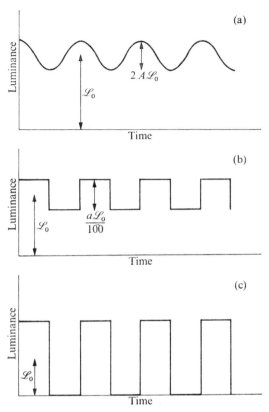

FIG. 11.1. (a) Sinusoidal modulation. (b) Square-wave modulation. (c) Intermittent illumination (square-wave).

exceed 1 since $\mathscr{L}$ cannot be negative. f is usually expressed in Hertz (1 Hz = 1 cycle per second). The period is $T = 2\pi/f$. Any other variation of $\mathscr{L}$ which has the same period T, (such as those shown in Figs. 11.1(b) and 11.1(c)) may be expressed as a Fourier series with f as fundamental frequency, i.e. we have

$$\mathscr{L} = \mathscr{L}_0\left\{1 + \sum_{n=1} A_n \sin(2\pi nft + \delta_n)\right\} \qquad (11.1\mathrm{b})$$

where n is a positive integer.

de Lange experimented with various waveforms and found that his results could be explained on the following assumptions:

(a) that the signals generated by modulation of the light were transmitted by a system equivalent to a low pass-filter whose attenuation characteristics are similar to the curves of Fig. 11.2;

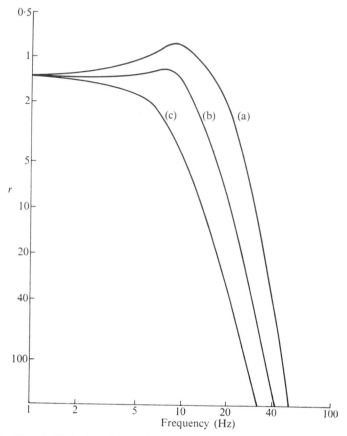

F IG. 11.2. Threshold values of r required for perception. Retinal illuminance (a) 430, (b) 43, and (c) 4·3 td. Each curve represents results obtained with modulation of more than one waveform, the appropriate value of *r* being calculated in each case. (After de Lange 1958*a*.)

(b) that for complex waveforms the effects of different Fourier components are additive provided that each is given the appropriate attenuation;

(c) the final 'discriminator' which decides that flicker is perceived, has a threshold signal that is independent of frequency; the whole variation with frequency is thus assigned to the attenuator.

Except when the frequency of modulation is very low, only the lowest Fourier component is effective because the higher components are completely suppressed by the filter. de Lange therefore defined the percentage ripple *r* by the relation

$$r = 100 \times \frac{\text{amplitude of fundamental Fourier component}}{\text{mean luminance}},$$

and showed r as a function of f. Some of his curves are shown in Fig. 11.2. For certain waveforms which include a period of total darkness in each cycle, r can reach the value 200 without $\mathscr{L}$ becoming negative.

A very large number of results obtained by de Lange (and by others) are consistent with the assumptions stated above, at least to a good approximation. It should, however, be noted that in these experiments the final response is made at the threshold of perception, i.e. the final 'signal' is very small. Many physical systems show linearity in respect of small differences,† and the technique used by de Lange is unlikely to reveal non-linearity. Evidence of non-linearity in the perception of flicker is given by Levinson (1964). We shall see below that there is evidence that, over a certain range, the effect of fluctuating illumination on vision with the S.R.I. is linear, but that in other conditions it is non-linear in a complicated way. This happens even when the second harmonic is far above f_c and would have no effect in a linear system.

11.3. Effect of eye-movements on perception of flicker

Kelly (1959, 1964) suggested that the effect of eye-movements should be considered in relation to the de Lange curves. If the target consists of a spot of light which covers a large number of receptor fields (Fig. 9.1), then some receptor fields will lie entirely within the illuminated area. These will give a rather small response because of the approximate balance between the opposed actions of the centre and the periphery of any one receptor field (§§ 7.28, 7.34–40). For receptor fields which are intercepted by the boundary the opposed effects are not equal and a higher net response should be obtained.

Receptors which are near a boundary are, in normal vision, continually undergoing changes of illuminance due to the eye-movements even when the light is steady. These changes have to be added to any change due to modulation of the light. It might therefore be expected that the measured sensitivity to flicker would be greater in normal vision than with a stabilized retinal image.

11.4. This effect should be largest at fairly low frequencies (1–10 Hz) because the eye-movements have relatively large amplitudes at these frequencies. The effect should be greater for a small circular target than for a large one, because the signal produced by the eye-movements is confined to receptors close to the boundary of the retinal image. Suppose that it is confined to an annular ring of width w min. arc and at the

† See Sperling (1963, 1964) for discussion of non-linearity.

edge of a target which is a circular disc of diameter D min. arc. Then the fraction of the total area for which the eye-movements are effective is $4w/D$. If $w = 3'$ then for $D = 240'$ diameter, this fraction is 0·05, but for $D = 60'$ it is 0·2. A given rate of angular movement will produce a larger rate of change of illumination with a sharp boundary than with a diffuse one (§ 11.10). This effect, therefore, should be greatest for a small target with a sharp boundary provided that the boundary lies within a region where the receptor fields are small and the acuity is good.

11.5. Keesey (1962) measured the de Lange curves for a target 240' in diameter with (a) normal vision and a sharp boundary, (b) normal vision and a diffuse boundary, and (c) stabilized vision. Sinusoidal modulation was used. The results are shown in Fig. 11.3. No significant differences were observed. In later experiments, she used targets of 30', 60', and

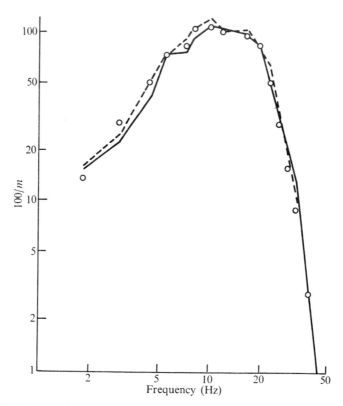

FIG. 11.3. Reciprocal of threshold modulation required for perception of flicker at various frequencies: target with sharp edge ———— ; with blurred edge ---------- ; stabilized image, 0 (from Keesey 1962).

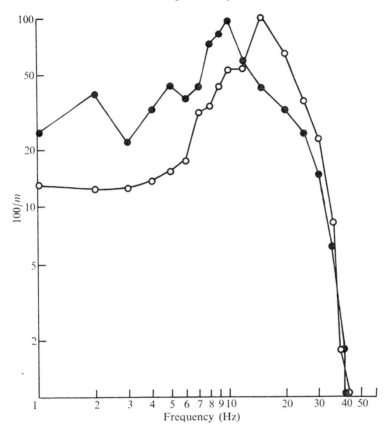

Fig. 11.4. Reciprocal of threshold modulation required for perception of flicker (minus-blue light): (a) normal eye-movements ●—●; (b) stabilized image ○—○. (From West 1968*b*).

120′ diameter. In a preliminary report† she stated that, using frequencies below 10 Hz, the curves obtained with a stabilized retinal image were lower than those obtained with normal vision. After further experiments she found no significant differences (Keesey 1970). West (1968*b*) used a circular field of 1·5° with minus-blue light (obtained with the filter specified in § 9.7) at an average luminance of 10⁴ cd m⁻². He obtained the curves shown in Fig. 11.4. At low frequencies the curve obtained with a stabilized image is lower than that obtained with normal vision, as Kelly predicted.

11.6. West (1968*b*) used minus-blue light because the results described in §§ 9.11 and 9.14 indicate that, even in the fovea, the size of receptor

† Meeting of Midwestern Psychological Association, Chicago, 1965.

fields for blue light is about 7'. Thus a vibration of amplitude less than 1' would have no effect. West thought that the blue component of white light would reduce any effect associated with the rest of the spectrum. The amount of light removed by the minus-blue filter is so small that if the dilution effect is proportional to the relative intensities of the different colours it would not account for the differences between the results obtained by Keesey and by West. However, the results described in § 11.17 suggest that the blue component of white light may have a larger effect than that expected from an estimate of its contribution to the total luminance.

West used high quality photographic lenses to obtain very sharp boundaries, and it is possible that the boundaries used by Keesey were not quite so sharp. On the whole, it appears probable that the effect predicted by Kelly does exist though possibly under a restricted range of conditions.

11.7. Vision of stabilized images when the luminance is slowly changed

Yarbus† (1960a) carried out experiments in which the logarithm L of the target luminance was made to change at a constant rate, so that:

$$\frac{dL}{dt} = \frac{d\,(\log_e \mathscr{L})}{dt} = \frac{1}{\mathscr{L}}\frac{d\mathscr{L}}{dt} = \mathscr{R}. \qquad (11.2)$$

t is measured in seconds and logarithms are to base e: $\mathscr{R}$ is constant in any one test. A fixed pupil of 1·5 mm was used so that $\mathscr{R}$ represents the rate of change of *retinal* illumination. Yarbus measured the minimum value of $\mathscr{R}$ for restoration of normal vision after the target had faded. We call this value $\mathscr{R}_m$. The apparatus is shown in Fig. 5.8. The target was a fine thread 3' wide seen against a bright circular field of diameter 11°. The luminance was altered by moving a logarithmic wedge. The second eye was occluded. Both the bar and the circular boundary were stabilized and, after a few seconds, the whole field became dark. Movement of the wedge began about 30 s later. When the wedge was moved with increasing velocity, the circular boundary appeared first, then parts of the thread, and finally the whole thread. The subject noticed that the luminance increased with time (§ 11.9). If the wedge was moved at a constant rate, the subject did not see the target immediately, but after the lapse of a small time T. It was found that parts of the thread appeared when $\mathscr{R}_m = 0\cdot3$, and the whole was seen clearly when

† See also Yarbus (1967, p. 64).

$\mathscr{R}_m = 1{\cdot}0$. These figures imply that change by a factor of $1{\cdot}3\ \mathrm{s}^{-1}$ is needed for moderately good vision, i.e. for the thread to be seen. $\mathscr{R}_m$ was the same for light increasing or decreasing and was independent of the initial luminance within the range† 3 cd m^{-2} to 250 cd m^{-2}.

11.8. The time-interval

The interval T between the first movement of the wedge and the time when the target was seen, was found to be about 1 s. It depended on the rate of change. It is probable that two kinds of process are involved in this situation: (a) a detector for rate of change (similar to the dimming detector described in § 7.44) and (b) a detector for total change in luminance. It is probable that both of these must be stimulated beyond their threshold level in order that the target may be seen. Obviously the target will not be seen if a very small change in luminance is made in zero time, although this would give an infinite value of $\mathscr{R}$. Also a very large change in log $\mathscr{L}$ does not make the target visible if the change is very slow. It would be interesting to have measurements of the minimum change of log $\mathscr{L}$ for vision of the target when the illumination is increased or decreased in a short time (0·05 s or less).

11.9. Perception of change of luminance in a ganzfeld

Waygood (1969) studied the perception of a slow change of illumination in a ganzfeld. A logarithmic wedge was moved at a uniform rate so as to change the illumination from 40 cd m^{-2} to 0·17 cd m^{-2} (or vice versa). This gives a difference of 2·3 in the logarithm to base 10 (or about 5 to base e). The time to make this change was varied from 18 s to 100 s so that $\mathscr{R}$ varied from 0·24 to 0·03. The pupil was not fixed but a correction was made to allow for change of the area of the pupil, so that $\mathscr{R}$ represents the rate of change of *retinal* illumination as in § 11.7. The relation between the percentage of time for which subjects perceived that the illumination was changing, and the rate of change $\mathscr{R}$, is shown in Fig. 11.5 curve (a). There was no significant difference between the values of $\mathscr{R}$ obtained for $\mathscr{L}$ increasing and those for $\mathscr{L}$ decreasing. The curve shows the mean of these values. It is found that when $\mathscr{R} = 0{\cdot}06$ the change was perceived 50 per cent of the time, and

† The retinal illumination varied from about 5 td to about 450 td.

when $\mathscr{R} = 0{\cdot}2$ the change was perceived 75 per cent of the time. The higher of these two values is close to the value of $\mathscr{R}_m = 0{\cdot}3$ which Yarbus obtained for partial visiblity of the retinal image. The observation that, in the experiments by Yarbus, the subjects noticed the change in luminance (§ 11.7) is in agreement with Waygood's results.

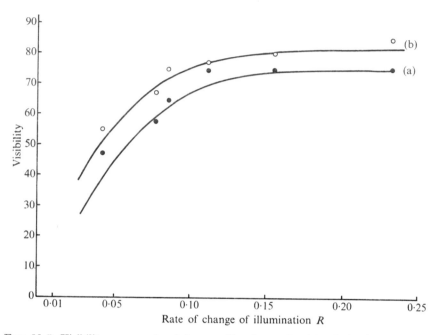

Fig. 11.5. Visibility versus rate of change of luminance for (a) 15° circular disc ● and (b) ganzfeld ○. (From Waygood 1969.)

Curve (b) of Fig. 11.5 shows the relation between rate of change of luminance and percentage of time for which a change is perceived when the field is limited by a sharp boundary to a central area of about 15°. Subjects are able to perceive the change more easily under this condition. Differences between the two curves are significant at $P = 0{\cdot}01$ level. Any signal depending solely on the area illuminated would be very much greater in the ganzfeld condition than with the limited area (which is only a small fraction of the whole area of the visual field). Since the boundaries of the limited area are unstabilized, the movement of the sharp boundary due to eye-movements produces rapid flucutations in the light received by receptors near the boundary (§ 11.10). These signals must be more than sufficient to compensate for the smaller area.

11.10. Change of illuminance due to movement of the target

Suppose that the variation of illuminance at a boundary between light and dark regions of a target is that shown in Fig. 9.7, and that the image is moved across the retina at a rate of v min. arc s^{-1}. Then the illumination of a receptor† situated at x will change at a rate

$$\mathscr{R} = v \frac{\mathrm{d} \log_e \mathscr{L}}{\mathrm{d}x} = vs, \tag{11.3}$$

where

$$s = \frac{\mathrm{d} \log_e \mathscr{L}}{\mathrm{d}x}$$

and x is a distance on the retina measured in minutes of arc. Suppose that the maximum values of s is $s_{\max}$ (corresponding to point A in Fig. 9.7).

It is of interest to compare the value of $\mathscr{R}_m$ required for vision when the illumination of the whole field is altered (§ 11.7), with that required when the illumination of receptors near a boundary is changed by moving the boundary (§§ 10.2 and 10.5). This comparison can be made only to within a factor of 3 because we do not know precisely the sharpness of the boundary of the meniscus (§ 10.3) or the sharpness of the target used by Ditchburn, Fender, and Mayne (§ 10.5). The latter was the image of a wire projected on to a ground-glass screen as shown in Fig. 5.10. We may estimate $s = 0.1$ (i.e. an edge blurred over 10′) for the meniscus, and $s = 0.3$ (i.e. an edge blurred over about 3′) for the image on the ground-glass screen. Taking $s = 0.1$ with $v = 4'$ s^{-1}, (§ 10.3) we obtain $\mathscr{R}_1 = 0.4$ for the rate of change of illumination on receptors near the boundary when the meniscus is seen. Taking $s = 0.3$ with $v = 5'$ s^{-1} (required for good vision according to the data given in § 10.6) we obtain $R_2 = 1.5$. The rates $\mathscr{R}_1$ and $\mathscr{R}_2$ agree, within a factor of 2, with $\mathscr{R}_m = 0.3$ for 'vision' and $R_m = 1.0$ for 'good vision' (§ 11.7) when the illumination of the whole field is changed. It may, at first, appear remarkable that these two rates of change should be of the same order of magnitude. In one experiment the illumination changes only at the boundaries, in the other it changes over the whole field. The fact that these rates are of the same order is in agreement with the hypothesis that, even when the illumination is varied over the whole field, the strongest signals come from receptor fields which are intercepted by boundaries (§ 11.3).

† For the calculation made in this paragraph, it is unnecessary to consider the effect of the finite area of the receptors. This becomes of importance in situations where the assumption of point detectors would lead to a very high value of $\mathscr{R}$.

11.11. Visibility of stabilized image with modulated illumination

In §§ 11.12–11.14 experiments on stabilized images with square-wave modulation (Fig. 11.1 (b) or (c)) and in §§ 11.15–11.17 with sinusoidal modulation, Fig. 11.1(a), are described. In these experiments the relation between the visibility V (defined in § 9.3) and the frequency f and relative amplitude A of the modulation is investigated.

It is known that a stabilized image is seen clearly when first presented, and becomes hazy in a time t_0 which is about 1–2 s. It may therefore be expected that, when the illumination is interrupted at very low frequency with period $T = 1/f$, the image will be clearly seen for a fraction t_0/T of the total time of presentation so that

$$V = t_0/T = t_0 f.$$

Thus, at very low frequencies, V should increase with f. At higher frequencies the effects of 'on' and 'off' stimulation will interfere with one another so that V should decrease again towards the value obtained with steady illumination.

11.12. Square-wave modulation (intermittent illumination)

Pritchard (1958a) measured (for each frequency) the value of a (§ 11.1) required to cause the visibility factor V to rise by 20 per cent. He used the ring pattern† (Fig. 5.4) extending over 25°, and a luminance of about 5 cd m^{-2}. The CFF for this target was 35 Hz. His results are shown in Fig. 11.6. They indicate that for red and green light the most efficient frequency for assisting vision with the S.R.I. is less than 2 Hz. There is a monotonic decrease as the frequency increases so that 100 per cent modulation is required to raise the visibility V by 20 per cent at 15 Hz. Small increases of visibility were obtained at higher frequencies up to 60 Hz. The increases of V for frequencies above f_c were not considered to be significant.

For blue light Pritchard found the maximum effect at 2·5 Hz i.e. an appreciably higher frequency than that found (by himself and other

---

† The rings close up towards the outer edge, and clear detail is seen only in the central region of about 15°—possibly a little less for blue.

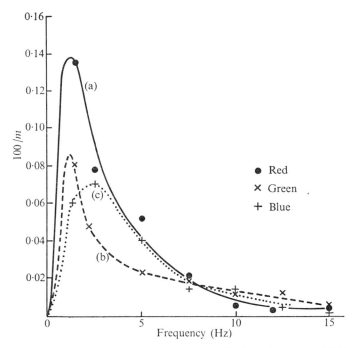

Fig. 11.6. Reciprocal of modulation ($\times$ 100) required to increase visibility by 20 versus frequency of modulation for red, green, and blue. (From Pritchard 1958a.)

workers) for white, red or green. This is probably associated with the observation that blue and blue-green stabilized images fade more rapidly than those which are white or red. Pritchard measured the variation of V with f for $a = 50$, $a = 100$, and $a = 200$ in a separate experiment with green light. There was no evidence of non-linearity.

11.13. Fiorentini and Ercoles (1960) examined the visibility of narrow bars 40′ long and 0·5′, 3′, and 12′ wide with intermittent illumination† with frequencies from 0·1 Hz to 28 Hz. The target luminance was fairly low ($\sim$1·5 cd m^{-2}). In these conditions the visibility increased with frequency of interruption at very low frequencies, and the target was seen during nearly all the light period when f was a little less than 1 Hz. The visibility fell back to that corresponding to steady illumination as f was increased. Since the approach to the value for steady illumination is asymptotic, there is no well-defined limiting frequency

---

† A variety of conditions were studied. For example in some experiments, the line was black and the background was modulated; in others the luminance of the line was modulated. Results included in Table 11.1 are typical.

f_s above which intermittency has no effect. However, in one series of experiments f_s may be estimated as between 8 Hz and 10 Hz. The CFF when the wire was intermittently illuminated and the field remained steady was 5 Hz, and when the whole field was flickered it was 15 Hz. Thus f_s and f_c were of the same order of magnitude. Similar results were obtained by Cornsweet (1956) at a much higher luminance (800 cd m^{-2}). Fender (1956) used a target consisting of a dark bar 60′ × 3′ seen on a bright field. A a luminance of 16 cd m^{-2} he found one peak at 20 Hz, and at a luminance of 160 cd m^{-2} there were peaks at about

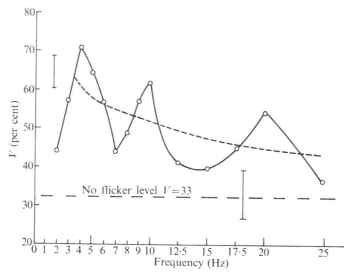

FIG. 11.7. Variation of V with frequency (intermittent illumination as in Fig. 11.1(a)) (r = 200 throughout). I represents error limits for single reading. (After West 1968a.) – – – 'Smoothed curve' showing only one peak.

18 Hz and 36 Hz. West (1965, 1968a) used as target a bipartite field with the two parts of different luminance (Fig. 9.2). The criterion of vision was that the subject should be able to perceive a difference of luminance between the two parts of the field. West made one experiment at 3·0 cd m^{-2} and obtained only one peak at about 3 Hz, but when the luminance was increased to 730 cd m^{-2} peaks were observed at 4 Hz, 10 Hz, and 20 Hz (Fig. 11.7). The existence of peaks at 10 Hz and 20 Hz is not established beyond doubt since the observations deviate from the dashed line by little more than the experimental error. However, even this curve implies a considerable effect of flicker in the range 15–22 Hz.

11.14. Summary of results on intermittent illumination

The results obtained on intermittent illumination by different workers are summarized in Table 11.1. At luminances below 10 cd m^{-2}, the low-

TABLE 11.1†

Intermittent illumination

Authors	Luminance (cd m^{-2})	Frequency range (Hz)	Hue	Size of target (min. arc)	Shape of Target	Peak Frequencies (Hz)
Ditchburn and Fender (1955)	80	5–60	White	60′ × 5′	Black Bar	18 (flat)
Fender (1956)	160	8–100	White	60′ × 3′	Black Bar	18, 36(?), 50(?)
	32	5–60	White	60′ × 8′	Bar	15
	16	5–80	White	60′ × 3′	Bar	20
Cornsweet (1956)	800	0·8–9·6	White	72′ × 0·1′	Black line	0·8
Pritchard (1958)	5	2–80	Red	1500′ diameter	Rings	1
			Green	1500′ diameter	Rings	1
			Blue	1500′ diameter	Rings	2·5
Fiorentini and Ercoles (1960)	0·7–7	0·5–28	White	40′ × 0·5′	Black line	2
	1·9	0·5–28	White	40′ × 0·5′		0·5–1·0
	1·2	0·5–28	White	40′ × 12′		1
	1·4	0·5–28	White	40′ × 3′		1
West (1965)	730	1–25	Green	90′ diameter	B.P.F.	4, 10, 20
	970	2–8	Green	180′ diameter	B.P.F.	3, 6
	3·0	2–20	Green	180′ diameter	B.P.F.	3
	540	2–20	Red	90′ diameter	B.P.F.	7, 15
	730	2–8	Red	180′ diameter	B.P.F.	4, 10
Yarbus (1962)	1000	1–50	White	60′ diameter	Circles	4 (or less), 11

† B.P.F. indicates bipartite field.

frequency effect discussed in § 11.11 is predominant. At high luminances an additional effect appears. There are peaks at higher frequencies which depend on the size of target and other experimental conditions. In any one condition the peak frequencies are approximately, but not exactly, multiples of the lowest frequency. It is possible that if the 'tail' of the low-frequency effect could be subtracted these peaks would all be seen to be multiples of a single frequency. In West's experiments this basic frequency is about 5 Hz.

11.15. Effect of sinusoidal modulation

West (1965, 1968a) arranged to modulate the light in accordance with the relation shown in Fig. 11.1(a). A typical curve of V versus f (when $A = 1$) for high luminance ($L_0 = 730$ cd m^{-2}) and a small target (1·5°) is shown in Fig. 11.8. Once again the criterion of vision is that the subject should be able to perceive the difference between the two parts of the field. There is a fairly broad maximum at about 5 Hz and no other peak. The curve shown in Fig. 11.8 is for green light, but similar results were obtained with red and white. The results for blue are very different (§ 11.17). Note that the maximum value of V is much less than 100 per cent, indicating that the maximum effect of sinusoidal variation is less than that of intermittent illumination. The results for a number of targets and for other experimental conditions are summarized in Table 11.2. The following generalizations can be made:

(a) The shape of curve is nearly the same for white, red, and green.

(b) The peak frequency is about the same for bipartite field and for line targets, provided that the target is within the fovea.

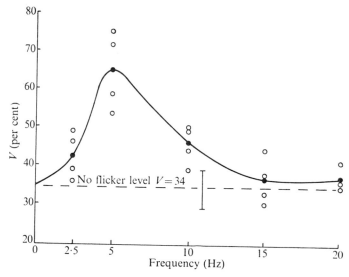

FIG. 11.8. Variation of V with frequency (sinusoidal modulation). Green light, bipartite field of diameter 1·5°, d$L = 0·15$, $\mathscr{L}_0 = 730$ cd m^{-2}. (After West 1968a.)

TABLE 11.2

Sinuisoidal fluctuation of luminance†

Luminance (cd m^{-2})	Hue	Target size	Target type	Subject	Peak frequencies (Hz)
730	White	90′	B.P.F.	W	3·5
2·4	White	90′	B.P.F.	B	No effect
730	Green	90′	B.P.F.	W	5
730	Red	90′	B.P.F.	W, B	4·5
92	Blue	90′	B.P.F.	W	4·5
145	Blue	90′	B.P.F.	B	2
92	Blue	45′	B.P.F.	W, B	6
92	Blue	240′	B.P.F.	W, B	1·5
730	Green	90′	B.P.F.	W	6
730	Green	90′	B.P.F.	W	8 (25 per cent modulation)
2·4	Green	90′	B.P.F.	W	4 (weak)
970	Green	180′	B.P.F.	B	7
3	Green	180′	B.P.F.	B	4 (weak)
730	White	90′	B.P.F.	W, B	5
730	White	90′	Dark bar	W, B	5
730	White	60′	Dark bar	P	2
730	White	240′	Dark bar	P	6
730	White		Bright bar 2′ or 4′ or 8′ wide		4
10–1000	White	60′	Bright bar 4′ wide	U.T.K., D.J.N.	2·5 and 6

† Results in last row due to Keesey (1969), remainder to West (1968a).

(c) If the target extends beyond the fovea (to 4°), or if a small target is placed 2° from the centre, the peak shifts to a lower frequency.

(d) If the luminance is reduced, the peak frequency falls by about 1 Hz for one log unit.

(e) The effect of modulation on V becomes less as the luminance is reduced, and is almost zero at 2·5 cd m^{-2}. Intermittent illumination of the eye which was not viewing the stabilized image produces no effect. When the frequency is constant, V increases with r (§ 11.2) from $r = 0$ to $r = 150$, and then remains unchanged when r is increased from 150 to 200.

11.16. Keesey (1969) describes experiments in which a vertical bar is seen against a circular background of 1° diameter. The boundaries of the bar and of the circular area were stabilized. The fixation mark was an unstabilized annulus (inner diameter 1·5°). In most of the experiments the bar was 5′ wide and was brighter than the background. White light with luminances in the range 10 cd m^{-2} to 1000 cd m^{-2} was used. The luminance of the bar was varied sinuisoidally; a range of

0–30 Hz was covered (with a few experiments at higher frequencies). Observations were confined to the first 20 s after presentation of the target. The bar was visible during the whole of this period for frequencies 2·5 Hz, 4 Hz, 5 Hz, and 6 Hz. As the frequency was increased the effect was reduced steadily, and in two subjects (out of three) there was no difference in visibility between steady illumination and fluctuation at any frequency above 20 Hz. Keesey and West agree that the largest effect of sinuisoidal fluctuation occurs at frequencies in the range 2–6 Hz, but the effect found by Keesey is larger. This suggests that the effect of fluctuation at a constant frequency decreases with time. This would correspond with observations of Campbell and Robson (§ 6.20) and Sharpe (§ 10.20), and with the electrophysiological experiments of Hübel and Wiesel (§ 7.41). Keesey's subjects reported that when the target could no longer be distinguished (at high frequencies) the field still appeared to flicker. Also, this subjective flicker appeared to cover the whole field, whereas in normal vision the subject could see clearly that only the bar was flickering.

11.17. Sinusoidal modulation (blue light)

The effect of sinusoidal modulation with a foveal target and blue light is shown in Fig. 11.9 (West 1968a). There appears to be a negative effect on V over the whole frequency range, together with a positive effect similar to that found for other colours. The criterion of vision is explained in § 11.15. The negative effect implies that under certain

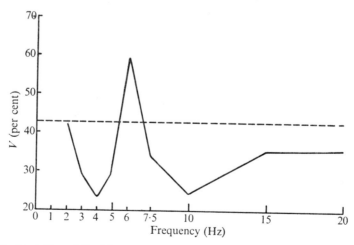

FIG. 11.9. Variation of V with frequency (sinusoidal modulation). Blue light, bipartite field of diameter 0·75°, $dL = 0·15$. (After West 1968a.)

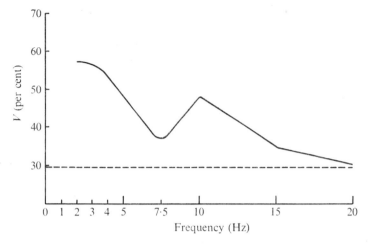

Fɪɢ. 11.10. Variation of *V* with frequency (sinusoidal modulation). Blue light bipartite field of diameter 4°, d*L* = 0·15. (After West 1968*a*.)

conditions it is more difficult to perceive a difference of luminance between two adjacent flickering areas than between two similar areas which are not flickering. The positive effect peaks rather sharply and, at its maximum, exceeds the negative effect, so that the over-all effect is then positive. The curve shown in Fig. 11.9 is for a target only 45′ in diameter placed as accurately as possible in the central fovea, and it shows the negative effect more strongly than a target 90′ in diameter. When the target diameter is increased to 240′ the effect is positive at all frequencies (Fig. 11.10). There is an indication of a peak at 10 Hz as well as the low frequency peak. The difference between subjects is greater for blue light than for another colour. Negative effects at certain frequencies were observed with green and white light. These were so small that they would not have been regarded as significant before the larger negative effect in blue light was obtained.

11.18. Possible artefacts with fluctuating illumination

The following three artefacts which would produce misleading effects in experiments with fluctuating light need consideration:

(a) It is possible the fluctuating illumination may induce an increase in large saccadic eye-movements causing the contact lens to slip, and so producing mechanical destabilization,

(b) The field may not darken uniformly so that in some part of the cycle there may be a moving 'shadow' in the field. This would increase V by a 'moving edge' effect,

(c) The waveform may not be exactly as designed, and harmonics or subharmonics of the nominal frequency may be producing some effect.

The first two of these are important because they suggest the possibility of an increase of V which has nothing to do with the change of retinal illuminance.

The first of these possibilities was examined by West and Boyce (§ 14.29). They found that if a subject fixates a source of light which is intermittent at a frequency of about 2·0 Hz, there is an increase in the frequency of saccadic movements. However, if the fixation mark is steadily illuminated there is no increase in frequency of saccades due to another intermittent source seen by the other eye. Also there is no increase of saccades when there is no precise fixation mark. Thus it does not appear that an increase of saccades would be produced in any of the experiments described above.

The second possibility arises with all methods in which a light beam is mechanically interrupted by a blade which cuts through it at a focus. The arrangement is similar to that used in the Foucault knife-edge test for concave mirrors.† Unless the optical system is very good and the blade cuts exactly through the focal plane, part of the field darkens first and a distinct shadow appears in the field. West used a reasonably good optical system to form an image of the source, and arranged that a blade moved slowly through the focal plane. It was found that, when care was taken with alignment and focus, the field darkened uniformly until near the end of the movement. Then one part became black first, and the moving shadow was seen momentarily before the light was extinguished over the whole field. The field was so dark when this happened that it seemed very unlikely that there would be any effect on V. In order to be quite sure, the effect was greatly increased by displacing the blade from the focal plane so that the shadow was much stronger. No change in V was produced.

In West's experiments the waveform of the fluctuating light beam was checked by allowing a small fraction to enter a photo-multiplier whose output went to a Fenlow analyser. The sine-wave was found to be contaminated with 1·3 per cent of second harmonic. The square wave had slightly less than the theoretically calculated proportion of the higher harmonics. (e.g. 10·94 per cent instead of 11.11 per cent of third harmonic). These differences from the nominal waveforms are so small that they cannot have any significant effect on the results.

† Ditchburn (1963, p. 327).

11.19. Discussion of effects of modulation

The considerations stated in the preceding paragraph show that the following must all be accepted as genuine effects of modulation:

(a) A low frequency effect which peaks at frequencies of 6 Hz or less for sinusoidal modulation, and at frequencies of 2 Hz or less for square-wave modulation,

(b) The complicated positive and negative effects obtained with sinusoidal modulation and blue light,

(c) The large difference (especially with blue light) between small targets viewed by the fovea and targets large enough for their boundaries to be entirely outside the fovea. It is very probable that square-wave modulation at high luminance gives effects at frequencies above 5 Hz including multiple peaks.

The results of the experiments of Pritchard (§ 11.12), who adjusted a to give a *small* change in V, are very similar to those of de Lange who adjusted r to give a just-perceptible flicker. In each case the measurement is made when the variation of luminance is adjusted to produce small signals near the limit of perception. Both the experiments on flicker fusion and those on vision with the stabilized image indicate that under this condition the system can be represented by a linear low-pass filter (§ 11.2).

It is common experience that a system which gives a linear response to small signals may be non-linear when larger signals are involved. A few experiments on flicker fusion (§ 11.2), and many of the experiments on stabilized images (§§ 11.13–11.15), indicate that the response of the human visual system to intermittent signals which are not small is non-linear and is very complicated. It is possible that, in this situation, Fourier analysis of signals is not very profitable. It may be better to consider the effect as due to an interaction of signals produced when the luminance is increasing ('on-signals'), with those produced when it is decreasing ('off-signals'). There is a good deal of electrophysiological evidence that 'on-signals' are very much larger than 'off-signals' when the luminance is low (Granit and Tansley 1948). It is therefore to be expected that complications due to their interaction would appear only at high luminance.

The results obtained with stabilized images suggest that further work on flicker fusion is required to extend our knowledge of the non-linear phenomena. Unfortunately, the simplest kind of experiments would involve asking subjects to say when two fields were flickering to an equal degree when both were giving an unpleasantly large flicker. This judgement would, at best, be much less accurate than the threshold judgments involved in the experiments of de Lange. Caution when using flicker near 10 Hz (i.e. near the alpha-rhythm frequency) would be needed. Further experiments on the electrophysiology of nerve signals generated by flicker at high intensities might be of considerable interest.

11.20. The results obtained with blue light are entirely unexpected. It appears that under certain conditions the signals which lead to perception of flicker can interfere with the signals which are associated with perception of contrast. This would produce the negative effect shown in Fig. 11.9. It might be possible to study this effect further by superimposing flickering illumination upon the after-image of a bipartite field. The striking differences between the results obtained with small blue sources viewed foveally, and those obtained with similar sources of white light, adds one more to the many anomalies associated with foveal vision in blue light.

To sum up, the existence of non-linear effects in the processing of visual signals produced by fluctuating illumination at photopic levels is clearly demonstrated. These effects are complicated and it is premature to form a detailed hypothesis. The further study of these effects will require experiments by many methods apart from the stabilized image. This study is likely to be difficult, but may be important both in regard to understanding the processing of visual information and for practical problems. Fluctuating illumination is used both for signalling, for attracting attention to advertisements, and in many lighting systems. It is desirable to understand its effects as completely as we can. In our present state of knowledge we cannot be sure that they are all favourable or even harmless.

11.21. Perception of structure and perception of flicker

Many observations on the effect of modulation of the light on stabilized images imply that the frequencies which enable the structure of the target to be seen are, in general, considerably lower than the appropriate CFF (§§ 11.12–11.16). Whether the criterion of vision is the perception of a bar or of a boundary between two parts of a bipartite field, there is a range of frequencies which are too high to have much effect on V but are still low enough to enable flicker to be perceived. As stated by Pritchard,[†] subjects report that, if the flicker rate is below the CFF, the

----

† Pritchard (1958a, p. 102). See also § 11.16 above.

stabilized image may still fade, but the field is seen to be illuminated *and flickering*. This suggests that the signals which convey information about the structure of the target (form-vision) are different from those which convey perception of a flickering source. The conclusion reached in Chapter 10, that the signals associated with form-vision are generated by changes of local retinal illumination due to the eye-movements of *low* frequency (1–8 Hz) is supported.

11.22. Perception of hue and perception of flicker

Pritchard† also stated that, for flicker frequencies between 15 Hz and the CFF, subjects reported that the fading S.R.I. leaves a field which is the same hue as the incident illumination, though desaturated. When the flicker rate is between 5 Hz and 15 Hz the field appears mono-chromatic (grey). The range of frequencies for which hue is not per-ceived probably depends on the size and retinal location of the S.R.I. and also on the target luminance. This observation may be compared with the phenomenon which is the basis of the flicker photometer method of comparing sources of different hue. Light from the two sources is presented to the observer alternately. At low frequencies of alternation both differences of luminance and differences of hue are observed. As the frequency is raised, a stage is reached at which the two colours fuse so that the alternation of hue is not perceived, though a fairly small difference of luminance causes an unpleasant flicker.‡ de Lange (1958*b*) has measured the value of r (a) to produce a perceived difference of luminance and (b) to produce a perceived difference of hue, when a fraction of the light is made to alternate between red and green. This fraction in superposed on a background of orange light which matches the red-green mixture. In each case r is measured as a function of f to yield an attenuation characteristic. The characteristics for the two functions are different especially at high frequencies (Fig. 11.11). This suggests the possibility of obtaining an attenuation char-acteristic for perception of hue in an S.R.I. by methods similar to those used by Pritchard (§ 11.12).

11.23. The preceding paragraph described conditions in which hue is perceived but structure is not. This was observed with a target which had no sharp boundaries. In § 9.28, an observation was described in

---

† Pritchard (1958*a*).

‡ In this discussion we are omitting a phase difference which, although interesting in other respects, does not appear to be relevant to the present discussion.

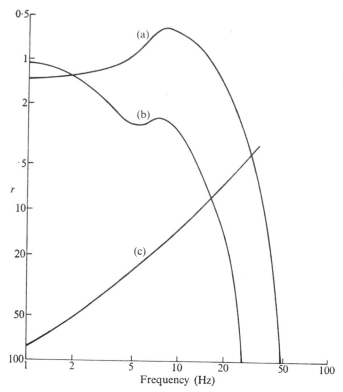

FIG. 11.11. Modulation required to perceive: (a) flicker when luminance is modulated, and (b) flicker when part of the light alternates between red and green; (c) shows (on a logarithmic scale) the ratio between r_1 (for luminance-difference perception) and r_c (for hue-difference perception). (After de Lange 1958b.)

which the structure of the target was seen but the field appeared to be monochromatic. This was obtained with a target which had sharp boundaries and very fine lines. It thus appears that form-vision and colour-vision can each be observed under a condition in which the other has disappeared.

The use of information in the visual system

12.1. Acquisition and processing of information

In this chapter and in Chapter 13 we are concerned with two very different kinds of experiments on the capacity of the human visual system to acquire and to process information. In the experiments considered in this chapter, the subject is presented with a simple target and makes a precise judgement in respect of the presence or absence of one well-defined feature. For example, in a vernier acuity test he decides whether two lines are collinear or not. In the experiments described in Chapter 13, the subject is presented with a more complicated kind of pattern and asked to describe what he sees. His description is made in terms of patterns previously seen, and this kind of judgement may be called 'pattern recognition'.

The acuity judgements are directly limited by the rate at which the visual system can accept information, and we can understand a considerable part of the process in terms of well-established physical theories. The pattern recognition judgements appear to use only a small fraction of the available information, and to be limited by the rate at which information can be processed or by the amount of information which can be held as available memory.

We can seek for points of contact between the results of the two kinds of experiments on visual information. One such point of contact is the way in which both kinds of subject-response are affected when the retinal image is stabilized.

The way in which information obtained by the retinal receptors is filtered and recoded is shown by the electrophysiological experiments described in §§ 7.22 to 7.45. It is almost certain that similar processes, and probably more complicated coding systems, operate in the human visual system. Since these electrophysiological experiments involve damage, human visual perception cannot be explored in detail by these methods.

12.2. Stages in visual perception

The process by which a person receives visual information may be divided into the following three stages.

(a) Formation of the retinal image by the dioptric system.

(b) Transference of information from the retinal image to the retinal receptors.

(c) Analysis, filtering, and coding in the retina, and transfer of information via the optic nerve for processing in the visual cortex.

Some loss of information in each stage is inevitable. In stage (a), loss occurs because spatial frequencies above a certain limit are not transmitted, and frequencies below that limit are attenuated by diffraction and by aberrations of the dioptric system. The amount of information† accepted is roughly proportional to the area‡ under the curve for the logarithm of modulation transfer-function (M.T.F.) versus spatial frequency (Fig. 1.21). In stage (b), there are losses due to the finite size of the retinal receptors and to the gaps between them. In stage (c), there are losses due to the finite time required to pass information from one part of a neural network to another, and to physiological 'noise' (i.e. random spikes not associated with a stimulus). It is also probable that any large neural system will contain a significant number of defective elements.

12.3. The optical quality of the dioptric system has been described in §§ 1.25–1.29. In §§ 12.6–12.21 we consider stage (b) and discuss whether scanning of the retinal image by the eye-movements is used to increase the amount of information which is extracted from the retinal image by the receptors. As an introduction to this problem an account of some theoretical work on fibre-optics is given in §§ 12.6–12.8. Stage (c) is considered in §§ 12.22–12.25, and the possibility of an edge-sharpening system is discussed in § 12.26. It must be emphasized that information, once lost, can never be retrieved. Neither scanning in stage (b), nor neural interaction in stage (c), can restore information which has been lost elsewhere in the system. Scanning and neural interaction may recode the available information in such a way that it is more readily accepted and more efficiently used by those parts of the brain which initiate action in response to visual information.

† The information content of optical images is treated by Fellgett and Linfoot (1955). An introduction to the subject is given in Chapter 8 and Chapter 20 of Ditchburn (1963).

‡ This rule applies to the targets of one dimensional structure discussed in §§ 1.28–1.31. For two dimensional targets, the logarithm of the M.T.F. should be multiplied by the frequency (p) before integrating.

12.4. Linearity of the visual system

Campbell and Robson (1968) present evidence that Fourier analysis may be applied to the discussion of contrast thresholds of sinusoidal gratings, square-wave gratings, etc. Predictions based on the assumption of linear addition of Fourier components are found to agree with the experimental results. It is reasonable to assume that there is a fairly wide range of luminance in which the human visual system, taken as a whole, may be regarded as a linear system. This over-all linearity might be achieved by one part of the system compensating non-linearity in another, but it is unlikely that this is so. Physical laws imply that stage (a) is linear, and make it nearly certain that stage (b) is also linear, except at very high luminance. If stage (a) and stage (b) are linear, then the over-all linearity implies that stage (c) is also linear. This does not mean that there are no conditions in which non-linearity will appear (see § 11.19 for discussion of a similar problem). We shall however assume, for the discussion of the results of experiments described in this chapter, that each stage of the human visual system may be regarded as an independent linear unit, i.e. each has an output which is directly proportional to its input.

We then define the following functions:

$M(p)$ is the M.T.F. of the dioptric system (§§ 1.28–1.29);

$A(p)$ is an *acceptance function* for transfer of information from the retinal image to the retinal mosaic;

$N(p)$ measures the efficiency of the neural processor in accepting and using information about a sinusoidal component of spatial frequency p;

$R(p)$ is the reciprocal of the threshold contrast when the subject views sinusoidal fringes of frequency p which are *external to the eye*.

$R'(p)$ is the corresponding reciprocal of the threshold contrast when the fringes are formed on the retina.

$M(p)$, $A(p)$, and $N(p)$ measure the efficiencies of stage (a), stage (b), and stage (c) respectively. $R(p)$ measures the over-all efficiency of the visual system.

These definitions, together with the assumption of independent linearity, imply that

$$R(p) = M(p)R'(p); \qquad (12.1a)$$
$$R'(p) = A(p)N(p); \qquad (12.1b)$$
$$R(p) = M(p)A(p)N(p). \qquad (12.1c)$$

In future we shall use M, A, etc. for $M(p)$, $A(p)$, etc.

12.5. The results of measurements of M are shown in Fig. 12.1. R has been measured by a number of workers including Schade (1948), Ooue (1959), Arnulf and Dupuy (1960), Campbell and Green (1965), Van Nes and Bouman (1967), Campbell and Robson (1968), and Gilbert and Fender (1969). Van Nes and Bouman made detailed measurements

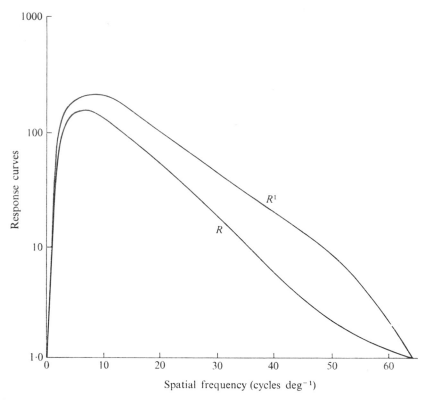

FIG. 12.1. Reciprocal of threshold contrast: R for fringes external to the eye, R' for interference fringes formed on the retina. (Data of Campbell and Green 1965.)

on the effect of luminance level for different colours. Campbell and Gubisch (1967) investigated the effect of chromatic aberrations on results obtained with white light. R' has been measured by the workers quoted in §§ 1.30 and 1.31. Mitchell, Freeman, and Westheimer (1967) have investigated the effect of orientation on M. Fig. 12.1 shows results for R and R' obtained by Campbell and Green *for the same subject.* The results of later investigations, especially the work of Campbell and Robson, have been used to extend the curves at very low frequencies. Nearly all observers find a maximum value of R at some frequency in the range 2 cycles deg^{-1} to 7 cycles deg^{-1}. This frequency decreases with

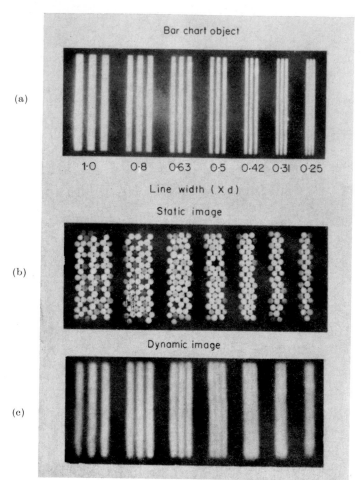

FIG. 12.3. Fibre optics: (a) object; (b) image formed by static system; (c) image formed by dynamic system (After Kapany.)

illumination (for any one observer), but at a given illumination there appears to be a fairly large inter-subject variation both in the magnitude and position of the maximum. Van Nes and Bouman find that, after making a fairly small correction for variation of diffraction with wavelength, the results are little affected by colour, provided the level of luminance is within the photopic range.

12.6. Fibre-optics

As an introduction to the theory of acceptance of information by the receptor mosaic, consider the physical system shown in Fig. 12.2. A

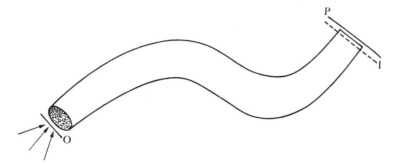

FIG. 12.2. Fibre optics system.

transluminated object O is placed in contact with the end of a bundle of glass fibres. If the fibres are suitably coated, the light which enters any one fibre is transmitted to the other end of that fibre, and there is no transfer of light between adjacent fibres. If the arrangement of fibres is preserved along the length of the bundle, an image I of the object O is obtained at the far end. This image may be recorded on a photographic plate P.

In the *static system* the fibre bundles and the photographic plate remain stationary. Fig. 12.3(b) shows the image of the grating object depicted in Fig. 12.3(a). The mosaic structure is seen but the resolution is not very good. In the *dynamic system*, the two ends of the fibre bundle are oscillated—one with respect to the object, and the other with respect to the photographic plate. In this system the two ends of the bundle are displaced at any instant, by equal amounts and in the same direction from their mean position. The image obtained in this way is sharper, and the mosaic structure is not seen (Fig. 12.3(c)). The mean amplitude of oscillation should be at least equal to the spacing of the fibres, and preferably about twice as large.

12.7. Acceptance function for a dynamic system (fibre-optics)

Drougard and Potter (1967) and Kapany (1967) discuss the quality of the images produced in fibre-optics systems, (a) with scanning, and (b) without scanning. When a single fibre scans a sinusoidal grating (§ 1.28) in a direction perpendicular to the lines, the image produced is a grating of the same spacing but lower contrast. It is thus possible to define a modulation transfer function analogous to the function M for a lens system (§ 1.28). This function may be expressed as the product of two equal factors. One factor is associated with the entry of light into the fibre, and the other with the exit of light from the fibre. One of these factors is

$$T(p) = \frac{2J_1(\pi pd)}{\pi pd} , \qquad (12.2)$$

where d is the diameter of the fibre, p is the spatial frequency of the grating, and J_1 stands for Bessel's function of order unity. $T(p)$, which is shown in Fig. 12.4 curve (a), is zero when p has the value p_1 given by

$$p_1 = 1 \cdot 22/d. \qquad (12.3)$$

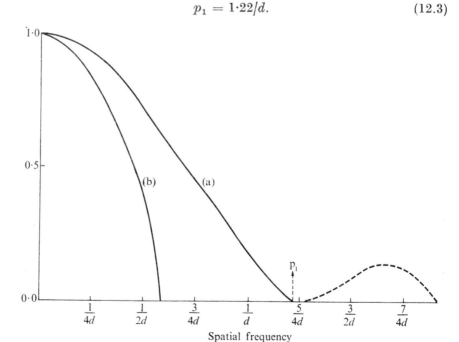

Fig. 12.4. Acceptance function, $T(p)$, for fibre optics; (a) scanning system, (b) static system, irregular mosaic.

T will be called the 'acceptance function'. True resolution is usually regarded as limited to frequencies less than p_1, though some structure is seen for frequencies between p_1 and $2p_1$. This is called 'spurious resolution' (§1.31).

Consider now a mosaic of fibres, which are not necessarily regularly arranged, but are fairly closely packed. If the ends of the bundle are oscillated together through at least twice the average distance between the centres of neighbouring fibres, then the whole area is scanned. The amount of information received per second is proportional to the number of fibres, but so is the area explored. Thus, to a good approximation, the acceptance function of the scanning bundle is the same as that of a single scanning fibre. This property is independent of the precise arrangement of the fibres and of the scanning path, within wide limits.

12.8. Acceptance function for a static system (fibre-optics)

A static system whose mosaic constitutes a regular array possesses characteristic spatial frequencies. For example, a square array has a frequency $p_m = 1/a$ (where a is the length of the side of a square). When this is superposed on a grating of spatial frequency p, beat fringes of frequency $(p_m - p)$ appear in the image (Fig. A.3 of Kapany 1967). Thus the image is not a linear representation of the object, and no acceptance function can be defined.

For an irregular mosaic superposed on a considerable area of an object, an approach to an acceptance function can be made in the following way. Loss of information is due to two causes. There is first a loss due to the finite diameter of the fibres, and this is given by eqn (12.2). There is a second loss due to the finite number of points at which the image is sampled. This may be estimated by applying the sampling theorem.† If there are N^2 fibres per unit area, then complete information about amplitude and phase may be obtained for spatial frequencies not greater than

$$p_2 = N/2. \tag{12.4}$$

When the frequency is between p_2 and $2p_2$, the field may be distinguished from an unstructured field, but the image does not directly represent the object.

Since for a bundle which is not close-packed, N will always be less than $1/d$, the highest spatial frequency which can be detected by a static

† An introduction to this application of the sampling theorem is given in Ditchburn, *Light* (2nd ed.), Chap. 20.

system will be about half the highest frequency detected by the same bundle operating as a scanning system. Kapany (1967) has shown that, in practice, the advantage of a scanning fibre system is usually larger than this. For gratings of low spatial frequencies, when there are many information points for each period, the static system will yield as much information as the scanning system. The acceptance function for a static system will be obtained by multiplying T by a function which is nearly unity for low spatial frequencies, and which begins to fall rather rapidly when p is about $0 \cdot 3p_1$ and reaches zero when $p = 0 \cdot 5p_1$. We do not know the precise value of this factor, but curve (b) of Fig. 12.4 is probably a reasonable approximation for the acceptance function of an irregular (but fairly close-packed) mosaic operating as a static system. This argument assumes that the systems are not limited by time. If the information can be stored only for a short time, then the static system makes an accurate measurement at a certain number of points, and the scanning system makes a less accurate measurement at a larger number of points. The latter is still better at very high spatial frequencies, but there may be little difference at low and medium frequencies.

12.9. Application of fibre-optics theory to vision

The mosaic of retinal receptors resembles a fibre-bundle in which the arrangement of the fibres is irregular but fairly close-packed. There is an appreciable 'dead space' between the sensitive areas of the cones. However, neither the mosaic structure nor the dead spaces are perceived, so the visual system must have some method of interpolation which suppresses the mosaic structure. Eye-movements have been shown to include components which oscillate the retinal image across the receptor-mosaic with an amplitude about equal to the smallest intercone separation. The hypothesis that these movements are used to increase the efficiency of transfer of information from the retinal image to the neural system, and at the same time eliminate the mosaic structure, is an attractive one (Marshall and Talbot 1942). We shall call this the *dynamic* theory of vision. This will be compared with the *static* theory, in which eye-movements of normal vision operate to maintain the visual signals and to prevent the fade-out observed with the stabilized image, but do not increase the amount of information accepted by the receptor mosaic.

12.10. Although the retinal receptors and fibre-optics bundle each have an optical input, their outputs are quite different. For fibre-optics the output is light, which reconstitutes the image if both ends of the bundle are stationary or are moved in the same way. In the visual system, the output from the retinal receptors is a set of electrical signals in a neural network. Some equivalent of the movement of the image end of the fibre-optics bundle must be provided. This may be achieved by continuous rearrangement of connections in the neural network, or by a computation process. Either way, the control system requires detailed knowledge of the eye-movements, including the tremor components in the frequency range 0–12 Hz. It is not impossible that this information should be available (§ 16.2), but the amount of information to be stored and processed is formidable. It is not true, as is sometimes assumed, that a static system requires *no* information about eye-movements. The visual scene appears stable despite the movements of the retinal image due to the saccades and drift movements as well as the much larger voluntary movements of normal vision. We shall discuss this stability in Chapter 16; here we are concerned only with the fact that any system which distinguishes displacements of the retinal image due to movements of an object in the external world, from displacements due to eye-movements, must use some information about eye-movements. The information needed for this purpose in a static system is considerably less detailed than the information about eye-movements required for a dynamic system.

12.11. Finite resolution time

It is generally accepted that the visual system has a finite resolution time τ which is about 30 ms for foveal vision at high luminance.† Thus, except when presented with targets which are shown for times much less than 30 ms, the static system 'views' a scene in which the boundaries are blurred by the eye-movements. To a first approximation, the blurring may be regarded as equivalent to an increase of cone diameter by an amount d, where d is the component of displacement (in a given direction), of the retinal image in time τ. The average *net* displacement of the eye from its initial position in a time of 30 ms is about 0·2′ (§ 4.17). This represents a minimum estimate of the effect of eye-movements since the largest excursus from the mean position is often greater than the *net* displacement.

---

† There is also a time delay (of about 200 ms) in initiating action based on visual information. This time delay is not relevant to problems discussed in this chapter.

12.12. Limiting spatial frequency

Polyak[†] (1941) gives 1·5 μm (equivalent to 0·30′) for the diameter of the smallest foveal cones at the base through which the light enters. After making the correction discussed in the preceding paragraph, the effective diameter is 0·5′, and from eqn. (12.3) we obtain

$$p_1 = 140 \text{ c deg}^{-1} \tag{12.5}$$

as the highest spatial frequency accepted by a dynamic system.

Polyak estimates 2500 cones in a central territory[‡] (called the foveola). The diameter of this region is 20′ so that the cone density is 29 000 per square degree. Inserting this datum in eqn (12.4) gives

$$p_2 = 85 \text{ c deg}^{-1}. \tag{12.6}$$

This value does not include any correction for the effect of eye-movements, and should apply to vision with a stabilized image when fading is prevented by intermittent illumination. For normal vision (static system), correction for movement during 30 ms is required, but the correction cannot be estimated very precisely because it depends on the detailed way in which the cones are arranged. It is unlikely to be less than 20 per cent, so that we may estimate

$$p_3 = 65 \text{ c deg}^{-1} \tag{12.7}$$

as the highest spatial frequency which can be detected in a static system. The above values apply to the foveola. If the corresponding data for size of cones in the outer region of the fovea are used, the calculated values are reduced to $p_1 = 50 \text{ c deg}^{-1}$, $p_2 = 30 \text{ c deg}^{-1}$, and $p_3 = 25 \text{ c deg}^{-1}$.

12.13. Experimental evidence on the effect of eye-movements

Three types of experimental evidence may be used to decide whether, in normal vision, eye-movements are used to improve the acceptance function of the retinal receptors. These are

[†] Summarized by Duke-Elder (1961) in *System of opthalmology*. Vol. 2. Henry Kimpton, London, pp. 264–9.

[‡] Polyak applied wht word 'foveola' to the central 60′ of the fovea. It is now commonly applied to a smaller area of 20′ diameter.

(a) Comparison of calculated acceptance functions for dynamic and for static systems with measurements on the visibility of interference fringes formed on the retina (§ 12.5);

(b) Comparison of visual acuity, vernier acuity, etc., in normal vision, and in vision with a stabilized image when the subject is given a time of 500 ms (or more) in which to make the response;

(c) Comparison of similar measurements when targets are presented for various times between 20 ms and 500 ms.

We shall consider these in the following paragraphs.

12.14. Interference fringes on the retina

The experiments whose results are presented in curve (b) of Fig. 12.1 show that R' is not zero for frequencies below 65 cycles deg^{-1}. Eqn (12.1) then implies that neither $A(p)$ nor $N(p)$ is zero for these frequencies. Thus, the limiting spatial frequency for $A(p)$ is equal to, or greater than 65 cycles deg^{-1}. According to eqns (12.5)–(12.7), this is the highest possible value for a static system, calculated from the smallest observed cone sizes. It is also within the range of values (150–50 cycles deg^{-1}) calculated for a dynamic system. Thus the results of these experiments are compatible with either system.

Byram (§ 1.32) observed structure with interference fringes on the retina up to 85 cycles deg^{-1} and could distinguish that the field was not uniform up to 150 cycles deg^{-1}. His results, if confirmed, would exclude the kind of static theory we have discussed in § 12.8, but would be compatible with a dynamic theory.

12.15. Normal vision and vision with a stabilized image

Experiments in which acuity judgements in normal vision and in vision with a stabilized image are compared, have been carried out by:

(1) Riggs, Ratliff, Cornsweet, and Cornsweet (1953) who measured the visibility of a dark line seen against a bright background;

(2) Keesey (1960) who measured (a) vernier acuity, (b) visibility of a dark line against a bright ground, and (c) limiting spatial frequency for visibility of gratings;

(3) Shortess and Krauskopf (1961) who measured stereoscopic acuity;

(4) Fender and Nye (1962) who measured vernier acuity under a variety of conditions;

(5) Gilbert and Fender (1969) who measured $R(p)$ for spatial frequencies from 0·3 cycle deg^{-1} to 30 cycles deg^{-1};

(6) Millodot (1966) who measured visual acuity with Landolt rings in the fovea and in parafoveal regions out to 7°;

(7) Kulikowski (1971) who measured $R(p)$ for spatial frequencies from 3 cycles deg^{-1} to 20 cycles deg^{-1}.

Several of these workers made measurements in which the targets were exposed for controlled times in the range 20 ms to 1 s. Others allowed the subject unlimited time to make the judgement. For the longer exposure times, some of the experimenters endeavoured to eliminate fading of the stabilized image by using intermittent illumination.

12.16. Let us first consider results obtained when the exposure time is 500 ms or longer. In this condition, some experimenters find no significant difference between normal vision and vision with the stabilized image (see experiments (2) and (3) listed in the preceding paragraph). In other experiments (1, 4, 5, and 6, above) normal vision is significantly better than vision with the stabilized image, but the difference is only about 0·1 log unit in the measured parameter. All the experiments listed in § 12.15 (except that of Gilbert *et al.*) involve targets which are not gratings and which contain a range of spatial frequencies from a few cycles per degree up to 100 cycles deg^{-1} or more. The limiting spatial frequency (above which R is zero) is about 50 cycles deg^{-1}, and this limit is set by the factor M, i.e. by aberration and diffraction in the lens system of the eye (Figs. 1.21 and 12.1). Thus, to the extent that subjects' judgements depend on information about high spatial frequencies, the experiments give no information about A, and no difference is to be expected between vision with a stabilized image and normal vision. This effect is shown clearly by the measurements of the upper limiting spatial frequency by Keesey (experiment 2(c)) and by Gilbert *et al.* (part of experiment 6). Each experiment gave a limit near to 45 cycles deg^{-1} which agrees with the limiting value of 50 cycles deg^{-1} for M as well as can be expected having regard to variation between subjects.

12.17. Gilbert *et al.* measured modulation thresholds for spatial frequencies from 3 cycles deg^{-1} to 40 cycles deg^{-1}. This includes a range (from about 3 cycles deg^{-1} to 40 cycles deg^{-1}) where M is fairly large ($>0·5$) so that differences due to scanning of the retinal image might produce significant changes in the observed results. When fading of the stabilized image was not prevented, normal vision was better by 0·5 log unit. When the illumination was occluded every other second, the

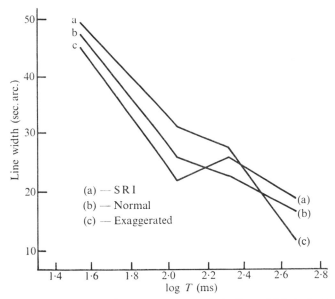

FIG. 12.5. Width of line (in seconds of arc) of dark line which is just visible; (a) stabilized image; (b) normal vision; (c) exaggerated eye-movements. (After Riggs *et al.* 1953.)

difference was only about 0·1 log unit. This residual difference was attributed to incomplete prevention of fading of the retinal image.

The residual difference is not as large as would be expected if normal vision uses scanning at full efficiency.† On the other hand, there is no indication that vision with a stabilized image is substantially *better* than normal vision, as would be expected if the visual system takes no account of eye-movements (§ 12.12 and § 12.19).

12.18. Experiments with brief exposure of target

The experiments of Riggs *et al.* (1953), of Keesey (1960), and of Shortess *et al.* (1961) show that, both for normal vision and for vision with a stabilized image, performance improves as T is increased from about 20 ms to about 200 ms. Improvement probably continues, though at a lower rate, from 200 ms to 500 ms. For normal vision, several other workers have found a similar variation with exposure-time, e.g. Ogle and Weil (1958) and Kahneman (1964). Rattle and Foley-Fisher (1968) found that vernier acuity was correlated with inter-saccadic interval. Their results are consistent with the hypothesis

† Kulikowski (1971) observed a larger difference (1·0 log unit), but attributes this partly to corneal oedema caused by his suction device.

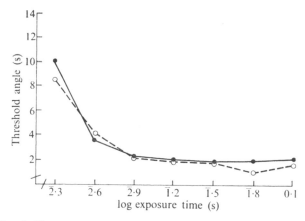

FIG. 12.6. Threshold angular width for detection of a black line as a function of exposure time: normal vision ●—●; stabilized image ○—○. (After Keesey 1960.)

that information can be efficiently integrated during the whole of an inter-saccadic interval (for intervals up to about 2·5 ms).

Riggs *et al* found that, for normal vision, performance improved more rapidly with T than it did for vision with a stabilized image (Fig. 12.5). No corresponding difference was found by Keesey (Fig. 12.6) and by Shortess *et al*.

12.19. Let us now consider how the available information might be expected to increase with T for (a) vision with a stabilized image, (b) normal vision (static system), and (c) normal vision (dynamic system).

(a) *Vision with a stabilized image.* Information should be received at a constant rate, so the available information should be proportional to T until T is so large that information is being 'forgotten' as rapidly as new information is received. An acuity parameter should improve as T is increased, and approach a limiting value asymptotically. In the simplest condition the parameter will vary with $T^{\frac{1}{2}}$ when T is small (curve (a) of Fig. 12.7).

(b) *Normal vision (static system).* Information should increase as with a stabilized image, but blurring of the image due to eye-movements should also increase with T. Since times of less than about 30 ms cannot be resolved, this blurring must increase with T up to 30 ms. The useful information is partially confused by this effect, and at 30 ms performance should be significantly less good than with a stabilized image (§ 12.12). If no account at all is to be taken of information about eye-movements, the best result will be obtained if signals which are

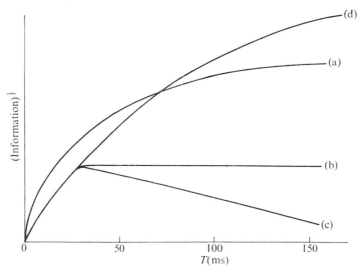

FIG. 12.7. Diagram to show qualitatively how available information should increase with T; (a) stabilized image; (b) normal vision (static system); (c) normal vision (static system operating without any information on eye-movements); (d) normal vision (ideal scanning system).

more than 30 ms out of date are deleted. Performance will then improve with T when T is less than 30 ms, and then remain unchanged as T is further increased (curve (b) of Fig. 12.7). If signals are integrated over periods much longer than 30 ms without taking account of eye-movements, performance will fall as shown in curve (c) of Fig. 12.7.

(c) *Normal vision (dynamic system)*. When T is less than 30 ms, the system will behave similarly to a static system, and at 30 ms performance will be less good than that obtained with a stabilized image. When T is increased, the scanning action should enable information to be acquired at a higher rate than with a stabilized image, and performance should improve until either, (a) it is limited by M as explained in § 12.16 or (b) temporal integration of information fails. For an experiment involving only fairly low spatial frequencies, performance should be significantly better than with a stabilized image when T is about 150 ms, as shown in curve (d).

12.20. The substantial improvement in performance obtained with normal vision for times between 30 ms and 200 ms is decisively against the simple static system. Since there are no experiments with brief exposure-time which use sinusoidal gratings of low frequency as targets, there is no strong evidence for or against a dynamic system. Further experiments of the type carried out by Gilbert *et al.*, but with short exposure of the target, are desirable. It would also be of considerable interest to have modulation threshold results for interference fringes formed on the retina and stabilized. Experiments on the threshold contrast for gratings when high frequency components of tremor movements are removed, but low frequency components are not, would also be valuable.

In the present state of our knowledge, it seems necessary to assume that the visual system uses information about low frequency components of eye-movements (up to at least 5 Hz) in order to be able to integrate information for periods at least up to 200 ms. The existence of a finite resolution time of about 30 ms makes it almost certain that information about components of frequencies greater than 15 Hz is not used, and there is direct evidence (§ 10.9) that components of these frequencies make visual judgements more difficult. It is probable that the visual system operates somewhere between the extremes of (a) no use of eye-movements (simple static system) and (b) complete use of eye-movements (simple dynamic system).

12.21. The structure of the retinal mosaic is not seen in vision with a stabilized image, nor in an after-image following a short flash. Thus at some stage in the analysis of visual signals, interpolation or spatial filtering must be used to suppress the mosaic structure. This must be achieved by a process which does not use eye-movements to increase the number of points at which the image is sampled.

12.22. Information capacity of the neural processor

Figure 12.1 (upper curve) represents R' which, according to eqn (12.1), is the product of two factors: (i) A which is the acceptance function for extraction of information from the retinal image by the retinal receptors and (ii) N which represents the efficiency with which information is taken from the receptors and analysed in the retina, L.G.B., and cortex before it appears as conscious perception and can be used to determine action. If the experimental evidence had supported the dynamical system in its simplest form, A would have the same form as T (shown in Fig. 12.4) with the scale of abscissa adjusted to place the first zero at 140 cycles deg^{-1} for the foveola (§ 12.12). For a static system, A should be nearly the same at low spatial frequencies because there are many information points per cycle (§ 12.8). Thus, up to about 10 cycles deg^{-1} the curve for A is unlikely to differ much from curve (b) of Fig. 12.4. For higher spatial frequencies, a static system would give a curve which dips sharply to zero at 65 cycles deg^{-1}.

The modified dynamic theory discussed in § 12.21 predicts that A falls to zero less rapidly and reaches zero at some frequency between 65 cycles deg^{-1} and 150 cycles deg^{-1}, though probably nearer to the lower value.

12.23. Since A is known within a fairly small margin of uncertainty at spatial frequencies up to 10 cycles deg^{-1}, N for this range may be deduced by dividing R' by A. The result is shown in Fig. 12.8. For

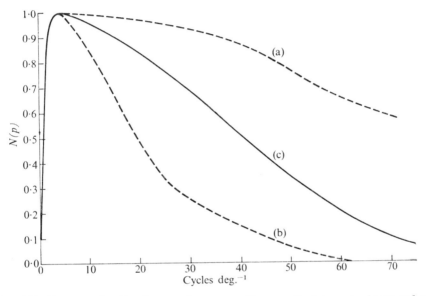

FIG. 12.8. Response function for neural processor N, normalized to a maximum value of unity. (a) highest values; (b) lowest values; (c) intermediate curve.

higher spatial frequencies N lies within the limits shown by the dotted lines. The upper curve (a) would imply the existence of a neural system with a large capacity for transmission and analysis of information about high spatial frequencies which are not transmitted by the dioptric system, and which the retinal receptors cannot accept. The lower curve (b) is consistent with a neural processor which is matched to the dioptric system of the eye, and to the limitations set by the structure of the retinal mosaic. For this, and for other reasons, the true curve for N is likely to be nearer to curve (b) at the high frequency end, as shown in curve (c) of Fig. 12.8. It should be emphasized that, whatever view is taken of the uncertainty of N at frequencies above 20 cycles deg^{-1} the existence of a maximum at about 7 cycles deg^{-1}, and a decrease at very low spatial frequencies, is not in doubt.

12.24. Effect of reduced illuminance

The preceding data and discussion apply to foveal vision at fairly high luminance (about 100–400 cd m^{-2}). Schade (1956) and Van Nes and Bouman (1967) find that the frequency at which R is a maximum, is less at lower light levels (e.g. at 1 cd m^{-2} it is about 3 cycles deg^{-1}). Part of this effect may be assigned to a change in M, due to increased aberrations associated with the expanded pupil. Some may be assigned to a change in A as larger cones become more important. Although these effects must certainly be taken into account, it is unlikely that they can explain the whole of the change. The main difference between visual function at high and at low illuminance is probably a change in the neural processor which operates so that, at low luminance, the effective size of receptor fields increases. This increases sensitivity to weak signals at the expense of reducing resolution of fine detail, i.e. at the expense of reducing ability to detect high spatial frequencies.

12.25. Moving targets

Schade also finds that, for moving gratings, the frequency at which R is maximum is less than that obtained with stationary gratings. Movement of the retinal image does not change M, and probably has only a minor effect on A. The observed change in R is almost certainly associated with a change in N due to an increase in the temporal rate of change of light received in any one receptor.

In the experiments of Schade, the moving gratings were allowed to drift through the field at a rate of one bar s^{-1}. The angular velocity is thus very small for gratings of high spatial frequency, e.g. for a grating of 40 cycles deg^{-1} the rate would be 1·5 min.arc s^{-1}. This velocity is lower than that required to produce an observable effect on the visibility of a target (§§ 10.3–10.6 and Fig. 10.3). For a grating of 6 cycles deg^{-1} the velocity is 10′, and this should have a significant effect. Thus for moving gratings, the maximum value of R is found at a lower value of p than that obtained with stationary gratings.

12.26. The Mach bands

If two areas of substantially different luminance are separated by a suitably graded boundary, the observer perceives dark and light bands as shown in Fig. 12.9. These are called Mach bands† after Ernst Mach (1838–1916) who discovered the phenomenon in 1865. They are not seen when the edge is extremely sharp, nor when it is too diffuse, but there is a considerable range from a width of about 2' to 300' over which the bands have been observed with stationary targets, and with the luminance in the photopic range. Within this range the bands become

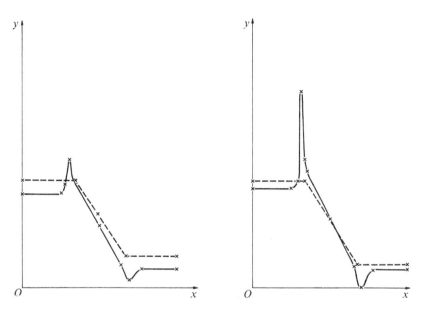

FIG. 12.9. Mach bands. Distribution of apparent luminance at edges of graded boundary————; real luminance – – – –. The curves on the right show the measured effect with a narrower transition region.

sharper and stronger as the gradient is increased by narrowing the transition region (Fig. 12.9).

12.27. Effect of eye-movements on the bands

Mach found that the patterns could be seen when the target was briefly illuminated by an electric spark, i.e. with an exposure-time much less than a millisecond. Fiorentini (1956) observed the bands when the exposure-time was a few milliseconds, but the gradient required was reduced when the exposure time was increased up to about 500 ms.

† Translations of six papers by Mach (published in 1865, 1866, 1868, and 1906) form part II of a book by Ratliff (1965) on the Mach bands (published by Holden-Day, San Francisco).

Fiorentini and Ercoles (1957) observed the bands in the stabilized image but they disappeared after 4–5 s and did not reappear so long as the image was stabilized. Riggs, Ratliff, and Keesey (1961) found that the bands disappeared in normal vision if the target was fixated. They disappeared more rapidly when the retinal image was stabilized. If a uniform field was suddenly substituted after the bands had faded (using a stabilized image), a strong negative after-image of the bands was seen.

These experiments show (a) that movements of the retinal image are not essential for the bands to be seen and (b) that the bands fade fairly rapidly when movements of the retinal image are reduced. The observation that they fade to a considerable extent, when the target is fixated (but not stabilized), indicates that the visual signals which lead to the bands being seen with steady illumination are maintained by the slow components of eye-movements. This is confirmed by the results of the experiments described in the following paragraph.

12.28. Effect of movements of the target

Bittini, Ercoles, Fiorentini, Ronchi, and Toraldo di Francia (1960) studied the effect on the bands of an oscillation of the target in a direction perpendicular to the boundary. A marked enhancement was observed when the amplitude was 2° and the frequency in the range 2–4 Hz. Bands could be seen when the transition region was up to 18° (Fig. 12.10). Oscillation at more than 4 Hz had an adverse effect when the amplitude was 2°, and oscillation at 8 Hz had an adverse effect when the amplitude was 0·5° or more. We should expect that the movements would have two effects: (a) an enhancement of the bands due to increased signals when the temporal change of illumination $(\mathrm{d}\mathscr{L}/\mathrm{d}t)$ on any one receptor is increased and (b) an adverse effect due to the boundary being spread over a wider region, so that the spatial gradients $(\mathrm{d}\mathscr{L}/\mathrm{d}x)$, $(\mathrm{d}^2\mathscr{L}/\mathrm{d}x^2)$, etc., are decreased. For very rapid movements, signals received when the boundary is in different positions are integrated, so that effect (a) is reduced and effect (b) becomes dominant.

12.29. Lateral interaction in relation to Mach bands

Mach (1866) postulated 'reciprocal interaction of neighbouring areas of the retina' to explain the existence of the bands. He suggested that this interaction manifested itself as a visual signal proportional† to

----

† $\mathscr{L}$ is luminance on a linear scale (§ 11.1).

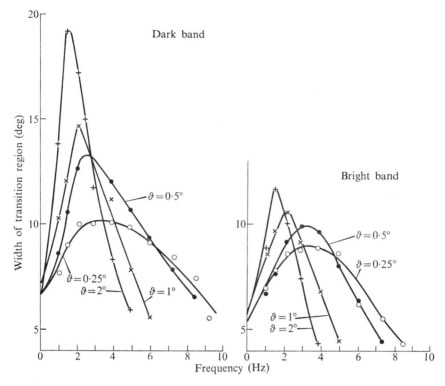

FIG. 12.10. Effect of movement on visibility of Mach bands. The curves show the width of the transition zone when the band is just visible for various amplitudes (ϑ) and frequencies of oscillation. (After Bittini *et al.* 1960.)

$-(\mathrm{d}^2\mathscr{L}/\mathrm{d}x^2)$. Ludvigh (1953) introduced a second term proportional to $(\mathrm{d}^4\mathscr{L}/\mathrm{d}x^4)$ and was able to explain the observations in more detail. Many other theories of the connection between lateral interaction and the bands have been proposed. These are discussed by Ratliff (1965). Here we are concerned to show that the bands are related to the existence of a maximum in the curves for R' and N, shown in Figs. 12.1 and 12.8, and that this maximum is itself a consequence of lateral interaction.

Suppose that the subject views a sinusoidal grating represented by

$$\mathscr{L} = 1 + G(p) \sin 2\pi p x. \tag{12.8}$$

We assume that the constant background is transmitted unchanged and that the fluctuating term is subject to the operator

$$\left\{ C_0 - C_2 \frac{\mathrm{d}^2}{\mathrm{d}x^2} - C_4 \frac{\mathrm{d}^4}{\mathrm{d}x^4} \right\}. \tag{12.9}$$

C_0, C_2, and C_4 are constants. This includes the terms postulated above, together with the constant term C_0 which is assumed to be small. Then the output is

$$\mathscr{L} = 1 + (C_0 + 4\pi^2 p^2 C_2 - 16\pi^4 p^4 C_4) G(p) \sin 2\pi p x. \quad (12.10)$$

This constitutes a linear reconstruction of the grating with a transfer factor given by

$$R''(p) = C_0 + 4\pi^2 p^2 C_2 - 16\pi^4 p^4 C_4. \quad (12.11)$$

This function has a maximum at

$$p_{\mathrm{m}} = \frac{1}{2\pi}\left(\frac{C_2}{2C_4}\right)^{\frac{1}{2}}, \quad (12.12)$$

and falls back to the value C_0 when $p = 1 \cdot 4 p_{\mathrm{m}}$.

12.30. R'' agrees qualitatively with the observed values of R, shown in Fig. 12.1, in that it rises (from a low value at $p = 0$) to a maximum, and then falls back when p is further increased. However, R'' falls much more rapidly than R when p is greater than p_{m}. This discrepancy arises because, by assuming that C_2 and C_4 are constant, we have ignored the finite size of the retinal receptors. If the retinal image is stationary, information from three adjacent receptors is needed to provide a value of $\mathrm{d}^2\mathscr{L}/\mathrm{d}x^2$. Thus, although C_2 is constant at low spatial frequencies (when the retinal mosaic provides many information points per cycle), it falls off to zero when one cycle no longer yields three information points, i.e. when p is about 40 cycles deg^{-1}. Similarly, $\mathrm{d}^4\mathscr{L}/\mathrm{d}x^4$ requires five information points, and will fall to zero when p is about 25 cycles deg^{-1}. Since C_4 falls off at a lower value of p than C_2, the information transfer function will fall off less rapidly as p increases than eqn (12.11) predicts. There may even be a subsidiary maximum. It is of interest that a second maximum is indicated by some of the observations (Lowry *et al.* 1961, Fig. 8; Campbell *et al.* 1965, Fig. 9; Gilbert *et al.* 1969, Fig. 4).

12.31. Lowry and De Palma (1961) calculated the transfer function required to change the input shown in Fig. 12.9(a) to the observed apparent luminance distribution shown in Fig. 12.9(b). They obtained the curve shown in Fig. 12.11 which agrees sufficiently well with the directly observed values of R shown in Fig. 12.1, having regard to the inherent difficulty of the measurements leading to the apparent luminance distribution shown in Fig. 12.9(b).

It thus appears that the maximum in R requires the existence of the Mach bands. The visual system emphasizes frequencies in the range

5 cycles deg⁻¹ to 10 cycles deg⁻¹ in comparison with both higher and lower frequency. This sharpens contours which are moderately diffuse. This effect should have some survival value in enabling certain kinds of objects to be detected against backgrounds which are not very different in luminance. The edge-sharpening does not operate either

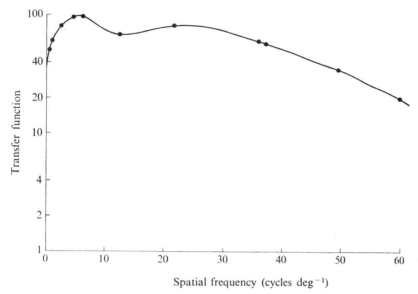

Fig. 12.11. Transfer function derived from measurements of apparent luminance in Mach bands. (After Lowry and De Palma 1961.)

when the boundary is already very sharp (and therefore easily seen), or extremely diffuse (so that a small sharpening would not help).

12.32. This edge-sharpening effect does not increase the information transmitted. It presents the available information in a form in which it is more readily used. From the point of view of information theory the Mach bands constitute a 'penalty', in as much as structure is perceived, which is not present in the target. This renders more difficult the interpretation of observations on diffuse boundaries seen in a microscope.

The changes in R found by Schade (1956) when the target is moving, are probably correlated with the changes in the visibility of the Mach bands found by Bittini *et al.* (1960), though further measurements on moving gratings are needed to test this hypothesis quantitatively.

13

Pattern perception

13.1. Information capacity of the visual system

The retinal receptors provide input signals to the fibres of the optic nerve which transmit information to the L.G.B. and then to the visual cortex. Ultimately there is an output which we may call 'conscious visual experience'. It is possible to evaluate both input and output in terms of the concepts of information theory, and to compare them. This comparison yields a result which is, at first, surprising, and is certainly interesting. The spatial-frequency transmission function of the lens system enables us to estimate the total number of points in the retinal image which could be distinguished if this image were scanned by an ideal physical instrument. This number is not less than 10^8. If 100 levels of luminance could be distinguished at each point, the image would contain 10^9 bits of information. The discussion of the preceding chapter implies that the fovea can extract a considerable fraction of the information in the central part of the retinal image but the fovea constitutes only a small fraction of the retinal area. In the parafoveal and peripheral regions of the retina, the receptors are organized into receptor fields whose size increases rapidly outside the fovea, so that the visual acuity falls. Making allowance for this factor, and for the finite resolving time of the visual system (of 30 ms to 100 ms), Jacobson (1951) has estimated that the retinal receptors accept information at a rate of at least 10^7 bits s^{-1}. Some of the factors involved in this calculation are not known with precision, and the rate may be ten times higher. It is unlikely to be lower. The optic nerve may be regarded as a set of parallel information channels, and its information capacity is of the order 10^7–10^8 bits s^{-1}.

13.2. The rate at which information becomes available in visual experience may be estimated from various behavioural experiments. These give values consistently less than 100 bits s^{-1} and usually about

40 bits s^{-1} (Jacobson 1951). This rate of information is still large (since 40 bits of information is sufficient to distinguish 10^{12} different visual scenes) but it is very small compared with the potential rate of acquisition of information and of transmission along the nerve fibres. The large difference between estimates of input and of output does not imply that the system is inefficient, nor can it be explained on the grounds of redundancy in the information received. There is probably some redundancy and, possibly, a large redundancy in some situations, but this can account for only a small part of the difference. The large difference exists because the visual system selects, at any moment, those items of information which are required to make a discrimination of value. In primitive conditions, survival depends on using information to provide a response which is both rapid and appropriate. In order that the response may be rapid the output must not contain more information than the higher centres can process in a very short time (100 ms or less). On the other hand what is transmitted must be sufficient to form the basis of a correct decision. In order to meet the demands of many different situations, the total amount of information collected must be very much larger than the amount of visual information used in making any one decision. Ability to select that part of the information which is useful in a given situation is an outstanding feature of the human visual perception (Ditchburn 1970).

13.3. Units of pattern perception

Electrophysiological experiments, some of which have been described in Chapter 7, show that coding and filtering of information begins in the retina. They also show that, in the visual cortex of a cat or ape, there is a complex process of recognition of units of pattern perception (§§ 7.37–7.40). This recognition is mediated through a hierarchy of cells. Each cell of one rank combines in its response information received from two or more cells in the next lower rank. It is virtually certain that processes of this kind are involved in human perception of pattern, and very likely that still more complicated ways of combining and filtering information remain to be discovered. The electrophysiological experiments involve damage and cannot be carried out on man. We must therefore seek to understand the visual process by combining what is known from the electrophysiological experiments on animals with psychophysical experiments on man. In this connection, any display which, without doing damage to the subject, deceives or limits the perception of pattern may be expected to give useful results.

13.4. Fragmentation of pattern seen as stationary images

At an early stage in observations of the stabilized image it was obvious that targets do not always appear and reappear as a whole.
Nor do they fragment in a purely random way. These effects were
systematically studied by Pritchard (1958a, 1961b) and by Pritchard,
Heron, and Hebb (1960). They described various kinds of fragmentation of patterns viewed as stabilized images. Evans (1965a, b and c)
made quantitative observations of frequency of disappearance for
various kinds of pattern seen as stabilized images. Bennet-Clark and
Evans (1963) produced after-images which were initially very sharp, in
the following way. Negatives of line diagrams, like the one shown in Fig.
6.1(a), are illuminated from behind through a translucent screen using
a photo-flash bulb. The flash lasts about 20 ms, and during this
period† the eye moves only about 0·3′ (Fig. 4.12), unless the flash
happens to occur when a large saccade is in progress. Except on these
fairly rare occasions, the after-image is initially sharp. It lasts up to
5 min and subjects report on the appearances seen at different times.
These observations were extended by Evans (1967, 1968). It will be
necessary, at some stage, to make experimental tests to see whether
the fragmentations obtained with after-images are the same as those
obtained with stabilized images. At present there is no evidence to
suggest that they are not, and we shall discuss all the results together.

13.5. It is convenient to begin with one of the later experiments
(Evans 1967) on unitary and fragmentary disappearance of short lines
seen as after-images. Disappearance was regarded as unitary if the line
disappeared as a whole, and fragmentary if either (a) one or more gaps
appeared in the middle of the line or (b) an obvious shortening of the
line (through loss of a fragment at one end) occurred. No distinction
was made between these two kinds of fragmentary disappearance.
Fig. 13.1 shows the percentage of different kinds of disappearance (as a
function of length of line) when the centre of the line is as near as
possible to the centre of the fovea. The percentage of unitary disappearances becomes smaller and the percentage of fragmentary disappearances become larger as the length of the line increases. Evans
interprets this result on the basis of a simple scheme of perpetual units
whose dimensions are twice the length of the line for which the percentage of unitary disappearance is equal to the percentage of fragmentary disappearance. It is very probable that further experiments

† Shorter flashes of 1 ms or less can be produced with photo-flash tubes.

will lead to a considerably more complicated model, but we may accept these results as showing the existence of a perceptual unit whose linear dimension is of the order of magnitude 20′ to 60′. This is very much larger than the separation between lines of a grating which is just resolved. It is also larger than the size of the 'central zone' which is

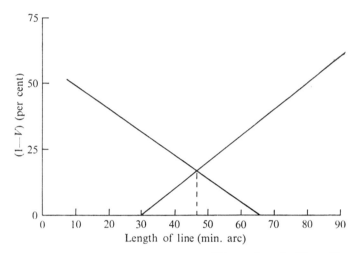

y-axis: $(1-V)$ (per cent), values 0, 25, 50, 75

x-axis: Length of line (min. arc), values 0, 10, 20, 30, 40, 50, 60, 70, 80, 90

Fɪɢ. 13.1. Percentage *disappearance* for lines of different lengths (From Evans 1967.)

obtained from experiments on eye-movements (§ 14.15). These considerations suggest that the units whose firing leads to perception of short lines in after-images are several stages up in the sort of hierarchy which is derived from the experiments of Hubel and Wiesel (§ 7.38). They combine information from cells which themselves combine information from groups of retinal receptors.

13.6. Location of perceptual units

Evans has shown that these units are not part of the retinal organization by the following interesting experiment. The test lines are placed so that their centres are 3° from the visual axis in a horizontal direction. This gives two positions in each eye, making four in all. If the units were part of the retinal organization we should expect results for the two nasal positions to agree, and to differ from the results for the two temporal positions. If, on the other hand, units are related to a part of the visual pathway which is higher than the chiasma (Fig. 7.5(b)), the results for the two left hemiretinas should agree, and should differ from those for the two right hemiretinas. The results, shown in Fig. 13.2,

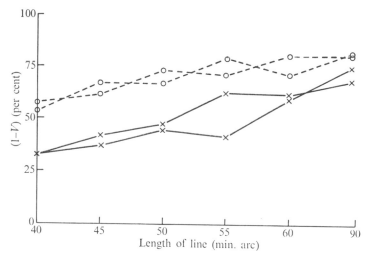

Fɪɢ. 13.2. Fragmentary disappearance for line targets 3° off axis. – – – – left hemiretinas (nasal and temporal), ——— right hemiretinas (nasal and temporal). (From Evans 1965a.)

are clearly in favour of the second hypothesis. This indicates that these perceptual units are either in the lateral geniculate body or in the visual cortex. The latter is much more probable in view of the experiments reported in § 7.38.

13.7. The size of the line for which fragmentation and total disappearance are equally possible is significantly greater in the parafovea than in the fovea. It is also found that, in the fovea, the percentage of fragmentation is independent of the orientation of the line. When small complex targets are viewed, independent fragmentation of vertical and horizontal lines is sometimes observed. This does not, by itself give any information about the shapes of the receptor fields, but it is very likely that their organization is very similar to that described in § 7.39. It should be remembered that the receptor fields for different kinds of detection may, and almost certainly do, use information from the same retinal receptors, but combine that information in different ways.

In order to stimulate a cell associated with the perception of a short line, it is desirable that the line should be long enough to stimulate all the receptors in the appropriate area of the retina. If a line becomes very short the unitary disappearance should increase towards 100 per cent at zero length. On the other hand if the line is long its perception involves many units, and the probability of signals to one or more of these units falling below threshold increases, and fragmentation becomes more and more probable. Thus one would expect that there would be an increase in total disappearance (unitary and fragmentary) both for very short and for very long lines. The results for subject B show this effect though the curve does not smoothly extrapolate to 100 per cent disappearance for a line of zero length. Subject D shows very little increase in total disappearance for short lines. This suggests that some other kind of perceptual unit comes into operation when the lines are very short.

13.8. Fragmentation of complex patterns

Since observations on single lines involve appreciable difficulties of interpretation, it is not surprising that observations on complex patterns, such as those shown in Fig. 13.3, give results which can be inter-

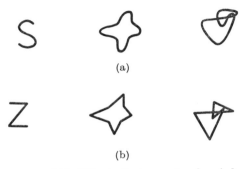

(a)

(b)

F IG. 13.3. Pairs of targets which differ in that one of each pair has sharp corners and the other smooth corners. (After Evans 1960.)

preted only in a rather general way. Pritchard†, Heron, and Hebb (1960) used targets which all fell within a 2° field, and were centred on the visual axis. They observed these as stabilized images using the apparatus shown in Fig. 5.6(a). They found that, most of the time, fragments of the targets were seen, and they emphasize the existence of organized fragments. For example, an array of circles (Fig. 13.4(a)) fades to give one of the appearances A′ or A″. The circle and triangle (Fig. 13.5) give appearances B′, or B″. Squares tend to fade so as to leave two parallel sides. Confusion lines which obscure a well-marked pattern sometimes disappear. At other times they appear to be in a plane behind the main figure. Irregular figures become more regular by shedding outlying parts. A circle with a gap in it is often seen as a complete circle. They found that:

  (i) a short straight line tends to appear and disappear as a unit;
  (ii) The activity of parallel lines in a figure is correlated;

† See also Pritchard (1961), Eagle and Klein (1962), Evans (1967), and Evans and Piggins (1963).

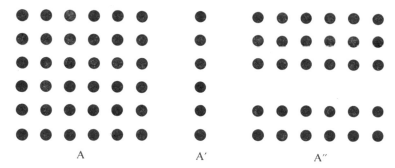

FIG. 13.4. Target and fragmentary appearances.

(iii) A meaningful diagram is visible longer than a meaningless one;
(iv) Jagged diagrams change their appearance more than rounded ones;
(v) There are marked 'field effects' in which the presence of a figure in one part of the field modifies the behaviour of parts of a neighbouring figure (§ 13.15).

Cardu and Gilbert (1967) displayed a variety of geometrical shapes and letters, with sizes of 30', 60' and 120' diameter. The targets were viewed centrally. Total disappearance, as opposed to fragmentary disappearance, increased with size of the figure for any one class of figures. The type of disappearance also depended on target structure. The authors discuss these differences in relation to the theory of pattern perception developed by Hebb (1963, 1966). This work has been extended to include the effect of thickness of line and spatial intervals on the mode of disappearance (Cardu, Gilbert, and Strobel 1971).

13.9. Fragmentation of after-images

Bennet-Clark and Evans (1963) studied fragmentation of afterimages of line diagrams. Usually only part of the pattern disappeared,

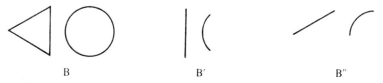

FIG. 13.5 Targets and fragmentary appearances. (After Pritchard *et al.* 1960.)

though occasionally the whole pattern was lost. When the whole pattern disappeared, it sometimes reappeared in part and sometimes as a whole. They confirmed observation (i) of the preceding paragraph, that short straight lines behave as units. For the circle and cross shown in Fig. 13.6 they observed the fragments shown in Fig. 13.6, A', A", A'" etc. These are very similar to the fragments observed by the author

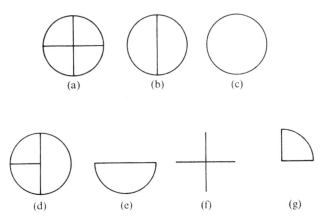

FIG. 13.6. Circle and cross target (a), and fragmentary appearances. (After Bennet-Clark and Evans 1963.)

with a rather similar target viewed as a stabilized image (Fig. 6.1). It is clear that the fragmentation observed in after-images is, at least qualitatively, similar to that obtained in stabilized images. None of the above observations included measurements of percentage time for fragmentary and total disappearance.

13.10. Evans (1965*b*) reported quantitative measurements on the percentage of time for which certain figures disappeared *in whole or in part*. He found that:

(i) a circle disappears less often than an ellipse of equal area;
(ii) 'spiky' figures with sharp corners forming acute angles disappear more than figures which are otherwise similar but rounded (Fig. 13.3);
(iii) complex figures disappear (at least partially) more often than simple figures, e.g. 40 per cent disappearance for a circle and 80 per cent for a circle with a cross in it, as shown in Fig. 13.6(a).

All the differences were obtained with at least two subjects and were highly significant (<0.001). These observations are consistent with the existence of specialized detectors (or perceptual units) for (a) circles,

(b) acute angles, and (c) straight lines. The circle-with-cross and the ellipse disappear (*completely or in part*) more often than the circle alone because they are seen completely only when *all* the associated units are active. If one fails then *part* of the complex target fades. Similarly if the rounded figures involve the cooperation of more units than the spiky ones, they will fade (in whole or in part) more often.

13.11. Evans (1965*b*) also found that the percentage of time for which targets fade (in whole or in part) in the stabilized image falls when the luminance is increased. He used an equilateral triangle (7·5° side) as target. His results are shown in Fig. 13.7. An increase in luminance by a factor of 16 reduces the disappearance rate from 82 per cent to 58 per cent. The fovea lies in the centre of the triangle so that the boundaries are entirely in the parafovea. He also attempted to distinguish between 'random' disappearances and 'structured' disappearances. He instructed subjects to signal 'random' when in doubt. On this basis he found that, under most conditions, more than half the disappearances were 'random'. This appears to conflict with the earlier reports (Pritchard, Heron, and Hebb 1960; Bennet-Clark and Evans 1963) which emphasized the predominance of meaningful and structured units of pattern. These earlier reports were all carried out with smaller targets

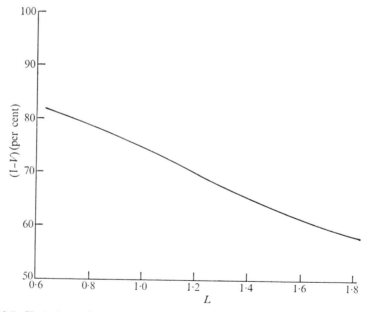

FIG. 13.7. Variation of percentage disappearance (i.e. 100 − *V*) with luminance. *L* = log (luminance in cd m⁻²).

falling mainly on the fovea, and it is possible that this is an important difference. On the other hand, the type of instruction given to subjects may have produced a strong bias in favour of structured disappearances in one case and against them in the other. It is quite probable that all disappearances are 'structured', in the sense that the patterns which remain involve finite numbers of perceptual units, each of which operates on an all-or-nothing basis. On this view, random disappearances are merely disappearances whose structure is too complicated to be understood without more knowledge about the perceptual units.

13.12. Fragmentation without stabilization

Evans and Piggins (1963) observed that most of the fragmentation effects obtained with stabilized images could be observed when trained subjects fixated carefully, using a dental-bite method to control head movements. In this condition, fragmentation occurred less often than with truly stabilized images or after-images, and 'fragmentations', which involved disappearance of most of the target, did not occur. Clarke and Belcher (1962) have also observed fragmentation in the peripheral field when subjects fixate. The experience of the present author suggests that only a small proportion of untrained subjects (perhaps 10 per cent) observe appreciable fragmentation of targets in the *centre* of the field when they fixate. A considerable number more can be trained so as to fixate well enough to see *some* of the fragmentations. It is likely that these subjects learn to reduce their drift movements, and that consequently the number of saccadic movements is reduced (§ 14.10). There may, however, be a more central effect. Evans (1968) has observed fragmentation with brief presentation of targets in a tachitoscope. About 50 subjects were used. Certain sub-patterns were seen much more frequently than others.

13.13. So long as the object of an experimenter is to discover and analyse perceptual units in the visual system, the choice of methods of producing fragmentation may reasonably be determined by experimental convenience. So far we have discussed four methods: (a) stabilized images, (b) intense after-images, (c) trained fixation, and (d) tachitoscope presentation. Of these, (b) and (d) have the important advantage that they involve no attachments to the eye and no lengthy training.† These are the most generally applicable methods at present available. Their convenience should not restrict the search for other

---

† Training is not only time consuming, it also involves a danger of 'indoctrination', i.e. subjects may come to know what the experimenter expects them to observe.

methods. The presentation of targets at low contrast offers another possibility.† This would create another kind of situation because breakdown of pattern perception in this condition would not be associated with absence of eye-movements. The study of perceptual units must involve the combination of information obtained by all these methods. It must not be assumed that different methods of making perception difficult will necessarily give the same result. Experiment may show that they do. If they do not, the differences will be of considerable interest.

13.14. A psychologist interested in 'units of visual perception' need not be interested in the physiological processes leading to fragmentation, but to many people this is the most interesting question. At the present stage it appears that, when information to the visual system is reduced in certain ways, some units of the type described in §§ 7.38–7.40 are kept activated at a level which is very near threshold, i.e. very near a 'noise' level. Thus the corresponding elements of pattern are intermittently perceived. It is clear that these units are above the chiasma and almost certain that they are in the visual cortex. The experiments on after-images make it quite certain that these units can be maintained in this near-threshold condition by signals which are still available when the image remains on the same part of the retina. It must be remembered that after-images change (a) by photo-chemical recovery producing a slow temporal change in the signals and (b) possibly by diffusion of photo-chemical products (Brindley 1962). It thus appears probable that the signals associated with lateral interaction without image movements can maintain this condition. It also seems likely that some independent process is needed to maintain the thing we have called 'attention' (§ 8.14).

Further understanding of the process may be obtained by the study of pattern perception in (a) binocular vision (§§ 13.15–13.20), and (b) with controlled movements of the retinal image (Chapter 10). So far all studies by the latter method have been concerned with the effect of movements on the perception of very simple boundaries.

13.15. Inter-ocular transfer with one stabilized and one unstabilized stimulus

The effect of contralateral stimulation on the percentage of time for which a black line 120′ long by 2′ wide could be seen as a stabilized

† A few tests made by the author suggest that this method is more difficult than the others.

image was studied by Cohen (1961). The stabilized image of this target was viewed by the right eye. The value of V, i.e. the percentage of time for which the target was seen, was 30 when the left eye was occluded, 51 when diffuse light (ganzfeld) was presented to the left eye, and 74 when 'patterned light' (unstabilized) was presented to the right eye.

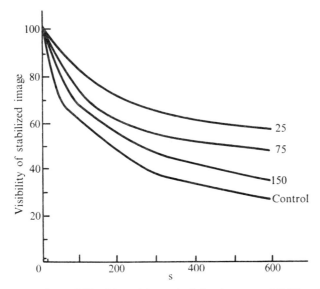

FIG. 13.8. Effect of unstabilized target in contralateral eye on visibility of narrow line seen as a stabilized image. 25', 75', 150 are mean distances of target in contralateral eye from position corresponding to stabilized image: actual distance fluctuates owing to variation of disparity of visual axes. (From Cohen 1961.)

He then presented to the left eye a vertical line geometrically similar to the one presented to the right eye—but *unstabilized*. Fig. 13.8 shows the effect of the target in the contralateral eye when it is placed at different distances from the position corresponding to the stabilized image.

This demonstration that an unstabilized image in one eye can affect perception of a stabilized image in the other indicates a central inter-action. It strengthens the belief that the interaction of different parts of a stabilized image seen in one eye is also central.

13.16. Inter-ocular transfer with stabilized images (successive presentation)

Dunlap (1921) carried out experiments in which a dim spot of light was presented to one eye peripherally. It disappeared, as would be expected (Troxler effect, § 6.21). If the same spot was then presented to the corresponding area of the other eye, it was not seen at all, although it would have been without previous stimulation of the other eye. Similar results were obtained by Guildford (1927), in a more extended investigation. Krauskopf and Riggs (1959) looked for a similar effect in the fovea using two stabilized images. Their stimulus was a small line 24′ × 6′, presented with its centre 9′ from the centre of the fovea. The logarithmic luminance difference between the line and background was about 0·2. In some experiments, the line was brighter than the background, in others it was darker. The stimulus was presented to one retina for the first 30 s of a viewing period and to the corresponding part of the other retina for the second 30 s. In control experiments the stimulus was presented 9′ on one side of the centre of the fovea in one eye for the first 30 s and 9′ on the other side of the foveal centre in the other eye for the second 30 s. The visibility was measured during the second 30 s in each case. In each of four replications of the experiment, the target was seen less often when the first presentation was on the corresponding part of the other retina than in the control experiment. The differences were small (V (test) = 20; V (control) = 22 approximately) but, in each experiment they were significant at a 5 per cent level. The conditions of this experiment are quite different from those of the experiments described in § 13.15 and of those to be described in § 13.17, and it is not surprising that the results are different.

13.17. Interaction of two stabilized images (simultaneous presentation)

The interaction of two stabilized images seen simultaneously in each eye was studied by Ditchburn and Pritchard (1960), who used the apparatus described in § 5.3, to produce the ring and cross pattern shown in Fig. 5.4. In order to distinguish the pattern seen in the left eye from that seen in the right eye the cross in one eye was set at 45° to the cross in the other so that the superposed patterns appeared as shown in Fig. 13.9. The first objective was to examine the suggestion that, in monocular experiments with stabilized images, the fading is essentially an example of retinal rivalry, i.e. that the stabilized image disappears when the signal of 'darkness' in the occluded eye becomes stronger than the weak signal from the stabilized image.

The values of V_L (percentage of time for which some part of the target is seen by the left eye) and V_R (corresponding datum for right eye) were measured for the variety of conditions listed in Table 13.1. If there were complete alternation between the two eyes, then $V_L + V_R$ should be

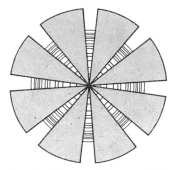

Fɪɢ. 13.9. Superposed ring-brush patterns with one set of brushes rotated through 45°
with respect to the other.

equal to 100. This is obviously not true. On the other hand, if the eyes
were acting independently, the percentage of time for which both
targets are seen would be $V_L V_R/100$, and the percentage of time for
which at least one image is not seen would be $P_c = (100 - V_L V_R/100)$.
The measured value of this quantity P_m is greater than P_c, indicating
that some interaction does take place. The percentages V_L and V_R are
both very much greater than the percentage V ($\sim$25) obtained when
this kind of target is viewed in one eye with the other eye occluded. It
should, however, be noted that, when the subject has to signal disappearances and reappearances of two stabilized images, he is forced
to make a strong effort to maintain attention, and this tends to increase V_L and V_R. This factor is not present in the experiments described in § 13.16. It was found that whenever the 'black field' appeared
in one eye it also appeared in the other.

TABLE 13.1

Hue	Luminance (cd/m⁻²) Left eye	Right eye	Visibility V_L	V_R	$V_L + V_R$	Measured P_M	Calculated P_c
White	10	3	74	79	153	44	42
White	10	3	80	82	162	34	34
White	10	3	72	83	155	44	40
Green	3	0·3	77	74	151	48	43
Green	0·6	0·3	64	70	134	65	55
Red	0·6	0·3	56	72	128	71	40
Red	0·6	0·3	69	65	134	66	55
Blue	0·6	0·3	47	44	91	87	79
Blue	0·6	0·3	55	55	110	73	70
Blue	0·6	0·3	57	43	100	74	64
Blue	3	1·5	62	75	137	57	53
Blue	3	1·5	74	62	136	62	54

The header for the two right-hand columns reads: "Percentage of time for which at least one target is not seen".

13.18. Binocular fusion of two stabilized images

In the above experiments, it was found that the targets could still be fused when they were misaligned by amounts up to about 60' (a distance about 10 times larger than the dimensions of Panum's area). This may be partly due to the fact that the patterns contain no sharp boundaries, but it suggests a failure to make a precise comparison of the location of the patterns seen in the two eyes, when the images are stabilized. Fender and Julesz (1967) found that random dot patterns can be fused when the misalignment is up to 130'. If two patterns which have been aligned (and fused) are slowly separated, a greater misalignment can be accepted for a short time. They, however, found it necessary to align the stabilized patterns within about 6' to produce fusion in the first place.

Evans and Clegg (1967) arranged to form sharp after-images of modified Julesz patterns on corresponding regions of the retina of each eye, by an extension of the method described in § 13.4. Of those subjects who had stereoscopic perception in normal vision, 85 per cent made correct judgements about depth relations in the combined after-image. Shortess and Krauskopf (§§ 12.15–12.18) had previously found that depth-discrimination with two stabilized images is as good, within experimental error, as in normal vision. These results all require that cortical cells which detect depth relations (§ 7.39) *can* be activated when the two images are both stationary on corresponding parts of the retina, i.e. without the intervention of scanning eye-movements. The eye-movements are, of course, needed for maintained depth-perception.

13.19. Pattern fragmentation associated with binocular stabilization

Evans and Wells (1967) presented to each eye one member of a stereoscopic pair which, when correctly fused, represented a truncated pyramid (Fig. 13.10(a)). These patterns were presented (a) as stabilized images of targets whose relative positions could be adjusted by the subject until he achieved fusion, and (b) as sharp after-images. In order to imprint the after-images on the corresponding parts of the retina the targets were first seen in weak light. When the subject achieved fusion, he pressed a button which fired two flash guns simultaneously, thus imprinting the image. The results obtained with the two kinds of stationary images were similar. Each monocular pattern was seen as a whole or fragmented. The binocular pattern was seen, as a whole and correctly fused, about 15 per cent of the time. For about an equal time, the binocular pattern fragmented, i.e. part was seen correctly fused, but part was missing (Fig. 13.10(b)). This is difficult to explain by reference to the images at retinal level. The missing lines are not present on either retina. This kind of fragmentation, however, is easily

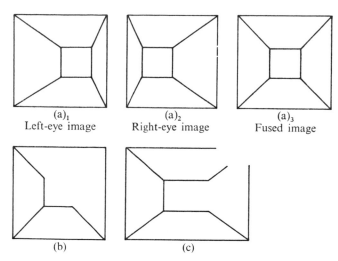

(a)$_1$
Left-eye image

(a)$_2$
Right-eye image

(a)$_3$
Fused image

(b)

(c)

FIG. 13.10. Pattern fragmentation with binocular stabilization. (a)$_3$ Stereoscopic pair correctly fused; (b) and (c) appearances of stationary images. (From Evans and Wells 1967.)

understood in terms of cortical depth detectors described in § 7.39. Another kind of appearance of the combined pattern (Fig. 13.10(c)) was compatible with the hypothesis that the left-hand side of the picture was dominant in one eye, and the right-hand side in the other. A corresponding effect with coloured images is described in the following paragraph.

13.20. Colour mixing in binocular vision

In normal vision, under suitable conditions, some observers can obtain additive colour mixing between the two eyes, e.g. if a patch of one retina is illuminated with green light and the corresponding patch of the other is illuminated with red, the additive colour (yellow) is perceived. Ditchburn and Pritchard (1960) obtained this effect, in normal vision, with patches of light and with the ring systems. The effect is not complete with the ring system because rings of different hues do not overlap completely.

With stabilized images and constant luminance, the additive colour was never seen. The hues were desaturated in the way observed with monocular vision (§ 9.18). When the ring system presented to the left eye was red, and that seen by the right eye was green, the whole field sometimes appeared red and sometimes green. This observation, which is similar to that described in § 13.16, is probably due to binocular rivalry. It is also possible that it might be due to mechanical de-stabilization occurring at different times in the two eyes but, very bad mechanical destabilization would be needed to cause regeneration of a ring-brush pattern which has no sharp boundaries. Although the field sometimes appeared of one hue, there were other occasions on which a rather peculiar type of fragmentation occurred. Sometimes, in the outer part of the ring system, patches of red were seen adjacent to patches of green. More frequently, when one eye received red light and the other green, the centre was perceived as green and the outer part of the field as red. If one was illuminated with red and the other with blue, then the centre appeared blue. These 'fragmentations' cannot be associated with mechanical destabilization. They indicate that, when the image is stabilized, the visual system has great difficulty in combining the colour signals from the two eyes. When the luminance is flickered at about 2 Hz, the additive colour is seen. In this condition the signals from the two eyes are more nearly 'normal' and can be combined at the appropriate level in the visual cortex.

13.21. Visual illusions viewed as stabilized images

Pritchard (1958*a*, *b*) studied three types of visual illusions shown in Figs. 13.11–13.13. These may be described in the following way.

FIG. 13.11. Geometrical illusions.

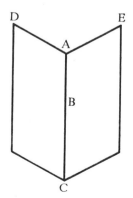

FIG. 13.12. Ambiguous perceptive figure.

Fɪɢ. 13.13. Regular stationary pattern illusions.

(i) *Geometrical illusions* in which some lines of the pattern appear distorted by the addition of 'conflicting' lines (e.g. in Fig. 13.11 the parallel vertical lines appear non-parallel).

(ii) *Regular stationary pattern illusions* in which the observer sees illusory shadow lines at right-angles to the main lines (Fig. 13.13); these illusory shadow lines generally appear to be moving (Mackay 1957). There also appears to be an illusory 'speckle' between the lines.

(iii) *Ambiguous perceptive figures* in which two different perceptual patterns are seen alternately (e.g. in Fig. 13.12 the corner A appears nearer or farther away than D and E).

The targets subtended a visual angle of about 5° and the luminance was 30 cd m^{-2}. The stabilized patterns were compared with similar un-stabilized patterns seen in the same apparatus and effectively at a distance of several metres so that accommodation was relaxed. Five subjects were used. The results are described in the following paragraphs.

13.22. Geometrical illusions

All five subjects could see the whole pattern part of the time, and they then saw the illusion just as clearly in the stabilized image as in normal vision. If only part of the pattern was seen, and especially if much of the conflicting lines disappeared, then the illusion was not seen.

13.23. Regular stationary patterns

None of the subjects saw these illusions in the stabilized image. Three of them found that, in normal vision, but with head movements restrained, the illusion became very weak. Slow movements of the pattern with an amplitude of 2° at 3 Hz restored the illusion. This suggests that slow movements of the retinal image are responsible for the illusion. Fender suggested that these illusory shadow lines may be Moiré fringes produced by superposition of the target and a short-lived after-image located in slightly different positions on the retina. It seems at least equally probable that the comparison is with a 'memory' held at a more central level.

13.24. Ambiguous perceptive figures

All five subjects found that this illusion remained in the stabilized image. The frequency of reversal with the stabilized image depended on the position of the image on the retina. If the point A on the figure was reasonably near to the centre of the visual field, the subject could decide to pay attention to it. Reversals were then nearly as frequent as in normal vision. If, however, the subject directed his attention towards B, the reversals stopped. If A was not sufficiently near to the centre of the visual field the reversals could not be obtained. This result is one of several observations which indicate that, in the centre of the visual field, there is a region in which the subject can affect what he sees by 'deciding to pay attention' to a given point. Outside this region he cannot, in stabilized vision, affect the situation by trying to pay attention to a feature of the pattern. In normal vision he would, of course, rotate his eye so as to bring the feature of interest into the central part of the retina.

13.25. Visual illusions seen as after-images

The three kinds of illusions were presented as sharp after-images (using the technique described in § 13.4) by Evans and Marsden (1966). About 20 subjects viewed a variety of geometrical illusions and nearly all subjects who saw the illusion in normal vision also saw it in the after-image, when the whole pattern was seen. The pattern depicted in Fig. 13.13 was shown to 32 subjects. All of them saw the illusion in normal vision and none in the after-image. The Neckar cube was seen to fluctuate in the after-image as in normal vision. The effect of placing the figure on different parts of the retina was not investigated.

13.26. General conclusions

The experiments in this chapter, taken as a whole, support the existence of pattern perception units in human visual perception. They show beyond reasonable doubt that central action is involved both in monocular and binocular pattern fragmentation. The fragmentations observed give some information about the pattern units. They do not, however, fit neatly into any logical scheme of useful detectors, of the type described in §§ 7.44–7.46, or of the cortical units described in §§ 7.38–7.40. It is satisfactory that the studies of pattern fragmentation by different methods are in agreement.

Control of small eye movements

14.1. Physiological control

Fixation is a voluntary act in that a subject can decide to fixate and can choose the point on which to direct his gaze. The subject is not aware of the eye-movements of fixation and does not consciously control the complicated and rapid movements described in Chapter 4. Nevertheless, fixation can be maintained within a median deviation of a few minutes of arc, and this implies the existence of a detailed and accurate system of control which is able to operate fairly rapidly. Uncontrolled movements would produce a displacement of the visual axis which, on average, would increase steadily with time. In the simplest situation the mean displacement would be proportional to the square-root of the time.

14.2. Control signals

The existence of a control system implies the existence of one or more 'signals' which give information upon which appropriate action may be based. For our problem, the simplest signal is an 'error signal'—proportional to the deviation θ_0 of the axis of the eye from some desired position. Other signals, such as the rate of rotation of the visual axis $(d\theta_0/dt)$ may also be involved. There are three obvious sources of signals: (a) the retina, (b) the proprioceptive nervous system associated with the extra-ocular muscles, and (c) the tissue round the eyeball.

The retina is obviously capable of giving fairly precise information about the position of the retinal image of the chosen fixation point relative to some point (or small region) of the retina which is regarded as central. The work of Barlow and Levick (§ 7.31) shows that, in some animals, the retina can also give a signal which depends on movement. The periphery of the human retina may give signals of this type. It is possible, but less likely, that foveal or parafoveal regions can also do so. The possibility of a retinal 'rate of movement detector' as an element in the control system should certainly be considered. It has been shown by Cooper, Daniel, and Whitteridge (1953) that signals proportional to $d\theta_0/dt$ are obtained from the proprioceptive system of the goat, and it is possible that there are similar signals related to the human extra-ocular muscles. Pressure on the eyeball can be felt, and large rotations of the eyes must alter pressures in the tissues around the eye and so produce a signal. This is small, even when the rotation is large, and is negligible in comparison with signals from the retina when the eye is within a few degrees of the primary position. If more than one signal is available, then it is possible that the control does not operate in exactly the same way in all subjects, i.e. one subject may use the different signals in very different proportions from another. The same subject may also use different control 'strategies' according to the requirements of the situation.

14.3. Control in the absence of retinal signals

The observations that the eyes rapidly deviate from the normal area of fixation when a target spot is extinguished (§ 14.11) show that information from the retina is essential for accurate fixation. This is also shown by observations with stabilized images. If a subject is able to see only a small bright spot which is stabilized and has been placed 30' or so from the mean direction which he usually accepts as the direction of fixation, he turns the visual axis in an attempt to correct the 'error'. The stabilized image moves in response to his movement and the error is not reduced. He moves several degrees before realizing that the correction is ineffective.

Although a subject loses *accurate* fixation in darkness, all control is not lost. The axis can be maintained within a few degrees of the primary position, even in darkness. Also, when viewing a stabilized target some subjects are able to direct their eyes and restrain oscillatory movements (14.28). Thus a weak control exists even in the absence of useful signals from the retina. It is likely that this weak control uses signals from the proprioceptive system. A velocity signal cannot, by itself, provide a stable control so there must be, even in the dark, a signal related to θ_0 as well as possible signals related to $d\theta/dt$ or $d^2\theta/dt^2$. It is probable that the signals which maintain some control over the visual axis in the dark are very weak when the eye is within a degree of the primary position. It is likely, although not quite certain, that the normal eye movements of fixation are thus controlled, almost entirely, by signals from the retina. We use this as a working hypothesis.

14.4. Random eye-movements and corrective eye-movements

The direction of the visual axis is determined by three pairs of opposed muscles. A very precise balance of forces between each agonist and antagonist is needed to keep the direction of the visual axis constant within a few minutes of arc. At least two kinds of failure of exact balance will occur, as follows.

(a) a short period variation of the resultant force, due to individual bundles of muscle fibre in one muscle losing tone (and ceasing to exert a force) without any corresponding instantaneous change in the antagonist. If this happens at random, in each of the three muscle pairs, then an irregular tremor of the axis will result.
(b) A slight excess of the mean force exerted by one muscle (over a period of a second or so) over the mean force exerted by its antagonist. This will produce drift movements.

The second of these movements (together with a small contribution from the first) will gradually displace the retinal image of the fixation mark from its original position on the retina, and an error signal will result. It is not *a priori* unlikely that this error signal might produce a change of innervation of the muscles and hence a reversal of the direction of drift (§ 14.12). Ditchburn and Ginsborg (1953) concluded from an examination of a considerable number of records that this does not usually happen but that the main correction is made by the saccades. Although any one drift is predominantly in one direction, there is no obvious relation between the directions of successive drifts or between direction of drift and mean position. It was found, that when saccades occur while the eye is fairly near to its mean position, they are random in direction. Saccades which occur when the displacement of the eye exceeds a few minutes from the extreme position are frequently directed towards a point nearer the mean position. The correction is not precise but it is effective in maintaining fixation within a small range. Retinal image movements due to head movements are adequately compensated (Gliem 1964).

Detailed studies (which will be described below) have shown that the situation is more complicated than that suggested by the early measurements but the following general conclusion is still valid. The direction of the visual axis is disturbed by the drifts and is restored *mainly* by saccades which are generated when the deviation exceeds a certain minimum. Drifts in certain directions may be used by some subjects to assist in maintaining fixation. It is also probable that some can *learn* to control drifts to some extent. Saccades can then be suppressed, or reduced in frequency, without losing all control of fixation (§ 14.10).

14.5. Target direction and mean direction

The purpose of a control system is to bring the visual axis back on target after it has wandered away through oculomotor instability, and to restore the image of the fixation point to a target region of the retina. In early discussions it was tacitly assumed:

(i) that the target direction of the visual axis is a precisely defined direction, i.e. the aim of the control system is to keep the retinal image of the fixation mark P_F as near as possible to a certain point P_c which may be called the 'perceptual centre of the retina';

(ii) that this target direction coincides with the mean direction of the eye over a record of reasonable length;†

(iii) that this target direction, being determined by the arrangement of retinal receptors, is constant.

The apparent simplicity of these assumptions is deceptive, as may be seen if one attempts to make them more precise. In order to discuss the second assumption we make the following provisos about the other two.

(a) If the fixation mark is a small area (e.g. the intersection of cross-wires which are not indefinitely narrow) then some point in this area is accepted by the subject as the fixation mark P_F. This point is not necessarily the true geometrical centre of the target but it remains unchanged over the time covered by one record.

(b) The 'perceptual centre' P_c remains constant over time intervals which are long enough to include several intersaccadic intervals, though it may change within the time of a single record of length 10 s or more.

The discussion of §§ 14.6–14.7 relates to times short enough for both P_F and P_c (and hence the target direction) to remain constant.

14.6. The mean position P_c and the target position P_F do not necessarily coincide. Suppose, for example, that the drift is always in one direction (Fig. 14.1(a)) and that a saccade returns the system to the

---

† The record should be long enough to give a reasonable mean direction of the eye, but not so long as to induce fatigue—different experimenters have considered that times in the range 10 s to 60 s are suitable.

target direction T_G whenever the deviation (due to drift) exceeds some value d_0. Then the mean direction is M, and the system is at the same distance from the mean position at the end of the saccade as at the beginning. In this situation there is no method of determining, from measurement of records, where the target direction is situated. It is impossible to say whether, (a) the drifts are due to imbalance and the

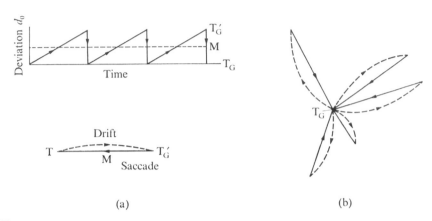

(a)   (b)

F IG. 14.1. (a) Unidirectional nystagmus; (b) Nystagmus with deviations in random directions and perfect correction.

saccades are corrective, or (b) these roles are interchanged. The records would show a nystagmus and would give the mean direction of the eye, but there would be no reason for regarding T_G, or any other point in the range $T_G T'_G$, as the 'target'.

The above is one extreme condition. At the other extreme, if the drifts were random in direction (and possibly in magnitude) and the saccades always returned the system to T_G, then the mean position M would coincide with T_G (Fig. 14.1(b)). The distances of the end points of the saccades from M would all be zero and the beginning points would constitute the extreme deviations from M. In this situation T_G would be unambiguously determined, and it would be clear that the saccades were recentring.

If the saccades, instead of recentring precisely, were to overcorrect by a small fraction of the mean drift, as shown in Fig. 14.2, the recentring effect of the saccades would still be obvious, and the target point, defined as the mean position at the end of the saccades, would nearly coincide with M. If, however, some saccades overcorrect and others undercorrect by amounts comparable with the mean drift excursus, and if the direction of saccade is not usually precisely 'on target', then the analysis of records becomes even more difficult.

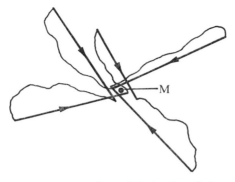

Fɪɢ. 14.2. Nystagmus with good, but not perfect, correction.

14.7. With these considerations in mind let us now consider an actual sequential map (Fender 1956) shown in Fig. 14.3. This shows the path followed by the direction of the visual axis. The initial points of the saccades all lie within the outer circle with centre C_1, and the final points are all within the smaller circle with centre C_2. The mean over-all position is somewhat to the right of C_1, approximately at M. Three of the five saccades bring the eye nearer to C_2, the other two leave it at the same distance from C_2 within error of measurement.

Four out of six drifts leave the eye direction further from C_1 or C_2 or M than it was at the beginning of the drift. Two make little difference. The mean position M is about equidistant from C_1 and C_2. It is clear that

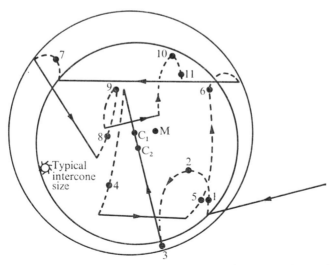

Fɪɢ. 14.3. Observed sequential map of eye-movements. Diameter of larger circle = 10′;
—— saccades; ------ drifts. (Data of Fender 1956.)

recentring is taking place and there is some indication that the drifts are random and that the saccades are recentring but in an imperfect way. Detailed analysis of considerable lengths of records is needed to determine whether the saccades are really recentring.

14.8. Saccades and drifts in relation to eye position

Using a vertical line as target, Cornsweet (1956) analyzed horizontal components of saccades and drifts. He found that the following were all functions of the direction of the visual axis:

(a) probability of occurrence of a saccade (Fig. 14.4);
(b) mean direction (right or left) of saccades (Fig. 14.5);
(c) mean magnitude of saccades (Fig. 14.6).

All these variations are of the type to be expected if the saccades are 'corrective' movements. On the other hand, the rate of drifts is not correlated with eye position. On average, the position of the eye (in regard to H-rotations) at the end of a drift is further from the mean position than at the beginning. When the retinal image is stabilized, the number of saccades falls and their relation to the deviation of the eye from the mean position is no longer clear (Fig. 14.4, curve (b)). This strongly supports the hypothesis of a corrective function of the saccades in regard to horizontal displacement. Cornsweet found that, on average, the saccades overcorrect horizontal displacements.

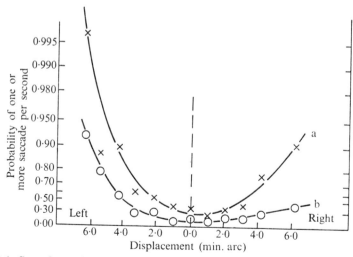

FIG. 14.4. Saccade probability as function of displacement from mean position; (a) normal vision; (b) vision with stabilized target. (From Cornsweet 1956.)

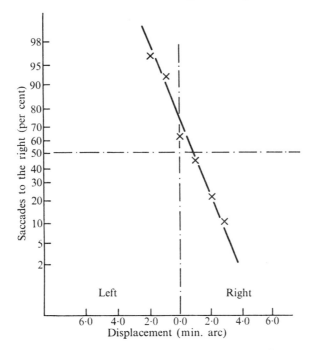

FIG. 14.5. Variation of saccade direction with displacement from mean position. (From Cornsweet 1956.)

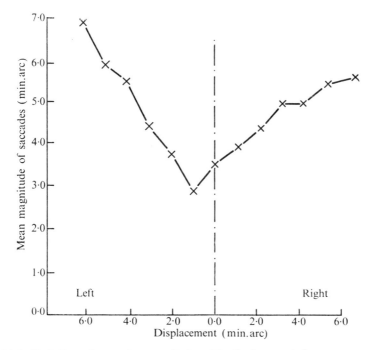

FIG. 14.6. Variation of saccade magnitude with displacement from mean position. (From Cornsweet 1956.)

14.9. Nachmias (1959 and 1961) recorded H- and V-components for subjects fixating on cross-hairs. He used a computer to derive position vectors and calculated bivariate distributions. At the beginning of saccades, the r.m.s. deviation (σ) of the eye from its mean position was above its average value over the whole period. This was true in each of five separate experiments. Polar plots of median directed magnitudes of drifts and saccades in different directions are shown in Fig. 14.7.

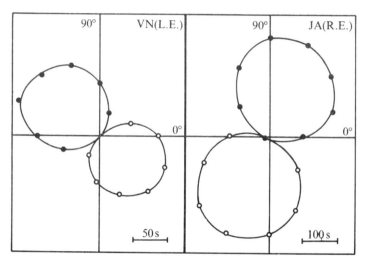

FIG. 14.7. Directed magnitudes of saccades (●) and drifts (○). (From Nachmias 1959.)

Nachmias calculated correlation coefficients for directed components of drift and of saccade motions in relation to the direction of the visual axis. He found that the directed magnitudes of saccade components along each meridian are significantly correlated with the directions of the visual axis at the beginning of the saccades. The coefficients were negative, indicating compensation. The variance of the direction of the visual axis at the ends of saccades was always less than at the beginning. This was true in respect of components along each meridian.

For one subject the drifts were not strongly correlated with position, and the variance of position at the end of the drifts was greater than at the beginning. For a second subject, drifts in directions near the vertical appeared to have a significant compensatory effect. At first consideration it appears impossible that both drifts and saccades should compensate along the same meridian, since this leaves no random motion. However, random disturbance in a vertical direction can be produced by drifts at angles intermediate between the vertical and horizontal meridia so that these movements may produce vertical movement which needs to be corrected. Nachmias suggests that, while saccades are predominantly corrective and drifts mainly random, there are circumstances in which drifts can also be corrective. This implies that the drifts are, to some extent, subject to control.

Nachmias (1961) and Boyce (1967) found that saccades were predominantly under-compensating, whereas Cornsweet (1956) and Ditchburn and Ginsborg (1953), found them to be over-compensating. This may be due to a difference of target but is more probably an inter-subject difference.

14.10. Suppression of saccades

One method of studying the effect of some action is to see what happens when it is withdrawn, other things remaining unchanged. Some subjects can increase or decrease the number of saccades while continuing to endeavour to maintain fixation (Clowes 1962; Fiorentini and Ercoles 1966; Steinman *et al.* 1967). Fiorentini and Ercoles studied the eye-movements of one such subject (a) during 'normal' periods of fixation with saccades and (b) during periods of 4 s without saccades. The results are shown in Fig. 14.8. Without the saccades, the distribution of eye position becomes more dispersed and also becomes bimodal. It appears, however, that even without the saccades, this subject is able to maintain a considerable degree of fixation because the deviation of the axis from the mean position is small in comparison with measurements (by other workers) of deviations in the dark (§ 14.11). Nye (1962) measured the rate of displacement of the visual axis (§ 4.17) and computed what the displacement would have been if the saccades had not occurred. The median difference between samples taken at 1·6 s apart increased from 4·7′ to 6·2′ for one subject, but remained unchanged for another. This implies that, over short periods, the saccades have only a weak corrective action.

14.11. Eye-movements in the dark or when viewing a stabilized image

All experimenters report that accurate fixation is lost when a fixation target is extinguished and the subject attempts to maintain the direction of gaze—he then has no retinal clue. It appears that the breakdown of fixation operates in slightly different ways in different subjects. Ditchburn and Ginsborg (1953) and Nachmias (1961) observed an increase in rate of drift. Cornsweet (1956) found no change in *rate* of

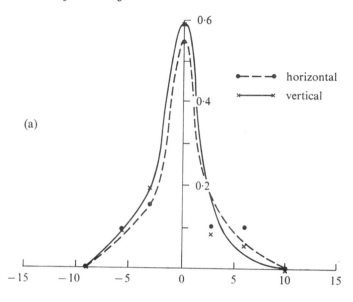

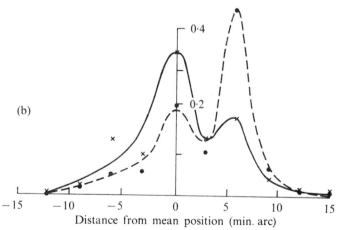

Fig. 14.8. Distribution of eye-position with time for (a) normal vision, (b) vision with voluntary partial suppression of saccades. (After Fiorentini and Ercoles 1966.)

drift. Nachmias observed that for one subject the prevailing direction of drift was reversed but for another remained unchanged.† Ditchburn and Ginsborg and Fiorentini and Ercoles (1966) find no change in intersaccadic interval, whereas Nachmias (1959) reported almost total disappearance of saccades in the dark. All experimenters are agreed

† It is possible that one subject was more precisely in the primary position.

that, in the dark, there is no correlation between the direction of the visual axis and the direction of saccades. Thus the corrective action of the saccades is lost, and the visual axis moves irregularly away from the direction it had at the moment when the fixation mark was extinguished (see also Gliem and Günther 1965).

14.12. Fiorentini and Ercoles (1966) report that, in the dark, there is a tendency for saccades to the left to be preceded by drifts to the right. This implies that there is a *velocity* correction. This observation is important because it implies that a signal, presumably from the proprioceptive system, is able to give information about the direction of movement even during the slow drifts. This effect is not found when viewing a stabilized image. Fiorentini and Ercoles attribute this to the fact that, when a stabilized image is viewed, the retina gives a false signal that the visual axis is stationary. They suggest that this overrules the weak signal from the proprioceptive system.

14.13. Latency of involuntary saccades

Many experiments have been carried out in which a subject attempts to follow a target which is, from time to time, moved sharply through distances subtending visual angles of a few degrees (Chapter 15). When time, direction, and magnitude of the pulsed movements are all randomized—so that the subject can make no rational prediction about any of them—there is a latency of response of (200 ± 50) ms. This latency is reduced when the pulse is partly predictable (§ 15.14).

It is not *a priori* obvious that there must be a latency in regard to the involuntary saccades of fixation. The drift during any one inter-saccadic interval is usually in the same direction and although the speed is not constant it does not vary much. There is thus the possibility that the position of the visual axis during a drift could be continuously monitored. The direction and magnitude of a correcting saccade could then be adjusted to allow for movement of the eye between the time when the error signal becomes large enough to initiate a saccade and the time when the saccade begins. Nachmias (1959) investigated the relation between directed magnitude of saccades and position at various times before the saccade occurred. He found a significant correlation for each of 8 meridia and for latency times from 0 ms to 200 ms (Fig. 14.9). On average, the best correlation was obtained for a latency time of about 100 ms. For all meridia the latency time† was less than 150 ms.

---

† Boyce (1965a) computed this latency in an equivalent way and found a latency in the range 130 ms to 160 ms.

Even allowing for inter-subject differences it seems nearly certain that the latency time is less than that obtained for voluntary saccades in response to unpredictable sharp movements of the target. It is, however, desirable that this experiment, which unfortunately is lengthy, should be repeated with several subjects. It is of interest to note that, if the

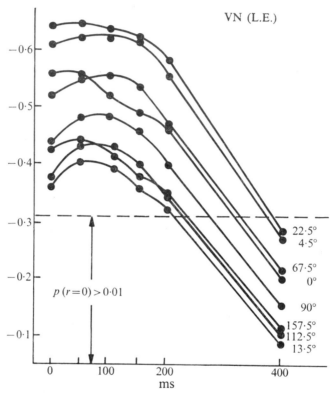

F IG. 14.9. Correlation of directed magnitude of saccade and direction of visual axis at various times before the saccade. (After Nachmias 1959.)

saccades shown in Fig. 14.3 are displaced backwards to the positions of the eye 100 ms earlier, the corrective action is improved and the ends of the saccades fall within a smaller circle. It must be regarded as fortuitous that this action is well illustrated by the piece of record chosen for another purpose.

Nachmias finds much larger correlations for some meridia than for others and attributes this to different velocity and magnitude of drift along different meridia. Boyce (1967) has found that when the direction of a target movement is known there is a change of drift velocity (in the appropriate direction) before the saccade. In this connection it may be noted that in Fig. 14.3 five out of six drifts have changed direction immediately before the saccade and at least three of these changes are corrective. This, also, needs examination on long records and for several subjects.

14.14. Hypothesis of a central insensitive zone

In the preceding paragraphs the control of the small eye-movements of fixation has been discussed in terms of an analogy with a mechanical servo-control which seeks to stabilize the value of a certain quantity (e.g. temperature), and does so within limitations determined by the sensitivity of its sensors, the latency of its response, and similar considerations. We shall now consider the hypothesis (Barlow 1952; Ditchburn and Ginsborg 1953) that there exists a central area A_c of the retina which has the following properties.

(a) When the image of the fixation mark is within A_c there is no error signal for position.
(b) This area A_c is divided into small sub-regions (A_1, A_2, etc.) each of which acts as the target P_c for the recentring process for a short time, after which another sub-region becomes the target for the recentring process.

Either of these two properties could exist by itself and most discussions have involved only one of them. We shall see, however, that both appear to be required to fit the detailed results now available.

14.15. Barlow (1952) suggested that an alteration of the fixation centre, from time to time, might be advantageous, and that the function of the recentring process over a long term might be to keep the visual axis within a certain range rather than to fix it as closely as possible. Ditchburn and Ginsborg (1953) fond that the directions of saccades originating within a central region of diameter 7' were not related to deviations of the eye from the mean position. Saccades originating outside this region usually ended within this region. They suggested that, for periods up to 4 s, the fixation direction moved around a sub-region of not more than 4' and then made a saccadic movement to another sub-region. Barlow and Ditchburn and Ginsborg wished to assimilate the area A_c with the 'central territory' of Polyak (§ 1.7), but the central territory has a diameter of about 20' and is thus much larger than A_c. The sub-areas are probably rather smaller than 4'.

Fender and Nye (1961) considered the existence of an area analogous to a 'dead-space' in a servo-mechanism. Glezer (1959) assumed that

P$_c$ could occupy any position within the central area and that saccades were always directed towards its instantaneous position. This theory accepts the second and rejects the first of the two properties stated in § 14.14. Although Glezer was able to account for the distribution of saccades shown in Fig. 14.5 (obtained by Cornsweet) and for similar results obtained by himself, it still appears that both properties are needed to fit the detailed measurements described below.

14.16. Sub-regions (short-period fixation areas)

The evidence for the existence of the sub-regions mentioned in the preceding paragraphs is of two kinds: visual inspection of records and computer analysis. First, there are sequential maps like the one shown in Fig. 14.3, but covering very much longer periods of fixation. The existence of temporary fixation regions appears obvious on many of these maps. However, it is easy to mistake random clustering for a genuine effect and some objective test is needed. Boyce (1967) devised a computer program for identifying the areas and eliminating random effects. The results were in favour of the existence of such areas, but this procedure was superseded by what appears to be a considerably better method of analysing the original records. This is an application of the cumulative sum technique (Woodward and Goldsmith 1964).

14.17. Cumulative sum analysis

Suppose that it is desired to distinguish systematic from random changes of a quantity which is being continuously recorded. The record is sampled at equal short intervals, each value is subtracted from an assumed mean and the resultants are summed. If only random variations are present, then the cumulative sum S_n of n resultants will fluctuate about zero in a random way. If the mean value of x changes then the curve of S_n versus n will change its slope upwards if x has increased, and downwards if it has decreased. This procedure was applied to records of H- and V-rotations, as shown in Fig. 14.10. Some changes of slope appear obvious but an objective test for systematic change of slope is needed. The test must have (i) a distance component and (ii) a time component. The former separates genuine changes of data-mean from changes due to errors of sampling. The latter is needed to eliminate cases where the fixation breaks down for a short period (possibly owing to an inhibited blink). Boyce used for (i) a requirement of a change of slope corresponding to a change in mean position of at least 3', and for (ii) the condition that the change in slope should last for at least 1 s (i.e. about 3 inter-saccadic intervals). Changes in slope which satisfy these conditions are marked with a dashed ver+ical line in Fig. 14.10. These tests strongly support the existence of short-period fixation areas. Most of the areas so found lie within the central region of 7′ in

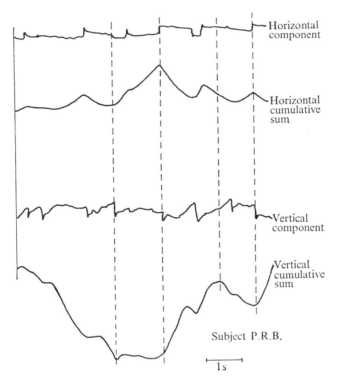

FIG. 14.10. Cumulative sum analysis (arbitrary vertical scale). (From Boyce 1967.)

diameter, but a few are well outside this region. These latter are not usually 'occupied' for long.

14.18. Analysis of saccades

It is found that nearly all the changes of fixation area are made by saccades, though a few are by rapid drifts. Saccades perform two functions: to recentre and to change the fixation area. Boyce estimated that about 85 per cent of saccades recentre and 15 per cent change the fixation area. There is probably a large inter-subject difference in this ratio.

When the short-period areas of fixation have been located and the saccades classified in respect of their functions, it is possible to examine in more detail the operation of the saccades which recentre. The following were calculated for these saccades only:

(a) distances D_{SB} and D_{SE} from the short-period mean at the beginnings and ends of saccades respectively;
(b) distances D_{OB} and D_{OE} from the over-all mean at the beginnings and ends of saccades respectively

Results are shown in Table 14.1 for two subjects.

TABLE 14.1

Recentring effect of certain saccades in respect of over-all mean position $(D_{OB}-D_{OE})$ and short-period mean $(D_{SB}-D_{SE})$.

Subject	P.R.B.	H.R.P.
D_{SB}	3·6	3·8
D_{SE}	3·0	3·2
D_{OB}	4·3	4·8
D_{OE}	3·5	4·6

The differences $D_{SB}-D_{SE}$ are significant ($P<0.01$) for both subjects. The differences $D_{OB}-D_{OE}$ is not significant ($P>0.1$) for one subject. The changes in bearing from the short-period and over-all mean positions between the beginning and ends of saccades are shown in Fig. 14.11, where $\Delta_S = \theta_{SE}-\theta_{SB}$ and $\Delta_0 = \theta_{OE}-\theta_{OB}$. The distribution of Δ_S shows peaks at 0° and 360° (which are the same direction), and also at 180°, indicating that many saccades are directed towards the short-period mean position and that some undercorrect and others overcorrect. The distribution of Δ_0 shows only one peak corresponding to undercorrection relative to the over-all mean (§ 14.8).

14.19. Probability of saccades as function of distances from the over-all and short-period means

The probability of a saccade occurring at a given distance r from a certain point is defined as the number of saccades in an annulus from $r-dr$ to $r+dr$ divided by the time spent in this annulus. The probabilities $P(r_0)$ and $P(r_s)$ for distances from the over-all and short-period

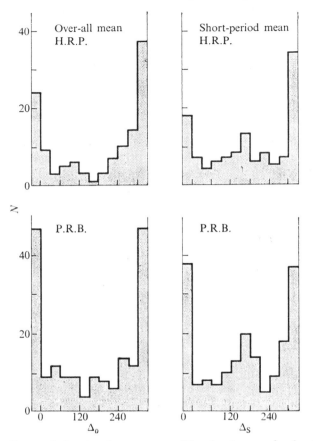

F IG. 14.11. Changes in bearing from mean position due to saccades for two subjects.
(From Boyce 1967.)

means respectively were computed (Fig. 14.12). For all three subjects $P(r_0)$ increases steadily with r_0, whereas $P(r_s)$ shows no definite trend. This supports the existence of an insensitive zone centred near to the over-all means. This computation, and also the one described in § 14.17, would be improved if an unambiguous way could be found of identifying short-period target points rather than short-period mean positions. When a short-period sub-region is 'occupied' for only a short time the difference between mean direction and target direction may be considerable (§ 14.6).

14.20. General description of control system

The experiments, taken as a whole, support the existence of a central region with both the properties described at the beginning of § 14.14.

They do not show that this area is circular nor that it has sharp boundaries. It is possible that an error signal exists even within the central area, but that it is very weak and rises fairly steeply at the edge of this area. In the above analysis, this edge would appear as the boundary of an insensitive zone. We may visualize the operation of the short-period regions by means of the imaginary sequential map shown in Fig. 14.13. We suppose that the large circle is the boundary of the central region, that C is its centre, and M_0 is the mean target position over a long record. M_0 is near to but does not coincide with C. The sequence starts at E_0 (the end of an earlier saccade), and T_1 is the target point. The visual axis drifts from E_0 across the boundary of the central region and a correction is ordered at O_1 (along the dotted line). The saccade occurs at B_1 and carried the eye to E_1. This saccade is an overcorrection in

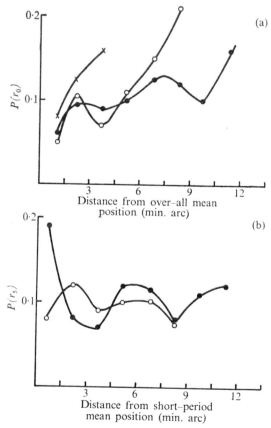

FIG. 14.12. Saccade probability as function of (a) distance from over-all mean position (three subjects), and (b) distances from local mean position (two subjects). (From Boyce 1967.)

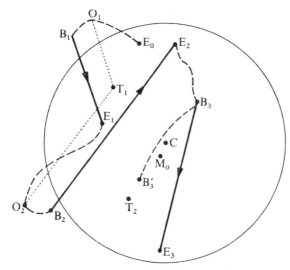

F ɪ ɢ. 14.13. Imaginary sequential map.

respect of T_1, but an undercorrection in respect of M_0. The eye then drifts out of the central region once more and a new correction is ordered at O_2 and made from B_2 to E_2. This too is an overcorrection in respect of T_1, but has almost no correcting effect in respect of M_0. A further drift from E_2 goes inward and is either terminated by a saccade to E_3 or an accelerated drift to B_3'. In either case a new period starts with T_2 as target point. Obviously the corrective action of the saccades in respect of M_0 or C is very small and only a very detailed analysis, such as we have described above, will reveal the corrective action in respect of T_1 and T_2. Yet the system as a whole is kept, for the majority of the time, within the central region.

14.21. Receptor fields

Barlow (1952) and Glezer (1959) have suggested that the central region may be a single receptor field and that signals arise only when the image of the point of fixation crosses into another receptor field. This would imply the existence of receptor fields of about 7' extent in the fovea. This is much greater than the estimates of 1' to 2' for colours other than blue (§ 9.14). It has been shown (§§ 7.35–7.43) that there are receptor fields at cortical level in respect of many detailed functions. It is, therefore, not difficult to believe that there may be one organization of the visual system with a structure about 7' for some purposes and another of range about 1' or 2' for others. The range of lateral interaction found in the experiments described in § 9.16 is about 7', so this structure may be responsible for more than one function. We should need to assume that another system was responsible for high resolving power etc. in light of colours other than blue.

Many of the observations on eye-movements are consistent with the hypothesis that, in the human fovea, each cone is the centre of a receptive field for some type of cortical cell, and each of these centres has an opposed periphery of diameter about 7'. Suppose that one area is labelled central. At any one moment a particular cone within this area is the target point for the recentering action. However, this pre-eminence is short-lived. After a few seconds the target point shifts to another of the central cones. This scheme fits much of the data in Chapter 4 and in this chapter, but until we have more detailed knowledge of retinal connections it cannot be regarded as established.

14.22. Circular targets of finite size

Most of the experiments described in Chapter 4, and in this chapter, have involved fixation on the intersection of fine cross-hairs or on small point targets. We can then speak of a point fixated and trace the movements of the image on the retina. Experiments in which the subject is asked to fixate the centre of a bright or dark spot of diameter much greater than 7' require further consideration. In this situation the boundaries from which information must be drawn are completely outside the central region, yet the accuracy of fixation falls only very slowly as the target size is increased (Fig. 4.13). The r.m.s. deviation (σ) for a target diameter D equal to 240' is only about twice the value obtained when $D = 2'$. There is an anomaly in that σ reaches a fairly sharp maximum when D is about 110', i.e. when the target is about the same size as the fovea. This suggests that two processes operate—one when the target is entirely within the fovea, and another when it is entirely outside. Both of these processes fail—or else their indications are, to some extent, conflicting when the target is about the same size as the fovea.

14.23. The general trend of the results shown in Fig. 4.13 (apart from the anomaly) can be explained in the following way. As the target becomes larger two effects operate:

(a) the boundary becomes larger, and
(b) the size of the receptor fields increase.

These two effects may operate so that the total number of fields intersected by the boundary does not change very rapidly. Therefore the number of channels giving information which locate the centre (and assess the error of fixation) change rather slowly. The provision of the information in any one channel falls as the size of the receptor fields increase, and this leads to the observed slow fall in the accuracy of fixation. However, the results described in the next paragraph indicate that the number of channels is not as important as might have been expected.

14.24. Fixation of the central point between two dots

Rattle (1968 and 1969) made a series of experiments in which a subject was asked to fixate the central point between two dots. In some experiments the separation of the dots was horizontal, in others it was vertical. The r.m.s. deviation σ was measured as a function of the angular distance d between the dots. The results for two subjects are displayed in Figs. 14.14 and 14.15. They show that the value of σ for the target with two dots (and separation d) is only about one and a half times the corresponding value for a circular target whose diameter is equal to d. Thus two small areas (and presumably two receptor fields) give nearly as much information as the whole circular boundary. The anomaly at about 110', shown in Fig. 4.13 is found also in Figs. 14.14 and 14.15, but one subject shows the anomaly clearly when the dots are on a horizontal line and the other when they are on a vertical line.

A plausible explanation of the anomaly is that from time to time the subject forgets the instruction to fixate the central point and fixates one of the dots instead. If this were so, the anomaly should be mainly in the H-component when the separation of the dots is horizontal. This is not in accord with the data, and this explanation must be rejected. Similarly, the anomaly observed with the circular targets cannot be due to occasional fixation of a point on the edge of the circular area.

14.25. High accuracy of fixation

The differences between the results obtained for two subjects (Figs. 14.14 and 14.15) constitute a warning against drawing detailed conclusions from experiments on a small number of subjects. Nevertheless, two over-all conclusions are valid. First, the accuracy of fixation of the central point of a circular target of diameter about 200',

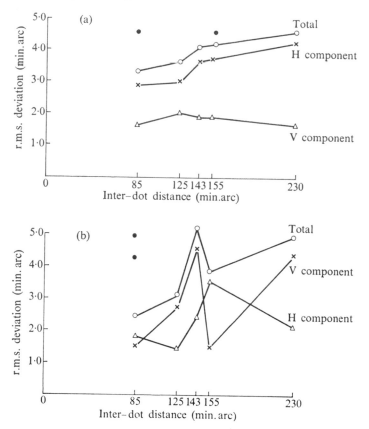

F IG. 14.14. Value of R.M.S. deviation σ as function of angular distance between two dots whose centre is fixated (subject J.F.). (a) Horizontal display; (b) vertical display of dots as indicated. (From Rattle 1968.)

or of two dots with this separation, is surprisingly good. It is equally remarkable that the accuracy of fixation in blue light is so good (§ 4.22). Second, there is an anomaly when the indicators which locate the centre are situated near the edge of the fovea. The results on eye-movements for circular targets of 4′ should also be noted (§ 4.18).

The accuracy of fixation of the centre of a circular target is consistent with accuracy obtained by a marksman shooting at the well-known target which has a central 'bull' and outer rings. A good marksman can hit the bull even when conditions are such that he can see only the outer rings. Further, his accuracy deteriorates little when positive lenses are used to blur the outlines of the target.†

† Private communication from Dr. F. W. Campbell.

Rattle carried out a few experiments in which he sought conditions in which the accuracy of fixation would be lost. He obtained an indication that fixation of the centre of a gap in a line is less accurate than fixation of the centre of two dots whose separation is equal to the length of the gap. The fixation of the centre of three dots, placed at the corners of an equilateral triangle, was much less precise than the fixation of the centre of a circle through the dots.

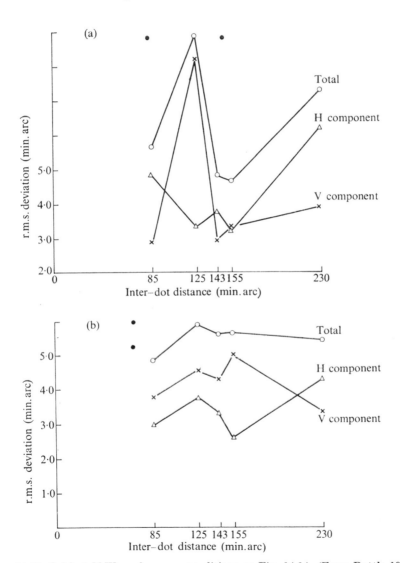

FIG. 14.15. Subject M.W. under same conditions as Fig. 14.14. (From Rattle 1968.)

14.26. Alteration of relation between movements of visual axis and movements of retinal image

The control of eye-movements during fixation may be regarded as a servo-system designed to control the directions of the visual axis. The movement of the retinal image is then regarded as a means of generating a signal which enables the visual system to correct deviations of the visual axis. Alternatively, the control of the visual axis may be regarded as designed to hold the image at the point of fixation P_F within a certain small region of the retina. So long as the relation between retinal-image movements and movements of the visual axis remains invariant, there is no important difference between the two approaches, though one may be more convenient than the other for the discussion of some experiments. Using the apparatus shown in Fig. 5.12, it is possible to alter the ratio F between movements of the visual axis and movements of the retinal image. This creates a novel situation since the error-signals from the retina do not correspond in the normal way with deviations of the visual axis from a target direction. The way in which the eye-movements and the retinal-image movements change when F is altered, should give some insight into the normal modus operandi of the control system.

14.27. Nye (1962) recorded eye-movements when F had the values 1, 2, and 5. The value $F = 1$ corresponds to normal vision. The values of the various parameters which describe eye-movements are shown in Table 14.2. The intersaccadic interval T_{is}, the median drift M_d, and the median saccade magnitude M_{se} have been defined in Chapter 4. $M_{se}(P)$ is the saccade power defined as the square root of the sum of squares of all saccades in 1 s. D_{re} is the drift rate calculated by Nye for drifts which lasted more than 500 ms. D_{ie} is the mean displacement of

TABLE 14.2
Movements of visual axis for different amounts of feedback

Subject	E.N.			P.N.		
F	1	2	5	1	2	5
T_{is} (s)	1·42	2·23	3·0	1·10	1·34	1·86
M_d (min. arc)	3·5	3·65	4·8	5·2	6·0	6·8
M_s (min. arc)	8·0	6·7	6·5	4·0	5·8	6·0
$M_s(P)$ (min. arc)	6·7	4·5	3·7	3·8	5·0	4·5
σ (min. arc)	2·4	2·1	1·8	2·8	2·6	2·4
D_{IE} (min. arc)	1·4	1·5	1·2	2·05	2·4	1·95
D_{RE} (min. arc s^{-1})	1·5	1·5	1·5	3·6	2·8	2·8

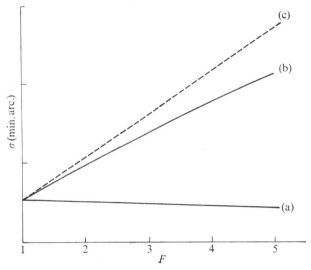

Fɪɢ. 14.16. R.M.S. deviation of (a) visual axis; (b) retinal image when F is varied; (c) calculated deviations of retinal image if visual axis displacement was independent of F. (Data of Nye 1962.)

the visual axis during 250 ms. The table shows that, when F is changed from 1 to 5:

(a) T_{is} increases by about a factor of 2;
(b) σ falls by about 20 per cent (Fig. 14.16);
(c) the drift parameters are unchanged;
(d) the saccade parameters increase a little for one subject, and fall for another; over all the differences are not significant.

The movements of the retinal image are given in Table 14.3. When F

TABLE 14.3

Movements of retinal image for different amounts of feedback.

Subject	E.N.			P.N.		
F	1	2	5	1	2	5
M_d (min. arc)	3·5	7·3	24	5·2	12·0	34
M_s (min. arc)	8·0	13·4	33	4·0	11·5	30
$M_s(P)$ (min. arc)	6·7	9·0	19	3·8	10	23
σ (min. arc)	2·4	4·2	9·0	2·8	5·2	12·0
D_{IE} (min. arc)	1·4	3·0	6·0	2·05	4·8	12·0
D_{RE} (min. arc s^{-1}	1·5	3·0	7·5	3·6	5·6	14

changes from 1 to 5, the retinal image movements increase approximately five-fold in speed and magnitude. The r.m.s. deviation σ increases by less than a factor of 5 but more than a factor of 4 (Fig. 14.16).

14.28. If the drifts are primarily due to muscular imbalance, then it is likely that a subject would have only a little control (conscious or unconscious) over this drift rate, and would be unable to alter it to meet a new situation. The results agree with this hypothesis. No other very simple deduction can be made. When F is increased, the image of the fixation point P_F drifts more rapidly out of the insensitive area, and saccades should become more frequent. Also, saccades of normal size should move the fixation point right across the insensitive zone and so generate further saccades until the system oscillates with a frequency of about 2 Hz. The results show that the control system makes a more subtle adaptation. It quickly learns that saccades overcorrect. It reduces their number and refuses to increase their size when the error-signal is large. The effect is the same as if the insensitive zone had been enlarged. In this way, the visual axis is controlled more closely by accepting the fact that the retinal image of P_F must be allowed to wander over a large region.

14.29. Effect of flicker on eye-movements

West and Boyce (1968) investigated eye-movements when the subject viewed a target which was intermittently illuminated. Some of the observations were made with the apparatus described in § 3.15, but most were made with an accelerometer (§ 3.20). This device gives saccade frequency and magnitude in a convenient way, but does not provide suitable data for calculating the r.m.s. deviation, σ, and so estimating the accuracy of fixation. The target illumination was subject to square-wave intermission (with equal periods of light and darkness). It was found that the saccade rate increased when the frequency of intermission was in the range 1–5 Hz, the largest effect being found at 2 Hz (Fig. 14.17). The distribution of saccades with saccade interval shows multiple peaks of which only one is found when the target is steadily illuminated. The extra saccades are normal in size, and the normal proportion have a recentering effect. The intersaccadic drifts are nearly the same in magnitude. This implies that the drift rate increases because the mean intersaccadic interval is shorter.

14.30. When a subject views a ganzfeld, flickering at frequencies 0–1·0 Hz, the saccade rate is substantially increased. The distribution of saccade interval is similar to that found with steady illumination. At

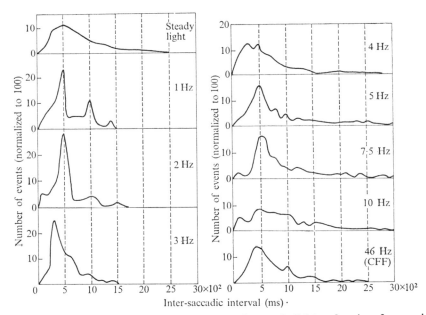

F IG. 14.17. Intersaccadic interval distributions for steady light and various frequencies of interruption. The increased saccade rate (e.g. at 2Hz) is indicated by the reduction of the proportion of long intervals. (After West and Boyce 1968.)

frequencies above 1·0 Hz there are no detectable effects. The 'photic shock' produced by flickering a ganzfeld should be greater than that produced in the experiments described in the preceding paragraph. It therefore appears nearly certain that the extra saccades described above are associated with the control system and are not due to 'photic shock'. This was confirmed by an experiment in which the target was seen steadily illuminated, but flickering luminance was presented either as a surround field or in the other eye.

During the dark intervals, the retina can give no information concerning eye-position. Any corrective action must be based on information received during the preceding light interval. West and Boyce suggest that the increased rate of drift and the extra saccades constitute an adaptation of the control system to the loss of information, i.e. the system makes the best possible use of the information still available. Further experiments, including measurements of the r.m.s. deviation σ, under various conditions, are needed to test their detailed explanation. The importance of the present results is to show beyond reasonable doubt, that the control system does respond to the loss of information, and to suggest that further experiments on targets with intermittent illumination may lead to a better understanding of the control system.

23

15

Small eye-movements in relation to voluntary movements

15.1. Introduction

This chapter is concerned with experiments on voluntary eye-movements made in response to lateral displacements of the target, on corresponding vergence changes made in response to changes in the distance of the target, and on the forces by which the extrinsic muscles rotate the eye. These experiments are considered in relation to the control of the involuntary movements and also to the dynamics of saccade and tremor movements. Much of the work on voluntary eye-movements refers to movements of 5° or more, and has been carried out with apparatus whose sensitivity limit is 10′–100′. Movements similar to the involuntary movements of fixation are either not observed or else appear as a minor source of error. Only certain rather general features of these experiments are of value in understanding the small involuntary movements. There are, however, some experiments on very small voluntary movements which have been carried out with more sensitive apparatus, and the results of these experiments are more directly relevant. From the extensive literature on larger voluntary movements, it has been necessary to select only those items which are of interest in regard to our main topic. Many experiments which are important in other connections, are omitted or only briefly mentioned.

15.2. Responses to changes in target position

A number of experiments have been carried out in which the target position is suddenly changed in one of the three following ways.

(a) The target is suddenly moved to the new position so rapidly that the movement appears instantaneous to the subject. This can be achieved conveniently when the target is a spot on a cathode-ray tube.

(b) One target is suddenly extinguished and another displayed simultaneously. This is conveniently done with two electric lamps, if the negrescence time is small, or with linked mechanical shutters.
(c) Two targets are displayed all the time but the subject is asked to change his gaze from one to the other on receipt of a signal, e.g. a click.

In each of these situations, the initial response is the same. After a latent period, which is usually 180 ms or more, the subject makes a saccadic movement in the general direction of the new target. § 15.3 is concerned with measurements of this initial saccade and of the movements by which the subject subsequently achieves good fixation in the new target direction, when the displacement is a few degrees. Measurements on eye-movements following smaller replacements, down to the smallest which evokes any response, are discussed in §§ 15.4–15.6.

15.3. Eye-movements associated with target replacement

Ginsborg (1953) examined the change in direction of the visual axis when the subject was asked to shift his gaze from one small bright spot A to another similar spot B when A was extinguished and B exposed. The angular separation of A and B was varied from 20' to 240'. The angular sensitivity of the apparatus was 0·2' and the time sensitivity was 5 ms. The following responses were found.

(i) The subject responds with a sharp saccade which may undershoot or overshoot the target and is not always directed precisely towards it. Overshoots are less common than undershoots. Sometimes the undershoot is large (up to half the distance from A to B). When there is an overshoot it is always small.
(ii) When there is either an overshoot or a large undershoot, the saccade is followed by a pause during which the eye drifts at a speed from 5' s⁻¹ to 120' s⁻¹ (i.e. from the normal drift rate of fixation upwards). This drift may be either towards or away from the target. It lasts for at least 150 ms, and may last up to 880 ms.
(iii) If the initial saccade leaves a large error, a correction is made by a second saccade which brings the visual axis within 10' of the correct direction of fixation (Westheimer 1954b). There is then a gradual drift towards the fixation point, and during this time small saccades occur more frequently than in prolonged periods of fixation (Barlow 1952). When the overshoot is small, or in most cases when the target movement is less than 60', the transfer is made by a single saccade followed by a drifting movement.

(iv) The difference between the mean position of the eye before change of target and the final mean position is equal to the angular separation of the targets as accurately as these means can be measured (within $\pm 3'$). Riggs and Niehl (1960) agree with this conclusion.

(v) The latency of the initial response (i.e. the time between the change of target and the beginning of the first saccade) is never less than 140 ms. There is, however, a small drift movement starting 60 ms after exposure of the second target.

(vi) The subject is unaware of the correction described in (iii) above and usually believes that he is fixating correctly after the first saccade, even when this is grossly in error. For a short time he accepts directions of the visual axis which differ by 50' or more from the normal mean position. He is satisfied that he is fixating accurately even while these large deviations exist. Similarly, when tracking a target, a subject is often unaware of a constant error (§ 15.8). This acceptance is, of course, only in regard to what he *consciously* perceives. The error is being corrected even while he is not aware of its existence.

The minimum latency of 140 ms is in agreement with observations on involuntary movements, as is also existence of drifts which are related to 'error' and which have a smaller latency (§§ 14.13, 15.9, and 15.14). Observation (vi) is unexpected. It tends to 'blurr' the sharpness of the concept of a central insensitive zone (§ 14.15). From the point of view of conscious perception the whole fovea sometimes appears to be an insensitive zone.

15.4. Smallest target movement which stimulates a response

Bennet-Clark (1964) investigated the oculomotor response to small changes in target position, with the intention of using them to estimate the diameter of the insensitive zone. He used two methods (a) an after-image method (§§ 2.8–2.10) with an angular resolution of about 4' and (b) cine-recording (§ 4.12) with an angular precision of about 1'. Time-resolution was about 100 ms. Method (a) was used with 27 subjects and method (b) with 2. The response of the subjects by an appropriate change of the visual axis was investigated.

Subjects were asked to change their direction between two targets whose directions were a few minutes of arc apart. Preliminary experiments showed that time of response is an important factor. This time was measured for all 27 subjects when they were asked to change their direction of fixation between two targets 7·5' apart. Both targets were displayed throughout. A histogram of response times is shown in Fig.

15.1. The range of variation is larger than for most visual functions though no larger than the range of intersaccadic intervals (Fig. 4.7). The response times of five subjects who played ball games for their University were 0·5 s, 0·5 s, 1s, 5 s, and 10 s, i.e. their response times for small movements were not significantly different from those of the

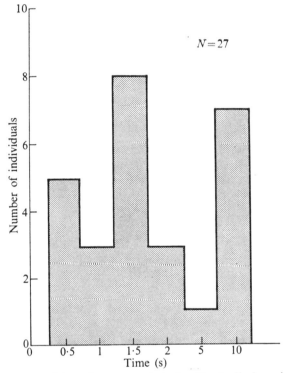

FIG. 15.1. Histogram of times for response to instruction to displace visual axis through 7·5′. (From Bennet-Clark 1964.)

other subjects. The existence of a threshold target displacement to stimulate movement had previously been noted but the suggested magnitude of this limit was considerably higher (e.g. Rashbass (1961*a*) suggested a limit in the range 15′–30′). Yarbus (1967) gives a limit of 8′.

15.5. The reciprocal of the response time T for greater angular movements was found to vary approximately linearly with the angle subtended by the targets. Extrapolation to $1/T = 0$ gives an infinite tracking time for a movement of 5·5′ for H.C.B-C. and of 9·8′ for C.R.E. Other subjects gave similar results. If the response is made after the target leaves the insensitive region then, since its most probable initial position is in the centre of the region, these figures represent radii of the region, and indicate diameters of 10′ and 20′ respectively. This indicates that the insensitive region for response to ordered changes of fixation is larger than the insensitive region postulated in relation to eye-movements of fixation. Much larger displacements are needed to produce a response in a time of about 150 ms. This is in agreement with the results of Ginsborg described in the preceding paragraph. It also is in qualitative agreement with the finding of Cornsweet (1956), that the probability of a correcting saccade increases with distance from the mean position up to a distance of 8′ (Fig. 14.4).

15.6. A second series of experiments by method (b) was carried out with two subjects. They were asked to track a target which moved (horizontally or vertically) with a regular motion at 0·5 Hz. It was found that one subject (D.C.W.) could track movements of 4′ to 16′ (horizontal or vertical) with an accuracy never worse than 4′ and usually much better. The other subject (H.C.B-C.) could track movements of 12′ and 16′ with about 2·5′ accuracy in the vertical direction, but was unable to track even a movement of 16′ in the horizontal direction. The first saccade (greater than 2′) after movement of the target was recorded for each subject. The average time for this was 200 ms for D.C.W. and 270 ms for H.C.B-C. The time interval did not alter significantly for different distances moved by the target. The magnitude (modal value) and range of saccade for each subject are shown in Table 15.1.

It may be seen that D.C.W. makes a saccade which is usually within about 3′ of the right magnitude. H.C.B-C. makes saccades which are nearly always in the right direction (except for the 4′ movement) but the magnitudes of his saccades are not correctly related to the magnitude of target movement. Thus, in these experimental conditions, D.C.W. refers the direction of fixation to a very small region of the retina, while H.C.B-C. does not. There are other experiments which indicate that D.C.W. is much above average in relation to certain visual tasks (e.g. he has very good vernier acuity) but, in relation to accuracy of fixation, he is not significantly better than H.C.B-C. It thus seems necessary to postulate that the process by which fixation is maintained is not, in detail, the same for all subjects. Some subjects have an extremely small central region. They are not satisfied with fixation unless the image of the fixation point lies within this area. Other subjects can accept a much wider variation of the position of the image of the point fixated but are still able to maintain the visual axis near to a mean direction. The variation which can be accepted alters with circumstances (§§ 15.3 and 15.14).

TABLE 15.1

Saccades made when tracking a target which has a small amplitude of oscillation at low frequency (0·5 Hz)

Subject	Tracking axis	Target movement	Modal saccade amplitude	Range including 50 per cent of saccades
H.C.B-C.	Horizontal	4 min. arc	6 min. arc	4–7 min. arc
		8 min. arc	4 min. arc	2–6 min. arc
		12 min. arc	4·5 min. arc	2–8 min. arc
		16 min. arc	11 min. arc	8–18 min. arc
H.C.B-C.	Vertical	4 min. arc	4 min. arc	3–6 min. arc
		8 min. arc	4 min. arc	3–5 min. arc
		12 min. arc	4 min. arc	3–6 min. arc
		16 min. arc	6 min. arc	3–8 min. arc
D.C.W.	Horizontal	4 min. arc	3 min. arc	2–5 min. arc
		8 min. arc	6·5 min. arc	5–9 min. arc
		12 min. arc	6 min. arc and 14 min. arc	6 min. arc and 14 min. arc
		16 min. arc	15 min. arc	13–18 min. arc
D.C.W.	Vertical	4 min. arc	2 min. arc	2–3 min. arc
		8 min. arc	4 min. arc	3–6 min. arc
		12 min. arc	9 min. arc	7–11 min. arc
		16 min. arc	14 min. arc	12–15 min. arc

15.7. Minimum perceived rate of target movement

Boyce (1965*a* and *b*) investigated the minimum rate of target movement which could be perceived *in the absence of a frame of reference*.† He found that it depended upon the velocity of movement and its time duration. At velocities above 8′–10′ s⁻¹ detection is independent of time of display,‡ but it is not certain whether the initial acceleration or the steady velocity is the clue for perception. Below this velocity time of display is important. Boyce considered that the subject has to distinguish retinal image movement due to movement of the target from the retinal image movements due to involuntary movements of the visual axis during fixation. The velocity of 8′–10′ s⁻¹ is faster than nearly all the drift movement and is easily distinguished. To explain the dependence on time (at lower velocities) Boyce proposes

---

† A general account of work on threshold of movements is given by Graham (1965), Chap. 20). Most of the earlier work is concerned with thresholds obtained when there is a fixation mark (or stable reference background), or with targets very different from those used in studies of small eye-movements.

‡ This agrees with much earlier work of Aubert (1886).

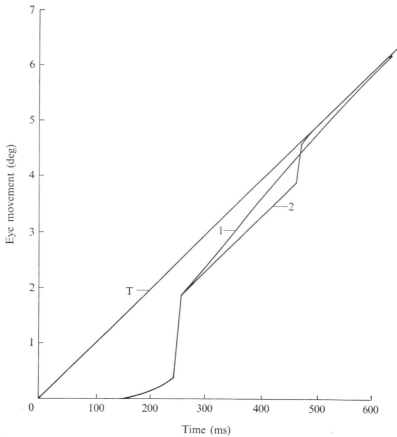

Fɪɢ. 15.2. Two types of eye-movements made while following a target which is suddenly accelerated from 0 to 10° s⁻¹. These are frequently observed. (After Robinson 1965.) T represents movement of target.

a sampled data system of distinguishing between the two kinds of movement.

15.8. Tracking a target moving with constant velocity

Eye-movements made when following a smoothly moving target have been studied by many experimenters including Dodge (1903), Westheimer (1965*a*, *b*), Westheimer and Conover (1954), Fender and Nye (1961), Rashbass (1961*a*, *b*), and Robinson (1965). The last of these includes a summary of most of the earlier work on eye-movements made while pursuing a target which is moving with constant angular velocity. Figure 15.2 shows two typical responses made when a stationary

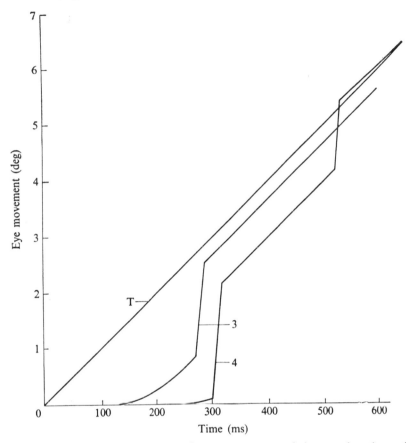

F IG. 15.3. Two less common sequences of eye-movements made in same situation as that which is described for Fig. 15.2. (After Robinson 1965.)

target is suddenly accelerated to a speed of $10°$ s^{-1}. In the first type, movement begins after 125 ms; there is an initial acceleration at a rate of $60°$ s^{-2} to a velocity of $6°$ s^{-1}. After 240 ms from the beginning of target movement, the eye has moved $0.4°$ and the target has moved $2.4°$ so that the eye is $2°$ behind the target. A saccade of $1.25°$ still leaves an error of $0.7°$. However, the eye leaves the saccade at a velocity of $12°$ s^{-1} and thus overtakes the target at about 600 ms, after which the eye-velocity is reduced to the target velocity. In the second type of response, after the saccade, the eye has the same velocity as the target. A second saccade corrects the remaining position error. The first response occurs in about 60 per cent of the trials and the second in about 30 per cent. Other types of response, which occur more rarely, include one in which the eye accelerates smoothly to near target velocity without any saccade, one in which the first saccade leaves a small error (of 0·25°) which is never corrected, and one in which the eye overshoots the target a little and reduces the velocity to allow the target to catch up (Fig. 15.3). Tests with higher target-speeds show that the eye can maintain smooth following up to a speed of about 25° s^{-1}.

15.9. Control of smooth and of saccadic pursuit

From the study of eye-movements made in following moving targets, it is generally accepted that the smooth pursuit eye-movements are made in response to target *movement*. Their function is to make the eye move at the same *rate* as the target. The saccadic movements, on the other hand, are made in response to positional errors. Their function is to bring the eye, as nearly as possible, to the instantaneous position of the target. Rashbass (1961a) describes two important experiments on this division of function. First he showed that the administration of a suitable dose of barbiturate completely eliminates the smooth pursuit movement while saccadic following remains (Fig. 15.4). This demonstrates that the nerve pathways involved in the control of smooth pursuit movements are to some extent independent of those used in the control of saccadic movements—since one can be blocked while the other is left in operation.

In a second experiment Rashbass made the target jump suddenly in one direction and immediately begin to move in the opposite direction. When the displacement was 3° and the rate $-3·5°$ s^{-1} the eye started to move smoothly in the direction in which the target was moving even though this movement increased the initial positional error. After a short interval a saccade (in the direction opposite to the smooth movement) corrected the positional error. In this experiment the smooth pursuit movement is a correct response to the steady movement and the saccade to the positional error. However, when the displacement was 1° and the rate was $-3·5°$ s^{-1}, the smooth pursuit operated but there was no saccade.

This last result somewhat blurs the simple division of control and function. If there had been no smooth movement a saccade would have occurred (§ 15.4). Thus the decision to make a saccade took into account the direction of movement as well as the positional error. There is other evidence that slow movements can occur in response to positional errors (§ 15.13).

Robinson (1965) gives 200–250 ms for the latency of the saccadic response and 125 ms for that of the smooth pursuit system. While there is a large inter-subject variation in these latencies and also a

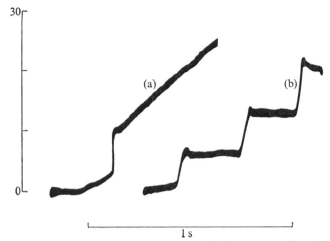

F IG. 15.4. (a) Pursuit by saccade and smooth following in normal conditions; (b) re-
movable of smooth following and pursuit by saccades alone, following administration of
barbiturates. (After Rashbass, 1961*a*.)

considerable alteration with experimental conditions (§ 15.14), it is
nearly certain that the latency of saccadic response is greater than
the latency of smooth pursuit movement.

15.10. Tracking of predictable motion

Eye-movements made when tracking a purely sinusoidal movement
of the target were studied by Fender and Nye (1961), Stark, Vossius,
and Young (1962), Dallos and Jones (1963), and Robinson (1965).
The response to movements of two different amplitudes, as a function
of frequency, is shown in Fig. 15.5. Either of these curves, taken by
itself, suggests that the control system constitutes a low-pass network
with a 'corner frequency' of about 1·5 Hz. The fact that the gain is a
function of amplitude shows that the system is non-linear. This conclusion is supported by measurements of phase-lag. Nevertheless,
Fender and Nye thought that, to a first approximation, the control
might be represented as a linear servo-system which used both a posi-
tion-error signal from the retina and a velocity-error signal from the
proprioceptive system (§ 1.24). By adjusting three constants, they were
able to fit their results over a reasonable range of conditions, including
some in which the value of F (§ 14.28) was altered. Stark *et al.* (1962)
proposed instead a linear control system using sampled data (§ 15.12)
instead of continuous control. Dallos and Jones (1963) and Robinson
(1965) proposed somewhat different linear control-systems and each
obtained a reasonable fit to the observed data.

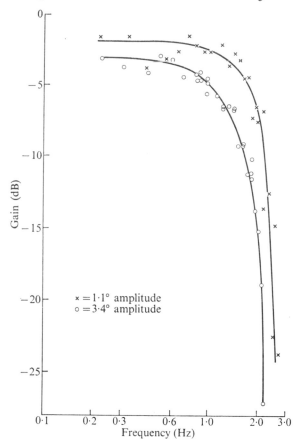

F IG. 15.5. Response to sinusoidal movements of different frequencies; (a) amplitude 1·1°; (b) amplitude 3·4°. (From Fender and Nye 1961.)

15.11. Tracking partly unpredictable motion

Stark *et al.* (1962) studied eye-movements made in response to target motion represented by the sum of several sinusoids. Dallos and Jones (1963) and Michael and Jones (1966) investigated response to band-limited random (Gaussian) motion of the target. In each of these situations, the movements of the target is not totally unpredictable, in principle. In practice, motion based on more than 2 or 3 sinusoids is effectively unpredictable as is the band-limited random motion. All these experimenters tried to fit their results to linear servo-control models.

St. Cyr and Fender (1969*b*, *c*) measured both H- and V-components of eye-movements in response to two-dimensional smooth movements of varying degrees of unpredictability. They made an elaborate analysis and concluded that the control is non-linear.

15.12. Response to sudden movements

Stark *et al.* (1962) also studied eye-movements made in response to sharp movements of the target of a few degrees. They found, in agreement with Rashbass (1961*a*) that the eye makes a saccade at about $t = 200$ where t is the time (in milliseconds) after the target movement. They also tested with pulses in which the target makes a movement in a certain direction and returns to its initial condition long before $t = 200$. In this situation the saccade is made, even though when it is made it takes the eye away from the position of the target. They put forward a theory of eye-movement control by data sampling at 200 ms intervals starting from $t = 0$. In the simplest form of this theory, information about target-movements between $t = 0$ and $t = 200$ cannot affect the saccade at $t = 200$ because that is determined by the sample taken at $t = 0$. They showed that when the target for a stabilized image is moved sharply there is a saccade at $t = 200$; the new sample shows the retinal disparity unchanged so a new saccade is made at $t = 400$. This process is iterative as shown in Fig. 15.6. Stark *et al.* also proposed a data-sampling system for the velocity control. They showed that the sampled data system gave correct predictions of behaviour when the factor F (§§ 5.15 and 14.26) is neither 0 nor 1.

15.13. Step-pulse responses

Boyce (1965*a*) studied the response to pulses of different length and found, that provided the return movement occurred within about 140 ms of the initial movement, the saccadic movement did not occur. He suggested that the interval of about 200 ms should be divided into two parts: 0–140 ms being used for 'calculating the saccade' and 60 ms for obeying an irrevocable order to make it. During the period of 140 ms further information about the error could be taken into account. This modification covered all the observations made by Boyce but he did not suggest that it would cover all the behaviour of a complex adaptive system. Wheeles, Boynton, and Cohen (1967) carried out similar experiments with step-pulses in which the return movement was not equal to the initial movement. They also used combinations of sharp movements and smooth movements, extending the work of Rashbass

(§ 15.9). It was shown that there is a period during which both position errors and velocity information can be used to decide whether a saccade is to be made and, if it is, to determine its magnitude. Thus the theory that saccades are controlled by position errors alone is not generally true. The observations of Robinson (§ 15.8) show that in some cases an excess velocity is used to correct a position error and is thus evoked by the position error.

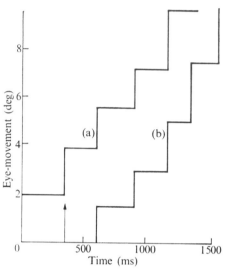

FIG. 15.6. Frustrated following by saccades; (a) target position; (b) eye position. Initial target movement is indicated by arrow. Eye-movements follow target movements at intervals of about 200 ms. (From Robinson 1965.)

The sampled-data system, with its successes and its difficulties is discussed in several papers included in the report of a symposium on eye-movement control (edited by Bach-y-Rita *et al.* 1971). The excellence of the model proposed by Young and Stark is clearly seen. It forms an admirable example of the application of servo-system analysis. Great ingenuity is used in attempting to join together sampled data control of velocity and position. Yet, at the end, it appears necessary to accept the conclusion, stated in different ways by Fuchs (pp. 357–8 loc. cit.) and by Fender (p. 539 ff), that it is not profitable to attempt to modify this system further in order to apply it to the more recent experimental results. Fuchs says 'it may be more appropriate to discard the notion of a sampler and to describe the system only as discontinuous. Further attempts to patch up the sampled data model rapidly leads to a very complicated system with no neurophysiological basis'. Fender and Nye made the first application of linear control theory and the first experiments in which the value of F was altered (§§ 14.26 and 15.10) but Fender now believes that the control cannot be represented as a linear system even as a first approximation, and all attempts to find a better linear system (specified by a better transfer function) are futile. He proposes a new model in which latency depends on information transfer, based partly on the experiments of St. Cyr and Fender (§ 15.11).

15.14. Factors affecting latency

Boyce (1965a) treated saccade time, direction, and magnitude as variables and measured the effect of giving the subject partial or complete advance information about the movement of the target. He also measured differences of latencies for response to outward and return movements. He investigated the effect of learning when pulses were given at regular intervals, extending some earlier measurements of Dallos and Jones (1963). The general tendency was that, as one would expect, latency increased when lack of advance information forced the brain to make a more complex calculation after the target moved. However, subjects did not all change their latencies in the same way, indicating that other factors are involved. Boyce also obtained evidence of an increase of drift rate during the period between a sharp movement of the target and the saccadic eye-movement. St. Cyr and Fender (1969c) analyse a wide range of situations leading to different measured latencies in the oculomotor system. They suggest that the time delay consists of two parts: a time required for signals to travel in nerve pathways, and a time dependent on target motion in the particular situation. They relate the latter to information transfer. The very long delays sometimes observed in vergence movements (§ 15.16), where the available information seems to be large, suggests that rate of acquisition of information may be only one of several conditions affecting latency.

15.15. Vergence tracking

Eye-movements made in response to a change in the apparent distance of a target have been recorded by Westheimer and Mitchell (1956), Riggs and Niehl (1960), and Rashbass and Westheimer (1961a, b). The apparent distance of the target may be varied by actual movement of the target or by presenting similar targets to each eye, and altering their positions so that different angles of convergence are needed to place their images on corresponding parts of the retina. The latter method was used by all the above experimenters. It is found that the response to a sudden change of apparent distance is a movement beginning about 150 ms after the stimulus and lasting several hundred milliseconds (typically 400 ms, not including the latency of 150 ms). Sometimes saccades occur during this movement. They are usually conjugate and do not, on average, assist the change in vergence.

The independence of the control of the mean direction of the visual axes and of the convergence is shown by Rashbass and Westheimer (1961a, b). If the two targets are moved so that tracking requires a change in mean position and a change in vergence, the former is made by saccades and the latter by the smooth movement described above. If the two targets are oscillated with different frequencies (1·0 and 0·66 Hz) then the vergence tracking deteriorates after a few cycles while the lateral tracking (partly by saccades) is maintained.

15.16. Westheimer and Mitchell (1956) who used spots of light as targets found that the subjects followed a change requiring a few degrees of increasing convergence with poor accuracy. Sometimes they accepted an error of as much as 1°. They sometimes did not make any change when the spots were moved so as to require reduction of vergence by 1·5°. They noticed only a momentary dyplopia and accepted the images as fused even when they were, for short periods, separated by distances large compared with the dimensions of Panum's area. Riggs and Niehl (1960) who used crosses as targets found that the correct movements for vergence were made within an accuracy of about 2′ (mean of 10 trials), and that the accuracy of lateral tracking was similar.

15.17. The experiments on vergence tracking, taken as a whole, show that the control is independent of the control for lateral tracking. Westheimer suggests that different pathways (which both use the final common pathways of the third, fourth, and sixth cranial nerves) are involved. It is easy to understand that the necessity for a large and sudden change in vergence very seldom occurs in any natural evolutionary situation and had little survival value. Therefore a rather sluggish control is sufficient. However, when both eyes are displaced from the target point by distances greatly in excess of the dimensions of the central insensitive zone, saccades do not occur *provided that the displacements are equal and opposite.* Much smaller displacements cause saccades if (a) one eye is occluded, (b) the displacements are in the same sense, or (c) the displacements are in the opposite sense and unequal by about 10′. This indicates that the decision to make a saccade and the decision whether the saccade is to be to right or to left is made by summating demands from the two eyes. When one eye demands a saccade to the left, and the other demands one to the right, then no saccade is made but the one eye moves rather slowly to the right and the other to the left thereby reducing the vergence error. Only on rare occasions, and only for some subjects, saccades to left and to right occur simultaneously and then they are unequal so that there is a lateral movement as well as a change of vergence.

15.18. Eye-movements during binocular fixation

The general character of eye-movements during binocular fixation is similar to that found for monocular fixation of stationary targets (§ 4.27 and Table 4.4). Lateral tracking also appears to operate in the same way. It is reasonable to assume that the processes operative in monocular fixation are still operative and that control of the two eyes is, to a considerable extent, independent since the eyes do not co-operate so as to cause a significant improvement in the accuracy of fixation (Table 4.4). We now wish to consider whether there is any independent control system which keeps the vergence as nearly at possible constant and equal to the angle appropriate to the distance of the target. Krauskopf, Cornsweet, and Riggs (1960) who have made a detailed study of this problem conclude that the only special control is associated with the synchronism of the saccades in the two eyes. They suggest that the eyes drift irregularly until one eye gives a sufficient error signal to 'demand' a saccade. There is then a saccadic movement for each eye, but the magnitude of the saccade for each eye is determined by the error signal for that eye. Thus the saccades will usually be of different magnitude and the difference will tend to correct the vergence error. This correction will be imperfect partly because of the saccade latency, but the standard deviation of the vergence is *less* than the standard deviation of the horizontal direction for one eye alone, whereas it would be about 1·4 times greater if the eyes were moving independently. This account of the process implies that the decision to make a saccade is controlled by one centre (which accepts information from both eyes) and the decision concerning the magnitude is made by another (which depends, wholly or mainly, on information from the eye which is to move). This is in agreement with evidence given in § 4.26.

24

15.19. Interplay of saccades and drifts in binocular fixation

St. Cyr and Fender (1969*a*) have made an extensive study of eye-movements when fixating small dots (2′ diameter), vertical lines, and horizontal lines. The lines were 7° long and the ends shaded into the background so as to make identification of the centre imprecise (§ 14.25). They used a modification of the method devised by Byford (§ 3.12) to record both H and V components for both eyes. They made records from both eyes when both eyes viewed targets whose positions had been adjusted so that, in the mean position of the visual axes, they were as nearly as possible on corresponding parts of the retina. They also made records from both eyes when one target was extinguished. They accept and extend the results obtained by Cornsweet, Krauskopf, and Riggs but criticize the analysis which tacitly assumes that only the saccades are corrective. The monocular processes of fixation must operate to control disparity of the visual axes when both eyes are fixating on a common point at infinity, or in an equivalent situation. St. Cyr and Fender find that there is an additional correction of horizontal disparity. This correction is made by drifts, i.e. by fairly slow vergence movements. They find no corresponding correction of vertical disparity.

Some records obtained by Ditchburn and Ginsborg (1953) suggested the existence of slow oscillations of horizontal disparity which they called convergence–divergence waves. It is possible that movements of this type, associated with small fluctuations of accommodation may operate to scan the visual scene in regard to depth. This would both assist depth perception and enable objects at different distances to be seen clearly most of the time. The analyses of Krauskopf, Cornsweet, and Riggs and of St. Cyr and Fender would not reveal these movements.

15.20. Function of drifts

Most of the experimenters on eye-movements in the period 1950 to 1965, believed that the wandering of the eye during fixation was primarily due to imperfect compensation of the actions of agonist and antagonist pairs manifested in the drift movements. The saccades were regarded as basically corrective though, partly owing to the latency, very imperfect in effect. Nachmias (§ 14.9), Boyce (§ 14.13), Fiorentini and Ercoles (§ 14.12) obtained evidence that, at least for some subjects and some directions, drift movements are corrective.

Several workers found that some subjects can reduce their saccade frequency very much and still maintain fairly good fixation (§ 14.10). This implies an ability to learn to control the drift movements.† St. Cyr and Fender (1969a) present the results of the analysis of eye-movements of two subjects. They computed the extent to which the average saccade and the average drift reduced the deviation from the over-all mean position of the eye which existed at the beginning of the saccade or drift. They found that, for one subject the average reduction was 0·33 (of the original deviation) for saccades and 0·25 for drifts. For the other it was 0·67 for saccades and 0·4 for drifts. Their analysis thus indicates that the drifts have a corrective action which, for one subject, is only a little smaller than the corresponding action of saccades.

15.21. The analysis of St. Cyr and Fender takes no account of the existence of short-period fixation targets (§§ 14.16–14.20). Boyce found that the corrective action of saccades in relation to short-period means was very much larger than the corresponding action in respect of over-all means. No corresponding effect was found for drifts. This suggests the possibility that changes in drift direction may be in response to position error signals related to the centre of the insensitive zone (§ 14.14). The saccades, on the other hand, may be controlled by deviations from short-period fixation centres. The analysis of St. Cyr and Fender deals only with differences of position at the beginning and ends of movements. It does not adequately represent those drifts which start by carrying the axis away from the mean position and change direction (§ 14.13). However, even though the method of analysis may over-emphasize the importance of correction by drifts, it leaves no doubt that this action is important.

15.22. Dynamics of eye-movements

In all the preceding discussion, eye-movements have been regarded as determined by commands from a central control system. The detailed course of eye-movements depends also on the force available to accelerate the globe, on its moment of inertia, and on visco-elastic resistances in the muscle and in the surrounding tissue. The most interesting problem is the acceleration and deceleration during a saccade. Much of the experimental work has been concerned with voluntary saccades of

---

† The extent to which the eye-movements of subjects whose eye-movements have been recorded are typical can only be conjectured. They may constitute a very non-typical 'educated' population.

5° to 40°. Several models, in which the eye is replaced by springs, dash-pots, etc. have been proposed. We shall give one example of such a model but will not be concerned with the variety of the proposed models or the details of the experiments upon which they are based. It is far from certain that the dynamical characteristics of the eye in respect of large saccades can be applied to the small saccades.

15.23. Moments of inertia

The moment of inertia of the globe, with any attachments used in measuring eye-movements, is an important parameter even if, in the end, it is decided that inertial forces are small compared with other forces. It is also a parameter which can be fairly closely defined. The moment of inertia of a solid body of the same densities and dimensions as the globe is about 4·3 g cm². (Robinson (1964) gives the value 4·12 g cm²; the author has calculated 4·4 g cm²). For rapid eye-movements the effective moment may be less because the vitreous humour may not follow the movement completely (Hilding 1954). A value of $2·5 \pm 1$ g cm² may be estimated.† These together with the moments added by various devices are shown in Table 15.2. The third column gives the additional moment as a percentage of the estimated effective moment. The lighter devices add only a negligible percentage. Many of those used for recording eye-movements add between 100 and 200 per cent.

TABLE 15.2
Moments of inertia

	gm cm²	Per cent addition to effective moment
The globe as a rigid body	4·3	—
Effective moment of globe (saccades)	2·5	—
Mirror resting on globe (§ 3.3)	0·05	2
Smaller caps used by Yarbus	0·05–0·1	2–4
Larger caps used by Yarbus	0·3–1	12–40
Plastic contact lens with mirror (§ 5.12)	1	40
Glass contact lens with mirror (§ 5.2)	2·5	100
Plastic contact lens with coil (§ 3.18)	2·5	100
Plastic contact lens with stalk and mirror	2·5–5	120–200
Plastic contact lens with targets mounted	5–10	200–400
Contact lens with accelerometer (§ 3.20)	5	200

† Stone, Thomas, and Zakian (1965) find that the effective moment of inertia of a dog's eye is about 90 per cent of the value calculated for a rigid body. This suggests a value of 3·8 g cm² for the human eye.

15.24. Properties of the extra-ocular muscles

Muscles have both a passive and an active part. In the extra-ocular muscle the passive part includes non-contractile elements of the muscle itself and of surrounding tissue (orbital fat, conjunctival tissue, suspensory ligaments, etc.). The active part may be further divided into a contractile part whose length changes in response to changes of nerve signals, and an elastic component. The latter is partly in series and, probably to a less extent, partly in parallel with the contractile material. When the eye is stationary in the primary position, the muscles are stretched so that when a saccade is ordered by the nerve impulses there is no backlash to be taken up. Stone, Thomas, and Zakian (1965) find that in the dog's eye each muscle is stretched by 2 mm. If one muscle were completely relaxed the eye would be deflected 8° by the contraction of the other. This 'zero-point force' is thus large compared with the forces involved in the involuntary movements of fixation.

15.25. Saccadic movements

When a stimulus, in the form of a change in innervation (i.e. in the frequency of spikes in the motor nerves) reaches the eye muscles, the agonist contracts. Since the opposed muscles are subject to reciprocal innervation,† the antagonist slackens at almost the same time (Sherrington 1897). No experiment, at any rate on an intact eye, can measure how much of the net force is due to the extra tension in the agonist and how much is due to reduced tension in the antagonist. This net force acts at a distance of about 14 mm from the centre of rotation to produce a couple. The angular acceleration is limited by (i) the inertia of the globe, (ii) the viscous resistance of the passive tissues, and (iii) the resistance to change of length of the elastic components which behave like opposing stretched springs. Westheimer (1954a), who made the first attempt at a quantitative account of the dynamics of eye-movements, thought the inertial resistance (i) was important. He postulated a system in which the eye was underdamped and was resonant at a frequency of 20 Hz. Measurements (not available to Westheimer) which will be described in § 15.27 indicate that (i) is negligible in comparison with (ii) and (iii) which are generally combined as visco-elastic resistance. It is found that when the muscles are cut, as the first step in surgical removal of an eye, the globe rotates freely (Childress

† See Fulton (1947).

and Jones 1967). This indicates that the viscous material is mainly in the muscle itself rather than in the surrounding tissue.

15.26. Duration of saccades

The data displayed in Fig. 4.2 show that, for saccades of 5° to 40°, the duration of a saccade increases linearly from 30 ms to 100 ms. Extrapolating the curve backwards gives a minimum duration of 25 ms which is nearly constant in the range 0–20′, i.e. in the range of the involuntary saccades. Cooper and Eccles (1930) found that the contraction time of the extra-ocular muscle for an isolated twitch is 7 ms. It is probable that the minimum time for contraction of the whole muscle *in vivo* is two or three times longer. Robinson (1964) estimates 20 ms. Thus the time of the main movement of one of the small involuntary saccades of fixation is fixed by the contraction of the muscle. Other considerations must determine the duration of larger saccades.

15.27. Dynamical measurements

Robinson (1964) used the method described in § 3.18 to measure saccadic movements. He also made measurements in which one eye was able to observe stimuli. The other was occluded and mechanically constrained so that forces could be applied to it. Alternatively, the force which the occluded eye exerted (against a stiff spring) when the other eye made a saccade, could be measured. He carried out the following series of experiments:

(a) recording displacement versus time for saccades in the range 5°–40°;

(b) similar records when the eye was loaded so as to increase the effective moment of inertia by a *factor* of nearly 100;

(c) observation of force exerted by the occluded eye versus time when the other eye made a saccade (Fig. 15.7);

(d) movement of the eye in response to a suddenly applied couple (or a suddenly removed couple) when the subject endeavoured to fixate.

He also measured the length-tension relation for the muscle of a cat. Stone, Thomas, and Zakian (1965) made measurements on passive rotatory characteristics of the dog's eye. Childress and Jones (1967) made measurements similar to (d) above but including an extensive study of response to steady loading. Thomas (1969) made records of saccades.

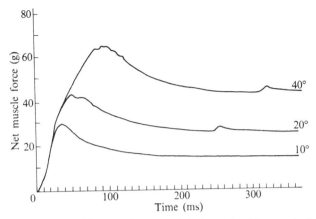

FIG. 15.7. Force exerted by muscles of occluded eye (pushing against a strong spring) when the other eye makes a voluntary saccade. Ordinate shows equivalent force at the moment arm of the radius of the eyeball. (From Robinson 1964.)

He also applied sinusoidal driving forces to the globe and measured the resulting angular accelerations using the accelerometer described in § 3.20.

15.28. Dynamical characteristics

From his measurements Robinson concluded the following.

(i) The net force exerted by the contractile part of the muscle (and controlled by the innervation) changes by 1·2 g deg^{-1} when the eye moves to a new position[†]. This balances the elastic forces due to change of muscle lengths.

(ii) During a saccade, there is an excess active tension of about 25 g; the magnitude of this force is independent of saccade magnitude from 5° to 40°.

(iii) The visco-elastic forces bring the eye to a rest when the active force falls near the end of a saccade; there is no active check, i.e. no temporary reversal of the active force (Fig. 15.7) to prevent or to reduce overshoot.

(iv) After the saccadic movement is nearly complete there is a slow readjustment to the new position lasting 200 ms during which the excess active force and the visco-elastic resistance both fall to zero.

(v) The active-tension of about 25 g is the maximum available; this limits the speed of large saccades. To produce a large movement the force must be used for a longer time.

† This is a revised value from Robinson (1965) and Childress and Jones (1967).

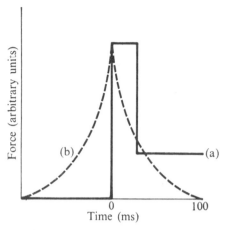

FIG. 15.8. Force vs time, in a saccadic movement: (a) Robinson, (b) Findlay.

15.29. Dynamical models

Robinson† (1964) set out a schematic diagram of springs, etc., to represent the eye. This leads to a fourth-order differential equation with seven adjustable constants. The frequency response curve is not very different from that shown in Fig. 2.1(c) for a heavily damped system. The cut-off frequency (at which the response is half that at zero frequency) is 1·1 Hz. At first sight it appears unlikely that such a sluggish system could execute rapid saccades. Robinson showed that pre-emphasis of the neural command causes the rapid movement. It is as though a 'short sharp tug' (plus a smaller permanent change of force) is applied (Fig. 15.8(a)). The heavily damped elastic system moves rapidly in response to the tug and stops quickly (with only a small overshoot) when it is over. In this model it is assumed that the visco-elastic forces consist of a fast part and a slow part, with time constants 12 ms and 285 ms.

Childress and Jones (1967) agree with Robinson that the eye is an overdamped system and that inertial forces are small. They propose the model shown in Fig. 15.9 which is simpler than that of Robinson, mainly in that all the damping is combined. They find that the series elastic forces $K_1 + K_2 = 9$ g deg^{-1}. The natural frequency of the system considered as a moment of inertia with two springs is 87 Hz.

15.30. Thomas (1967, 1969) measured the velocity response to sinusoidal driving and obtained a strong resonance at 37 Hz (with a

† See also Robinson (1965) and Robinson *et al.* (1969).

bandwidth of 40 Hz). This leads to a response function which rises to a maximum at 40 Hz and falls rapidly at higher frequencies (Fig. 15.10). It is possible that this resonance is found by Thomas and colleagues and not by other workers because his accelerometer is more suitable for investigating the dynamics of fast movements than the displacement records. However, the repeated movement when the eye is driven at angular velocities up to $250°$ s^{-1} leaves no time for the recovery stage of 200 ms (§ 15.28). It is possible that this modifies the properties of the muscle so as to reduce the effective damping. In any case the

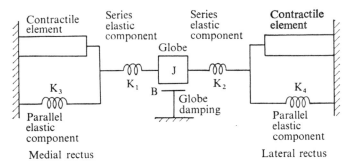

FIG. 15.9. Mechanical model to simulate action of eye-muscles. J = inertia of eyeball, B = damping of eyeball. The Ks are spring coefficients. (From Childress and Jones 1967.)

effective damping when the muscle is stretched and contracted by an applied force may not be the same as it is when its length changes in response to a change in innervation and the energy has to be derived from metabolic processes.

15.31. Involuntary tremor

Each of the extrinsic eye-muscles consists of about 10^5 fibres, and there is one associated nerve fibre for every 2·5 muscle fibres (§ 1.24). Most of these nerve fibres are used to supply discharges which activate the associated muscle fibres. If these discharges are subject to independent random fluctuations, then the number of activated muscle fibres will vary. The agonist and antagonist may then be, on average, in balance but with a fluctuation about the balance point. The frequency spectrum of the changes of force generated in this way would be flat up to very high frequencies. Breinin (1955) has found, in electromyograms, discrete non-synchronous firing of motor neurons up to several hundred Hertz.

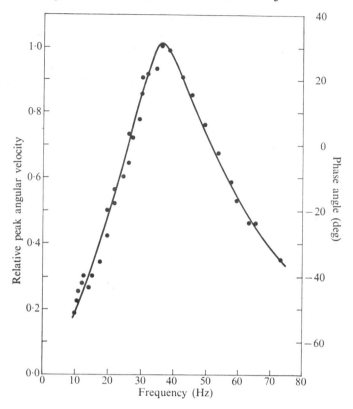

FIG. 15.10. Velocity response function. (After Thomas 1967.)

15.32. If the spectrum of the input is flat up to 200 Hz or more, then the response function of the muscle system is proportional to the frequency spectrum of the tremor shown in Fig. 4.8. This function is represented on a log versus log scale in Fig. 15.11. It is a reasonably good fit to an overdamped second-order system with time constants of 2 ms and 20 ms. In the model of Robinson (1964), time constants of 285 ms and 12 ms are required (§ 15.28) to represent the behaviour of the eye in saccades of 5°–40°. It is possible that the 20 ms time of Findlay is associated with the same visco-elastic elements as the 12 ms time of Robinson. Close agreement of time would not be expected since the system is not linear and the amplitudes are very different. It is also likely that the 285 ms process has not sufficient effect on the small amplitude movements to show up in the frequency range 5–100 Hz. In this connection, it may be observed that Robinson (1965) found that analysis of smooth pursuit required the introduction of at least one time constant longer than any which had been used in the analysis of saccades.

Collins (1971) gives a preliminary account of measurements on the ocular-rotatory systems of cats and of human subjects. The measurements are more detailed and the models more complicated than those described in §§ 15.27–30. Collins isolates some of the individual elements and finds their properties more non-linear than the system as

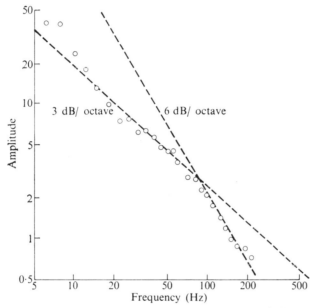

Fig. 15.11. Tremor spectrum on log–log scale. (From Findlay 1971.)

a whole. He describes a 'simplified linear model' which resembles Robinson's model. The 'constants' of this model have to be regarded as variables in relation to large movements of the globe. For the very small displacements of fixation, the predictions of his model do not appear to differ very much from those of the simpler models. Note that the linearity of the dynamical system is a separate question from the linearity of the control system. The linearity of the dynamical system depends on such things as whether the extension of a band of muscle-fibre in response to an applied force is proportional to that force in accordance with Hooke's Law. For the small displacements associated with involuntary eye-movements, extension (or contraction) probably is linear. Non-linearity enters, if at all, through the complicated viscous forces.

15.33. Involuntary saccades

Two problems arise in connection with the involuntary saccades of fixation: (a) the form of the response function, and (b) the form of the nerve input by which they are stimulated.

With regard to (a), there are two possible (alternative) assumptions: (i) that the response function is the same as that of the voluntary saccades and (ii) that it is the same as that of the tremor. The amplitude of about 5′ for a median involuntary saccade is about 50 times larger than the tremor amplitudes, and 60 times smaller than that of 5° voluntary saccades. Thus neither assumption (i) nor assumption (ii) can be accepted with confidence. If (i) is accepted then there is the further problem that the response functions for voluntary saccades found by Robinson (1965) and by Thomas are considerably different. Findlay (1971) accepts assumption (ii), i.e. he assumes that the function shown in Fig. 4.8 and Fig. 15.11 applies also to the saccades. He also assumes that the saccade spectrum shown in Fig. 4.8, which represents all the saccades in one record, applies also to each individual saccade. This is true, at least for the higher frequencies, if the inter-saccadic intervals have a random distribution. It is not certain that this is true for records of moderate length. With these assumptions he derives the spectrum of the input, and with a further assumption about phases he obtains the form of the input shown in Fig. 15.8 (curve (b)). When the rate of pulses in a nerve-fibre changes suddenly about 10 pulses must be received before the new rate can be recognized. A rate of 1000 pulses a second, which is very high (§ 7.5), cannot be regarded as established in less than about 10 ms. Thus there must be a finite rise-time for the input. It is also likely that, for the involuntary saccades, maximum innervation is operative only for a very short time. Almost as soon as the maximum is reached, the active input begins to fall sharply towards its new equilibrium value. Thus the exponential rise and decay found by Findlay appears more suitable to describe the changes of input operative for the involuntary saccades than the scheme which Robinson postulated for the larger saccades (Fig. 15.8, curve (a)). However, the rate of rise obtained by Findlay is too slow for the involuntary saccades by a factor of 4 or 5.

15.34. The time course of voluntary saccades appears to be determined by the maximum available excess force (§ 15.28). For a 40° saccade this force must be applied longer than for a 5° saccade. It is nearly certain that the time course of saccades of 100′ and less is nearly constant, and is determined by the minimum time required for a rise of muscle tension (§ 15.26). The force applied in making these saccades is less than the maximum available force and is roughly proportional to the magnitude of the saccade.

The two problems mentioned at the beginning of § 15.33 require for their solution further detailed records of involuntary saccades of different sizes. If the viscous elements of the muscle operate like non-Newtonian fluids (or gels), then their dissipative power for very small displacements may be very different from that for larger displacements which involve larger angular velocities. The importance of inertial resistance relative to viscous resistance may be much greater for the small movements than for the large.

More detailed discussion of the dynamics of eye-movements involves the detailed anatomy and physiology of muscle contraction together with the general system of motor control (Granit 1970).

16

Conclusion

16.1. Real and apparent movement

The physiological systems described in Chapter 7 are suitable for detecting displacement of the boundaries in a retinal image from one receptor field to another. It is also probable that the human visual system includes specific movement detectors broadly similar to those described in §§ 7.30–7.31. Additional information is needed to distinguish between 'real' movement (i.e. retinal image movement due to movement of the target) and 'apparent' movement (i.e. retinal image movement due to eye-movements). The system which makes this distinction must also be able to deal with the very common situation in which retinal image movement is due partly to eye-movements and partly to movement of the target. It must then be able to extract the real movement which may be greater or less than the movement derived from the retinal image movement.

We shall be mainly concerned with the absence of apparent movement related to saccades—both the small saccades of fixation and the larger saccades made when scanning the visual scene. General reviews of work on real and apparent movement are given by Spigel (1965), Duke-Elder (1968, pp. 671–7), Graham (1965, pp. 575–88), Le Grand (1967, pp. 178–92), and MacKay (1973).

16.2. Outflow and inflow theories

For a long time two kinds of theory of how the visual system compensates for eye-movements have been current: these are known as the 'outflow' and 'inflow' theories. Helmholtz† stated the 'outflow' theory which postulates that when the eye-muscles are ordered to move the eyes a simultaneous instruction is given to 'offset' the resulting movement of the retinal-image. The 'inflow' theory was precisely formulated

† See pp. 243–70 of the Dover Edition of a translation of Helmholtz, *Physiological Optics* (1866).

by Sherrington (1918) though it was known, in general terms, to Helmholtz. It assumes that the information used to offset the effect of eye-movements comes from the proprioceptive nerves which send to the cortex precise information about the way in which the eye has moved. This theory is now generally rejected because there is good evidence that the proprioceptive system does not give any information about the deviation of the eyes from the primary position. A subject whose eye-muscles have been paralysed can attempt to move the eyes and when he does so he perceives a movement of the target. This movement is in the direction to be expected if compensation has been made for the desired movement which has not taken place. This was known to Helmholtz. The conclusion is confirmed and extended by a series of experiments by Brindley and Merton (1960). These are consistent with some kind of 'outflow' theory but not with an 'inflow' theory.

16.3. Suppression of vision associated with saccades

A subject who is attempting to fixate is often aware that the direction of his gaze is wandering a little but a naïve subject does not usually know that he is making saccadic movements. Even the large saccadic movements, made when viewing a landscape or when viewing a picture, are often not consciously perceived (Yarbus 1967, p. 146). The alternation of saccades and fixation pauses in reading is not noticed by most people. The rapidity of saccadic movements requires that any compensatory system must operate very rapidly; also in addition to extracting the real movement from the apparent movement the system must prevent the subject from seeing a blurred picture of the visual scene while a saccade is in progress. It has, for a long time, been supposed, usually without very direct evidence, that visual information is accepted only during the fixation pauses. This has led to the hypothesis that vision is wholly or partially suppressed during the saccades (Dodge 1900, 1905). It has been suggested that

(a) suppression is due simply to rapid movement of the retinal image so that no one group of receptors is stimulated by the moving boundaries (Dodge 1905);
(b) there is a central inhibition (Holt 1903);
(c) there is an inhibition at retinal level (Richards 1968), or
(d) there is a psychological 'withdrawal of attention' (Bell and Weir 1949; Woodworth and Schlossberg 1954).

A general discussion of this topic[†] is given by Lévy-Schoen (1969, p. 151).

[†] See also Le Grand (1967, p. 192).

16.4. The small saccades of fixation

These are sometimes called microsaccades, but they are quite large enough to be noticed, in the absence of some compensation, and they are fast enough to blur the image seriously. The median saccade is about 5′ and many saccades of fixation are over 10′ (§ 4.8 and Fig. 4.7). The moon's angular diameter is about 30′. If the moon were subject to sharp movements of up to a third of its diameter we should be well aware of this phenomenon. The duration of the involuntary saccades (some 25 ms) is about the same as the integration time of the visual system (§ 4.4 and 12.11). The blur which would occur in the absence of some kind of suppression or compensation is of order 10 times the intercone distance in the centre of the fovea. The mean velocity in a saccade of 10′ is about 400′ s^{-1} (§ 4.4).

Fender and the author found that a subject did not see most of the saccadic movements of a spot of light reflected from his eye-mirror on to a white screen. In another experiment Fender made a saccade control the movement of a spot of light on a cathode-ray tube. A subject could not see the 'blip' produced by his own saccade. In each of these experiments the movement was easily visible to a second observer.† This experiment formed the basis of an extended investigation by Ebbers (1965) who found that the 'blip' could be seen by the subject if it was made bright enough. He adjusted the luminance until the subject could not see the 'blip' and found that it was still visible to a second observer. The latter then looked through a filter followed by two polaroids whose angle could be altered so that the combination formed a filter of variable density. In this way the ratio of the sensitivity of the observer to that of the subject (in respect of the 'blip') was measured. This ratio varied from 6 : 1 to 125 : 1, i.e. the mean log difference was about 1·2. This considerable difference in threshold was confirmed by other experiments in which precautions were taken to eliminate possible sources of error. In further experiments Ebbers measured the impairment of the subjects vision,

(a) when the spot on the cathode-ray tube moved with the eye, and
(b) when it moved against the eye,

and found less impairment in the first case. Hence he concluded that suppression is mainly due to the rapid movement of the retinal image. This part of the experiment is not entirely satisfactory because only

† The second of these experiments was mentioned in a lecture given at Florence (Ditchburn 1956).

one component of the eye-movement controls the cathode-ray tube and the two movements are not, in general, parallel.

16.5. Lettvin (1962) and his students made a practical test of suppression during involuntary saccades. The subject attempted to read the headlines of a newspaper during a flash of light. The flashes were presented at random. Times of flashes and saccades were recorded. When a flash occurred in an intersaccadic interval the headline could be read easily, but it could not be read either directly or as an after-image if the flash happened to coincide with an involuntary saccade. The author, together with A. E. Drysdale, has recently been making observations on the visibility of structure of after-images of gratings of different spatial frequencies. It is found that, in a few tests, the structure of a grating of fairly high spatial frequency is not seen at all even though the contrast is high enough for it to be seen clearly in more than four-fifths of the tests. This, like the effect found by Lettvin, may be due to blurring of the after-image by a saccadic eye-movement which happens to be in progress at the time of the flash.

It is known (Sperling 1963) that discrimination of the structure of a briefly presented target can be inhibited by a flash of light given up to 40 ms *after* the presentation of the target. Lettvin found that this inhibition did not occur if the masking flash coincided with a saccade.

16.6. Vision of flashes presented during involuntary saccades

Several experiments have been carried out to test whether the threshold for vision of brief flashes of light, presented during a saccade, is higher than the threshold for flashes presented during an intersaccadic interval. The flashes are so brief that blurring of the retinal image of a flash (due to the eye-movement) is not significant. Krauskopf, Graf, and Gaarder (1966) used a signal derived from the saccade to trigger an 'immediate' flash or a 'delayed' flash. The latter usually fell in an intersaccadic interval. They found no significant difference of threshold. Zuber, Crider, and Stark (1964) presented flashes at times before, after, and during saccades, and made records of time of flash in relation to the time of saccade. For one intensity, the flash was never seen when it occurred within a time interval of 50 ms centred on the *beginning* of the flash. One flash in eight was seen during the intervals −50 to −25 ms and +25 to +50 ms (relative to the beginning of the flash), and all flashes were seen during intersaccadic intervals†. Thus

---

† A number of flashes thought to be associated with blinks etc. were discarded, but their inclusion would not effect the general result.

total suppression during the flash was found for flashes of this intensity. Zuber, Horrocks, Lorber, and Stark (1964) also found suppression during the fast phase of vestibular nystagmus. These saccades are involuntary but are larger than the saccades of fixation.

The saccades presented by Krauskopf *et al.* were triggered by a signal derived from the velocity of the eye-movement. This signal does not become strong until the saccade is well advanced (Fig. 4.1). Thus the

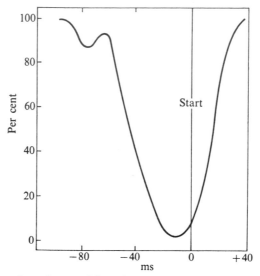

Fɪɢ. 16.1. Percentage chance of detecting flash as a function of time from beginning of a saccade. (From Latour 1966.)

flashes could not occur before the saccade or during the early part of the saccade when suppression appears to be at its strongest. A delay of even 10 ms would put the flash so near the end of the saccade that suppression would be very weak. (Fig. 16.1). The disagreement between different experimenters makes further tests desirable. At present, in view of the results obtained for voluntary saccades (§ 16.7), it appears reasonable to accept the suppression obtained by Zuber *et al.* for involuntary saccades.

16.7. Suppression associated with voluntary saccades

Latour (1962, 1966) measured the visibility of flashes as a function of intensity and of time (relative to the beginning of a voluntary saccade).

For a flash of suitable intensity he found suppression starting about 60 ms before the saccade and reaching a maximum near the beginning of the saccade. The suppression decayed rapidly during the saccade and was zero at the end of the saccade (magnitude 15°) (Fig. 16.1). All these results were confirmed by Zuber, Michael, and Stark (1964) who studied the effect of voluntary saccades of 20° magnitude. Zuber (1964) found that suppression is maintained up to the end of a 20° saccade which lasts 45 ms. Latour found that colour, size, position, and monocular or binocular presentation of the flash did not significantly affect the results. Latour also expressed his results in the form of an increase in threshold luminance for perception of the flash and found that the increase was about 0·5 log units (i.e. a ratio of 3.1). Volkmann (1962) obtained the same rise of threshold.

The results of Latour and of Zuber *et al.* show that with voluntary saccades there is a specific inhibition which operates on stimuli which are presented during a period when the eye is stationary and is thus not due to blurring by the rapid movement of the retinal image. It is probable that a similar, though possibly weaker, inhibition operates during the involuntary saccades. Lorber, Zuber, and Stark (1964) found that the pupil reflex is suppressed during a voluntary saccade of 10°. Richards (1968) found suppression during passive saccades produced by tapping the eyeball near the outer canthus. Matin, Pearce, and Kibler (1964), and Matin and Pearce (1965 and 1967) report experiments in which the subject is asked to state the location of a flash presented during a saccade relative to a fixation mark which is extinguished 3 s earlier. They find no evidence of the use of information from the proprioceptive system. This result would be expected in view of the experiments of Brindley and Merton (§ 16.2).

16.8. After-images

Yarbus (1967, p. 145) states that, when a subject views an after-image, nearly every large saccadic movement is accompanied by a temporary disappearance of the after-image if it is weak, or a change in the colour if it is strong. Fiorentini and Mazzantini (1965) find that all saccades of amplitude greater than 1° cause disappearance of the after-image. The time of disappearance depends both on the amplitude and the velocity of the eye-movement. The author has observed this effect but finds also that occasionally an after-image which has faded out is seen again immediately after a large saccade. The temporary disappearance or reappearance of the after-image lasts much longer

than the saccade. It is possible that this effect is due to a slight movement of the retina relative to the sclera causing a change in the electrical polarization which is manifested in the E.R.G. (Richards 1968;
Yarbus loc. cit.).

The experiment described in § 2.10 shows that there is an apparent
movement of the after-image associated with voluntary or involuntary
movements of the eye when a suitable structured background is present. It is also found that when the background does not contain well-
marked structure small movements of the eyes do not produce an
apparent movement of the after-image, and the apparent movement due
to a large saccade of 50° is not very noticeable.

16.9. Elevation of threshold associated with displacement of background

MacKay (1970*a*, *b*, *c*) designed experiments to test the hypothesis
that the elevation of threshold associated with saccades (§§ 16.3–16.8)
is due to inflow of signals, generated by rapidly moving boundaries,
from retina to cortex. This is an alternative to the theory previously
accepted that there is an instruction for suppression, of central origin
and, indeed, forming part of the instruction which orders the saccade.
Such an instruction would have to flow outwards from the cortex in
order to control the pupil reflex (§ 16.7).

The stimulus display used by MacKay is shown in Fig. 16.2. A
steadily illuminated circular patch (10° in diameter) can be moved 3°,
in a time which can be varied from 10 ms to 40 ms. The test stimulus
is a 2° spot which can be presented in various positions relative to the
position of fixation which itself can be at X (the initial centre of the
background), or at Y (the final position), or at an intermediate position F. The interval T from onset of motion to flash can be varied in
the range −60 ms to +120 ms.

Fig. 16.3(a) shows results obtained with a flash of suitable intensity
and with fixation at Y. It is obviously similar to the curve for saccadic
suppression shown in Fig. 16.1. MacKay (1970*b*) found that the effect
he observed is transferred interocularly. He also found (MacKay
1970*c*) that there is mislocation of flashes, which are strong enough to be
perceived. These last results are comparable with the results of Matin
and Pearce (1967) on mislocations associated with saccades (§ 16.7).

16.10. The results obtained by MacKay show that the existence of
suppression of a flash presented before a saccadic movement begins
does not necessarily imply that there is a central instruction to suppress

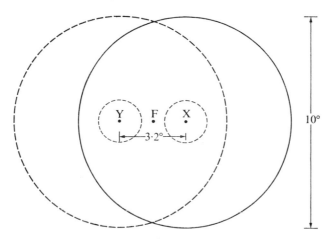

FIG. 16.2. (From Mackay 1970a.)

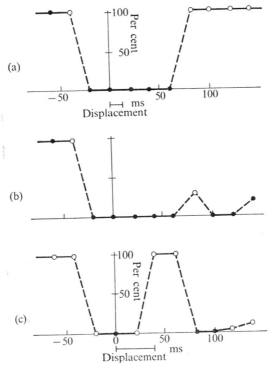

FIG. 16.3. Percentage chance of detecting flash as a function of time from beginning of displacement: (a) fixation at Y; (b) fixation at X; (c) fixation at F and larger displacement time. (From Mackay 1970a.)

visual signals which takes effect when the saccade is ordered rather than when the movement begins. It is possible that confusion-signals generated by moving boundaries may arrive at the cortex in time to upset the processing of information about a target which was briefly presented before the movement began. On this view, the results are analogous to the suppression of a briefly presented target by a 'blank' flash presented *after* the target (Baker 1963).

Although the time of onset of partial suppression for moving bound-aries is about the same as that obtained with saccades, the recovery time is usually considerably different. In many conditions, recovery does not occur within 100 ms after the beginning of the motion (Fig. 16.3(b)), and some curves indicate that the recovery process may 'rebound' (Fig. 16.3(c)). In MacKay's experiments the velocity V of the moving boundaries is in the range $100°$ s^{-1} to $500°$ s^{-1}. The mislocation effect for $V = 100°$ s^{-1} is so much smaller than that for $V = 500°$ s^{-1} as to suggest that there may be no observable effect for X less than $20°$ s^{-1}. The maximum velocity associated with a saccade of $10'$ magnitude is $10°$ s^{-1} (§ 4.4). Thus, although the effect described by MacKay is of considerable interest in itself, there is some doubt whether it is the same as the suppression associated with saccades. Measure-ments of the elevation of threshold using movements of different amplitude down to $3'$ and of different speeds would be of value.

16.11. Cortical and retinal potentials associated with saccades

A number of workers have reported changes in E.E.G. records (of potentials from the occipital region of the scalp) associated with voluntary saccades. These changes are complicated and the results of different experimenters are not completely in agreement. The existence of these effects is doubted by some workers. It appears, however, from the average of many records by the CAT method, that there are changes (called the λ-wave or λ-complex). These changes are partly at the time when the subject receives the stimulus for a saccade and partly at the time when the saccade begins (Evans 1952; Gastaut and Alvim Costa 1957; Remond, Lesèvre, and Torres 1965). These changes are associated with the saccade itself rather than with the pattern displayed.

Armington, Gaarder, and Schick (1967) have observed both E.E.G. potentials (from the occipital area) and E.R.G. potentials associated with saccades when the subjects viewed gratings of different spatial frequencies. A computer was used to average 100 samples each taken during the interval 15 ms to 265 ms after the beginning of a saccade.

In the E.R.G. a saccade produced a positive deflection at about 50 ms followed by a negative deflection at about 100 ms from the beginning of the saccade. In the E.E.G. record there was activity starting at about 100 ms. The response amplitudes showed a maximum at a spatial frequency of about 4 cycles deg^{-1} decreasing to low values at 40 cycles deg^{-1} and at 1·5 cycles deg^{-1}. The curve for the E.E.G. amplitude versus spatial frequency agrees with the visual sensitivity as well as can be expected in view of the E.E.G. noise-level. This suggests that signals similar to those by which the structure of these gratings are normally discriminated are generated by the saccades. There are a number of experiments on visual evoked electrical responses (VER) associated with flashes and brief pattern stimuli presented during saccadic movements (Gross *et al.* 1967; Mitrani *et al.* 1970; Chase and Kahil 1972). The results are not entirely in agreement and further work is in progress.

16.12. Relation of saccades to visual function

Let us consider what kind of suppression, if any, is needed to opti-mise visual perception when saccades are present. If the visual scene were perceived to move sharply, or if a blurred image was seen, there would be distraction extending far outside the time occupied by the saccade and vision would be seriously impaired. Total suppression of visual signals during the saccadic movements would be better than this. Each saccade would then create a 'temporal blind-spot'. Con-tinuity of vision could be preserved by interpolation (from times before and after) so that the temporal blind-spots would not be perceived—as happens with the spatial blind-spot. This, however, implies a delay at best—and sometimes a total failure—in perceiving a danger signal which appears during the saccade. The median intersaccadic interval is about 600 ms and the duration of the suppression associated with an involuntary saccade is 70 ms (§ 16.6). Thus the suppression is in operation 10 per cent of the time for the 'median observer'. The larger saccades made in searching the visual scene last longer (Fig. 4.2) and it appears probable that, for many people, suppression operates for 20 per cent of the time.† For some, whose vision is not very bad, the percentage of time for which suppression operates must be considerably higher though there is evidence that high frequency of saccades is associated with some impairment of visual function (Rattle and Foley-Fisher 1968).

16.13. From the data given in the preceding paragraph, it appears that the penalty incurred by total suppression of visual signals during

† The suppression described in §§ 16.9–16.10 lasts even longer.

saccades would be significant, though blurred vision would be worse. In the hierarchy of cortical cells described in §§ 7.37–7.41, there are some which have a very selective response to structure and are little affected by precise localization of the structure with respect to the visual axis. At this level information is integrated over times of 30 ms or longer. They should retain the information about structure which existed immediately before a saccade, provided that the information concerning the 'blurred image' (which is coming in during the saccade) is attenuated, so that it does not spoil the clear picture derived from information in the preceding intersaccadic interval. A blurred picture is, in itself, less conspicuous than a clear picture, and a rise of visual threshold by a factor of two or three (§ 16.7) should be sufficient for this purpose. Attenuation to this extent would not prevent a danger signal from being perceived unless it happened to be near threshold. In § 15.13 it is suggested that instructions in regard to saccade direction and magnitude are issued about 60 ms before the saccade begins. The results shown in Fig. 16.1 are consistent with the view that an instruction for suppression is issued at this time but the experiments described in §§ 16.9–16.10 show that this is not necessarily so. If there are cells which respond to movement then either they must be insensitive to movements of the size and velocity associated with the involuntary saccades, or else perception of movement must be strongly suppressed during these saccades. The latter seems probable since the saccades include a fairly wide range of velocity. The visual system must include an operation which downgrades or cancels the information content of the after-images relative to information about the present scene. In the absence of such an operation, the eye-movements would continually generate blurred after-images, and their information content would interfere with the processing of the most recent information. The fading of the photo-chemical record (due to pigment regeneration) does not operate fast enough and must be supplemented by a neural process which operates in times of a few hundred milliseconds at most. It is possible that this process is associated with saccadic eye-movements (§§ 12.18 and 16.18).

16.14. After-effects of movement

After gazing at a moving scene (e.g. a waterfall) for 20 s to 30 s, stationary objects appear to be moving in the opposite direction. This illusion which was known to Aristotle and was described in detail by Purkinje (1825) is called the *waterfall effect*. It may be seen by looking at a series of black and white stripes moving perpendicular to their length produced by rotating a spiral behind a rectangular aperture in a mask (Fig. 16.4(a)). When the rotation is suddenly stopped, the stripes appear to move backward. Helmholtz thought that this illusion might be due to eye-movements. The observer tends to rotate his eyes so as to follow the movement and to return to the centre of the field by sharp movements (of which he is often unaware). The nystagmus established in this way continues for a short time after the motion has stopped. If

FIG. 16.4. After effects of movement: (a) Waterfall-effect (boundaries moving vertically downwards), the rotating spiral is covered except for lower half of area in rectangle; (b) to observe parallel boundaries with some moving upward and others downward, the whole area within the rectangle is viewed; (c) to observe the spiral effect the mask is removed.

the observer sees little or nothing during the saccadic movements and is not conscious of the slow movements (so that he does not compensate for them) then he will see the illusory motion. Fender (1964) recorded eye-movements of a person who was seeing a similar illusory movement after he had been rotated about a vertical axis (the *ocular-gyro illusion*). The nystagmoid eye-movements did exist but they decayed long before the illusion itself died out and the eye-movements could not be directly associated with the illusion.

16.15. The spiral after-effect

When the aperture is extended across the spiral two sets of bars moving in opposite directions are seen, e.g. both may be seen moving towards the centre. When the movement stops both sets then move out-wards. This shows that the explanation in terms of eye-movements given in § 16.14 cannot be correct. This conclusion is reinforced if the subject is allowed to see the whole spiral and instructed to gaze first at the centre of the spiral and then at a neighbouring object. The object appears to expand if the rotation of the spiral was such that boundaries appear to move inwards. When the spiral is rotated in the opposite direction, the object subsequently viewed appears to contract. This is known as the spiral after-effect.†

16.16. Sekuler and Ganz (1963) have studied the after-effect of seen motion when the target is viewed through a stabilization apparatus so that the rate of movement of boundaries across the retina is not affected by eye-movements. They subsequently observed the threshold of luminance for striped patterns, (a) moving in the original direction, and (b) moving in the opposite direction. The threshold for (a) was higher than the threshold for (b). This is consistent with the hypothesis that there are separate movement detectors for opposite directions of motion and that these can be independently fatigued. The eye-move-ments which operate when a subject approximately fixates a station-ary field are sometimes in one direction and sometimes in the other. On average, in normal vision, they excite both sets of detectors equally and the signals cancel. When, however, one set of detectors is fatigued, the signals from the other predominate and there is an illusion of movement. Thus although the simple explanation of the waterfall effect given in § 16.14 is untenable, eye-movements do appear to have some relevance to the phenomenon. It would be desirable to see if the illusory movement is obtained when the retinal image is stabilized but prevented from fading by intermittent illumination.

16.17. Limits of discrimination between real and apparent movement

MacKay (1973) proposes that the distinction between real and apparent movement is not made simply by ordering the effects of move-ment of the visual axis (and of translation of the head) to be subtracted from the observed movement of the retinal image. This would leave an apparent irregular movement of a stable scene due to the errors of the system. He suggests that the comparison is made between a template of the original scene and the computation of the 'new' scene allowing for eye-movements. The external scene is then assumed to be stationary

† A monograph by Holland (1965) gives about 200 references to work on this subject.

unless the two 'scenes' differ by more than the error of the system.†
If this is so then the small eye-movements of fixation, in some situations, form one source of the 'error' which determines the smallest real movement that can be discriminated in the absence of a stationary frame of reference. The results described in § 15.7 indicate that in one situation the magnitude of the minimum perceived real motion is about equal to that expected if the small eye-movements of fixation constitute the main error. It must, however, be expected that there will be other situations, where different sources of 'error' predominate.

16.18. Conclusions

In the remainder of this chapter some of the more important conclusions arising from the study of small eye-movements and of stabilized images are summarized. A valid criticism of the whole body of experiments is that the number of subjects is too small and too many of them are trained. This has happened because the demands on a subject's time are rather large and because the cost of individually worked contact lenses is considerable. The measured accuracy of fixation must be regarded as typical of trained subjects and may be significantly better than that of untrained subjects.

In regard to experiments on stabilized images, there is a variety of possible experiments and it has seldom happened that two experimenters have made observations under precisely the same conditions. In this situation, a large number of interesting ideas emerge but there are relatively few quantitative results supported by two or more independent, and exactly comparable, measurements.

16.19. Eye-movements of fixation

Since the work of Adler and Fliegelman (1934), the eye-movements of fixation have been classified into three types, usually named saccades, drifts, and tremor. Each type of movement has been observed by

† The author accepts this view with the addition that a state of continuous motion of the whole, or part, of the external scene, can come to be accepted as the 'norm'; e.g. the steady stimulation of detectors of moving boundaries (by the waterfall or the spiral) becomes 'normal'. The sudden withdrawal of these signals is assumed to imply movement in the opposite direction for a short time until the general presumption of a stable external word resumes its dominance. Other clues can also affect what is accepted as the 'norm'. A skater appears to be moving gracefully and rapidly when the real motion (on a television screen) is a slight wobble. This continues to happen, even when the scene has been 'zoomed' so that there is very little background. The presumption of motion, supported by clues from the attitude of the skater, is more powerful than the direct signals (or absence of signals) from the motion detectors.

several experimenters using a variety of experimental methods some of which involve no attachment to the eye. The tremor excursus seldom exceeds 1' and movements of more than 2' can almost always be un-ambiguously classified as drifts (or slow movements) or saccades. The magnitudes of saccades and drifts and the intersaccadic interval are well-defined parameters (§§ 4.3 and 4.6). The range of values listed in Table 4.1 is (almost certainly) mainly a representation of inter-subject differences. The values of intersaccadic interval recorded by Lord (1950) for seven subjects span nearly the whole range of values obtained by the other experimenters. There is no reason to assign any significant part of the differences obtained by different experimenters to different experimental conditions.

16.20. Accuracy of fixation

The accuracy of fixation may be represented by the quantity σ, defined by eqn (4.3), which, in the simplest situation, is the r.m.s. deviation of the visual axis from the mean direction. Table 4.3 lists measured values of σ which vary from 1·4' to 3·2' (for subjects fixating a distant target). This deviation is surprisingly small, and the range of variation is reasonable considered as an inter-subject variation. It is well established that, when the fixation target is the centre of a circular disc, σ increases by less than a factor of 2 when the diameter D of the disc changes from 20' to 240'. There is also agreement in regard to the existence of an anomaly when D is about 100', i.e. about equal to the diameter of the fovea.

16.21. Tremor spectrum

It is generally accepted that the power spectrum of the tremor includes a part which decreases smoothly from the lowest frequency to which the analysis can be applied (2–5 Hz) to a frequency of about 150 Hz where it is too small to be distinguished from 'noise' in the recording system. Several of the early experimenters thought that there was a resonance or 'dominant frequency' in the frequency range 30–80 Hz but this was not supported by any objective analysis. Fender and Nye (1961) and Findlay (1971) find no resonance (larger than the experimental error) in the displacement spectrum. Bengi and Thomas (1968b) find a sharp resonance in the velocity spectrum at 40 Hz. Movement at this frequency would appear to be disadvantageous in that it would operate to blur the retinal image. It is thus important to know whether a lightly damped resonance at a frequency higher than the CFF is present and further work is needed.

16.22. The control system

The ability of subjects to hold the direction of the visual axis within a very small r.m.s. deviation from a mean direction implies the existence of a control system operating with very accurate information and capable of very rapid response. This information must come from the retina since fixation is rapidly lost when retinal information is absent. The power to fixate the centre of a disc 240′ in diameter implies an ability to combine information from regions of the retina whose separation is much larger than the intercone distance.

No correlation has been found between the tremor movements of the two eyes or between the tremor direction and the displacement of the visual axis from its mean position. It is likely that the tremor arises from the random firing of individual nerve fibres operating on a system whose damping increases with frequency, as described in §§ 15.31–15.32. The tremor is thus the irreducible 'noise' of the occulomotor system. The saccades and drifts, on the other hand, interact in a complicated way to maintain accurate fixation. It is likely that there are many points of similarity between the control of these small movements and the control of the large movements of ocular pursuits. It is, nevertheless, necessary to be cautious in applying theories developed from observations of voluntary movements of 5°–25° to the control of the small involuntary eye-movements of 2′–20′.

16.23. The following three ideas about the control of small eye-movements were put forward in 1952–3:

(a) that the function of the control is not to maintain the most accurate fixation of which the system is capable, but to keep the visual axis most of the time within a small range of angles and to move it about within this range;
(b) that when the fixating eye is within a small central range no control signals, or very weak signals, are available;
(c) that the drifts arise from imperfect balance of opposed extraocular muscle pairs and are uncontrolled; the flicks, on the other hand, are controlled (though imperfectly), some of them to recentre, others to move the visual axis within the central area.

The first of these ideas is supported by a fair amount of experimental evidence and the author knows of no contrary evidence. The eye-movement records do not prove beyond reasonable doubt that this hypothesis is necessary, and it might be vulnerable to Occam's razor if it were not for the evidence from experiments on stabilized images. These require a movement larger than the excursus of the tremor for long-term maintenance of normal visual function. This is supported by the electrophysiological experiment described in § 7.41. The second idea has undergone considerable modification since it was proposed in the form described in § 14.14. A minor change is to suppose that the control is not zero, but is very small, in the central region, as suggested by Fig. 14.4. A more fundamental modification is required if it is accepted that the control of fixation on the centre of a circular disc of 50′ diameter is essentially the same as the control when the fixation target is the intersection of two cross-hairs. It then becomes necessary to assign the property not to a small area of the retina, as suggested in § 14.14, but to a small range of deviation of the visual axis from the mean direction. A control system whose signals are a non-linear function of the error is more difficult to describe and to investigate than a linear system, but is not, in itself, less probable.

16.24. The third idea mentioned in the preceding paragraph has been the subject of some controversy and no clear consensus of opinion has been established. It has been shown that saccades can be suppressed and that tolerably good fixation can be maintained when they are. This result, together with other evidence (§§ 14.12–14.13) shows that drifts; can be controlled. No one has suggested that, in normal conditions, fixation is maintained entirely by controlled drifts, the saccades operating purely at random. Opinion differs only in regard to the way in which saccades and drifts interact to maintain fixation. The author believes that this third proposition is nearly correct in regard to normal fixation by untrained subjects. Most saccades are 'commanded', though not all are recentering. Those that are ordered to recentre do so imperfectly; they are particularly liable to overshoot. The drifts, on the other hand, are primarily due to muscle imbalance but they can be controlled by altering their direction. Some subjects can learn to improve this control to such an extent that the visual axis can be moved around the central zone without the intervention of saccades which can then be suppressed. Whether the movement of the visual axis due to drifts and tremor is sufficient to maintain full visual function (over a long period) remains an open question.

16.25. Stabilized images

Observations of stabilized images show, that when the illumination of the target is steady, movement of the retinal image is essential for normal vision. When the retinal image movements are reduced below a certain level visual targets are, at best, seen intermittently; they appear hazy and pattern fragmentation occurs—as in the later stages of an after-image. Under the conditions stated in §§ 6.10 and 8.14 total loss of vision is experienced.

The experiments on stabilized images indicate that one function of eye-movements is to operate on spatial gradients of illuminance in the retinal image and so generate time-varying signals in the optic nerve. This system emphasizes sharp boundaries between areas of different illuminance or different hue. When information concerning some boundaries is removed (or greatly reduced) the visual system organizes the available information so as to produce 'pictures' which may be very different from what is seen in normal vision (Chapter 9).

The experiments on pattern perception (Chapter 13) show the existence of pattern perception units but no experimenter has so far been able to devise an experiment which analyses the perception of a complex pattern in terms of unambiguously determined pattern units. In this field it may be best to advance by means of experiments in which the effects of eye-movements are removed either by using a tachistoscope or by observing flash-imprinted after-images and so avoid the more difficult technique of image stabilization.

16.26. When an image has been stabilized, vision may be restored either by imposing controlled movements which regenerate time-varying signals, or by modulating the target luminance so as to produce time-varying signals directly.

The minimum movement required for regeneration of the retinal image depends in a complicated way on the visual structure, on the luminance, and on the part of the retina under study. For unidirectional movements, there is a minimum *rate* of movement as well as a minimum movement. For oscillatory movements there is a preferred frequency-band (Chapter 10). Similarly, the amount of modulation required depends on a number of variables (Chapter 11).

The experiments described in Chapter 9–11 have yielded a good deal of information about the minimum signals required for vision under various conditions. Further experiments of this kind, combined with electrophysiological data on single cells in animals, should lead to a more detailed understanding of the basic signals which carry information in the human visual system. Apparatus giving both good stabilization and retinal images of high optical quality will be required for the further investigation of foveal vision.

Photometric units

Luminance measures the amount of light emitted by a surface per unit area. The term illuminance is used for a measure of the amount of light received per unit area. It replaces the term illumination, which is now restricted to a descriptive, non-quantitative application.

The units used by different authors have been converted to candelas per metres^2 (abbreviation cd m^{-2}) for *luminance* ($\mathscr{L}$). The logarithm, to base 10, of the luminance in cd m^{-2} (sometimes called the luminance in log-units), is denoted by L.

The *retinal illuminance* is measured in trolands (abbreviation td). One troland is equal to the retinal illuminance obtained by looking at a matt surface whose luminance is 1 cd m^{-2} through an artificial pupil of area 1 mm^{-2}.

Appendix

Contact lens-systems and suction devices

A.1. Requirements

A suitable device for attachment to the eye, in measurements of eye-movements, or in experiments with stabilized images should satisfy the following conditions:

(a) the optical parts should be of adequate quality and precisely adjusted (§ A.2);

(b) the optical parts should be fixed to each other, and to the lens or suction device, with sufficiently strong components to avoid significant vibration, but the whole assembly should not be so heavy as to cause an important increase in the moment of inertia of the eye (§ A.3 and § 15.23);

(c) the device should follow the small movements of the eye without slip of more than a few micrometres; 4 μm corresponds to an angular movement of 1' (§ 2.21);

(d) it should be tolerable for periods of 30 min or more, preferably without the use of an anaesthetic.

The use of an anaesthetic is undesirable for two reasons. First, it may affect the eye-movements or the process of visual discrimination. Second, the pain which the anaesthetic removes may be 'early warning' of processes, such as the abrasion reported by Barlow (1963), which are dangerous if allowed to continue. If an anaesthetic is used, it is desirable to choose one whose effect normally passes off in about an hour. The eye should be washed out with contact lens fluid, before the lens or suction device is inserted. Without this precaution, amethocaine may affect the size of the pupil for more than 12 h, though its effect normally disappears in about an hour. This is probably due to greater penetration of the drug, owing to the surface of the cornea being rubbed by the lens.

The requirements in regard to following the movement of the eye for adequate stabilization of the retinal image (§§ 5.31–5.33) are about the same as those required for satisfactory records of the tremor and detailed records of the saccades. The requirements for recording the number, direction, and approximate size of the saccades (together with the intersaccadic drifts) are much less stringent.

A.2. Size and quality of the eye-mirror

It is necessary to make the spot of light at the eye-mirror smaller than the mirror itself in order to ensure that, for all positions of the eye, the edge of the spot does not fall outside the edge of the mirror. This would cause spurious

changes of current when the photo-transducers are used. In photographic recording methods there is no corresponding error but, if the spot overlaps the edge
of the mirror, stray light usually enters the eye.

It is convenient to make the spot of light about 3 mm in diameter and the
mirror about 6 mm. Two sources of error need to be considered:

(a) spread of the beam due to diffraction, and
(b) deviation of the beam (if the mirror is slightly concave or convex) due to
movement of the beam from one part of the mirror to another.

If the diameter of the beam at the mirror is d, then the diffraction pattern has
appreciable intensity over a range of angles somewhat greater than $\pm \lambda/d$, i.e. a
range of about $\pm 1\cdot 6 \times 10^{-4}$ radians or $\pm 0\cdot 6'$ for $d = 3$ mm and $\lambda = 550$ nm.
This implies some inaccuracy in reading from the blurred edge of a photographic
record but, with suitable photographic processing, the edge can be sharpened
and the error reduced to about $0\cdot 1'$. In a photo-electric method, a standard point
in the diffraction pattern can be identified and measurements made to an accuracy very much better than $0\cdot 1'$ (R. V. Jones 1960). Thus the error due to diffraction
is not serious when d is about 3 mm, but would become appreciable if d were
reduced to 1 mm or less. If the mirror is convex or concave with a radius of r
mm, then a 1 mm movement of the spot of light across the mirror will cause a
spurious deflection of $1/r$ i.e. $0\cdot 1'$ for $r = 3 \times 10^4$ mm. This implies a departure
from planarity of $0\cdot 3\lambda$ over a circular area of diameter 6 mm. For recording of
saccades and drifts, a mirror of moderate quality which gives a sharp image is
sufficient, but a mirror for recording tremor must be tested by interference
against an optical flat. There will usually be some defect within a millimetre of
the edge; ignoring this error (and arranging that the light does not fall on this
region) the rest of the mirror should be plane to $0\cdot 1\ \lambda$. These considerations show
that, for satisfactory records of tremor, the mirror must be clear of the tear
fluids which would spoil its optical quality.

The requirements of high optical quality apply, of course, to the rest of the
optical system. In most telescopic stabilization systems it is not difficult to obtain
images of high quality provided that reasonably good optical components are used
and are accurately aligned. In rigid stabilization systems the quality of the high
power lens used to focus the target (e.g. L in Fig. 5.6(a)) is of critical importance
when the target is viewed by the fovea. This lens should be corrected for spherical
aberration and unless used with monochromatic light, for chromatic aberation.

A.3. Adjustment of mirror

It is sufficient to adjust the angle between the normal to the mirror and the
visual axis to be less than $1°$. Most errors due to imperfect alignment are pro-
portional to $(1 - \cos \theta)$ whose value for $\theta = 1°$ is about $1\cdot 5 \times 10^{-4}$. Fig. A.1 shows
a simple autocollimation method of checking the alignment. The subject sup-
ports his head on a chin rest and fixates a brightly illuminated point of light P
which is in the centre of a screen covered with graph paper. The pinhole
is at the focus of a good quality lens L, whose focal length is about 60 cm.
The beam reflected from the mirror M is seen as a bright spot of light C on the
graph paper, and its coordinates measure the error in angular adjustment. Small
translations of the head have no effect in this situation. If a permanently fixed
mirror is required, the error is measured and then the lens is mounted on a jig

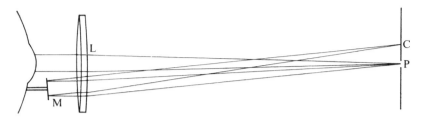

F IG. A.1. Collimator for testing alignment of mirrors.

and placed in the autocollimator again. The jig is then adjusted so that the spot occupies the same position as before. The plastic stalk is heated and bent until the spot is central. The lens is replaced on the eye and the adjustment checked. Owing to the small eye-movements, the spot is always in motion but the mean position can be set to within 5′.

It is often convenient to adjust the angle of the mirror while the lens is worn by the subject. Fender (1956) used a ball and socket connection. Fig. 3.4(a) shows an improved arrangement used by West (1965). A very stiff grease is used between the spherical surfaces so that the mirror can be moved by hand but remains in position once it has been set.

A.4. Stiffness of stalk assembly

If the stalk system has a resonance below 150 Hz, distortion of a record of tremor is probable. Byford (1962a) devised a precision method of testing mirror-stalk assemblies for vibration at various frequencies. Fig. A.2 shows the principle of the apparatus. The assembly under test is attached to a steel ball which is mounted in spherical cups so as to be able to rotate about any axis. A small medical lamp is fixed to the assembly and the instantaneous position of this lamp

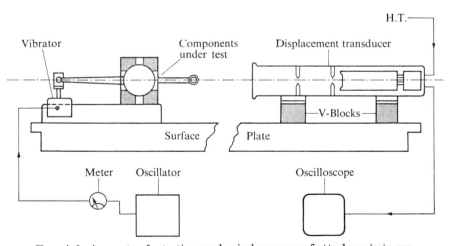

F IG. A.2. Apparatus for testing mechanical response of attachments to eye.

is monitored by the photo-transducer system on the right. This is similar to the one shown in Fig. 3.8. An oscillatory rotation, about an axis perpendicular to the plane of the paper, can be applied by means of the vibrator shown at the left. The amplitude and frequency of the oscillation can be varied to cover the whole range of eye-movements. The input and output can be displayed on an oscilloscope. The apparatus itself is tested by substituting a stiff steel rod for the assembly under test and verifying that, in this condition, there are no resonances within the appropriate frequency range.

A.5. This apparatus was used by Byford, and later by Boyce, to test a variety of assemblies, including plastic stalks of various thicknesses and lengths and also stalks made of thin metal tubes. It was found that all the metal tube assemblies which were tested had no resonances below about 200 Hz. Some of the thinner plastic stalks were not satisfactory but the thicker stalks similar to those used by Fender and Pritchard were generally satisfactory. Boyce found that some stalks had resonances at much lower frequencies than the 'natural resonances' calculated from the elastic constants. These arise from non-linear interaction of different frequencies associated with asymmetries in the stalk or in its loading. It is thus unsafe to assume that the resonance frequency can be calculated from known constants. Pritchard (1958a, p. 51) made a direct 'user test' by loading the mirror and reducing the thickness of the stalk so that the error due to vibration should be increased more than one hundredfold. No difference was obtained in the behaviour of the stabilized images and he concluded that, in his normal arrangement, there was no error due to vibration of the stalk. Byford's apparatus was used for static tests on linearity of response. Most systems were satisfactory in this respect.

A.6. Plastics vary considerably in their elastic properties and to be sure of obtaining sufficient rigidity it is necessary to use a fairly thick plastic stalk. For the study of eye-movements, by the methods described in Chapter 3, a stalk about 2·5 cm long carrying a mirror assembly weighing 0·4 g is needed. The plastic stalk for this application should be 4 mm in diameter. Thin-walled duralumin tubes of this diameter are also satisfactory and are much lighter. For some stabilization systems (§§ 5.5–5.8) heavier components are mounted at a somewhat greater distance from the eye and it is easier to obtain sufficient rigidity with metal tubes rather than plastic stalks. In an apparatus like that shown in Fig. 5.6(a) it is desirable to attach the lens assembly to the stalk by means of copper wire or strip, rather than thin steel or phosphor bronze, because the elastic viscosity of the copper damps high frequency vibrations. If possible, new systems should be tested for resonances up to 100 Hz.

A.7. Slip of contact lenses and suction devices

The normal methods of manufacture of contact lenses for correcting refraction are designed to produce lenses which are comfortable when worn continuously. Most haptic lenses do not touch the cornea, which is usually rather sensitive. They rest on the sclera, with a film of liquid between the lens and the eye (Fig. A.3). The lens floats on this film and is expected to move to assist transport of oxygen to the cornea. Movement of the lens shown in Fig. A.3 from position (a) to position (b) is resisted by viscous friction but not by any positive force. Bier

(a)   (b)

FIG. A.3. Contact lens with corneal radius greater than radius of cornea; (a) central (correct) position; (b) slipped to left.

(1957) advocates a clearance of about 0·1 mm between lens and cornea (after the lens has settled on to the eye) for lenses worn for correction of refractive errors. The corresponding angular movement of 'easy slip' is over 15′. Obviously slip of this magnitude is unacceptable for studies of small eye-movements, or for experiments with stabilized images.

A.8. Suction

The slip may be reduced either by using a lens which touches the cornea as shown in Fig. A.4 or Fig. A.5 or by bringing the lens into closer contact with the globe by means of suction. These methods can be combined, to some extent. A small suction applied to a lens which is a moderately close fit may yield a result which is as good as that obtained by applying a larger suction to a lens which has a large central clearance. The amount of suction which can safely be applied is limited. The cornea is only 1 mm thick and may be deformed by the negative pressure due to suction; this effect is progressive and a large deformation is not always reversible. It is desirable to apply suction in such a way that the negative pressure is known and can be smoothly adjusted. Fig. A.6 shows a contact lens assembly in which suction is applied by filling the rubber tube with contact lens fluid and then altering the height of the free end. With a tube 30 cm long the negative pressure is continuously variable between 0 cm and 2·5 cm of mercury (an equal positive pressure can be applied to assist removal of the lens.) This method of applying suction may be contrasted with two other methods which have been used. These are (a) the use of a rubber sucker, and (b) a method in which the lens or suction device is filled with liquid and pressed on to the eye so

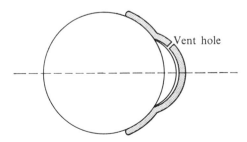

FIG. A.4. Contact lens with tight fit at limbus.

F ɪ ɢ. A.5. Contact lens with ring fit on part of cornea and transcurves (more than one transcurve may be needed for comfort). The main pressure is on the sclera. The difference between lens radius and corneal radius is exaggerated

that some fluid is expelled at the edges. Both of these methods apply a variable and unknown amount of suction. A rough calculation applied to one device indicates that the suction may exceed 10 cm Hg. The corresponding negative pressure acting on the cornea is 1 N (or 100 g weight).

A.9. Suction may be used either to reduce the gap at the cornea as described above or with a device which rests on a small area of the sclera. This area may be an annular ring, as shown in Fig. A.5, or local patches of the sclera under a haptic contact lens. The pressure of the atmosphere on a haptic contact lens, (or on a suction device of the same area) is about 4 Kg. In normal contact lens use, this pressure is opposed by the atmospheric pressure acting on the free surface of the liquid at the edge of the lens. Surface tensional forces balance the forces due to the weight of the device and there is usually a small negative pressure

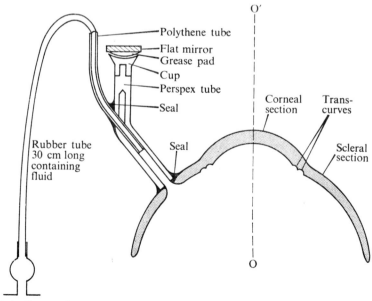

F ɪ ɢ. A.6. Contact lens assembly with rubber tube for applying known amounts of suction. ○—○' is the optical axis.

in the fluid. With one contact lens this pressure was found to be -2.5 cm Hg. If a contact lens or device touches the sclera only in small regions the liquid may be forced out and a substantial fraction of the force of 4 kg weight then acts on these areas. The lens can then stick to these areas. Slip is stopped completely, but there is likely to be some damage to the conjunctiva when the lens is removed. This effect will depend very much on how long the lens has been worn. A device which touches only the sclera is more likely to be tolerable for an hour without an anaesthetic than one which rests on the cornea. However it leaves the cornea completely unsupported so that a large negative pressure may cause a temporary or even a permanent deformation of the cornea.

A.10. Mechanical tests for slip

Byford (1962b) measured the rotation of the contact lens when the subject fixated, in turn, three targets spaced at intervals of 30'. He analysed the results to estimate backlash and concluded that backlash could be detected when the eye moved 1° but not when it moved 30'. Differences of 1' were statistically significant. Byford carried out further experiments in which a square of cigarette paper placed on the cornea was observed through a large engineering microscope mounted on a milling table. A series of measurements, without a contact lens, revealed no relative motion between the edge of the paper and small irregularities in the region of the limbus. Measurements were made of the displacement of the paper, and also of a scratch on a contact lens, when the subject fixated, in turn, a series of ten targets placed at intervals of 1°. The lens lagged by 7', i.e. rather less than 1' per degree of eye-movement. Further measurements by a different method (Byford 1962b) confirmed these results. Towards the end of the series of tests Byford obtained some contact lenses worked to fit the corneal bulge. On fluoroscopic test these lenses appeared to fit closely both on cornea and sclera. No lag could now be detected when the eye moved through $\pm 1°$. Tests were not made for larger angles. From these data it appears that geometrical measurements can measure a lag of 1' but probably not much better. Lenses can be made such that, even without suction, the lag is less than 1' when the eye remains within $\pm 30'$. This is a larger range than that found in normal fixation (Table 4.3).

A.11. After-image tests for slip

Fender (1956) tested the accuracy of his apparatus for stabilizing the retinal image by moving the direction of fixation between two positions A and B. If the image is perfectly stabilized then the after-image due to an exposure made when fixating A should coincide with the retinal image seen when fixating B. This kind of test was frequently used by the author and colleagues. It was found that on some days the subject made many large saccades, and movement between the after-image and the stabilized image was then obvious. When this occurred, it was necessary to remove the lens and give an hour or two for the irritation to subside. When, however, the lens was well seated, and the subject comfortable, eye-movements when viewing the stabilized image became less than in normal vision, and observable displacement of the retinal image relative to the after-image was rare.

Barlow (1963) investigated slip by an adaptation of the method described in § 2.8. The target was mounted on a contact lens as shown in Fig. 5.8(a). Half the target was illuminated with a bright flash of light and the other half was exposed 5–10 s later. The contact lens was then removed, and the subject inspected the after-images against a white surface. The median displacement between the two after-images was 3·4′. Bennet-Clark and Ditchburn (1963) using the same technique obtained up to ten displacements of 3′ to 8′ in a 20 s period; blinks caused displacements of 15′ to 30′. In one case, violent movement of the eyes following the flash lifted the contact lens from the eyeball. West (1965) used a modification of Barlow's method. During fixation he observed slip, but infrequently. If voluntary saccades of $\pm2°$ or more were made, slip of about 2′ was observed.

A.12. An evaluation of the accuracy of stabilization that is obtained by tightly-fitting contact lenses without suction was made by Riggs and Schick (1968). They printed, on the retina, a strong after-image of a line and made repeated determinations of the alignment between this after-image and the stabilized image of a line, over a period of up to 30 min. Since only a small area of the retina is illuminated by the flash, the induced movements of the eye are relatively small and there is enough time for them to die out before the main part of the observations. They found short-period irregular movements of 0·3′ and a standard deviation of 0·4′ during a 1 min period. These irregular movements were superposed upon a slow drift of $(2–5) \times 10^{-3}$ min. arc s^{-1}. This was attributed to a slow change in the shape of the eyeball when a contact lens is worn. It is unlikely that either the irregular movement or the drift have any effect in stabilization experiments or in the observations of tremor. The slow drift does imply that the stimulus cannot be held on one set of retinal receptors for more than about 5 min.

A.13. Effect of suction

Bennet-Clark and Ditchburn (1963) applied suction in the range 0–5 cm Hg to lenses of the type shown in Fig. A.7. After a bright flash, displacments could be observed for up to 10 s. Thereafter movement was less than 1′ and it was not certain that there was any movement. The displacement associated with voluntary movements of $\pm15°$ was reduced from 30′ to about 3′. This suggests that movement associated with a involuntary saccade of 30′ would be much less than 1′. West (1965) who used a modified form of the after-image method observed only infrequent displacements of about 1′ during fixation, without suction, and none when suction ($\sim$3 cm Hg) was used. Bennet-Clark and Ditchburn measured the percentage of time for which a target, with sharp boundaries, disappeared when viewed as a stabilized image. Suction was varied in the range 0–6 cm Hg. A considerable increase in time of disappearance was obtained when suction of 2 cm Hg was applied, but no further change when stronger suction was applied. West (1965) obtained a qualitatively similar result. Barlow (1963) applied suction of up to 15 cm to his lens and produced total and permanent fading of the stabilized image. This amount of suction caused adverse effects on vision of unstabilized images.

A.14. Boyce (§ 4.5) observed the effect of suction on the overshoot in a saccade. The negative pressure was 3 cm Hg. The results, shown in Fig. 4.3, may be explained in the following way. When no suction is used, the lens follows the movement of the eye in the early stages of a saccade but, when the acceleration

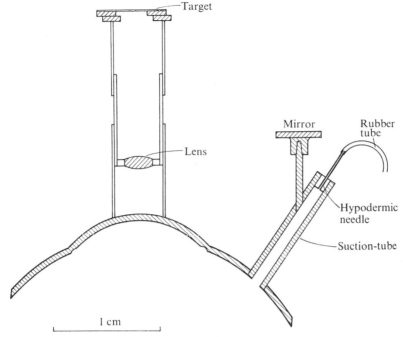

F<small>IG</small>. A.7.

reaches a certain value the lens slips and moves until it hits the corneal bulge. If the saccade is small ($<2'$), the lens slowly returns to the central position when the eye stops and no overshoot is observed. If the saccade is a large one, the lens slips a second time, and continues to move forward under its own inertia after the eye has begun to slow down. This leads to a spurious overshoot whose magnitude increases with the size of the saccade (up to a maximum value). If this interpretation is correct, Fig. 4.3 indicates that, when suction was applied, slip had been reduced to less than $0.2'$ and that a true overshoot of $0.6'$, independent of the size of the saccade, was obtained. There is reason to believe (§ 15.29) that the true overshoot should vary very little with the size of the saccade, for saccades from $0'$ to $10'$.

A.15. Summary

The practical conclusions of the foregoing discussion are as follows.

(a) Certain requirements of stiffness of attachments mounted on the eye and of optical quality are important both for records of tremor and for experiments on stabilized images viewed by the fovea; these requirements apply both to contact lenses and to suction devices.

(b) By careful attention to certain details contact lenses can be made to fit so well that slip is reduced to less than $0.5'$ even without suction; it is, however, easier to make contact lenses of good, rather than excellent, fit and to apply a

27

known suction of 2–3 cm Hg. Slip may then be reduced below the limits of measurement (0·3′).

(c) Rubber or metal devices, with stronger suction (10 cm Hg or more) also give good adhesion to the eye but should be used only when continuous medical supervision is available. Strong suction is liable to cause deterioration of image quality (Barlow 1963).

Many of the early experiments on stabilization were carried out at a time when the necessary conditions for obtaining a satisfactory fit were not understood, so that displacements of about 1′ were associated with saccades of 15′ or more. On the other hand, many of the suction devices which gave good adhesion were associated with optical components which were not good enough to give stabilized images with sharp boundaries. Defective stabilization causes the target to be seen more of the time; targets with diffuse boundaries disappear more easily than targets with sharp boundaries. Thus both the merits and the faults of suction devices combined to increase the extent to which the target disappeared and to produce the black field appearance (Chapter 6).

It is desirable that some of the early experiments should be repeated, both with well fitting contact lens and small suction and with suction devices using controlled and measured suction. In each case optical systems of adequate quality should be used. Tests for accuracy of stabilization and for image quality are both necessary.

References

ADLER, F. H. (1965). *Physiology of the eye* (4th ed.). C. V. Mosby, St. Louis, U.S.A.
—— and FLIEGELMAN, M. (1934). *Archs Ophthal., N.Y.* **12,** 475.
ADRIAN, E. D. (1928). *The basis of sensation.* Norton, New York.
—— and MATTHEWS, B. H. C. (1934). *Brain* **57,** 335.
—— and MATTHEWS, R. (1927). *J. Physiol,* **63,** 357.
—— —— (1928). *J. Physiol.* **64,** 278.
—— —— (1929). *J. Physiol.* **65,** 273.
AGUILAR, M. and STILES, W. S. (1954). *Optica Acta* **1,** 59.
ALPERN, M. (1962). In *The eye* (ed. H. Davson). Vol. 3. Academic Press, New York.
—— and BARR, L. (1962). *J. opt. Soc. Am.* **52,** 219.
ANDERSON, E. E. and WEYMOUTH, F. W. (1923). *Am. J. Physiol.* **64,** 561.
ARDEN, G. B. (1963a). *J. Physiol.* **166,** 468.
—— (1963b). *J. Physiol.* **166,** 449.
—— and WEALE, R. A. (1954). *J. Physiol.* **125,** 417.
ARMINGTON, J. C., GAARDER, K., and SCHICK, A. M. L. (1967). *J. opt. Soc. Am.* **57,** 1534.
ARNULF, A., DUPUY, O., and FLAMANT, F. (1951). *C. r. hebd. Séanc. Acad. Sci., Paris.* **232,** 438.
——, ——, —— (1955). *Annls Opt. ocul.* **3,** 109.
——, ——, —— (1960). *Revue Opt. théor. instrum.* **39,** 195.
AUBERT, H. (1886). *Pflügers Arch. ges. Physiol.* **39,** 347.
AUTRUM, H. (1959). *Naturwissenschaften* **13,** 435.
AVERILL, H. L. and WEYMOUTH, F. W. (1925). *J. comp. Psychol.* **5,** 147.
BACH-Y-RITA, P., COLLINS, C. C., and HYDE, J. E. (1971). *The control of eye-movements.* Academic Press, New York and London.
BAKER, H. D. (1963). *J. opt. soc. Am.* **53,** 98.
BARLOW, H. B. (1952). *J. Physiol.* **116,** 290.
—— (1953). *J. Physiol.* **119,** 169.
—— (1956). *J. opt. Soc. Am.* **46,** 635.
—— (1957). *J. Physiol.* **136,** 469.
—— (1958). *J. Physiol.* **141,** 337.
—— (1962). *J. Physiol.* **160,** 169.
—— (1963). *Quart. J. exp. Psychol.* **15,** 36.
——, FITZHUGH, R., and KUFFLER, W. (1957a). *J. Physiol.* **137,** 327.
——, ——, —— (1957b). *J. Physiol.* **137,** 338.
—— HILL, R. N., and LEVICK, W. R. (1964). *J. Physiol.* **173,** 377.
—— and LEVICK, W. R. (1965). *J. Physiol.* **178,** 477.
—— and SPARROCK, J. M. B. (1964). *Science* **144,** 1309.
BAUMGARDT, E. (1959). *Nature* **184,** 1951.
—— and HILLMAN, B. (1961). *J. opt. Soc. Am.* **51,** 340.
BAUMGARTNER, G., BROWN, J. L., and SCHULZ, A. (1965). *J. Neurophysiol.* **28,** 1.
BAYLOR, D. A. and O'BRIEN, P. M. (1971). *Proc. Fed. Am. Soc. exp. Biol.* **30,** 79.

BEELER, G. W., FENDER, D. H., NOBEL, P. S., and EVANS, C. R. (1964). *Nature* **203**, 4950.

BELL, G. A. and WEIR, J. B. (1949). *Arch. Ophthal.* **42**, 856.

BENGI, H. and THOMAS, J. G. (1968a). *Med. and biol. Eng.* **6**, 171.

—— —— (1968b). *Nature* **217**, 773.

BENNET-CLARK, H. C. (1964). *Optica Acta* **11**, 301.

—— and DITCHBURN, R. W. (1963). *Optica Acta* **10**, 367.

—— and EVANS, C. R. (1963). *Nature* **199**, 1215.

BIER, N. (1957). *Contact lens practice* (2nd ed.). Butterworth, London.

BISHOP, P. O. (1962a). *J. Physiol.* **162**, 409.

—— (1962b). *J. Physiol.* **162**, 432.

——, KOZAK, W., LEVICK, W. R., and VAKKUR, G. J. (1962). *J. Physiol.* **163**, 503.

BITTINI, M., ERCOLES, A. M., FIORENTINI, A., RONCHI, L., and TORALDO DI FRANCIA, G. (1960). *Atti. Fond. Giorgio Ronchi* **15**, 62.

BOYCE, P. R. (1965a). Thesis (Reading University).

—— (1965b). *Optica Acta* **12**, 47.

—— (1967). *Proc. R. Soc.* B. **167**, 293.

—— and WEST, D. C. (1967). *Optica Acta* **14**, 119.

BREININ, G. M. (1955). *Brain mechanisms and consciousness* (ed. J. F. Delafresnaye for UNESCO and WHO). Blackwell, Oxford.

BRINDLEY, G. S. (1954). *J. Physiol.* **124**, 400.

—— (1959). *J. Physiol.* **147**, 194.

—— (1960). *Physiology of the retina and visual pathways.* Edward Arnold, London. (Second Edition 1970)

—— (1962). *J. Physiol.* **164**, 168.

—— and MERTON, P. A. (1960). *J. Physiol.* **153**, 127.

BROWN, J. L. (1965). In *Vision and visual perception* (ed. C. H. Graham). Wiley, New York, pp. 251–320.

BROWN, P. K. and WALD, G. (1963). *Nature* **200**, 37.

—— —— (1964). *Science* **144**, 45.

BRYNGDAHL, O. (1961). *Optica Acta* **8**, 1.

—— and RIWEBERG, L. (1964). *Optica Acta* **11**, 117.

BURKHARDT, D. A. (1966). *J. opt. Soc. Am.* **56**, 979.

BURNS, B. DESLISLE (1968). *The uncertain nervous system.* Edward Arnold, London.

BURNS, B. D., HERON, W., and PRITCHARD, R. M. (1962). *J. Neurophysiol.* **25**, 165.

—— and PRITCHARD, R. M. (1964). *J. Physiol.* **175**, 445.

—— and WEBB, A. C. (1970). *Nature* **225**, 469.

—— —— (1971). *Proc. R. Soc.* B **178**, 63.

BYFORD, G. H. (1959). *Nature* **184**, 1493.

—— (1960). Thesis (Reading University).

—— (1961). *Br. Commun. Electron.* **334**.

—— (1962a). *I.R.E. Trans. med. Electron.* **9**, 236.

—— (1962b). *Optica Acta* **9**, 223.

BYRAM, G. M. (1944a). *J. opt. Soc. Am.* **34**, 571.

—— (1944b). *J. opt. Soc. Am.* **34**, 718.

CAMPBELL, F. W. (1960). *J. opt. Soc. Am.* **50**, 738.

—— and GREEN, D. G. (1965). *J. Physiol.* **181**, 576.

—— and GUBISCH, R. W. (1966). *J. Physiol.* **186**, 558.

—— —— (1967). *J. Physiol.* **192**, 345.

—— and ROBSON, J. G. (1961). *J. Physiol.* **158**, 11P.

—— —— (1968). *J. Physiol.* **197**, 551.

CAMPBELL, F. W., ROBSON, J. G., and WESTHEIMER, G. (1959). *J. Physiol.* **145**, 579.

CARDU, B. and GILBERT, M. (1967). *Can. J. Psychol./Rev. Can. Psychol.* **21**, 526.

——, ——, and STROBEL, M. (1971). *Vision Res.* **11**, 671.

CARMICHAEL, L. and DEARBORN, W. F. (1948). *Reading and visual fatigue.* Harrap, London.

CHARNWOOD, LORD (1950). *Nature* **166**, 348.

CHASE, R. and KAHIL, R. E. (1972). *Vision Res.* **12**, 215.

CHILDRESS, D. S. and JONES, R. W. (1967). *J. Physiol.* **188**, 273.

CLARK, B. (1936). *Am. Acad. Opt.* **10**, 120.

—— (1936). *J. exp. Psychol.* **19**, 505.

—— (1936). *Am. J. Psychol.* **48**, 82.

CLARK, see BENNET-CLARK, H. C.

CLARKE, F. J. J. (1957). *Optica Acta* **4**, 69.

—— (1959). Thesis (London University).

—— and BELCHER, S. J. (1962). *Vision Res.* **2**, 68.

—— and EVANS, C. R. (1964). *Science* **144**, 1359.

CLOWES, M. B. (1959). Thesis (Reading University).

—— (1961). *Optica Acta* **8**, 81.

—— (1962). *Optica Acta* **9**, 65.

—— and DITCHBURN, R. W. (1959). *Optica Acta* **6**, 252.

COHEN, H. B. (1961). *Can. J. Psychol.* **15**, 212.

COLLINS, C. C. (1971). In *The control of eye-movements* (ed. Bach-y-rita *et al.*).

COOPER, S. and DANIEL, P. M. (1949). *Brain* **72**, 1.

——, ——, and WHITTERIDGE, D. (1953). *J. Physiol.* **120**, 491.

——, ——, —— (1954). *Trans. ophthal. Soc. U.K.* **74**, 435.

—— and ECCLES, J. C. (1930). *J. Physiol.* **69**, 377.

CORNSWEET, T. N. (1956). *J. opt. Soc. Am.* **46**, 987.

—— (1958). *J. Opt. Soc. Am.* **48**, 808.

—— (1962). *Am. J. Psychol.* **75**, 653.

—— (1966). In *Recent developments in vision research*, (Publication 1972) N.R.C., Washington, D.C., p. 171.

—— (1970). *Visual perception.* Academic Press, New York and London.

CRAIK, K. J. W. (1940). *Nature* **145**, 512.

CRAWFORD, B. H. (1937). *Proc. R. Soc.* B **123**, 69.

—— (1947). *Proc. R. Soc.* B **134**, 283.

CUGELL, see ENROTH-CUGELL.

CYR, see ST-CYR.

DALLOS, P. J. and JONES, R. W. (1963). *Inst. elect. electron. Engrs Trans. Automatic Control* **8**, 218.

DANIEL, P. M., KERR, D. I. B., SENEVIRATNE, K. N., and WHITTERIDGE, D. (1961). *J. Physiol.* **159**, 87P.

DAVIES, T. and MERTON, P. A. (1957). *J. Physiol.* **140**, 27P.

DAVIS, J. R. and SHACKEL, B. (1960). *Br. J. Ophthal.* **44**, 606.

DAVSON, H. (1962). *The eye.* Vols. 1, 2, 3, and 4. Pergamon Press, Oxford.

DAW, N. W. (1968). *J. Physiol.* **197**, 567.

DELAFRESNAYE, J. F. (1964). *Brain mechanisms and consciousness.* Blackwell, Oxford.

DE LANGE, H. (1957). Thesis (Delft University).

—— (1958a). *J. opt. Soc. Am.* **48**, 777.

—— (1958b). *J. opt. Soc. Am.* **48**, 784.

DE PALMA, J. J. and LOWRY, E. M. (1962). *J. opt. Soc. Am.* **52**, 328.

DE VALOIS, R. L. (1960). *J. gen Physiol.* **43** (part II), 115.
DE VALOIS, R. L. CARR, N., and CIANCI, S. (1959). *Am. J. Psychol.* **14**, 412.
——, JACOBS, G. H., and ABRAMOV, I. (1964). *Science* **146**, 1184.
——, SMITH, C. J., KITAI, S. T., and KAROLY, A. J. (1958). *Science* **127**, 238.
DITCHBURN, R. W. (1956). *Research* **9**, 466.
—— (1956). In *Problems in contemporary optics.* Istituto Nationale di Ottica, Firenze. p. 609.
—— (1957). *N.P.L. Symposium on problems of colour vision.* H.M. Stationery Office. p. 415.
—— (1959). Thomas Young oration. *Phys. Soc. Yb.* p. 66.
—— (1963). *Nature* **198**, 630.
—— (1963). *Optica Acta* **10**, 325.
—— (1963). *Light* (2nd ed.). Blackie, London.
—— (1969). Eye-movements. In *Encyclopaedia of linguistic information and control* (ed. A. P. Meethan and R. A. Hudson). Pergamon Press, Oxford.
—— (1969/70). Sight and survival. *Advant. Sci., London.* **26**, 1.
—— and FENDER, D. H. (1955). *Optica Acta* **2**, 128.
——, ——, and MAYNE, S. M. (1959). *J. Physiol.* **145**, 98.
——, ——, ——, and PRITCHARD, R. M. (1956). *Proc. Phys. Soc.* **69**, 1165.
—— and FOLEY-FISHER, J. A. (1967). *Optica Acta* **14**, 13.
—— and GINSBORG, B. L. (1953). *J. Physiol.* **119**, 1.
——, —— (1952). *Nature* **170**, 36.
—— and PRITCHARD, R. M. (1956). *Nature* **177**, 434.
——, —— (1960). *Quart. J. exp. Psychol.* **12**, 26.
DODGE, R. (1900). *Psychol. Rev.* **1**, 454.
—— (1903). *Psychol. Rev.* **5**, 307.
—— (1905). *Psychol. Bull.* **2**, 193.
DONDERS, F. C. (1847). *A. F. Holland Beitr.* **1**.
—— (1864). *Anomalies of refraction and accommodation.*
DOWLING, J. F. and BOYCOTT, B. B. (1966). *Proc. R. Soc.* B **166**, 80.
DROUGARD, R. (1964). *J. opt. Soc. Am.* **54**, 907.
—— and POTTER, R. J. (1967). In *Advanced optical techniques.* (ed. A. C. S. Van Heel). North-Holland, Amsterdam.
DUKE-ELDER, W. S. (1939). *Textbook of ophthalmology.* (2nd ed.). C. V. Mosby, St. Louis, U.S.A.
—— (1961). *System of opthalmology.* Vol. 1. Kimpton, London.
—— (1962). *System of opthalmology.* Vol. 4. Kimpton, London.
DUNLAP, E. (1921). *Am. J. Physiol.* **55**, 201.
EAGLE, M. N. and KLEIN, G. S. (1962). *Percept. Mot. Skills* **15**, 579.
EBBERS, R. W. (1965). *J. opt. Soc. Am.* **55**, 1577.
—— (1965). Thesis (Indiana University, U.S.A.).
ENROTH-CUGELL, C. and JONES, R. W. (1963). *J. Neurophysiol.* **26**, 877.
ERULKAR, S. D. and FILENZ, M. (1960). *J. Physiol.* **154**, 206.
EVANS, C. C. (1952). *Electroenceph. clin. Neurophysiol.* **4**, 371.
EVANS, C. R. (1965a). *Br. J. physiol. Optics* **22**, 39.
—— (1965b). *Br. J. Psychol.* **56**, 121.
—— (1965c). Thesis (Reading University).
—— (1967). *Br. J. Psychol.* **58**, 315.
—— (1968). *Report of I.E.E./N.P.L. Conference on Pattern Recognition*, p. 250.
—— and CLEGG, J. M. (1967). *Nature* **215**, 893.
—— and MARSDEN, R. P. (1966). *Br. J. physiol. Optics* **23**, 242.
—— and PIGGINS, D. J. (1963). *Br. J. physiol. Optics* **20**, 1.

EVANS, C. R. and SMITH, G. K. (1964). *Nature* **204**, 303.
—— and WELLS, A. M. (1967). *Br. J. physiol. Optics* **24**, 45.
FELLGETT, P. B. and LINFOOT, E. H. (1955). *Phil. Trans. R. Soc.* **247**, 369.
FENDER, D. H. (1955a). *Brit. J. Ophthal.* **39**, 65.
—— (1965b). *Br. J. Ophthal.* **39**, 294.
—— (1956). Thesis (Reading University).
—— and GILBERT, D. S. (1966). *Sci. Prog.* **54**, 41.
—— and JULESCZ, B. (1967). *J. opt. Soc. Am.* **57**, 819.
—— and NYE, P. W. (1962). *Kybernetik* **1**, 81.
——, —— (1962). *Kybernetik* **1**, 192.
FINDLAY, J. M. (1967) Thesis, Cambridge.
—— (1969a). *Optica Acta* **16**, 65.
—— (1969b). *Vision Res.* **9**, 157.
—— (1971). *Kybernetik* **8**, 207.
FIORENTINI, A. (1956). *Problems in contemporary optics.* Istituto Nationale di Ottica, Firenze. p. 600.
—— and ERCOLES, A. M. (1957). *Optica Acta* **4**, 150.
——, —— (1960). *Atti. Fond. Giorgio Ronchi* **15**, 618.
——, —— (1963). *Atti. Fond. Giorgio Ronchi* **18**, 548.
——, —— (1966). *Atti. Fond. Giorgio Ronchi* **21**, 199.
——, JEANNE, M., and TORALDO DI FRANCIA, G. (1955). *Atti. Fond. Giorgio Ronchi.* **10**, 3.
—— and RADICI, T. (1957). *Atti. Fond. Giorgio Ronchi* **12**, 45.
—— and MAZZINTINI, L. (1965). *Atti. Fond. Giorgio Ronchi* **20**, 307.
FISCHER, M. H. (1932). *Pflügers. Arch. ges. Physiol.* **230**, 161.
FLAMANT, F. (1955). *Revue Opt. theor. instrum.*, **34**, 433.
FOLEY-FISHER, J. (1968). *Vision Res.* **8**, 1055.
FRIEDMAN, B. (1931). *Arch. Ophthal.* **6**, 633.
FRY, G. A. (1969). *J. opt. Soc. Am.* **59**, 618.
FULTON, J. F. (1931). *Physiology of the nervous system.* Oxford University Press, New York.
FUORTES, M. G. F. and HODGKIN, A. L. (1964). *J. Physiol.* **172**, 239.
GAARDER, K. (1960). *Science* **132**, 471.
——, KROPFL, W., and KORESKO, R. (1966). *Electroenceph. clin. neurophysiol.* **21**, 544.
——, ——, KRAUSKOPF, J., GRAF, V., and ARMINGTON, J. C. (1964). *Science* **146**, 1481.
GASTAUT, H. and ALVIM COSTA, P. (1957). *Acta physiol. pharmac. néerl.* **6**, 515.
GAZE, R. M. (1958). *Quart. J. exp. Physiol.* **43**, 209.
GERRITS, H. J. M. and VENDRIK, A. J. H. (1970a). *Vision Res.* **10**, 1443.
—— —— (1970b). *Exp. brain Res.* **11**, 411.
——, DE HAAN, B., and VENDRIK, A. J. H. (1966). *Vision Res.* **6**, 427.
—— and TIMMERMAN, G. J. M. (1969). *Vision Res.* **9**, 439.
GILBERT, G. S. and FENDER, D. H. (1969). *Optica Acta* **16**, 191.
GINSBORG, B. L. (1952). *Nature* **169**, 412.
—— (1953). *Br. J. Ophthal.* **37**, 746.
—— and HEAVENS, O. S. (1951). *Rev. Scient. Instrum.* **22**, 114.
GLEZER, V. D. (1959). *Sechenov physiol. J. USSR* **45**, 211.
GLIEM, H. (1964). *V. Graefes Arch. Klin. Exp. Ophthal.* **167**, 307.
—— and GÜNTHER, G. (1965). *V. Graefes Arch. Klin. Exp. Ophthal.* **168**, 322.
—— (1967). *Klin. Mbl. Augenheilk.* **150**, 334.
GRAF, V. and GAARDER, K. (1966). *Am. J. Psychol.* **79**, 73.

GRAHAM, C. H. (Ed.) (1965). *Vision and visual perception.* Wiley, New York, Sydney, and London.

GRAND, see LE GRAND.

GRANIT, R. (1930). *Am. J. Physiol.* **94**, 41.

—— (1947). *Sensory mechanisms of the retina.* Oxford University Press, London.

—— (1955). *Receptors and sensory perception.* Yale University Press, Yale and Oxford University Press, London.

—— (1962). In *The eye* (ed. H. Davson). Vol. 2. Academic Press, New York and London. pp. 537–778.

—— (1970). *Basis of motor control.* Academic Press, New York and London.

—— and TANSLEY, K. (1948). *J. Physiol.* **107**, 54.

GREGORY, R. L. (1958). *Nature* **182**, 1214.

GROSS, E. G. and WALENSTEIN, E. (1967). *Electroenceph. clin. Neurophysiol.* **22**, 204.

GUBISCH, R. (1967). *J. opt. Soc. Am.* **57**, 507.

GUILDFORD, J. P. (1927). *Am. J. Psychol.* **38**, 534.

HAGINS, W. A. and RÜPPEL, H. (1971). *Proc. Am. Fed. Soc. exp. Biol.* **30**, 57.

HALLETT, P. E. (1963). *Vision Res.* **3**, 9.

HAMMOND, P. (1971). *J. Physiol.* **213**, 476.

HARTLINE, H. K. (1938). *Am. J. Physiol.* **121**, 400.

—— (1940). *J. opt. Soc. Am.* **30**, 239.

—— (1942). The Harvey lectures, **37**, 39.

—— (1949). *Fed. Proc.* **8**, 69.

—— (1968). *Les Prix Nobel.* Kungl. Boktr., Stockholm. p. 242.

—— and GRAHAM, C. H. (1932). *J. cell. comp. Physiol.* **1**, 277.

—— and RATLIFF, F. (1957). *J. gen. Physiol.* **40**, 357.

—— —— (1958). *J. gen. Physiol.* **41**, 1049.

——, WAYNE, H. G., and RATLIFF, F. (1956). *J. gen. Physiol.* **39**, 651.

HARTRIDGE, H. and THOMSON, L. C. (1948). *Br. J. Opthal.* **32**, 581.

HEBB, D. O. (1963). *Am. Psychol.* **15**, 36.

—— (1966). *A textbook of psychology.* Saunders, Philadelphia and London.

HEBBARD, F. W. and MARG, E. (1960). *J. opt. Soc. Am.* **50**, 151.

HECHT, S., SHLAER, S., and PIRENNE, M. N. (1942). *J. gen. Physiol.* **25**, 819.

HELMHOLTZ, H. VON (1866). *Physiological Optics.* Translation published 1962 by Dover Publications, New York.

HERING, E. (1875). *Sber. Akad. Wiss. Wien* **70**, 169.

—— (1879). *Spatial sense and movements of the eye.* Translation published 1942 by American Academy of Optometry, Baltimore.

—— (1899). *Ber. maths-phys. Kl. K. Sachs, Ges. Wiss., Leipzig*, p. 18.

HIGGINS, G. C. and STULTZ, K. F. (1953). *J. opt. Soc. Am.* **43**, 1136.

—— —— (1954). *J. opt. Soc. Am.* **44**, 315.

HILDING, A. C. (1954). *A.M.A. Arch. Ophthal.* **160**, 47.

HILL, R. M. and MARG, E. (1963). *J. Neurophysiol.* **26**, 249.

HODGSON, F. and LORD, M. P. (1954). *Nature* **174**, 75.

HOLLAND, H. C. (1965). *The spiral after-effect.* Pergamon, Oxford.

HOLT, E. B. (1903). *Psychol. Monogr.* **4**, 3.

HUBEL, D. H. (1963). *Scient. Am.* **209**(5), 57.

—— and WIESEL, T. N. (1959). *J. Physiol.* **148**, 574.

—— —— (1960). *J. Physiol.* **154**, 572.

—— —— (1961). *J. Physiol.* **155**, 385.

—— —— (1962). *J. Physiol.* **160**, 106.

—— —— (1965). *J. Neurophysiol.* **28**, 229.

IARBUS, see YARBUS, A. L.

JACOBSON, H. (1951). *Science* **113**, 292.

JOHANSSON, G. and BACKLUND, F. (1960a). *Rep. Psychol. Lab., Uppsala.*

—— —— (1960b). *Scand. J. Psychol.* **1**, 181.

JONES, C. (1959). *J. opt. Soc. Am.* **49**, 645.

JONES, F. MELVILLE, see MELVILLE JONES.

JONES, L. A. and HIGGINS, G. C. (1947). *J. opt. Soc. Am.* **37**, 217.

JONES, R. M., WEBSTER, J. G., and KEESEY, U. T. (1972). *IEEE Trans. B.M.E.* **19**, 29.

JONES, R. V. (1960). *J. scient. Instrum.* **36**, 90.

JURY, E. I. and PAVLIDIS, T. (1963). *Inst. elect. electron. Engrs. Trans-Automatic Control* AC-8. **210**. HECKENMULLER, E. G. (1965) *Psychol. Bull.* **633**, 157.

KAHNEMAN, D. (1964) *Vision Res.* **4**, 557.

KAPANY, N. S. (1967). *Fiber optics.* Academic Press, New York and London.

——, EYER, J. A., and KEIM, R. E. (1957). *J. opt. Soc. Am.* **47**, 423.

KEESEY, U. T. (1960). *J. opt. Soc. Am.* **50**, 769.

—— (1962). Paper presented at April meeting of Western Psychological Association, reported in *Documenta Ophth.* **18**, 16.

—— (1965). *J. opt. Soc. Am.* **55**, 1577.

—— (1969). *J. opt. Soc. Am.* **59**, 604.

—— (1970). *J. opt. Soc. Am.* **60**, 390.

—— and NICHOLS, D. J. (1966). *J. opt. Soc. Am.* **56**, 543.

—— —— (1967). *Vision Res.* **7**, 859.

—— —— (1969). *Electroenceph. and clin. Neurophysiol.* **27**, 248.

—— and RIGGS, L. A. (1962). *J. opt. Soc. Am.* **52**, 719.

KELLY, D. H. (1959). *J. opt. Soc. Am.* **49**, 730.

—— (1964). *Documenta Ophth.* **18**, 16.

—— and CRANE, H. D. (1970). *Research study of a fundus tracer.* Report of the Stanford Technical Institute, Menlo Park, Stanford, California, U.S.A.

——, ——, HILL, J. W., and CORNSWEET, T. N. (1969). *J. opt. Soc. Am.* **59**, 508.

KISE, K. HATAKEYAMA, A., and MATZUMARA, T. (1961). *Act. Soc. Ophth, Japan.* **65**, 9.

KOZAK, W., RODIECK, R. W., and BISHOP, P. O. (1965). *J. Neurophysiol.* **28**, 19.

KRAUSKOPF, J. (1957). *J. opt. Soc. Am.* **47**, 740.

—— (1960). *Am. J. Psychol.* **73**, 204.

—— (1960). *Am. J. Psychol.* **73**, 294.

—— (1963). *J. opt. Soc. Am.* **53**, 744.

—— and COLEMAN, P. D. (1956). *Army Med. Res. Lab. Report 218.*

——, GRAF, V., and GAARDER, K. (1966). *Am. J. Psychol.* **79**, 73.

—— and CORNSWEET, T. N., and RIGGS, L. R. (1960). *J. opt. Soc. Am.* **50**, 572.

—— and RIGGS, L. A. (1959). *Am. J. Psychol.* **72**, 248.

KRIS, E. C. (1958). *W.A.D.C. Tech. Report 58–660. Astia Document A D. 209385.*

KUFFLER, S. W. (1953). *J. Physiol.* **16**, 37.

—— FITZHUGH, R., and BARLOW, H. B. (1957). *J. gen. Physiol.* **40**, 925.

KULIKOWSKI, J. J. (1971). *Vision Res.* **11**, 261.

LAND, E. H. (1971). *J. opt. Soc. Am.* **61**, 1.

LANDOLT, A. (1891). *Archs Ophthal.*, N.Y. **11**, 385.

LANGE, see DE LANGE.

LATOUR, P. L. (1962). *Vision Res.* **2**, 161.

—— (1966). *Cortical control of eye-movements.* Royal Van Gorcum (Netherlands) for the Institute for Perception Rvo-Tno.

LE GRAND, Y. (1933). *Revue Opt. théor. instrum.* **12**, 145.

LE GRAND, Y. (1935). *C.r. hebd Séanc. Acad. Sci.*, *Paris*. **200**, 490.
—— (1967). *Form and space vision*. Indiana Press, Bloomington, U.S.A. and London.
LEHMANN, D., BEELER, G. W., and FENDER, D. H. (1965a). *Electroenceph. clin. neurophysiol.* **18**, 527.
——, ——, —— (1965b). *Electroenceph. clin. neurophysiol.* **19**, 336.
——, ——, —— (1966). *Electroenceph. clin. neurophysiol.* **20**, 274.
——, ——, —— (1967). *Electroenceph. clin. neurophysiol.* **22**, 636.
LETTVIN, J. Y. (1961). *Sensory communication* (ed. W. Rosenblith), p. 757 M.I.T. Press Boston, U.S.A.
—— (1962). *M.I.T. Res. Lab. Electron. Quart. prog. Rep.* **67**, 254.
——, MATURANA, H. R., McCULLOUGH, W. S., and PITTS, W. H. (1959). *Proc. Inst. Radio Engrs* N.Y. **47**, 1940.
LEVINSON, J. (1964). *Documenta Ophth.* **18**, 36.
LÉVY-SCHOEN, A. (1969). *Étude des mouvement oculaires*. Dunod, Paris.
LISTING, J. B. (1853). *Zeitschrift Dioptrik des Auges*.
LLEWELLYN THOMAS, E. and MACKWORTH, N. H. (1960). *J. Inst. elec. Engr.* **2**, 331.
——, ——, and HOWAT, M. R. (1960). *I.R.E. Trans. med. Electron.* **7**, 196.
LORBER, R. M., ZUBER, B. L., and STARK, L. (1964). *M.I.T. Electron. Res. Lab. Quart. prog. Rep.* **74**, 250.
—— (1965). *Nature* **208**, 558.
LORD, M. P. (1948). *Proc. Phys. Soc.* **61**, 489.
—— (1950). *Nature* **166**, 349.
—— (1951). *Proc. Phys. Soc.* B **64**, 171.
—— (1952). *Nature* **170**, 670.
—— and WRIGHT, W. D. (1948). *Nature* **162**, 25.
—— —— (1949). *Nature* **163**, 803.
—— —— (1950). *Nature* **166**, 1036.
—— —— (1950). *Prog. Rep. Phys. Soc.* **13**, 1.
LOWRY, E. M. and DE PALMA, J. J. (1961). *J. opt. Soc. Am.* **51**, 740.
LUDVIGH, E. (1948). *Science* **108**, 63.
—— (1953). *Joint Project Reports Nos. 4 and 5. U.S. School of Aviation Medicine*, Pensacola, Fla., U.S.A.
McCREE, K. J. (1960). *Optica Acta* **7**, 281.
McILWAIN, J. T. (1964). *J. Neurophysiol.* **27**, 1154.
MACKAY, D. M. (1957). *Nature* **180**, 849.
—— (1970a). *Nature* **225**, 90.
—— (1970b). *Nature* **225**, 731.
—— (1970c). *Nature* **225**, 872.
—— (1973). *Handbook of sensory physiology* (ed. R. Jung). Vol. VII, 3.
MACKENSEN, G. (1958). *V. Graefes Arch. Klin. Exp. Ophthal.* **160**, 47.
MACKWORTH, J. F. and LLEWELLYN THOMAS, E. (1962). *J. opt. Soc. Am.* **52**, 713.
—— and MACKWORTH, N. H. (1958). *J. opt. Soc. Am.* **48**, 439.
MAGOUN, H. W. (1964). In *Brain mechanisms and consciousness* (ed. Delafresnaye)
MALIS, L. C. and KRUGER, L. (1956). *J. Neurophysiol.* **19**, 172.
MARG, E. (1951). *A.M.A. Arch. Ophth.* **45**, 169.
MARX, E. and TRENDELENBURG, W. (1911). *Z. Sinnesphysiol.* **45**, 87.
MARKS, W. B., DOBELLE, W. H., and MACNICHOL, E. F. (1964). *Science* **143**, 1181.
MARSHALL, W. H. and TALBOT, S. A. (1941). *Am. J. Physiol.* **133**, 418.
—— —— (1942). *Biol. Sym.* **7**, 117.

MATIN, L. (1964). *J. opt. Soc. Am.* **54**, 1008.
—— and MAKINNON, G. E. (1964). *Science* **143**, 147.
—— and PEARCE, D. G. (1965). *Science* **148**, 1485.
——, ——, and KIBLER, G. (1964). *J. opt. Soc. Am.* **54**, 1398.
——, ——, MATIN, E., and KIBLER, G. (1966). *Vision Res.* **6**, 453.
MATURANA, H. R. and FRANK, S. (1963). *Science* **142**, 977.
——, LETTVIN, J. Y., McCULLOUGH, W. S., and PITTS, W. H. (1960). *J. gen. Physiol.* **43** (Sup. 2), 129.
MELVILLE JONES, F. and FREE, W. T. (1960). *F.P.R.C. Report 1156.* Air Ministry, London.
MERTON, P. A. (1956). *J. Physiol.* **132**, 25P.
—— (1961). *J. Physiol.* **156**, 555.
MICHAEL, J. A. and STARK, L. (1967). *Expl. Neurol.* **17**, 233.
—— and JONES, G. M. (1966). *Vision Res.* **6**, 707.
MILLMAN, J. and TAUB, R. (1956). *Pulse and digital circuits.* McGraw-Hill, London.
MILLODOT, M. (1966). *Br. J. Physiol. Optics.* **23**, 75.
MITCHELL, D. E., FREEMAN, R. D., and WESTHEIMER, G. (1967). *J. opt. Soc. Am.* **57**, 246.
MITRANI, L., MATEEF, ST., and YAMIKOFF, N. (1970). *Vision Res.* **10**, 405; 411; 417.
——, ——, —— (1971). *Vision Res.* **11**, 1157.
MORUZZI, G. and MAGOUN, H. W. (1949). *Electroenceph. clin. Neurophysiol.* **1**, 455.
NACHMIAS, J. (1958). *J. opt. Soc. Am.* **48**, 726.
—— (1959). *J. opt. Soc. Am.* **49**, 901.
—— (1961). *J. opt. Soc. Am.* **51**, 761.
NES, see VAN NES.
NYE, P. W. (1962). Thesis (Reading University).
NOTON, D. and STARK, L. (1971a). *Scient. Am.* **224**(6), 34.
—— —— (1971b). *Vision Res.* **11**, 929.
OGLE, K. N. and WEIL, M. P. (1958). *Archs Ophthal.*, N.Y. **59**, 4.
OOUE, S. (1959). *J. appl. Phys., Japan.* **29**, 531.
ORCHANSKY, J. (1899). *Zentbl. Physiol.* **12**, 787.
PARK, G. E. and PARK, R. S. (1933). *Am. J. Physiol.* **104**, 545.
PEDLER, C. and TILLY, R. (1964). *Vision Res.* **4**, 499.
——, —— (1965). *Expl. Eye Res.* **4**, 370.
PIRENNE, M. H. (1962a). In *The eye.* (ed. H. Davson). Vol. 2. Pergamon Press, Oxford. p. 13ff.
—— (1962b) In *The eye* (ed. H. Davson). Vol. 2. Pergamon Press, Oxford. p. 134.
PLATT, J. R. (1956). *Am. Scientist.* **44**, 180.
—— (1960). *Scient. Am.* **202**(6), 121.
POLYAK, S. L. (1941). *The retina.* University of Chicago Press, Chicago, Illinois, U.S.A.
—— (1957). *The vertebrate visual system.* University of Chicago Press, Chicago, Illinois.
PRITCHARD, R. M. (1958a). Thesis (Reading University).
—— (1958b). *Quart. J. exp. Psychol.* **10**, 77.
—— (1961a). *Quart. J. exp. Psychol.* **13**, 181.
—— (1961b). *Scient. Am.* **204**(5), 1.
—— and HERON, W. (1960). *Can. J. Psychol.* **14**, 131.
——, ——, and HEBB, D. O. (1960). *Can. J. Psychol.* **14**, 67.

PUCKETT, J. DE W. and STEINMAN, R. M. (1969). *Vision Res.* **9,** 694.

PURKINJE, J. E. (1825). *Beobachtungen und Versuche zur Physiologie der Sinne* **2,** 60.

QUEREAU, J. V. (1955). *A.M.A. Arch. Ophthal.* **53,** 807.

RASHBASS, C. (1960). *J. opt. Soc. Am.* **50,** 642.

—— (1961a). *J. Physiol.* **159,** 326.

—— (1961b). *J. Physiol.* **159,** 361.

—— and WESTHEIMER, G. (1961a). *J. Physiol.* **159,** 339.

—— —— (1961b). *J. Physiol.* **159,** 361.

RATLIFF, F. (1952). *J. exp. Psychol.* **43,** 163.

—— (1965). *Mach bands: quantitative studies on neural networks in the retina.* Holden-Day, San Francisco, U.S.A.

—— and HARTLINE, H. K. (1959). *J. gen. Physiol.* **42,** 1241.

——, MILLER, W. H., and HARTLINE, H. K. (1958). *Ann. N.Y. Acad. Sci.* **74,** 210.

—— and MUELLER, C. G. (1957). *Science* **126,** 840.

—— and RIGGS, L. A. (1950). *J. exp. Psychol.* **46,** 687.

RATTLE, J. D. (1968). Thesis (Reading University).

—— (1969). *Optica Acta* **16,** 184.

—— and FOLEY-FISHER, J. A. (1968). *Optica Acta* **15,** 617.

REICHARDT, T. (1961a). In *Sensory communication* (ed. W. Rosenblith). M.I.T. Press. Boston, U.S.A. p. 303.

—— (1961b). *Kybernetik.* **1,** 57–9.

REMOND, A., LESÈVRE, N., and TORRES, F. (1965). *Rev. Neurobiol.* **113,** 193.

RICHARDS, W. (1968). *J. opt. Soc. Am.* **58,** 1159.

RIGGS, L. A. (1958). *A. Rev. Psychol.* **9,** 19.

——, ARMINGTON, J. C., and RATLIFF, F. (1954). *J. opt. Soc. Am.* **44,** 315.

——, JOHNSON, E. P., and SCHICK, A. M. L. (1964). *Science* **144,** 567.

—— and RATLIFF, F. (1951). *Science* **114,** 17.

——, ——, CORNSWEET, J. C., and CORNSWEET, T. N. (1953). *J. opt. Soc. Am.* **43,** 495.

——, ——, and KEESEY, U. T. (1961). *J. opt. Soc. Am.* **51,** 702.

—— and SCHICK, A. M. L. (1968). *Vision Res.* **8,** 159.

—— and TULUNAY, S. U. (1959). *J. opt. Soc. Am.* **49,** 741.

—— and WHITTLE, P. (1967). *Vision Res.* **7,** 441.

—— and NIEHL, E. W. (1960). *J. opt. Soc. Am.* **50,** 913.

ROBINSON, D. A. (1963). *Inst. elect. electron. Engr. Trans. Med. electron.* **10,** 137.

—— (1964). *J. Physiol.* **174,** 245.

—— (1965). *J. Physiol.* **180,** 569.

——, O'MEARA, D., SCOTT, A. B., and COLLINS, C. C. (1969). *J. appl. Physiol.* **26,** 548.

ROSE, A. (1942). *Proc. Inst. Radio Engrs., N.Y.* **30,** 295.

—— (1947). *J. opt. Soc. Am.* **37,** 908.

ROSENBLITH, W. (1961). *Sensory communication.* M.I.T. Press, Boston, U.S.A.

RUSHTON, W. A. H. (1956a). *J. Physiol.* **134,** 11.

—— (1956b). *J. Physiol,* **134,** 30.

—— (1958a). *Ann. N.Y. Acad. Sci.* **74,** 291.

—— (1962). *Visual pigments in man.* Liverpool University Press, Liverpool.

—— (1965). (Ferrier Lecture, 1962). *Proc. R. Soc. B.* **162,** 20.

RUTLEY, K. S. (1972). *Med. biol. Eng.* **10,** 101.

ST. CYR, G. J. and FENDER, D. H. (1969a). *Vision Res.* **9,** 245.

—— —— (1969b). *Vision Res.* **9,** 1235.

St. Cyr, G. J. and Fender D. H. (1969c). *Vision Res.* **9**, 1491.

Schade, O. H. (1948). *R.C.A. Rev.* **9**, 5; 245; 490; 653.

—— (1956). *J. opt. Soc. Am.* **46**, 721.

Schoen, see Lévy Schoen.

Sekuler, R. W. and Ganz, L. (1963). *Science* **139**, 419.

Shackel, F. (1960a). *Br. J. Ophthal.* **44**, 89.

—— (1960b). *J. opt. Soc. Am.* **50**, 763.

—— and Davis, J. R. (1960). *Br. J. Ophthal.* **44**, 337.

Sharpe, C. R. (1972). *J. Physiol.* **222**, 1.

Sherrington, C. S. (1918). *Brain* **41**, 233.

—— (1897). *Proc. R. Soc.* **61**, 247.

—— (1918). *Brain* **41**, 233.

Shortess, G. K. and Krauskopf, J. (1961). *J. opt. Soc. Am.* **51**, 555.

Smith, W. M. and Warter, P. J. (1960). *J. opt. Soc. Am.* **50**, 245.

Sparrock, J. M. B. (1969). *J. opt. Soc. Am.* **59**, 872.

Sperling, H. G. (1963). *J. opt. Soc. Am.* **53**, 521.

—— (1964). *Documenta Ophth.* **18**, 3.

—— and Hawerth, R. S. (1971). *Science* **172**, 180.

Spigel, I. M. (1965). *Visually perceived moment.* Harper and Row, New York.

Stark, L., Vossius, F., and Young, L. R. (1962). *I.R.E. Trans. Hum. Factors Eng.* **3**, 52.

Stark, L., Michael, J. A., and Zuber, B. L. (1969). In *Attention in Neurophysiology* (ed. C. R. Evans and T. B. Mullholland), Butterworth, London. p. 281.

Steinman, R. M. (1965). *J. opt. Soc. Am.* **55**, 1158.

—— and Cunitz, R. J. (1968). *Vision Res.* **8**, 277.

——, —— Timberlake, G. T., and Herman, M. (1967). *Science* **155**, 1577.

——, Skavenski, A. A., and Sansbury, R. V. (1969). *Vision Res.* **8**, 1167.

Stiles, W. S. (1949). *Revue Opt. théor. instrum* **28**, 215.

—— and Crawford, B. H. (1937). *Proc. R. Soc.* B **122**, 255.

Stone, S. L., Thomas, J. G., and Zakian, V. (1965). *J. Physiol.* **181**, 337.

Stenstrom, S. (1948). *Am. J. Optom.* **25**, 5.

Sunderhauf, A. (1960). *Klin. Mbl. Augenheilk.* **136**, 837.

Talbot, S. A. and Marshall, W. H. (1941). *Am. J. Ophthal.* **24**, 1255.

Taylor, C. A. and Thompson, B. J. (1957). *J. scient. Instrum.* **34**, 439.

Teller, D. Y., Andrews, D. P., and Barlow, II. B. (1966). *Vision Res.* **6**, 701.

Tepas, D. I. (1962). In *Visual problems of the armed forces* (ed. M. A. Whitcomb). NAS-NRC Publication, 21–25 Washington, D.C., U.S.A.

Thomas, J. G. (1958). *J. Physiol.* **141**, 7P.

—— (1961). *Nature* **189**, 842.

—— (1967). *Kybernetik* **3**, 254.

—— (1969). *J. Physiol.* **200**, 109.

Thomson, L. C. and Wright, W. D. (1947). *J. Physiol.* **105**, 316.

Toussant, D., Kuwabara, T., and Cogan, D. G. (1961) *Archs. Ophthal.*, N.Y. **65**, 575.

Troxler, D. (1804). In *Ophthal. Bibliothek.* Vol. 2, part 2, p. 1.

Tulunay, U., see Keesey, U. T.

Valois, see De Valois.

Van Heel, A. C. S. (1967). *Advanced optical techniques.* North-Holland, Amsterdam.

Van Nes, F. L. and Bouman M. A. (1967). *J. opt. Soc. Am.* **57**, 401.

Verheijen, F. J. (1961). *Optica Acta* **8**, 309.

VERNON, M. D. (1928). *Br. J. Ophthal.* **12,** 113.

VERNON, M. D. (1930). *The movement of the eyes in reading.* Medical Research Council Report. No. 148. H.M. Stationery Office, London.

VILTER, V. C. (1949). *C.r. Séanc. Soc. Biol.* **143,** 830.

VOLKMAN, F. C. (1962). *J. opt. Soc. Am.* **52,** 571.

——, SCHICK, A. M. L., and RIGGS, L. A. (1968). *J. Opt. Soc. Am.* **58,** 562.

VON HELMHOLTZ, see HELMHOLTZ, H. VON.

WAGNER, H. G., MACNICHOL, E. F., and WOLBARSHT, M. L. (1960). *J. gen. Physiol.* **43** (part 2), 45.

——, ——, —— (1963). *J. opt. Soc. Am.* **53,** 66.

WALD, G. (1964). *Science* **145,** 1007.

WAYGOOD, M. (1969). *Optica Acta* **16,** 64.

WEST, D. C. (1965). Thesis (Reading University).

—— (1967). *Vision Res.* **7,** 949.

—— (1968a). *Vision Res.* **8,** 719.

—— (1968b). *Optica Acta* **15,** 317.

—— and BOYCE, P. R. (1968). *Vision Res.* **8,** 171.

WESTHEIMER, G. (1954a). *A.M.A. Arch. Ophthal.* **44,** 710.

—— (1954b). *A.M.A. Arch. Ophthal.* **52,** 932.

—— (1957). *J. opt. Soc. Am.* **47,** 967.

—— (1958). *Bull. of math. Biophys.* **20,** 149.

—— (1963). *J. opt. Soc. Am.* **53,** 86.

—— (1965). *J. Physiol.* **181,** 881.

—— and CONOVER, D. W. (1954). *J. exp. Psychol.* **47,** 283.

—— and MITCHELL, A. M. (1956). *A.M.A. Arch. Ophthal.* **55,** 842.

WHEELES, L. L., COHEN, G. H., and BOYNTON, R. M. (1967). *J. opt. Soc. Am.* **57,** 394.

——, ——, ——, and GAUSTELLA, M. J. (1966). *J. opt. Soc. Am.* **56,** 960.

WHITTERIDGE, D. (1959). *Quart. J. exp. Physiol.* **44,** 385.

—— (1960). *Handbook of Physiology.* Section 1. Neurophysiology, Vol. 2, 1089. Am. Physiol. Soc. Washington, D.C.

WIESEL, T. N. (1960). *J. Physiol.* **153,** 583.

—— and HUBEL, D. H. (1963a). *J. Neurophysiol.* **26,** 978.

—— —— (1963b). *J. Neurophysiol.* **26,** 1003.

—— —— (1966). *J. Neurophysiol.* **29,** 1115.

WOLBARSHT, M. L., WAGNER, H. G., and MACNICHOL, E. F. (1961). In *The visual system. Neurophysiology and Psychophysics.* (ed. Jung R. and Kornhuber, H.) Springer-Verlag, Berlin.

WOLTER, J. R. (1955). *A.M.A. Arch. Ophthal.* **53,** 201.

WOODWARD, R. H. and GOLDSMITH, P. V. (1964). *Cumulative sum technique.* I.C.I. Monograph No. 3., Oliver and Boyd, Edinburgh.

WOODWORTH, R. S. and SCHLOSBERG, H. (1954). *Experimental psychology.* Holt, New York.

WORTHINGTON, C. R. (1971). *Proc. Fed. Am. Soc. exp. Biol.* **30,** 57.

WRIGHT, W. D. (1937). *Proc. R. Soc. B.* **122,** 220.

YARBUS,† A. L. (1954). *Dokl. Akad. Nauk SSSR* **96,** 732.

—— (1955a). *Trudy Inst. Biol. Fiziki.* 1.

—— (1956a). *Biofizika* **1,** 76.

—— (1956b). *Biofizika* **1,** 435.

—— (1956c). *Biofizika* **1,** 593.

—— (1956d). *Biofizika* **1,** 713.

—— (1957a). *Biofizika* **2,** 163.

YARBUS,† A. L. (1957b). *Biofizika* **2**, 698.
—— (1957c). *Biofizika* **2**, 703.
—— (1959a). *Biofizika* **4**, 320.
—— (1959b). *Biofizika* **4**, 757.
—— (1960a). *Biofizika* **5**, 158.
—— (1960b). *Biofizika* **5**, 293.
—— (1961). *Biofizika* **6**, 297.
—— (1962a). *Biofizika* **7**, 64.
—— (1962b). *Biofizika* **7**, 207.
—— (1962c). *Biofizika* **7**, 333.
—— (1962d). *Biofizika* **7**, 615.
—— (1967). *Eye-movements and vision.* Published in Moscow 1965. English translation published by Plenum Press, New York.
YOUNG, L. R. and STARK, L. (1963). *I.R.E. Trans. Hum. Factors Eng.* **4**, 38.
ZUBER, B. L. (1964). *M.I.T. Electron. Res. Lab. Quart. Prog. Rep.*‡ **75**, 190.
——, CRIDER, A., and STARK, L. (1964). *M.I.T. Electron. Res. Lab. Quart. Prog. Rep.*‡ **74**, 244.
——, HORROCKS, A., LORBER, M., and STARK, L. (1964). *M.I.T. Electron. Res. Lab. Quart. Prog. Rep.*‡ **73**, 221.
——, MICHAEL, J. A., and STARK, L. (1964). *M.I.T. Electron. Res. Lab. Quart. Prog. Rep.*‡ **74**, 217.
—— and STARK, L. (1965). *Science* **150**, 1459.
——, —— (1966). *Exp. Neurobiol.* **16**, 65.
——, ——, and LORBER, M. (1966). *Exp. Neurobiol.* **14**, 351.
——, ——, and SEMMLOW, J. L. (1968). *Biophys. J.* **8**, 1288.

ADDITIONAL REFERENCES

ZINCHENKO, V. P. and VERGILES, N. YU. (1972). *Formation of visual images (Studies of Stabilized Images).* Research Report translated from Russian. Consultants' Bureau, New York, London.
ZIKMUND, V. (Ed.) (1973). *The oculomotor system and brain functions.* Butterworth, London, and the Publishing House of the Slovak Academy, Bratislava. Includes contributions on after-images (Ditchburn, R. W.), pattern fragmentation (Evans, C. R.), and many on eye-movements (by Jeannerod, M., Kornhuber, H., Lesèvre, N., Remond, A., Lévy-Schoen, A., and others).
SANSBURY, R. V., SKAVENSKI, A. A., HADDAD, G. M., and STEINMAN, R. M. (1973). *J. opt. Soc. Am.* **63**, 612.
HADDAD G. M. and STEINMAN, R. M. (1973). *Vision Res.* **13**, 1075.

† Page numbers given refer to the original publication. Page numbers in the English translation of some volumes of *Biofizika* are a little different. Almost all the material in the papers is included in the book.

‡ Nearly all the material quoted in the M.I.T. Progress Reports was subsequently published in the journal references listed above under the names of Lorber, Michael, Stark, and Zuber.

Author index

Subject index

References are to paragraphs except when figures or tables are indicated. A stands for appendix. S.R.I. stands for stabilized retinal image.

DATE DUE

DEC 19 '77
DEC 19 '77
NOV 28 78
MAY 7 '79
JO 19 81
MY 2 '86
MR 24 88
AP 18 '88
MR 28 '89
DE 16 '91
DE 13 '94

GAYLORD